THE SHAH'S
LAST RIDE

The Story of the
Exile, Misadventures and Death
of
the Emperor

William Shawcross

Chatto & Windus
LONDON

Published in 1989 by
Chatto & Windus Ltd
30 Bedford Square
London WC1B 3RP

A CIP catalogue record for this book
is available from the British Library

ISBN 0 7011 3254 X

Printed in Great Britain by
Redwood Burn Limited, Trowbridge, Wiltshire

THE SHAH'S LAST RIDE

This book is for
Christiane,
with my love,
and in happy memory
of her sparkling friendship
with my mother,
Joan

Contents

Farewell, King!
Cover your heads, and mock not flesh and blood
With solemn reverence; throw away respect,
Tradition, form, and ceremonious duty;
For you have but mistook me all this while.
I live with bread like you, feel want,
Taste grief, need friends; subjected thus,
How can you say to me I am a king?

RICHARD II, ACT 3, SCENE 2

Prologue

In April 1979, the Shah of Iran was gone three months from his throne and, denied entry into the United States and almost everywhere else, was camping on an island in the Bahamas. Dr. Henry Kissinger, speaking at a Harvard Business School dinner in New York, declared that it was quite wrong for the United States to treat the Shah, a friend for thirty-five years, "like a Flying Dutchman looking for a port of call."

The eternal wanderer is one of the oldest myths. Kissinger's eloquent evocation of the legend was intended to elicit sympathy for the Shah. However, central to all the stories of the Dutchman is that his lack of refuge is a punishment for his own misdeeds or folly. He is adrift not so much because of the callousness of the world as because of his own conduct.

In most tales, the Dutchman has been condemned to endless voyaging either for committing murder or for challenging God. And what is more, anyone who comes into contact with him or with his phantom ship is cursed.

Thus Walter Scott sings in *Rokeby*,

> *Full spread and crowded every sail,*
> *The Demon Frigate braves the gale:*
> *And well the doom'd spectators know*
> *The harbinger of wreck and woe.*

This book is the story of a journey, the Shah's forlorn journey into exile and death, and of various elements of his rule—his relations with the British and Americans, his secret police, SAVAK, the CIA, oil, the arms trade. The tale of the fall and exile of the Shah is one which illustrates the nature of relationship between states and leaders. It is a story of loyalty and convenience. *"Les états sont des monstres froids,"* said Charles de Gaulle.

CHAPTER ONE

The Ending

January 16, 1979, Mehrabad Airport, Teheran. A bitter wind from the Elburz Mountains sweeps around two 707s parked in front of the low, white, thickly carpeted Imperial Pavilion where, in happier days, the Shah of Iran welcomed or bade farewell to the monarchs and statesmen who came to pay him court, nurture his ambitions, and ask for alliances, money, or other tokens of his kingship. The planes have been tested and are now being loaded and prepared for flight. The Shah himself is about to leave.

There is not much other activity at the airport. Rows and rows of planes of Iran Air—"the caviar airline"—are grounded by strikes. In recent months, as the Islamic revolution has gathered force, almost all the country has been stopped by strikes. They have all been directed at just one target: the Shah.

In Teheran, there have been power cuts, and even basic foodstuffs have been short. Oil, the fount of the country's wealth and of the crash modernization and militarization on which the Shah, encouraged by his allies, had embarked in the 1970s, has at times stopped flowing altogether. Iran has even had to import heating oil from the United States in recent months. Now the armed forces are working the oil fields. In Teheran poor people wait in long lines in the snow for paraffin. Drivers are lining up for hours in front of gas stations guarded by sullen, sometimes angry soldiers who keep control by firing their automatic weapons into the air. Soldiers, drivers, and attendants alike are cursing the snow and the cold—and the Shah.

Gray-black smoke rises from bonfires of tires and rubbish set alight by gangs of youths who roam the streets, stop expensive cars like BMWs or Mercedeses, and siphon out the gas. Drivers are unwise to protest, especially if they are foreign. The Americans, in particular, are afraid of being beaten up. The best insurance is to have on a window a sticker of the Shah's great enemy, the turbulent, intransigent priest, Ayatollah Khomeini, or, even better, to play one of the tapes on which, from his exile near Paris, he exhorts the Shah's overthrow.

The city this morning is relatively calm, far quieter than it has been on many days in recent months. But it is an uneasy calm, expectant of imminent, enormous change. The Shah has already announced that he will leave the country for a holiday and for medical treatment. Only the actual day of his departure is, to the people, unknown.

As in all revolutionary crises, there is no real news. No one knows what is being plotted, what pressures are being applied, who will turn where. Almost the entire population listens to the Persian service of the BBC, and the BBC reports the latest broadside from the ayatollah in Paris and such information from Teheran as correspondents have been able to sift from rumor.

Together the rumors and the snippets of information, the suspicions and the lies, make a pretty fearful brew. According to one story, the Shah's announcement that he will leave is only a bluff, and soon the Army will strike. All the generals, the admirals, and the air force commanders, quite apart from the secret policemen from SAVAK—which is now a byword both at home and abroad for torture and repression—have everything to lose if he goes. So the logic is that they will prevent him. It is all being organized. That is one story.

Some think that he will go abroad for a few days and that the CIA will then engineer his return in a countercoup, just as it did in 1953. Others say no—for this time it is the British and the Americans who are throwing him out. This is a view that is widely held by those around the court itself. If the British were not behind Khomeini, why would the BBC broadcast his strictures and sermons? Everyone knows the old saying, "If you lift a mullah's beard you'll find 'Made in Britain' stamped on his chin."

The Shah himself has tried to have the British government curb the BBC. He sees its refusal as a clear British betrayal of him. The Americans' position is said to be more complicated. If they wanted the Shah to stay they would already have told him to order the Army to destroy the revolution, not just peck at it. Instead, President Carter has sent over a senior U.S. general, Robert E. Huyser, to keep the Army quiet. That is what is being said by many.

Palaces and rich houses all over town are echoing emptily now. For weeks, for months even, members of the royal family and the royal court have been getting out. The exodus has been a little undignified. Sometimes it seemed that those who had profited most successfully from the bonanza that the Shah had unleashed were the first to go—with members of the Pahlavi dynasty leading the rush to the exit.

The Shah had actually asked his twin sister, Princess Ashraf, to leave the country—she was too much the symbol of the royal family's excesses. The walls and the floors of her newly redecorated palace—rather garish, many thought—are bare. The carpets and the pictures have been crated and flown to one of her other homes—perhaps to Juan-les-Pins, perhaps to one of her two places in Manhattan, perhaps to her house on the Avenue Montaigne in Paris, perhaps to the house of her fabulously rich businessman son in London, or perhaps to his island in the Seychelles. Her other son, a naval officer who will later pass, briefly and tragically, through this story, dined in his mother's palace one night in October 1978 and, pointing to the one picture remaining on the wall, said, "There's one they forgot to take."

From the Shah's Niavaran Palace on the slopes of North Teheran, where all the rich villas are clustered, the Queen, Farah Diba, has sent a planeload of clothes and what others might call household effects to the United States.

It has been a strange time for customs officers throughout Western Europe and North America. How could they possibly assess the value of the trinkets being imported—suitcases and crates crammed with carpets, pictures, furniture, diamonds, strings of pearls, ruby rings, emerald earrings, tiaras, silver services. Teheran banks have been swamped with requests for money transfers —almost every rich person in the country suddenly wants his or

her money telexed to accounts in Switzerland, Paris, London,
New York, the Cayman Islands. Employees of the Central Bank
have gone on strike, refused to send any more telexes, and circulated documents accusing two of the Shah's nephews and an army
general, among others, of transferring $2.4 billion to banks out-
side Iran.

It is a time for journals and diaries. In London the Shah's ambassador, Parviz Radji, who had been, inter alia, the lover of
Princess Ashraf, has been agonizing daily over the turn that his
country has taken, the corruption of the court of which he was a
part, and the inglorious way in which it has now all collapsed. He
recounts a rumor—false, it later seems—that the Shah in his despair now goes to a friend's house to smoke opium three times a
week. He wonders whether anyone now has sympathy for the
Shah, or whether his vanity, his vainglory, his hectoring, his in-
sensitivity, his military obsessions, have not lost him all goodwill,
at home and abroad.

Radji thinks he ought to go back to Teheran so as not to be
"lumped with the more infamous of the Shah's associates" in people's minds. A friend warns him not to do so. "The current joke
in Teheran is about the fox who was hurrying out of town. Someone asked the reason for such haste. The fox said: 'In that town
they kill all foxes that have three balls.' 'But have you got three
balls?' he was asked. 'No,' replied the fox, 'but they kill you first
and count your balls afterwards.' "

In the town of frightened foxes, a British diplomat phoned one
of the richest businessmen in the country. "Is he in?" "No, he's
in prison," came the answer. The diplomat knew that was untrue
but asked why the man was imprisoned. "Because he sent a
hundred and fifty million dollars out of the country," came the
reply. "Who are you?" asked the diplomat. "One of his servants,"
the voice stated. "The oddest things can happen," noted the diplomat in his diary.

A few senior officials, including a former prime minister and
the former head of the secret police, SAVAK, have been arrested
on the Shah's orders. But these were little more than futile, almost
feckless, gestures of appeasement (and personal betrayal) by the
Shah. In these last months of 1978 almost all the golden people of
Iran and the international wheeler-dealers who had fed off them
and with them have vanished—westward. One of the most fabulously rich of the Shah's ministers, Hushang Ansary, has obtained

permission to leave on the grounds that he had an urgent appointment with Henry Kissinger. From the airport he called the U.S.
ambassador to say he would be back within three days. "This may
not be *savoir faire*, but it looks like *sang froid*," commented the
ambassador in a cable to Washington. Ansary never returned.

In the old days it was hard to get an audience with the Shah.
The palace bustled with courtiers, officials, cronies, and those
whom the French call *affairistes*. (Sadly, there is no exactly equivalent expression in English; the French have in mind businessmen
whose fingers seem to stick everywhere.) Everyone was then seeking the monarch's presence. His appointments were rigidly controlled. It was his imprimatur rather than his ear that people
wanted. The Shah was not known as a great listener—not at least
to Iranians. He suffered foreigners more gladly. In any case, in
the old days, no Iranian ever came to give him advice. Everyone
knew that the only source of political acumen was the Shah himself. But by the end of 1978, all that had changed. The old crowds
had largely fled, the King was seeking counsel, and almost anyone
could drop by.

All at once in the anterooms of the palace were scores of people
who had not been seen or allowed anywhere near the place in
recent years. Members of the National Front, the opposition the
Shah had crushed in the fifties and ignored ever since, leftists,
rightists, monarchists, republicans, dentists, doctors, lawyers—
almost anyone it seems could finally get in to see His Imperial
Majesty. Each of them had his pet theories on what had caused
the massive, popular Islamic uprising, and on how the situation
should now develop.

Even "intellectuals" were allowed in. The Shah had sometimes
shown disdain for many such people. He and his courtiers used
the French word *"intellectuel"* to refer to them. The first syllable,
pronounced *an*, means "shit" in Persian. The Shah used to stress
that syllable, *"ANtellectuel,"* when referring to anyone with education who was thought not to embrace everything the Pahlavis
embodied.

There came one day to the palace a certain Dr. Shakhar. He was
a lawyer who had not seen the Shah for the last twenty years. He
asked the master of the horse, whom he knew, to arrange an
audience. The master of the horse, Kambiz Atabai, obliged, and
Dr. Shakhar was shown into His Majesty's presence. When he

emerged, Dr. Shakhar seemed to think that the talk had gone well and he asked for another audience. This too he was granted; he spent another two hours with the Shah. Triumphantly he told the master of the horse that he had the solution to everything "in my back pocket."

Kambiz Atabai, a slim, good-looking man, asked him if he would share his secret, and Dr. Shakhar said by all means. He had, he said, advised the Shah to erect a hundred scaffolds in Teheran and to hang on them a hundred people, starting with his former prime minister. Then all would be well.

The master of the horse said later that he had not been overly impressed by this proposal. Everyone's solution was subjective, he thought, based on the resentments and jealousies festered in the long, bitter years of internal exile that the Shah had imposed on all those who would not recognize his sole and divinely inspired leadership of Iran. Now the Shah was getting each of those personal, often vindictive views one by one. Never before had he been subjected to such a plethora of opinions—often from people with whom he had no real relationship, many of whom bore him and his family substantial grudges. "We all wanted to save the country. We all had a solution and we all wanted to present it to one man alone," said Kambiz Atabai.

A few weeks before he left Iran, the Shah had asked one of the most respected members of the opposition that he had crushed in the fifties to try to form a government. This man, Gholam Hussein Saddiqi, tried and failed. When he told the Shah he could not find anyone to serve under him, the Shah was astonished and asked "Why?"

Saddiqi, a learned and formidable *intellectuel*, was embarrassed if not frightened, because his answer could never before have been given by a subject to the Shahanshah, King of Kings, Light of the Aryans, Mohammed Reza Pahlavi. Hesitantly, he said it was because no one wanted to be associated with the Shah. At this the Shah snapped forward, flung out his arms, and shouted, "Why? Why? I do not understand."

Until only months before, the Shah had genuinely believed that he was beloved by the Iranian people. Perhaps this meant no more than that he believed the propaganda, the lies, and the flattery of those who surrounded him; still, his belief had been complete. But in the last twelve months the fury of the entire nation had been aroused against him by an aged, exiled cleric for whom he had only contempt. Suddenly the people, his people, were expressing only loathing for all that he had achieved in his thirty-seven years on the throne. It was impossible for him to comprehend.

Only a year ago the Shah had seemed to himself and to his allies to be utterly secure. President Jimmy Carter had spent New Year's Eve 1977–78 with him and praised him extravagantly. And then the Shah had allowed the publication of a scurrilous attack on his clerical enemy, Ayatollah Khomeini. To everyone's astonishment, this had opened a whole wellspring of bitterness against his regime and precipitated a cycle of protests, killings, mournings, more protests, more killings, throughout the spring and summer.

Two terrible climaxes occurred. One, in August 1978, was a fire in a cinema in Abadan. The doors were locked from the outside. Four hundred people perished. The government blamed the inferno on Muslim fundamentalists. The opposition said it was the work of SAVAK, the secret police. That was what most people believed. Then at the beginning of September, troops opened fire on demonstrators in Jaleh Square in South Teheran. Hundreds were killed or wounded.

This last event had a catastrophic effect on the Shah. When President Carter called him soon after it, the Shah spoke as if shell-shocked by the diabolical conspiracy against him. Those who saw him then say he seemed to shrink into himself and lose whatever vestige of certainty he had till then retained.

A few days after the massacre, the Shah had an opportunity to show himself as a compassionate leader after an earthquake destroyed the town of Tabas and killed about twenty thousand people. But instead of going into the streets where mullahs, students, and soldiers were desperately digging people out, he merely flew into the airport, where the military rescue operation was being organized. He stood around, stiff, resplendent, and uncomfortable in the brilliant plumage of a field marshal's uniform. Then he flew out again. In terms of identifying himself with the people's suffering, it was a disaster.

At around the same time, Michael Blumenthal, the U.S. treasury secretary, visited him while on a swing through the Middle East in search of petrodollars for investment in the States. He had met the Shah a year before, and the Shah had lectured him imperiously on the need for law and order in affairs of state. "You in the United States don't understand how a country should be run," the Shah had declared.

Blumenthal went to the palace for lunch. He barely recognized the Shah. The athletic, arrogant, and handsome monarch of 1977 had been replaced by a sick, befuddled man who had no idea what was happening. "I don't know what to do," he told Blumenthal. "I don't know what they want me to do." He repeated this over and over, as if he believed that if only "they," whoever they were, told him how to act, then everything would be all right. In between such anguished pleas, there were long and embarrassing silences while he simply stared at the floor. To Blumenthal he seemed like a ghost.

Back in Washington Blumenthal went straight to see Zbigniew Brzezinski, Jimmy Carter's national security adviser. "You've got a zombie out there," he said. "What are we doing in Iran? Have we got some fallback position? You've got to understand that we can't count on the Shah anymore."

But there was no one else. For at least twenty-five years, Western policy had been to help the Shah destroy all alternatives to his own rule.

Soon after Blumenthal's visit, the Shah's naval commander, Admiral Kamilladin Habib Olahi, one of the more thoughtful senior officers, came to see his King. He brought with him a thirty-page document proposing a military takeover of the country. After he was shown into the King's presence, the admiral kept his eyes lowered, as was normal in audiences with the Shah, stood to attention, and read from his memorandum. The Shah paced up and down the room. The admiral suggested that the revolution was coming to a head and the Shah must order the military to take control. They would have to arrest everyone responsible for the present crisis. This included perhaps five thousand of the most corrupt courtiers and businessmen—to calm the millions of people who wanted the government overthrown—and five thousand mullahs and revolutionaries.

Sitting much later in the genteel coffee shop of a Holiday Inn in suburban Virginia, Habib Olahi recalled that as the Shah walked to and fro, he said, "This is against the constitution."

"But it is the only way to save the country. The revolution is already in an advanced state. Nothing can save Iran except an equal force in the opposite direction."

"You think I should act against the constitution?"

"Yes, Your Majesty. It is the only way to save the country."

There was silence. It lasted for about five minutes. The Shah kept on walking back and forth. Habib Olahi, a stocky man, still stood at attention, his eyes fixed on the rich carpet. Neither man spoke. Finally the naval commander realized that the Shah was not going to approve his plan. He started to talk about something quite different.

Habib Olahi left the palace very pessimistic. "Every book on revolutions shows that they succeed when the head of state loses his nerve. The Shah was so indecisive." Habib Olahi thought part of the blame lay with Iran's allies—particularly the Americans and the British, who were giving him differing advice. Others around the Shah agreed with that. All through his life, the Shah had depended on the counsel of foreigners. Now he was not getting it.

The Shah had at court a tall, slim, well-dressed man, a former ambassador to Washington, Vienna, and Bonn. He was now the grand master of ceremonies. His name was Amir Aslan Afshar.

Mr. Afshar was not an *intellectuel* and his position did not afford him great administrative power. But it did give him unique access to the Shah. There were those who might have used that access to greater effect than Afshar, some who might have been more ruthless, perhaps, for he was not really an aggressive man. He was a courtier. But he was with the Shah constantly throughout those final months of 1978 and early 1979.

For weeks now Afshar's office had been chaotic, besieged every day by rich men and rich women reminding him of past favors, promising him future ones. Some wanted to see the Shah; others were more interested in fleeing the whirlwind then reaping it. Some of them already had homes abroad, as did Afshar himself. Many of them were, with reason, frightened of the Shah's desperate attempt to find scapegoats to appease the mobs. In the last months of 1978 several of his former servants were arrested in this vain hope.

On November 5, 1978, four generals called Afshar saying they must see him at once. November 5 was a particularly bad day, the day, in the words of the British ambassador, that "the balloon went up." An ayatollah had been released from three years' detention and mobs took to the streets to celebrate. Thousands of young men attacked government buildings, banks, offices of state enterprises, liquor shops—anything associated with the regime. Windows were smashed. Furniture was dragged into the streets and burned along with cars and buses. Young men danced around the flames and slapped onto those cars that did dare pass stickers proclaiming "Death to the Shah." The chancery of the British embassy was attacked and part of it was burned down.

Since the massacre in Jaleh Square, the soldiers had been under orders—from the Shah himself—to avoid bloodshed. The Shah constantly said to those around him that while a dictator could survive by massacring the people, a king could never do so. This is not to say that force was thereafter eschewed. It was used in Isfahan, in the north, and in the west—but less in Teheran. Within the government and the court there was a constant debate as to how many deaths the United States, and other allies of the Shah, would tolerate. "Would you accept five thousand deaths? Ten thousand? Twenty thousand?" was a question frequently asked of American officials by Iranian ambassadors and other emissaries.

In the last three months of 1978, the Army in Teheran was patrolling under restraint. Stuck out on the streets day after day, taunted and mocked, the troops became demoralized. No one would take a decision. The master of the horse, Kambiz Atabai, later told the story of how one day a lieutenant and his men were caught in a hostile crowd at the university. The lieutenant was screaming into his walkie-talkie for advice. No one would give it. His plight went all the way up to his general, who was in the palace. Even he would not give an order. The lieutenant was shouting, "What must I do? I have to defend my soldiers." The general replied, "Tell him to use his initiative. There must be no bloodshed. I will report to His Majesty and come back to him."

Now, on November 5, one of the generals urged Afshar, "The whole city is burning; you must tell His Imperial Majesty to do something."

"You are generals, you should talk to him," Afshar replied. But, by his own account, he agreed he would speak to the Shah if they too would do so. So when the Shah left his office to drive back to the residence in the palace grounds, Afshar rushed toward him. He fell on his knees and grasped his monarch around his legs.

"What is going on?" asked the Shah.

Afshar replied, "Your Majesty, you have to do something. The people are very unhappy. They are burning shops and are in the streets. Something has to be done."

Behind the figure of Afshar hugging the Shah's legs, the four generals also fell to their knees. "I really wanted to stop the Shah, to get him to do something," said Afshar long afterward.

The Shah replied, "But the troops are in the city."

To which one general, later killed, stood up, saluted the Shah, and, with tears in his eyes, said, "Majesty, the soldiers do nothing. They are not allowed to shoot. People make fun of them and spit on them and laugh at them."

Then, recalled Afshar, "The generals and I said, 'Majesty, it is time to put a strong man in charge of government.' " Afshar and the others wanted General Gholam Ali Oveissi, the governor of Teheran, to be made prime minister. He was known as "The Butcher of Teheran" because of the massacre of Jaleh Square. He was reckoned to be one of the officers prepared to use force to put down the revolution.

The Shah said, "OK, OK. It's all right. Get up and I will see what I can do."

But that night, he summoned the British and American ambassadors, and after talking to them he appointed as prime minister his chief of staff, General Gholamreza Azhari, a mild-mannered man who was absolutely opposed to the use of force.

When the Shah informed Afshar of this, his grand master of ceremonies said nothing. "He was the Shah. I could not question his judgments or decisions." But a few months later, in exile, he did ask the Shah why he had not chosen Oveissi. The Shah, according to Afshar, replied that the British and American ambassadors had been against it; they thought it was better to have a quiet man like Azhari, who could discuss problems with the mullahs leading the revolutionary ferment.

Afshar drew his own conclusions from this. "I think," he said much later in his apartment overlooking the Mediterranean in France, "that this was another of the West's attempts to undermine the Shah. With Oveissi we could have ended the whole thing. We had a list of three to four hundred people who were the key organizers. We could have arrested them. Having Azhari was another way of trying to destabilize Iran, to bring the Shah's rule to an end."

· · ·

In Afshar's attitude, one senses one of the many paradoxes of the Iranian revolution. Millions of Iranians—perhaps the majority, it is hard to tell—saw the Shah as did Ayatollah Khomeini: he was an agent of the Great Satan, as Khomeini called the United States. The idea that the U.S. and Britain were actually conspiring against the Shah was less pervasive. But it was strongly felt by many in the court, and indeed by the Shah himself.

All through his life the Shah had been obsessed by the way other nations controlled or manipulated Iran, particularly the British, the Russians, and the Americans. This was understandable enough. After all, it was the British and the Russians who had dominated Iran through the nineteenth and much of the twentieth centuries. The British had encouraged his father to seize power in the 1920s. Then they and the Russians had deposed him and installed the Shah himself on the throne in 1941. For many years the British had tried to run him, or so it seemed to many. Since the 1950s they had lost a good deal of their influence over him to the Americans. Many Iranians around the Shah believed that the British resented this and blamed the Shah for it.

Nonetheless, faced with the greatest crisis of his reign, and unable to sift through the unfathomable views and motives of his countrymen, the Shah had turned increasingly to foreign advisers.

One of those who visited him was the Comte Alexandre de Marenches, the conservative head of the French secret service, who had known and admired the Shah for years. At the end of 1978, when he realized the danger that Khomeini was inflicting on the Shah from France, Marenches says he tried to have him expelled from the country. He flew to Teheran to consult the Shah. After driving through streets filled with angry demonstrators, he found the Shah in a darkened room of the palace, wearing large sunglasses that hid half his face. The Shah said he wanted the French to keep Khomeini; if he went to Syria or Libya he would be even more dangerous.

For Marenches the most dramatic moment of the interview was when the Shah turned to him and said, "You do understand, my dear count, that I can never fire on my own people." Thinking of the crowds "spreading terror in Teheran," Marenches says he replied, "Sire, in that case you are lost."

When the audience was over, the Shah led Marenches with great courtesy to the door. He took off his glasses to shake hands, and the light fell upon his face. Marenches thought he looked ravaged.

Next day in Paris, Marenches called on President Giscard d'Estaing. The president rose to greet him and asked, *"Alors?"*
"C'est Louis XVI," said Marenches.
"Alors, c'est la fin," said Giscard.

More frequent visitors to the palace in the last months were the American and British ambassadors, William Sullivan and Anthony Parsons. Both of them have published their accounts of the Shah's final days and their frequent meetings with him. What emerges is the Shah's complete inability to understand what had gone wrong, what mistakes he had made.

But they too managed only to confuse him. Did they want further liberalization? Did they want him to crack down on the rioters? Would they put up with thousands of imprisonments and deaths? He could not tell. The messages from Washington and London were discordant. Some American officials wanted force. Others did not. The British seemed to be against it, but the British could never be trusted.

The British ambassador, Anthony Parsons, a man whose heavy spectacles gave him an amiable academic appearance, was an Arabist who had been in Iran since 1974. Parsons was equivocal about the regime. He liked the Shah personally, but, as he later acknowledged, he had been so intent on promoting British exports to Iran that he had given too little weight to many of the country's problems. His wife had been much more critical of Pahlavi excesses than he.

In the crucial summer months of 1978, as the Shah disintegrated, Parsons had gone on home leave, as had the U.S. ambassador. Since his return, Parsons had become heavily involved with the Shah, attempting to advise him and to answer his questions as to why the people had turned against him. Parsons had said that among the causes was the fact that the massive influx into the cities following the mid-seventies oil boom had created a rootless, unhappy proletariat.

In Teheran thousands of workers spent their days building villas or even palaces for the rich and their nights in hovels or holes in the ground. The materialism was crass, everyone's expectations had been aroused, and few people had been satisfied. There was no confidence between the government and people. Little wonder people turned to their traditional leaders, the mullahs, said Parsons. The Shah did not disagree.

Parsons was due to leave Iran for London in early 1979. He found his last meeting with the Shah a profoundly emotional experience and told the Shah he was so moved by the tragedy of it all that he would rather not speak. The Shah smiled and put his hand on Parsons' arm as the ambassador faltered, tears in his eyes. "Never mind, I know how you feel. But we must have one last talk," said the Shah.

He said he was getting three different sets of advice: to stay and "tough it out," to retire to a naval base and let the Army put down the people in his absence, or to leave. What did Parsons think?

Parsons said he was loath to answer, because anything he said would be seen as a British plot.*

The Shah insisted. Reluctantly, and stressing this was only his "personal" opinion, nothing to do with the British government, the British ambassador replied that a crackdown could not work, that if the Shah was now forced to withdraw to a naval base, he would soon have to leave altogether anyway, but that if he did now leave Iran, the chances of his coming back were slight.

The Shah then made a strange gesture. He looked at his watch and said, "If it was up to me I would leave in—ten minutes." But he had to stay, he said—because the parliament had not yet confirmed his new prime minister, Shapour Bakhtiar. (The previous premier, General Azhari, had suffered a heart attack after only a few weeks in office.)

Parsons thought this was ridiculous, but he realized that even days before he would flee, the Shah was unable to acknowledge that power had slid from him like snow from the mountains in spring.

Till now Iran had, on paper, a constitutional monarchy, but in reality all power was exercised by the Shah. He had controlled the government and the parliament. Now, he had just appointed a new Cabinet and he insisted that he would not leave until it had been formally approved by the Majles, or parliament, as the constitution demanded. Only then could the new prime minister formally take up the vast burden of his office. Parsons considered this absurd. As if anyone any longer cared for such constitutional

---

* When a former British foreign secretary, Lord George-Brown, visited the Shah at the end of 1978 and told him he thought he should leave the country, the Shah took this as being an instruction from the British government. So far as is known, Lord George-Brown was acting in a strictly personal capacity.

niceties. This was a revolution. It was not a picnic. But it was the Shah's way.

The U.S. ambassador, William Sullivan, was very different from Parsons. With a bushy crop of gray-white hair, burly, ramrod straight, he was a veteran of Laos and the Philippines, and by his own account neither very knowledgeable about nor very sympathetic to Iran.

Like Parsons, he had been out of Teheran as the Shah's power crumbled in the summer of 1978. After his return, he went dozens of times to the palace. Often the Shah summoned him and Parsons together. On some of these visits the atmosphere in the palace had been macabre.

On one occasion in the early fall, the Shah had turned on Sullivan, recited almost every incident of unrest, and declared that it was all so sophisticated that it must be the result of foreign intrigue against him. The KGB were not capable of coordinating such protests, he said, so it must be the work of British intelligence and the CIA. Well, he said to Sullivan, he knew that the British had never liked him. But why had the CIA turned on him? Had he done something wrong? Or had Washington and Moscow reached some grand design in which Iran was divided between them as part of a plan for world condominium?

The Shah's tone was plaintive, hurt, inquiring, rather than angry. Sullivan found it almost pathetic—as well as astounding. The ambassador tried to explain what he knew of the sources of unrest and said he thought the mullahs were getting their money from the merchants in the bazaars, not from the CIA. The Shah seemed surprised. Sullivan realized that he had almost no one to talk to, except, of course, Sullivan himself, and Parsons. He did talk to his wife, Empress Farah, but otherwise he had never been at ease with Iranians.

On another occasion, Sullivan arrived in his armor-plated Chrysler (which an enraged mob had once found too heavy to overturn) to find the palace surrounded by tanks (sold to the Shah by the British) and by units of the Imperial Guard heavily armed with machine guns and antiaircraft weapons. But the usual doorman was not on duty. Sullivan opened the door himself and went in alone.

There were no soft-footed, tailcoated aides-de-camp in the hall. He wandered along the thick carpets through to the main drawing room. Still there was no one. The whole palace seemed deserted, as if the royal family and all the staff had already taken the road to Varennes.

Eventually the lost ambassador was found by Empress Farah. She was as surprised as he was, and went off to look for some servants. Finally he was taken upstairs to the Shah's study.

In some of their talks the Shah had seemed drained by events. Sometimes he was nervous; at other times, strangely calm. At all times he was uncomprehending and desperate for advice. Just what did Washington want? This was a tough question for Sullivan. Washington was divided, with the national security adviser, Zbigniew Brzezinski, arguing for a crackdown, and the secretary of state, Cyrus Vance, urging restraint. So the ambassador could not take a single firm line.

At the end of December Sullivan went to the palace on a mission that, he says, was rather unusual for an ambassador. It was to tell the head of state to whom he was accredited that he ought to leave the country. But their relationship had become so close over the last few months that even this advice did not seem all that "surrealistic" to Sullivan.

The Shah listened quietly and then turned to Sullivan "almost beseechingly, throwing out his hands and saying, 'Yes, but where will I go?' "

Sullivan later claimed that he had been given no instructions on this point. But he remembered that the Shah had a house in Switzerland. Every winter for years the popular illustrated papers of Europe had devoted great color spreads to the Shah and his wife and four children on the ski slopes. For après-ski, half the finance ministers or even heads of European governments used to come to pay court, to seek this or that contract, some one or other loan —anything to divert some of the Shah's new oil wealth back to Europe. And for après-après-ski there were always the lovely blond women flown in from Madame Claude's famous establishment in Paris.

But Switzerland the Shah now dismissed, saying the security was no good.

"We also have a home in England," he said, "but the weather is so bad." He might also have said, as he had on countless occasions, that although he had constantly looked to the British for advice, he distrusted them acutely. Instead, he just kept looking at the American ambassador with what Sullivan describes as "soulful eyes."

So Sullivan asked, "Your Majesty, would you like me to seek an invitation for you to go to the United States?"

At that the Shah leaned forward, almost like a little boy in his eagerness, and said, "Would you, would you really?"

The Shah's version of this meeting was somewhat different. After Sullivan left, he talked to Iranians who had come to the palace to see him. He said to them in wonderment, "Do you know what Sullivan has just said to me? That I must leave."

Amir Aslan Afshar, the grand master of ceremonies, said later, "He didn't want to leave. I know. I was the closest to him. I was with him twenty-four hours a day and he called me all the time. At the beginning of January he decided to go to the U.S. for two months and then come back. He said to me, 'Prepare yourself for two months.' I sent my suitcase to the palace. From the Protocol Department I packed some small gifts, carpets and things like that. We sent a small planeload of things ahead of us to the States.

"The Shah wanted to go to America because he didn't know what Sullivan was reporting and didn't know what was happening in the U.S. He wanted to talk to Carter and the Senate and the CIA. 'I'm going to explain to them all the importance of Iran to the U.S. and the danger of it falling to extremists,' he said."

Within twenty-four hours Washington told Sullivan that the Shah would be welcome to come to the United States. He could stay at the Palm Springs home of Walter Annenberg, newspaper publisher, millionaire, friend of the Shah's friend Richard Nixon, former ambassador to the Court of St. James. Sullivan was told to convey the invitation in the name of the president and to ask how many people would be traveling with the Shah. At this time Ayatollah Khomeini was declaring that any country which took the Shah out of Iran would be doing the revolution a favor. So Sullivan actually thought that by taking the Shah, the U.S. might gain points with the opposition, whose triumph he now regarded as inevitable.

On January 12 Sullivan went to see the Shah again. According to the Shah's subsequent account, "The atmosphere was grim. My departure was no longer a matter of days, Sullivan said, but of hours." The Shah recalled that Sullivan "looked meaningfully at his watch."

Sullivan remembers the meeting rather differently. Indeed, throughout the story of the Shah's last year, recollections differ enormously. There is no one version on which everyone agrees, no single destination, no unity of perception or goal. Nor could there be. This was a revolution in which allegiances constantly shifted, perceptions changed, unexpected futures suddenly beckoned, and equally unforeseen punishments became dreadful threats. Accounts are bound to differ.

As far as Sullivan recalled, the Shah seemed relieved to be invited to the U.S. and suggested he should fly to Andrews Air Force base outside Washington. This is where state visitors usually land, and Sullivan thought the Shah hoped that he might then be given an official welcome by President Carter or other senior U.S. officials. There were ample precedents for such a notion. The Shah had repeatedly been to America during the last thirty years; he had been welcomed with full honors as not only an important chief of state but also a vital ally by every single president since Harry Truman.

But Sullivan did not think that such a grand welcome would now be appropriate. It was one thing to ease the Shah's passing out of Iran, quite another to accord him full honors on arrival in the United States. Washington would require a good relationship with the new Iranian authorities, Iran being the strategically vital country it was. The president was supposed to be disassociating himself from the Shah, not encouraging him.

So Sullivan recommended rather that the Shah enter the States through an obsure air force base in either Maine or South Carolina, and best of all at night. He could fly on to Travis Air Force base in California and then take a helicopter to the Annenberg estate. In other words, he was supposed to slip through the back door into the country, unseen, unheard, and unsung.

The Shah seemed to Sullivan to accept the proposal. But the Shah was not happy. In his memoirs, he later quoted one of his generals saying, as he faced his trial and firing squad, that the Americans "threw the Shah out of the country like a dead mouse."

The Shah's office was in the grounds of Niavaran Palace. Part of the palace was a rather plain, square, white building put up in the early 1960s for state visitors. The subsequent growth of Teheran had made the previous royal quarters in town too cramped, and after an attempt on the Shah's life in 1965, one of several that he survived, the family had moved to Niavaran. From the iron gates that gave onto the road the palace was visible through tall plane trees, but it was not easily accessible. Banks of guards, telephones, TV monitors, and electronic friskers kept out unwelcome visitors and made the grounds secure for the Shah, his wife, their children, their dogs, and their courtiers.

The Shah's main office was altogether prettier. It was on the slope of the gardens in a tiny old palace built by the previous (Qajar) dynasty. It had since been rebuilt; its arched windows and steep roofs made it look like a Russian provincial home.

There the Shah worked in a large salon that looked out through tall windows onto the city below. It was furnished with gilt, beveled mirrors, chandeliers, gold-plated telephones, gold cigarette boxes studded with jewels, gold pens and inkwells. This was in keeping with the style of the palace itself. But in the office, such traditional "Versailles-kitsch" furniture was offset by charts, radios, tape recorders, and other modern gadgetry, including an illuminated wall map.

Outside this office was a smaller room, little more than an antechamber. It contained a large white marble bust of the Shah's father, Reza Shah, who had dominated his son as much as he had his country.

Now, just before he left the country for what would be the last time, the Shah went in there and paused in front of the graven image of the ruthless and brilliant army officer who had seized power in 1921, and ended the Qajar dynasty, proclaimed himself the new Shah, the first of the Pahlavi dynasty, and begun to re-create Iran.

A vast and awesome leader, Reza Shah had ruled despotically, trying to force the factions, oligarchies, and tribes of Iran to accept centralized authority and the appurtenances of the twentieth century.

In the old days, the courtiers who clucked around his son, Mohammed Reza, would constantly invoke the name of the old man. They would tell Mohammed Reza that his achievements were even greater than those of his father. No praise could be higher.

But during the trauma of 1978, the Shah's courtiers no longer mentioned his father's name. They were concerned lest the Shah

should think that they were rebuking him or comparing him un-
favorably with the man of steel. They did not want him to make
the comparison himself.

Privately people made another, even more invidious comparison among themselves. They said that Reza Shah was a man to
whom no one dared to lie. With his son, no one dared to tell the
truth.

Now, as the son came to see the marble bust for the last time,
court photographers crowded around to capture the poignancy of
the son saying good-bye, presumably with a sense of terrible failure, to the father for whom he had never been good enough.
There stood the Shah, impeccable as ever in a well-cut gray suit
and rather loud tie, ramrod straight, his face, as always, expressionless before the cold white stare of his father.

Then he turned on his heel and walked down the stairs.

On January 16 the Shah and the Empress, Farah Diba, left the
Niavaran Palace for the last time. Instead of flying straight to the
United States, the Shah had decided at the last minute to accept an
invitation from Anwar Sadat of Egypt to pause briefly in Aswan.

For the Queen the last few months had been perhaps harder
than for the Shah himself. "There wasn't really five minutes of
breathing calmly," she said later. "If we had ten to twenty minutes, we were happy." While the court crumbled around them
and advisers fled, she had become more and more vital to the
Shah, lending him continual strength. In 1978 he came to depend
on her almost completely.

Like him, she had been against destroying the revolution with
massive bloodshed. And like him, she was uncertain whether they
should leave. At one stage she says she suggested that he go and
she stay, for the sake of those who believed in them. He refused
and said they must leave together.

Officers of the Imperial Guard and the servants lined up on the
palace steps, weeping, to say good-bye. Some of them held the
Koran over the Shah's head, to give him its customary protection
on his journey, and wailed as the royal party left by helicopter for
the airport. It had been literally years since the Shah had driven in
the streets of Teheran. Occasionally he went by car to the nearby
homes of members of his family. Otherwise it was everywhere by
air. His view of Iran had almost always been from the sky.

They landed close to the Imperial Pavilion. The Shah said later that he noticed the terrible wind and the gloomy sight of the planes grounded by strikes.

In the pavilion he made a little speech to a few reporters. "As I said when this [new] government was formed, I am feeling tired and need a rest. I also stated that when I felt that things were going well and the government was settled I would take a trip and that trip starts now. . . ."

Asked how long he would be away he said softly, "I don't know."

He then waited for his new prime minister, Shapour Bakhtiar, who had been imprisoned several times during his reign, and in whose hands he was now leaving the country.

The Shah did not like Bakhtiar—"I had always considered him an Anglophile and an agent of British Petroleum." (Perhaps therefore he thought his appointment would please the British.) But he still would not leave until Bakhtiar had been confirmed by the Majles. He asked his staff to telephone back to the city, but all the lines from his pavilion at the airport were cut. They had to use the guards' radio, which was patched through to army headquarters and thence to the Majles.

Finally the news crackled through that Bakhtiar had indeed been confirmed. A helicopter was sent for him and shortly afterwards it clattered down on the tarmac. Bakhtiar, a thin, nervous but very elegant man who looked like a French aristocrat, with a trim mustache and superbly cut clothes, entered the pavilion and bowed before his King.

"Now you have everything in your hands," said the Shah. "I hope you will succeed. I entrust Iran to you and to God." Within days Bakhtiar would be swept away in the whirlwind of the ayatollah's return. He was the Kerensky of the Iranian revolution.

The Shah and his party, dressed against the wind, began to walk toward the plane. In front of the blue-and-white 707, he stopped for the final farewells. As neatly dressed as ever, his striped tie showing through the lapels of his overcoat, he stood stiffly, his left foot slightly forward, as if ready to walk quickly away. Several generals soon to lose their lives bent to kiss his right hand. One fell on the ground to kiss his feet and the Shah bent awkwardly to fetch him up. In his left hand, the Shah gripped his spectacles. He had barely slept for days and his white face was dominated by his broad, dark eyebrows, which were locked together in an expression suggesting both grief and incomprehension. Beside him the

Empress's face was stretched taut with misery.

Almost everyone was weeping, even Bakhtiar, who, perhaps alone of those on the tarmac, had wanted the Shah to leave. Al-

most all the military men had begged him to stay. The Shah's own eyes were wet. This was not the first time that his officers had seen him show such emotion. He said to the commander of the Imperial Guard, "Do whatever you consider necessary. I hope people are not killed." Later he wrote, "I was completely overwhelmed by the expressions of loyalty given to me when I left. There was a poignant silence broken by sobs."

It was just two in the afternoon when the Shah and the Empress and their small entourage finally took off. When the news was broadcast on Teheran radio a few moments later, the city erupted in joy. Car horns were blared for minutes on end, headlights were flashed, people danced and sang and shouted, "The Shah is gone. He's not coming back." Boys gave V signs; girls and young women in chadors laughed, danced, and shouted, "Everyone is free now." People waved gladiolus, carnations, portraits of Ayatollah Khomeini, crying, "By the force of Khomeini, the Shah has fled."

Statues of the Shah and his father were torn to the ground; newspapers with huge headlines "THE SHAH HAS GONE" were at once printed and distributed by the armload, to be enthusiastically seized and read.

Meanwhile, the Shah's 707, with the Shah himself at the controls, climbed and turned away toward the West, the source of many of his dreams and illusions, and now the object of hatred of many of his people.

CHAPTER TWO

The Party

In October 1971, Mohammed Reza Pahlavi gave a party to excel all parties. He invited the leaders of the world. Not all of them came, and many of those who did attend represented the panoply of power rather than its reality.

The party was held in the ruins of Persepolis, which was built by Darius and burned by Alexander the Great. It was supposed to mark the 2500th anniversary of the original Persian empire founded by Cyrus the Great in the sixth century B.C. In retrospect it can be seen to mark the beginning of the end of the Pahlavi dynasty, which the Shah's father had founded just fifty years before.

In 1971 the Shah was also celebrating his own thirtieth anniversary on the throne, and the tenth anniversary of his reform program, which he called the White Revolution, and which was supposed to introduce land reform, increase literacy, enfranchise women, modernize industry and the infrastructure, redistribute at least some wealth, and lessen the power of the Muslim clergy, the mullahs. Inevitably, therefore, this "revolution" had infuriated the clergy.

Nineteen seventy-one also marked the emergence of Iran as a regional force. On St. Valentine's Day that year, the oil cartel,

OPEC, had just had its first major success in forcing up oil prices. The Shah had taken a leading role in this process. Perhaps even more importantly, the British government was now completing its announced intention to withdraw its troops from "east of Suez" and, together with the Americans, had quietly been encouraging the Shah to take over the British role as the "policeman of the Gulf."

In 1971 there was a sense of self-confidence about both the Shah and his government. But, as Persepolis itself showed, it was a mood that was beginning to degenerate into unreal arrogance. The Shah had imagined it as a modern version of the Congress of Vienna of 1815, where the rulers of the world could meet and discuss matters of great import. One government handout predicted of the party that "this august, universal assembly will make Persepolis, during the unforgettable day of October 15, 1971, the center of gravity of the world."

Persepolis was a pageant in which the Shah's dreams and ambitions were unfolded. Many of those who wrote about it at the time recalled Christopher Marlowe's line, "Is it not fine to be a King and ride in triumph in Persepolis?" Triumphant it was, in a sense, for the Shah; but it was also somewhat bathetic. As with so much of what he envisaged, the reality did not quite match the vision.

Nine kings journeyed to Persepolis, three ruling princes, two crown princes, thirteen presidents, ten sheikhs, and two sultans, together with clutches of vice presidents, prime ministers, foreign ministers, ambassadors, and other friends of the court from many parts of the world.

The Shah decided to follow nineteenth-century rules of protocol, which meant that the senior guest was his friend and ally Haile Selassie, emperor of Ethiopia, Lion of Judah. President Georges Pompidou of France refused to come unless he could be seated above Haile Selassie and Francophone heads of state; the Shah refused, so, in a huff, Pompidou sent his prime minister instead. The Shah never forgave Pompidou for this insult.

The king and queen of Denmark were there. So were the kings of Jordan, Belgium, and the former king of Greece. The queen of England did not come, but she sent instead her husband, Prince Philip, and her daughter, Princess Anne. Prince Bernhard of the Netherlands represented his wife, Queen Juliana. Perhaps most disappointing to the Shah was that President Nixon did not attend. (Mrs. Nixon had been honorary chairman of the U.S. committee for the 2500th anniversary.) Vice President Spiro Agnew represented the United States—and was outranked by nearly everyone save the ambassador from Peking.

The guests aside, almost everything at the party had been brought from Paris. An encampment of tents was constructed on the dry, high plateau of Persepolis by the French decorator Jansen. The house of Jansen had, over decades, decorated the royal palace in Belgrade in 1920, the private apartments of Edward VIII (later the Duke of Windsor) at Buckingham Palace in 1935, villas in Cap d'Antibes and apartments on Fifth Avenue. Jansen's classic Parisian "style-Palais-style-Ritz, sub-Louis Quatorze" was very much the Shah's taste.

At the center of Jansen's sumptuous tent city was a sort of Big Top, where receptions and dinners were to take place. It was draped with ruby velvet and furnished with gilded chairs. The Shah and the Empress had their apartments there.

Around the main tent were scores of smaller tents for the famous and not-so-famous guests, many of whom were the important or merely rich foreign friends of various members of the court. They were cleverly designed, in France, and contained two bedrooms, two marble bathrooms, and a small, chic sitting room. There were hot plates for breakfast, refrigerators for drinks, and ironing boards for the frantic maids. The plumbing must have been a great feat of civil engineering.

Only the highest or the most favored guests were to live in the tent city, and so, inevitably, the fighting between socialites to ensure places there was fierce. Imelda Marcos gave Christina Ford space in her tent. The less fortunate guests had to come daily from the new hotel in Persepolis or even from Shiraz, forty miles away. That town had been given a face-lift. The prison, where some of the dissidents who opposed the Shah's rule were held by SAVAK, was painted up, the streets were cleaned, pots of flowers were placed all along the main roads, birds in cages were hung from lampposts, shopkeepers were given blue coats to wear. As soon as the party was over, all the finery, even the shopkeepers' jackets, was taken away. Only the painted prison remained.

Top hairdressers flew in from the Paris salons of Carita and Alexandre; Elizabeth Arden created a new makeup named Farah, to be given in kits to the guests; Baccarat designed the crystal goblets; Ceralene fashioned the place settings after a fifth-century B.C. Persian ceramic; Robert Havilland produced a cup-and-saucer service to be used just once by arriving guests; and Porthault, one of the great French linen makers, made the private and state linens. Lanvin created new uniforms for the gentlemen of the court. The coats were ornately if not fabulously stitched with over a mile of gold thread. Each took about five hundred hours of work.

The food at Persepolis was prepared by Maxim's aided by other leading French and Swiss chefs and caterers. The year before, Maxim's services had been tried out when the Ministry of the Court commissioned them to provide a banquet in the desert for a hundred people. M. Louis Vaudable of Maxim's personally supervised that affair and created an exquisite new dish of caviar and poached quails' eggs. Unfortunately the Shah never ate caviar and would not touch his food. So no one else could do so either. Eventually Maxim's improvised and placed some leeks, which had been used for consommé, in front of the King. He began to eat and everyone else could then do so. This time the dish was repeated for the guests and the Shah had an artichoke. The only food on the menu that was Iranian was the caviar; almost everything else came from France.

The menu for the main banquet was printed in black, with intricate gold filigrees, on vellum pages and bound in a little book whose covers were in blue silk and gold. *Oeufs de Cailles aux Perles de Bandar Pahlavi* was followed by *Mousse de Queues d'Écrevisses, Sauce Nantua*. The principal course was *Selle d'Agneau des grands plateaux, farcie et rôtie dans son jus*. To refresh the palate there was then a *Sorbet au Vieux Champagne* (Moët 1911). Then came *Paon à l'Impériale, Salade Composée selon Alexandre Dumas, Turban de Figues garni de Framboises au Porto,* and finally *Café Moka*.

The wines were appropriate. Vin Nature de la Champagne, Château de Saran; Château Haut-Brion blanc 1964; Château Lafite-Rothschild 1945; Musigny Comte de Vogüé 1945; Dom Pérignon Rosé 1959 Cuvée Ravissime; and, with the coffee, Cognac Prince Eugène, *Réserve des Caves Maxim's*.

After the banquet, other French experts had created a *son et lumière* spectacle and a fireworks display. Still other French artists helped devise the "authentic" uniforms in which the Iranian Army could parade dressed as Persians of centuries gone by. The guests sat with rugs and hot water bottles watching the parade of the Shah's own incomplete vision of Iranian history.

Like any other country, the history and the passion of Iran has been the product of its location. The Shah liked to call it "the crossroads of civilization," situated as it is between Russia and the Persian Gulf, midway between Europe and the Far East. Iran is much larger than any country of Western Europe; its territory today covers about 636,000 square miles, about the same area as Western Europe from Spain to Germany. It has borders with the Soviet Union, Turkey, Iraq, Pakistan, and Afghanistan. To the north is the Caspian Sea; to the south and west, the Persian Gulf, through which most of the world's oil has passed in the twentieth century.

Iran has always been inhabited by many different peoples or tribes. If its history is taken as stretching back 2,500 years, Iran has had periods of imperial greatness, but Iranians have also experienced successive waves of invasion, intervention, and occupation, which have left them understandably fearful or suspicious of foreigners. It was the greatness of the ancient empire to which the Shah was attracted and with which he constantly compared his own achievements and ambitions.

That empire was founded by Cyrus the Great, the first of the Achaemenids, a man of great character. He conquered Lydia, now Turkey, in 546 B.C. and his domain covered almost all the eastern Mediterranean—including Babylonia, Syria, and Phoenicia. His son Cambyses drove into Egypt, and the empire was then extended by his successor Darius as far as the valley of the Indus. Darius proved to be a superb administrator. He built a canal between the Nile and the Red Sea, established a system of taxation, and constructed a fifteen-hundred-mile royal road from Sardis to Susa. It was a mammoth and indeed crippling undertaking, and by the end of Darius's reign the vast empire was in decline. In 330 B.C. Persia was conquered by Alexander the Great.

Alexander was much struck by the quality of the learning and the administration of the country; he treated the royal family he had overthrown with esteem. He ordered the tomb of Cyrus at Pasargadae to be well preserved, and he was infuriated when he later discovered that it had been vandalized. But in Iran he is remembered more for the fact that he destroyed Persepolis by fire.*

Alexander's death was followed by years of savage internecine fighting between his own commanders. Finally the nomadic Parthians moved from northeast Iran, defeated the Seleucids, and established themselves on the high plateau of Persia. The Parthians were followed, two centuries after Christ, by the Sassanians, whose Shahanshah, or king, still ruled over a vast area, including parts of what are now Georgia, Armenia, Afghanistan, Bahrain, and Iraq. The Sassanian empire survived until Iran's conquest by the Muslim Arabs in the seventh century A.D.

It was this fantastic history that the Shah celebrated at Persepolis in 1971. He had persuaded himself that he was the spiritual heir to Cyrus, and that he too would extend and advance the Persian empire.

---

* There are several theories as to why Alexander did this. One is that it was in revenge for the burning of the Acropolis by Xerxes some 150 years earlier. Another is that Thaïs, the mistress of Ptolemy, one of Alexander's generals, suggested that if Alexander burned Persepolis, Persian culture would be extinguished forever. In a drunken frenzy, Alexander did as was proposed. Persian culture survived; Hellenistic influence in the area did not.

For the celebration, soldiers of his Army had been forbidden to shave for the last month so that their faces would more nearly represent those of warriors of old. Lesley Blanch, an official biographer of the Queen, later described the scene.

The tight crimped beards of the Medes and the Persians; the small pointed beards of the Safavids, or the fierce moustaches of Qajar troops. Shields, lances, pennons, broadswords and daggers of earlier warriors, all were there. Beneath a scorching sun, but shielded by parasols for those in need, the guests, who were seated on a rostrum below the pillared ruins of Cyrus' might, watched this impressive defile. Achaemenian foot guards, Parthian warriors, the cavalry of Xerxes, litters, chariots, tanks, Bactrian camels. Fath Ali Shah's artillery, warriors from the Caspian or the Persian Gulf, the Air Force, the new Women's contingents of the armed forces . . . all were there at Persepolis; all attested to Iran's glories, past and present.

Many Iranians were less impressed. Later one of the Shah's ambassadors who eventually denounced him gave a different description: "It was as if some Technicolor epic of Cecil B. De Mille's was being projected onto the screen of the vast plain." Perhaps more significantly, many felt that by celebrating the Iran of Cyrus and Darius, the Shah completely and deliberately ignored a part of Iran's history that was far more relevant to the twentieth century A.D.—the teachings of the prophet Mohammed.

Unlike Jesus Christ, who is for Christians the Son of God, Mohammed, who was born in A.D. 570, is seen by his followers as God's messenger. God's messages, imparted to him in visions, are embodied in the Koran, which itself represents God's law. From the beginning Islam was a political as well as a religious movement, and in the Koran are gathered political or legal revelations as well as spiritual ones. By the end of Mohammed s life, his followers had become the dominant power in all Arabia. Within a hundred years Islam was "a mighty empire stretched from the Punjab to the Pyrenees and from Samarkand to the Sahara." In Iran, Islam saw its role as being the guardian of the people against the authority of the Shahs. The mullahs remained a dominant influence until the twentieth century when the Pahlavis attempted to curb them.

• • •

Apart from the Shah's particular version of Iranian history, there was another aspect of Persia that was indeed celebrated at Persepolis. That was the lure of Persia—the fantastic attraction it has held for Westerners ever since the seventeenth century, when traders, ambassadors, and princes began to bring back exotic spices, silks, and tales.*

Gradually, the Europeans came to see Persia as an ally against the Ottomans. The Safavid Shahs encouraged commerce and built roads, caravanseries, and workshops to produce·silk and pottery to be sent to the countries to the west.

During the eighteenth century, Persia's economy began to decline, partly because the Europeans had begun to use the sea route rather than the land route to the East. The country was conquered by the Afghans, but by the middle of the century the Persians had not only thrown out the Afghans but also marched through the Khyber Pass and captured India. Delhi was sacked and many of the Moghul treasures were carried back to Iran, including a Peacock Throne, which was lost en route and then copied by Iranian craftsmen. Almost all the Moghul jewels were also taken to Iran; they became the crown jewels of Iran's kings.

The British became a dominant influence in Persian life during

---

* Among the earliest English travelers were Anthony and Robert Sherley, from Sussex, who arrived in Persia in late 1598. Anthony convinced Shah Abbas that he would be able to persuade European monarchs to ally themselves with him against the Turks. Shah Abbas made him an ambassador, and some scholars believe that he returned to England in 1599 bearing rich gifts. It seems possible that he may have met William Shakespeare, or that Shakespeare at least heard of his adventures. In about 1600 Shakespeare wrote *Twelfth Night*, which contains several references to the Persian king and his fabulous wealth. (Sherley's sponsor, the Earl of Essex, was a friend of Shakespeare's patron, the Earl of Southampton.)

Another early European traveler was Jean Chardin, a Parisian jeweler, who reached Persia in 1665. His journal did much to introduce Persia to Europeans. He saw that the Safavid dynasty was in decay and thought Shah Abbas II a cruel man—he had burned one of his wives who had refused to sleep with him. Altogether Chardin considered Persian kings both too powerful and too indifferent to the people's welfare. He related that Shah Abbas II invited foreign dignitaries to polo matches but would not allow Europeans wine, on the grounds that their tolerance of alcohol was low. (It seemed that the Russian ambassador had once become intoxicated and insulted other guests.) The Persians themselves drank a good deal of wine and had an extensive nightlife; Chardin quotes the prices that obtained prostitutes and courtesans.

Chardin considered that poetry was a natural medium for the Persians because of their lively imaginations and because Persian was such a supple language. He quotes a Persian story that has the Serpent in the Garden of Eden speaking Arabic, the language of elegance and persuasion. Adam and Eve spoke Persian because it was so soft and insinuating. When the Angel Gabriel ordered them out of the garden, he used first Arabic and then Persian; neither had the desired effect. So he resorted to Turkish, which was a threatening language, and the sinners left at once.

the nineteenth century; but to this day many Persians believe that Britain merely exploited Persia for the sake of India throughout the nineteenth and early twentieth centuries.

In Britain itself intellectual fascination with Persia grew again in the middle of the nineteenth century after the publication of Edward FitzGerald's translation of the *Rubáiyát of Omar Khayyám*. This work was enthusiastically adopted by Richard Burton, Dante Gabriel Rossetti, William Morris, and John Ruskin. Ruskin reviewed it in 1869, saying that "it is the work of a poet inspired by the works of a poet; not a copy, but a reproduction; not a translation but the redelivery of a poetic inspiration."

Among FitzGerald's friends was Alfred Tennyson. He also became interested in Persian literature and began to study the language, intending to translate the poetry of Hafez. But his wife thought the characters of the Persian alphabet were "peculiar" and harmful to his eyes. When she discovered also that Persian was written from right to left, she became convinced that his eyesight would suffer irreparable damage. So she hid all his Persian textbooks and persuaded him to take up badminton instead.

Khayyám was not one of the greatest Persian poets, nor the best loved in Persia, but FitzGerald's translation made large Western audiences aware for the first time of Persian poetry. FitzGerald understood Khayyám's nihilism and his rage:

> *Ah love! Could thou and I with fate conspire*
> *to grasp this sorry scheme of things entire,*
> *would we not shatter it to bits—and then*
> *remold it nearer to the heart's desire!*

At Persepolis, Mohammed Reza Shah remolded Persian history to his own heart's desire. He was delighted with his party. It had, he said, helped immeasurably to establish Iran anew in Western perceptions. For him the high point of the ceremony was when he stood before the empty but impressive tomb of Cyrus the Great and addressed it grandiloquently in his flat, featureless voice:

> To you Cyrus, Great King, King of Kings, from Myself, Shahanshah of Iran, and from my people, hail! . . .
> We are here at the moment when Iran renews its pledge to History to bear witness to the immense gratitude of an entire people

to you, immortal Hero of History, founder of the world's oldest empire, great liberator of all time, worthy son of mankind.

Cyrus we stand before your eternal dwelling place to speak these solemn words: Sleep on in peace forever, for we are awake and we remain to watch over your glorious heritage.

The Shah, a shy, almost taciturn man, showed unaccustomed emotion as he spoke, pausing before he could complete his address to the dead monarch. After he finished, it is said, a wind suddenly arose from the floor of the desert and blew sand across the spectators.

This was widely thought to be a good omen. It was not.

Seven years later, many of the men and women who emerged in 1978 to express such vocal opposition to the Shah cited Persepolis as one intolerable example of Pahlavi excess. Some Iranians disliked the event because of its expense. Others, including the Queen herself, by her own later account, were unhappy that it was so French and had so little Iranian personality to it. The whole affair cost anything up to $300 million (estimates differ) and that in a country where per capita income, though rising, was still only about $500 a year. Moreover, the event seemed to be much more a paean to the Pahlavi family than to Iran.

At the time no one denounced it more fiercely than Ayatollah Khomeini, whom the Shah had exiled in 1964 for his fierce opposition to the Pahlavi regime. Khomeini seemed then only a very small voice in the wilderness. But in retrospect, the party at Persepolis can be seen to symbolize the end of the most successful years of the Shah's reign.

From now on the Shah would be far more interested in military than in social matters. Oil price rises were about to bring Iran colossal, unimagined wealth. But rather than helping the development of the country, these petrodollars would spread chaos and disappointment among millions of people, while offering fabulous opportunities of corruption to the court, the Shah's family, and many foreign companies and merchants.

For the Shah himself it would bring a complete divorce from reality. He became more and more obsessed with his own kingship and the importance of his direct succession from Cyrus. In an interview in 1975 he declared that during his Persepolis party, "the whole world, from the United Nations to every capital, paid tribute to Cyrus and his kingdom. . . . The seeds of international cooperation were well sown at Persepolis . . ."

In the next few years no one would try to temper this vision or even to relate it to reality. None of the Shah's own officials or courtiers dared to contradict him. And foreign statesmen were far more eager to have him spread Iran's wealth in their direction than to advise restraint. French leaders would humbly seek absolution for Pompidou's awful error in failing to attend Persepolis, and seek contracts for nuclear power stations. The Americans would give him the key to the U.S. armory. The British, the West Germans, the Italians, the Dutch, the Japanese, all the countries of the socialist world save Albania—these and many more joined in the line. Everyone competed to flatter him, to encourage him, and to take Iran's money. A folly would be an inspiration, dreams would be visions, propaganda would be perfect sense. Until January 16, 1979.

CHAPTER THREE

The Flight into Egypt

The flight into Egypt took less than three hours. The Shah, who had always loved flying, remained in the cockpit until his 707 was out of Iranian airspace. A few miles behind him followed his backup plane. As usual on his visits abroad, it carried the luggage —for reasons of security. When the plane passed out of Iranian airspace, the Shah turned over the controls to his pilot, Captain Behzad Moezzi, and went back to his suite for lunch with the Queen. The food had been prepared in the palace and was now served by the Shah's own cook, Ali Kabiri.

The Shah's plane had a sumptuous section at the front for the royal family and seats at the back for the entourage. In the old days it had carried a full complement of aides, courtiers, ministers, secretaries, and bodyguards. On this flight, the plane was almost empty.

The senior functionary on board was Amir Aslan Afshar, the grand master of ceremonies. He had not wanted the Shah to depart. But he was reassured by the fact that the Shah had promised that they were leaving only for a few weeks' "vacation."

Sitting close by him was Colonel Kiumars Jahanbini, the Shah's chief bodyguard. Jahanbini did not look like the sort of gorilla who often protects important men. He was rather short, he wore glasses, and he had receding hair. He had been trained in England, at Sandhurst, and for the past fifteen years he had been an officer in the Imperial Guard. His formal title was commander of the Special Security Unit, and he was the shadow of the Shah, traveling with him almost everywhere he went. Jahanbini had been one of the few people to have known for almost a month that they were going to leave Iran. "I had a lot of time to prepare myself. But I simply could not believe that we were not coming back. I left almost everything I had."

There were several other guards aboard, including the Queen's bodyguard, Colonel Yazdan Nevissi; there was a Sergeant Ali Shahbazi, and there were two of the Shah's valets, Amir Pourshoja and Mahmoud Eliassi. Finally there was Dr. Lucy Pirnia.

Dr. Pirnia had been the pediatrician of the four children. (They had all left Iran for the United States a few weeks before their parents.) She was a small, attractive woman with red hair. She had not had any idea of leaving her family in Iran. But she was loyal to the Queen, and in January 1979 she had realized that the Queen had a serious problem. There were almost no women left in the palace.

Most of the Queen's friends and ladies-in-waiting had already left the country. Her mother was gone from Teheran. One of her maids was married and did not wish to leave; another had become very religious. "She went from wearing a miniskirt to the veil," said the Queen later. "She begged me to take her with me in the end. She said, 'I have nobody, you are my mother, please take me.' But I felt I could not handle another nervous wreck. I needed someone quieter." Dr. Pirnia came to the palace a few days before the departure to say good-bye to the Queen. Instead she agreed to fly out with her.

From among this small group of people were to be found the only Iranians who remained with the Shah and Queen in the months to come. They would no doubt have been astonished, if not appalled, if they had been able to glimpse the bitterness and pain of the long voyage that lay ahead. In some ways the exile on which the Shah was now embarked echoed not only his first exile in 1953, but even that of his father, Reza Shah, before him.

Reza Shah was a colossal figure, in every sense. He attempted to stride Persia as a Bismarck, changing its face, uniting it and freeing it from foreign domination. But in the end he was toppled by those very same foreigners who had for so long manipulated Iranian life.

He was born in 1878, the child of a poor Persian officer. Persia was then one of the most backward countries of the Middle East, divided into tribal fiefdoms over which the shahs, now the Qajar dynasty, had less and less influence. The country was still almost untouched by the political and industrial revolution that had gradually spread from its core in Europe. Persia's bureaucracy was still tiny and the Qajars had embarked on almost no public works. They did not even create a national army, and such institutions as schools and the courts remained, as in most Islamic states, in the hands of religious leaders.

The most powerful forces in the land were the British and the Russians. The overriding concern of the British was to protect the route to India and to secure their hold on Afghanistan, the buffer between Persia and India. It was also vital to them that Persia should be able to prevent any Russian drive to the south. And so for the Qajars, British involvement was a mixed blessing. They disliked British interference, but at the same time they appreciated that the British presence in Persia countered what would otherwise have been overwhelming Russian influence. To differentiate, one might say that Persians held the British more responsible for Iran's misfortunes, but the Russians were more feared.

For much of the latter part of the nineteenth century, the British dominated the court. They were granted the right to build telegraph lines across the country so that London could be in closer touch with India. In 1872 Baron Julius de Reuter, a British subject, was given an exclusive concession to build railroads and to mine almost all of Persia's minerals. Lord Curzon later called this the most complete surrender of a country's resources to foreign interests that could ever be imagined. Protest within Persia was such that the Shah was compelled to void the concession. The British then used Reuter's unsettled claims to block Russian railroad concessions. Intense competition between the two great powers continued and by the end of the century both were deeply involved in different aspects of Persian life. This became increasingly unpopular, and when the British were granted a monopoly over the sale of Iranian tobacco, massive protests followed and the government was forced to cancel the agreement. For a time Russian influence increased.

• • •

One of Russia's means of exerting its power was the Iranian Cossack Brigade, which the Shah had founded after a visit to Russia and which had Russian officers. Some time before the turn of the century, Reza Khan joined the Cossacks, as a tall teenager of fifteen or sixteen.

This was shortly before another concession had been granted— once more to the British at the expense of the Russians. In 1901, an Englishman, William Knox D'Arcy, was given the right "to search for, obtain, exploit, . . . carry away and sell" all Iranian oil save that of the five northern provinces. Those provinces were excepted out of deference to Russian sensibilities. Russian opposition to the concession even as it stood was defused by presenting the Persian text to the Russian delegation when the Russians' translator was known to be out of town.

In 1907 the British sent troops to protect the oil-drilling operation without regard to Iran's sovereignty. Oil was discovered in the southwest in 1908 and the Anglo-Persian Oil Company was founded the following year. The British Navy converted from coal to oil-fired boilers, and with the outbreak of World War I, the British had an even more pressing need for Persia's new and invaluable resource. The British government bought a controlling interest in Anglo-Persian, which from then on operated in Iran on terms much more favorable to the British than to the Iranians.

Iran declared its neutrality in World War I, but most Iranian sympathy lay with Germany because she was fighting Great Britain and Russia. Iran became a battleground. Germany's allies, the Turks, moved into Azerbaijan and western Iran; the Kaiser was presented as a supporter of Islam. German agents were allowed to act freely in what the British had hitherto considered their own area of influence.

The British sent troops to defend the Abadan refinery and made a secret deal with the Russians whereby at the end of the war the Russians would have control of Istanbul and the Dardanelles, and Iran would be divided between them, the Russians in the North, the British in the South, and the British influential in the "neutral" zone, where the oil was to be found. By 1917 the British and the Russians between them occupied most of Iran.

Then came the Russian revolution; late in 1917, the new Soviet leaders renounced what they considered the czar's unequal treaties and subsequently the Cossack officers were withdrawn from Iran. The British were determined to consolidate their own control over the country and in 1919 they imposed an Anglo-Persian treaty that virtually made Iran a British protectorate. It aroused fury among the educated classes in Teheran, and it was never ratified by the Majles. It was at this time that the same Iranian nationalists began to look to the United States for support against British exploitation.

The British officer in charge of the British troops in Iran at the end of 1920 was Major General Sir Edmund Ironside, a substantial figure. He had fought in the Boer War and he was John Buchan's model for Richard Hannay in *The Thirty-Nine Steps*.

Ironside was greatly struck by the personality (and physique) of Reza Khan, who was now a colonel in his early forties. In his diary he noted, "He is a man and the straightest I have met yet. . . ." Before he left Persia in February 1921, Ironside told Reza Khan that the British would not oppose his seizing power so long as the reigning Qajar shah was not actually deposed. The British were then looking for a "strongman solution" to the problem of keeping their influence in Iran.

Reza Khan joined forces with a civilian, Sayyed Zia ad-Din, to mount a coup and to impose a new government on the weak Qajar leadership. Reza Khan was thought to be pro-British and the British minister in Teheran simply told the Qajar shah that he must cooperate; so he did. Ironside, who had by now left the country, noted in his diary, "I fancy that all the people think I engineered the coup d'état. I suppose I did strictly speaking."

In fact the new government did not develop as a British creature and, in the words of one historian, Nikki Keddie, it marked "a turning point in Iranian history." It showed an unprecedented independence of the West, and promised agricultural development, national independence, a modern industrialized economy, and other social reforms. Relations with the Soviet Union were normalized.

Soon after the coup, Reza Khan became minister of war and de facto commander in chief of the armed forces. He began to modernize the Army; in 1923 he became prime minister and started to strengthen the central government against the tribes. Reza Khan had promised Ironside that he would not depose Ahmad shah and for a time he did not. But in 1925 he did overthrow the Qajars. He had considered creating a republic, but he was persuaded by many of the leading clergy that the monarchy should be preserved. The mullahs were concerned that in a republic the Muslim clergy might be disestablished, as had recently happened in Turkey. So on April 25, 1926, he crowned himself Reza Shah Pahlavi, Shahanshah of Iran. The Qajar dynasty had ended; the Pahlavi dynasty had begun.

Accepting kingship was almost the only time that Reza Shah listened to the advice of the Muslim clergy. Throughout his rule he sought to unite Persia under a strong national Army and forced it to modernize and accept many of the attributes and conventions of the twentieth century. The protests of the religious establishment were largely ignored.

His model and hero was his neighbor Mustafa Kemal Atatürk; he strove to implement the same reforms in Iran as were being achieved in Turkey. He enjoyed considerable success; in the first ten years of his rule Iran probably progressed more than in the entire Qajar period of the last hundred and twenty years. He built roads, schools, hospitals, and sent students abroad for further education, most to France and some to Germany, which many Iranians still saw as their friend simply because it was the traditional enemy of both Britain and Russia. He built up the textile, sugar, and cement industries, he introduced electrification, and he embarked on a vastly ambitious railroad across the country, linking the Persian Gulf to the Caspian. He curbed the tribal chiefs and imposed a secular legal code. He insisted that foreigners call the country Iran rather than Persia.*

But he was less successful than Atatürk in forging a stong national ideology. Atatürk was able to control the mullahs and to find a place for them as well as for merchants and intellectuals in the new Turkey. He governed as an autocrat but also as a twentieth-century politician. By contrast, Reza Shah ruled as a monarch, proving adept at centralization but not at delegation. He saw the clergy, rightly, as a hindrance to his plans for modernization. He banned many of their rites and their passion plays, and he forbade women to wear in public the chador, the long, black seamless garment in which they were covered from scalp to toe. Reza Shah exiled one ayatollah who dared to criticize the Shah's female relations for entering a shrine unveiled. Indeed, one of his

---

* The origin of Reza Shah's 1935 order on the country's name is somewhat obscure. It appears that the Germans had a hand in it. In their attempt to win Iranian friendship, German officials harped on the theme that Iranians too were "Aryans" and that colonialists, particularly the British, were degrading the country by calling it Persia. Reza Shah himself had no idea that the country was known abroad as anything but Iran. Hence his order.

Reza Shah and three of his children, including Mohammed Reza on his knee. Princess Ashraf is on the right.

military aides was said to have violated the sanctuary of the shrine by marching in and dragging the ayatollah out by his beard, so that the Shah could whip him for his lèse-majesté.

Reza Shah also seized land from the clergy and other great landowners. Much of it he kept for himself and his family. Indeed, by the thirties his family was almost certainly the largest landowner in Iran, owning perhaps one-sixth of the usable land. Apart from that, Reza Shah undertook very little effective agricultural reform. As a result, agricultural productivity and peasant living standards remained stagnant. No national market for consumer or industrial goods was created and thus industrialization was hindered.

Reza Shah acknowledged eleven children, though he may have had many more. His heir, Mohammed Reza, was born to his second wife, Queen Taj ol Molok, on October 26, 1919. A few hours later he was followed by a twin sister, who was named Ashraf, and whose relationship with her brother remained passionate and painful all of their lives. Other children by Taj ol Molok were an elder daughter, Shams, and a son, Ali Reza, who died in a plane crash in 1954.

When Reza Shah crowned himself in 1926, Mohammed Reza was anointed Crown Prince, or Valiahd, and everyone was thenceforth required to address him as "Your Highness." It was not easy to grow up under the shadow of his overwhelming father as he lashed Iran into a nation. Like almost everyone else in Iran, the Crown Prince was very much afraid of him.

His mother, Queen Taj ol Molok, appeared different—tiny and delicate. But she was equally fierce and unbending; in later years she was frequently described as a harridan. She was not easily appeased when, after the birth of the twins, Reza Shah took two more wives, with whom he had six more children.

Mohammed Reza was timid, even gentle and self-questioning, quite unlike his twin sister, Ashraf. When he was seven the boy almost died of typhoid. There were virtually no drugs to be had in Teheran in those days; the doctors dithered and the family prayed around the bed. Then, when the fever reached its crisis, Mohammed Reza apparently had a dream in which he saw Ali, the son-in-law of the prophet Mohammed and, to Shiites, the second most holy of men, hand him a bowl of liquid. He drank. Next day the fever had abated and he began to recover. This was a story he told all his life; it was just the first of many miracles with which he believed he was blessed. He considered himself divinely protected. (But he never considered the mullahs to have divine guidance.)

Reza Shah was literate but scarcely educated. He was determined that his children be well schooled. He sent the Crown Prince to school at Le Rosey, the famous Swiss establishment for the young international rich. It was often said later that it was in Switzerland that Mohammed Reza acquired a sympathy for aspects of democracy, and that his subsequent attempts to reconcile such notions with the governance of Iran proved to be difficult. He later declared that his years in Switzerland were "the most important of my whole life. . . . I learned what democracy is . . . I still believe in democracy but not without discipline. [Without discipline] it is anarchy."

When the seventeen-year-old boy returned to Iran after five years in Switzerland, much had changed under the impact of his father's modernization. Teheran now had boulevards and electric lights. Iran was beginning to have some of the appurtenances of the world to the West. The entire country was strictly controlled by his father. Even village officials were appointed by Teheran.

Tribal independence was being crushed by the new might of the Army.

Reza Shah did not give his son much of substance to do. But Mohammed Reza enrolled in Teheran's Officers' Academy, learned to fly, and began to acquire the reputation of a playboy. When he was nineteen, Reza Shah decided that the Crown Prince's marriage was due and so he began trawling the Middle East for the most suitable wife—from a dynastic point of view.

"With his characteristic forthrightness—perhaps better adapted to engineering projects than affairs of the heart—he started his investigations," wrote his son later. The most desirable candidate was Fawzia, only seventeen, but the loveliest and favorite sister of King Farouk of Egypt. The two young people were informed of the arrangement and they were married in spring 1939.

The wedding of the future Shah and Princess Fawzia. King Farouk gave his sister away.

At first all went well; the princess was fun as well as beautiful. Cecil Beaton once declared of her:

> If ever Botticelli were reincarnated and wished to paint an Asiatic Venus or Primavera here is his subject. He would delight in the Queen's features contained in a perfect heart-shaped face: strangely pale but piercing blue eyes; crimson-colored lips curling like wrought-iron volutes; and the way in which the dark chestnut hair grows beautifully from the forehead.

Their only child, Princess Shahnaz, was born in 1940, but from then on the marriage appears to have disintegrated. The royal court in Egypt was then one of the most cosmopolitan in the world; Fawzia was sophisticated and had been accustomed to great luxury and pampering, not least from her doting brother. Teheran, by contrast, was a poor and primitive society in those days. It was like being exiled from Paris to a small provincial town.

When World War II broke out, Iran was closely linked to Germany. The Nazis had assiduously courted Reza Shah, exploiting his desire to see Iran become more independent of both the British and the Russians. In his early years Reza Shah had reached a series of agreements with Moscow and ended the system of extraterritoriality, by which Westerners in Iran were outside the jurisdiction of the Iranian courts. This the British accepted, but they were infuriated when, in 1932, Reza Shah canceled the oil concession to the Anglo-Persian Oil Company. A new sixty-year agreement was signed with the company in 1933, but the British never trusted Reza Shah again. They began to see him as an increasingly unreliable tyrant—which to some extent was true. By the mid-1930s, he had begun to rule as a royal dictator without the benefit of independent counsel.

The British diplomat John Colville, appointed to the Eastern Department of the Foreign Office in September 1937, wrote later, "My parish . . . was Turkey and Persia. Persia was just a little tiresome, as the Shah, Reza Pahlavi, was a temperamental despot. We had to be particularly polite to him because of the enormous interests of the Anglo-Persian Oil Company (now BP) in the country . . . Turkey was more exciting."

Throughout the thirties the Germans had been eager to displace the British. Apart from declaring that the Persians were true Aryans, they had become Iran's most important trading partner. Much of the heavy equipment with which Reza Shah was industrializing the country, building ports and roads, came from Germany. The Germans helped construct his railway. With the rolling stock and engineers came German agents, bribes, and propaganda. By the end of the decade, the Russians saw German economic links as threatening the Soviet rear in Central Asia. The British became increasingly alarmed at the numbers of German "advisers" and their political activities in Iran.

When war came, Reza Shah declared that Iran would remain neutral, but the German invasion of the U.S.S.R. rendered that impossible. The large German presence in Iran at once became a hostile force to the Russians as well as to the British. The Allied Arctic convoys were under such heavy German pressure that an alternative route into the U.S.S.R. was needed. What better path could there be than through Iran and, indeed, along Reza Shah's new railway? In July 1941 the British and the Russians demanded the expulsion of all German agents and influence. Unusually for him, Reza Shah hesitated—and was lost.

In August 1941 the British and the Russians invaded Iran. Reza Shah abdicated, saying to his son Mohammed Reza, "I cannot be the nominal head of an occupied land, to be dictated to by a minor English or Russian officer." The old man was bundled off, with little ceremony and less dignity, into exile with his favorite wife—not Queen Taj—and most of his children. He had wanted to go to Canada, but the British did not allow him even that choice; they dispatched him first to Mauritius and then to South Africa where, on July 26, 1944, he died.

Once again the ruler of Iran was determined in London. Although his son Mohammed Reza was Reza Shah's designated heir and had been groomed to succeed his father—albeit in happier circumstances—the British paused. Members of the British Cabinet actually considered restoring a member of the old Qajar dynasty to the throne; unfortunately it emerged that the man in question did not speak a word of Persian. Even in London this was thought to be a drawback.

Some British officials considered Mohammed Reza a weak playboy "hand in glove with the German Legation." But in the end they and the Russians decided to install him on his father's throne; they reasoned that he could always be replaced if he did not do as was required. After all, he would have no real power. Iran would be ruled by the British in the south and the Russians in the north. Convenient nineteenth-century rules would be restored, so long as the war lasted.

Thus the new Shah began his reign in the shadow of his father's humiliation, and as an Anglo-Soviet puppet. He was not quite twenty-two.

His position was not helped by the fact that the Queen Mother and his twin sister, Princess Ashraf, had not accompanied Reza Shah into exile. They were both powerful personalities. Ashraf claimed later that she had wanted to leave with her father but he insisted that she remain because "your brother needs you more." Princess Fawzia found life in a court controlled by her scheming mother-in-law and jealous sister-in-law intolerable.

Mohammed Reza deeply resented the way in which his country was once again being governed by its old enemies. After American troops joined the Allied occupation of Iran, he observed that American policies were independent of both Britain and Russia and so he appealed to President Roosevelt for help. As a result, the United States encouraged the British and the Russians to join with it in signing a treaty with Iran promising that all three countries would withdraw their troops within six months of the end of the war. For the Shah it demonstrated how useful the United States could be against Iran's old exploiters.

In 1944 the State Department advised Roosevelt that Iran should be strengthened after the war so that she could resist the encroachments of Britain and Russia. The notion appealed to Roosevelt. He wrote what became a celebrated memorandum to Cordell Hull, the secretary of state, in which he declared that he was "thrilled by the idea of using Iran as an example of what we could do by an unselfish American policy. We could not take on a more difficult nation than Iran. I should like, however, to have a try at it."

Roosevelt sent Winston Churchill a report on Iran by Major General Patrick Hurley, who had been President Hoover's secretary of war, and had visited Iran in May 1943. He attacked both the British and the Russians for their "imperialist" policies in Iran and called for a free, independent Iran with a constitutional monarchy. He thought Iran had been too long governed by a "powerful and greedy minority" and that "the people have been subjected to foreign exploitation and monopoly." Churchill was not pleased and replied to FDR that there need be no conflict between imperialism and democracy. "British imperialism has spread and is spreading democracy more widely than any other system of government since the beginning of time."

After the war, the British did withdraw in accordance with their treaty obligations, but the Soviets set up puppet regimes in the northern provinces of Azerbaijan and Kurdistan. The Shah and, in particular, his prime minister, stood firm, the new United Nations procedures were mobilized against Moscow, President Truman made threats, and eventually the Russians withdrew. It was another lesson in American power and friendship which the nervous young Shah appreciated.

In 1947 Princess Fawzia returned to Egypt. The following year she and the Shah were divorced. Alone in Teheran, the Shah was once agan free to indulge his habit of nightclubbing. Two years later, he married Soraya Esfandiari, the beautiful eighteen-year-old daughter of a Baktiari father and a German mother.

In 1949 he narrowly escaped the first of three attempts on his life. The attacker was a young man who appeared to be aligned with both the Communist-controlled Tudeh (People's) Party and with what the Shah called "archconservative religious fanatics." Martial law was declared and Communists were arrested.

• • •

Queen Soraya with the Shah and his sisters.

In the early 1950s, the Shah endured his greatest test, one that committed him much more strongly to the United States. The crisis embraced oil and nationalism and Western fear of Communist encroachment. It also fundamentally changed the nature of the Shah's relations with his government and people. Till 1953 he was far from all powerful. After 1953 he became determined to allow no rivals in the Iranian political firmament.

The drama stemmed from the Iranian fury at the Anglo-Iranian Oil Company, which held a monopoly of all Iranian oil production and which many Iranians thought, with good reason, profited Britain rather more than Iran. Royalties paid to Iran were lower than the taxes Anglo-Iranian paid to the British government, and the company kept most skilled jobs for British expatriates. After nearly fifty years, there were still almost no Iranian technicians in the industry. All in all, Anglo-Iranian was seen as a major tool in British control over Iran.

During the late forties Anglo-Iranian had made some concessions to growing Iranian anger but they were far from meeting the popular demands. A prime minister who sought to push an unpopular agreement through was assassinated by a religious nationalist in March 1951. That same month the Majles approved nationalization of the oil industry. Then the National Front leader, Dr. Mossadeq, who had long been one of the most fiery and articulate proponents of nationalization, was appointed prime minister over the objections of the Shah, and became an extraordinary actor on the stage of the world.

Mohammed Mossadeq came from a wealthy family of landowners who had served as ministers to the Qajars. By comparison, the Pahlavis were nothing. Born in the 1880s, he had been educated in Switzerland long before Reza Shah seized power. He was a lawyer and during the early 1920s he had served in various Cabinets. Then he had opposed Reza Shah's establishment of a dynasty in his own name, and had been exiled to the northeast of Iran. In 1944 he had resisted Soviet efforts to gain an oil concession in northern Iran. But his principal dislike was for the British. He apparently once told the Shah that the Russians did not count. "It is the British who decide everything in this country." By the 1950s, he saw his country's salvation in keeping a proper distance, a real neutrality, between East and West. But in the midst of the Cold War, with most of Eastern Europe now under fearful Stalinist rule, such views were heresy in both London and Washington.

It was for his style as much as for his opinions that Mossadeq became notorious in the West. Like Khomeini a quarter of a century later, he was almost totally incomprehensible to many Western Europeans and Americans. By the time he came to power in 1951 he was already seventy. He exploited his age, like all his other attributes, to great dramatic effect. He would weep, he would faint, he would rant, he would laugh, moan, or shriek—as he thought the situation demanded. He often appeared in pajamas, and he received delegations in his bed. He walked with a stick, but sometimes he would throw it away and skip. For Iranians he was charismatic, but for most foreigners he seemed rather strange. It was not hard for the British, whose influence remained powerful in Teheran, and who had a spy in Mossadeq's own Council of Ministers, to portray him as a madman likely to lead Iran into the Soviet camp.

His nationalism and his fury at British exploitation made it impossible for him to compromise even if it was clear that his policies were self-destructive. At first many American officials in the Truman administration were sympathetic to his cause and exasperated by British greed. Dean Acheson described Mossadeq as "a most conservative, rich, reactionary, feudal-minded Persian, who also just happened to hate the British." But gradually Washington became concerned that he was becoming dependent upon the Tudeh Party. (This was a Soviet instrument, but in some ways it was the only real political party in Iran; the others were the factions of certain politicians.)

The Labour government in Britain, with Herbert Morrison as its combative foreign secretary, was able to lead the Americans out of neutrality into a worldwide boycott of Iranian oil. The Iranian economy began to collapse. The United States refused Mossadeq loans until the dispute was settled. Mossadeq declared that Iran did not need a settlement anyway; much better that the country proceed as if it had no oil—at least that way it would not be exploited. He proclaimed an age of austerity.

By mid-1952 the middle class began to drift away from him, but his fierce nationalism remained popular with poorer people and the clergy. The Shah detested the way in which Mossadeq rather than he was coming to symbolize Iran, and he tried in the summer of 1952 to remove him from office. But massive public protests enabled Mossadeq to return and to assume greater powers and authority than ever. He broke diplomatic relations with Britain and banished the Shah's mother and Princess Ashraf. His thought, undoubtedly, was that while he could not hope to control those two strong women, the Shah himself was more pliable.

The Shah now showed himself incapable of decisive action. Dispatches from both the British and the American embassies at the time commented on him with patronizing contempt. Thus a British embassy official reported on a three-hour lunch with the distressed Shah: ". . . One reason for the length of the audience was, I think, that he found some comfort in being offered a number of more or less obvious platitudes regarding the transitory nature of the present political muddle." In a joint Anglo-American paper on the crisis, the Shah was described as "well-meaning, naturally well disposed toward Britain and the U.S., aware of the Communist danger, but vacillating and weak. Recently he has shown himself to be too easily swayed by Mossadeq's threats . . ."

Washington tried at first to mediate between Britain and Iran. In July 1951, Averell Harriman traveled to Teheran. Mossadeq received him in bed; he fluttered his hands as Harriman came into the room and launched into a fluting tirade against the British. "You don't know how crafty they are. You don't know how evil they are. They sully everything they touch." Harriman remarked that he had fought with the British in two world wars, and he thought there were some good things about them too. Harriman and his interpreter, Vernon Walters, found Mossadeq engaging but almost impossible as an interlocutor. On one occasion he remarked, "Iran's problems have always been caused by foreigners. The whole thing began with that Greek, Alexander."

In his palace, the Shah had very little idea of what was happening. Shorn of more and more of his powers by Mossadeq, who tended to ignore him, the Shah retreated into alternating bouts of gloom and high spirits which involved playing practical jokes on guests. Queen Soraya later recalled that sometimes he would try to amuse everyone by barking like a dog during the screening of a film (film shows remained a favorite form of palace relaxation till the end). On other occasions he would try to frighten ladies of the court by planting plastic frogs and spiders on their laps as they played bridge. There was not much else for him to do.

At the end of 1952, the British government (now Conservative) decided that Mossadeq had to be removed. The British already had substantial intelligence "assets" in Teheran. Now they tried to enlist the CIA. Kermit (Kim) Roosevelt, grandson of Theodore, veteran of the OSS and the head of the Agency's Middle Eastern operations, was invited to London to discuss a British plan. The British were concerned primarily about the Anglo-Iranian Oil Company. The Americans were much more interested in a possible Soviet threat to Iran.

The British plan to overthrow Mossadeq was put on hold until after General Eisenhower's inauguration in January 1953. A group of British officials flew to Washington to explore the matter further with Allen Dulles, the new director of the CIA, and his brother, John Foster, the new secretary of state. The British recommended that Kim Roosevelt be in charge of any operation and be sent to Iran to explore the possibilities. It was so agreed.

In Iran Roosevelt noted that the economic blockade was losing Mossadeq his support, both among the mullahs and among the merchants in the bazaar. Indeed, his erratic and increasingly dogmatic responses to the crisis meant that even some of his own National Front supporters were defecting from him. Roosevelt reckoned that the Army was still loyal to the Shah and that a strong coalition could be mounted against Mossadeq. He recruited two Iranian brothers who were already British agents and brought them secretly to the United States for further training.

One problem for any coup plotters was what to do with the Shah if Mossadeq were removed. At this stage, the Shah himself had little idea what was being planned. Indeed, he even suspected the British of conspiring with Mossadeq against him.*

His uncertainty is visible in the diplomatic cable traffic. After diplomatic relations with Britain were broken, he remained in touch with London through the offices of the American ambassador, Loy Henderson. In May 1953 the State Department told the British that the Shah wanted to know what the British expected of him. He was

> harping on the theme that the British had thrown out the Qajar dynasty, had brought in his father and had thrown his father out. Now they could keep him in power or remove him in turn as they saw fit. If they desired that he should stay and that the crown should retain the powers given to it by the constitution he should

---

* British intentions were, as ever, widely debated in Iran. C. M. Wodehouse, one of the British officials most heavily involved in the clandestine campaign to overthrow Mossadeq, wrote later that many prominent Iranians believed that the British had brought Mossadeq to power because the Abadan refinery was uneconomic. Therefore London wanted it nationalized in order to be able to claim compensation.

be informed. If on the other hand they wished him to go, he should be told immediately so that he could leave quietly.

The Foreign Office drafted and sent a personal reply from Churchill that may have given the Shah wry amusement as well as comfort: ". . . while we do not interfere in Persian politics we should be very sorry to see the Shah driven out. Perhaps Mr. Henderson, the United States ambassador at Teheran, will convey this assurance to the Shah and say that it comes personally from me."

When Henderson went next to see the Shah, they walked around the palace garden to avoid being overheard by Mossadeq's spies or microphones. The Shah seemed very pleased by Churchill's message. He thought it meant the British attitude was changing. Previously they had urged him to be a purely constitutional monarch; now perhaps they wanted him to involve himself more in Iranian politics. He thought he must do that—otherwise there would be confusion and chaos.

By midsummer 1953, all attempts to negotiate a settlement of the oil crisis had foundered on Mossadeq's stubbornness. Churchill was determined that he must be overthrown. Anthony Eden, the foreign secretary, was more cautious. On June 22 the Americans, who were also exasperated by Mossadeq, and were increasingly concerned about Soviet influence, decided to unleash Kim Roosevelt and the other CIA and MI6 operatives.

In London, Eden fell sick and Churchill took over the Foreign Office. He gave final permission for what the British called Operation Boot to proceed. (To the CIA it was Operation Ajax.) Churchill sent an even stronger message encouraging the Shah to act against Mossadeq. It was a masterpiece of instruction, indirect but utterly clear, and deserves to be recalled in full.

> I should be glad if Mr. Henderson, U.S.A., would transmit to the Shah the following observation of a general character which I believe is correct and in accordance with democratic principles.
> Begins. It is the duty of a constitutional monarch or President when faced with violent tyrannical action by individuals or a minority party to take the necessary steps to secure the well-being of the toiling masses and the continuity of an ordered state. Ends.

In the event the message was not delivered until after Mossadeq had been overthrown.

Kim Roosevelt was sent back to Teheran. He arrived soon after Princess Ashraf—who had been in touch with the CIA and MI6 in Europe—slipped secretly into the country, in order to, in Queen Soraya's words, "encourage us to act." Furious, Mossadeq had ordered her to leave.

The Shah was still nervous and undecided. Kim Roosevelt went to see him, driven through the palace gates lying under a blanket in the back of a car. The Shah climbed in beside him. Roosevelt told him of the plan. The Shah was thrilled. Till now he had not fully believed that the Americans wished to get rid of Mossadeq. British support alone would have been at best a mixed blessing.*

The plan involved having the Shah issue two firmans, or decrees, dismissing Mossadeq and appointing one of his own supporters, General Fazlollah Zahedi, as prime minister. He was then to fly to a town on the Caspian and wait. Meanwhile, Roosevelt would give two agents several hundred thousand dollars out of a substantial slush fund the CIA had established in Teheran. This money was to be handed out to thugs from athletic clubs and the poor of the South Teheran slums to encourage them to demonstrate in favor of the Shah.

General Zahedi, a tall and good-looking man, was not always a British favorite. Indeed during World War II a British officer of some distinction, Fitzroy Maclean, had actually arrested Zahedi on grounds he had been intriguing with German agents. In his famous book *Eastern Approaches,* Maclean includes an account of his capture of the general, in whose home he said he found many photographs of his women friends. (Women were an interest Zahedi pursued all his life. Queen Soraya later described him as "half swashbuckler and half Don Juan.") By 1953 his war record was forgotten; though the British had misgivings, Zahedi was deemed preferable to the dangerous Mossadeq.

In the last few days before the coup, Mossadeq assumed more and more dictatorial powers. To Roosevelt's irritation, the Shah still dithered. A referendum to dissolve parliament was held and

---

* Just before the Shah's second exile in 1979, Kim Roosevelt published a glamorous account of his own role in the earlier affair, with the consent not only of the CIA but also of the Shah. He did not, however, have the consent of the British. When the CIA screened the book for him, officials suggested he attribute actions to the Anglo-Iranian Oil Company, so as to avoid upsetting the British government. Anglo-Iranian's successor, British Petroleum, immediately threatened to sue and the book had to be withdrawn and rewritten.

was said to be accepted by 99.9 percent of the people. Parliament was duly dissolved. On August 12, the Shah issued his firmans.

At first the plan did not go well. Mossadeq simply arrested the Shah's messenger, Colonel Nematollah Nassiri, an officer of the Imperial Palace Guard. Mossadeq declared that he had forestalled a coup and issued orders for Zahedi's arrest. But the general was already in hiding on a friend's estate. He appealed to the Army, still largely loyal to the Shah. At first, the streets of Teheran were held by Mossadeq supporters and members of the Tudeh Party. Mobs with red flags tore down the graven images of the Shah's father, Reza Shah, and cried "Yankees go home."

Thinking the attempt had failed, the Shah himself panicked and fled with Soraya in a small plane to Iraq. When they arrived in Baghdad, disheveled, tired, their clothes and a couple of bags and a jewel box flung hastily across the seats of the plane, the Iraqi authorities arranged a secret meeting for the Shah with the U.S. ambassador. The Shah was desperate for advice from the Americans and the British. Should he publicly denounce Mossadeq? What was to be done? Should he stay here or go to Europe? He insisted he had not abdicated, but what should he do now?*

Before any advice could be given, at least by the British, the Shah and Soraya flew on to Rome—perhaps because King Faisal was embarrassed by his presence in Baghdad and perhaps because the Shah thought they would be safer and more comfortable in the Italian capital.

In Rome, the Iranian chargé d'affaires rushed off to the seaside rather than commit himself to the Shah's uncertain cause. He even refused to let the Shah have the keys to the personal car he kept in Rome. (A junior embassy employee was more loyal and handed them over. The Shah later dismissed the chargé.)

The Italian press made much of the fact that the royal couple

---

* Next day the American ambassador to Baghdad gave his British colleague the Shah's account of what had happened. The cable to the Foreign Office gives some flavor of the Shah's personality and his predicament. The Shah said that "some time ago it had been suggested to him that coup against Mossadeq was desirable. He had agreed in view of Mossadeq's increasingly unconstitutional actions and insane jealousy. On reconsideration the Shah had, however, felt that he must act as constitutional monarch and had decided to issue letters dismissing Mossadeq and appointing General Zahedi Prime Minister. . . . The Shah had so informed those in his confidence." He had gone to the Caspian to avoid suspicion and there he learned to his horror that the plan had failed—Mossadeq had simply refused to be dismissed. "He had then decided that as a constitutional ruler he should not resort to force as that would lead to bloodshed, chaos, and Soviet infiltration. He had therefore come to Baghdad."

The Shah and Soraya
arrive in Rome.

had almost no clothes, no staff, and appeared to have no money.
They were hard-pressed even to get a hotel room. A British embassy official wrote to the Foreign Office, "It seems that they
only got a fourth-floor berth at the Excelsior . . . because some
Persian industrialist vacated his suite." (All those Iranians who
helped the Shah in these days were subsequently rewarded a thou-
sandfold.)

For the Shah, the real problem was still to discover what the
British and Americans wanted of him next.

On instructions from State, the U.S. ambassador in Rome advised him to give a press conference in which he stressed his constitutional rights and the illegality of Mossadeq's actions. He
should explain that he left the country only because his authority
was no longer respected and because he desired to avoid bloodshed. But at the same time State thought the U.S. might make
some "minor concessions" to Mossadeq, in case the Shah did not
return.

The British were becoming more wary of the Shah. He had not
behaved with courage so far, and some British officials considered
that he was a weak card that should be played no longer. Notes in
Winston Churchill's files suggested that Britain's options were
either to send a "correct" reply to the Shah, commiserating with
him but declining to advise him, or to encourage him along the
American line, or to urge him to undertake an all-out campaign
against Mossadeq. One possibility was "to write off the Shah and
proceed on the unpalatable assumption that Mossadeq is the indis-
putable ruler of Persia and the only bulwark against Communism." In the end, however, the prime minister's advisers decided
that it was most prudent for Britain to follow the American line.
"By doing so, we shall strengthen our hand with the Americans
in arguing that it would be a mistake to cultivate Mossadeq."

For the next couple of days the Shah and Soraya had all their meals in the hotel's public rooms. While Soraya wandered apparently penniless around the shops, the Shah gave innumerable informal press conferences in which he repeated the message the Americans had suggested. The AP correspondent would then read out the latest dispatch from Teheran and, according to the British embassy, "The Shah would then put on his spectacles and, in a charming manner which endeared him to all present, would comment in his quiet English on the news. Later, as the Shah began to get news of his own, he repaid their kindness by giving them the stop press himself. The number of journalists who claim to have sat on the same sofa and had private speech with His Majesty is legion. While he may not have said in so many words that these encounters with the press had been an 'eye-opener,' he did remember that he had been sincerely treated by the journalists' courtesy and by the beneficent power of journalism in the modern world."

At first the mobs in Teheran had all been anti-Shah. Gradually, however, the tide began to turn. Soldiers appeared in the streets and showed that the Army was still loyal to the Shah and to Zahedi. Then the CIA's paid demonstrators, organized by Roosevelt's two intelligence brothers, marched up from South Teheran and shouts of "Long live America" began to prevail over "Yankees go home."* The Shah's picture was plastered on walls and windows. Pro-Shah and anti-Shah groups fought in the streets. Mossadeq was toppled; Zahedi was embraced by the crowds and assumed the premiership.

It was lunchtime on August 19, 1953, when the news arrived in Rome. The AP man rushed up to the Shah with a wire that announced: "Teheran: Mossadeq overthrown. Imperial troops control Teheran. Zahedi Premier." Soraya burst into tears; the Shah went white and then declared, "I knew that they loved me."

Then, drinking champagne with journalists, he flew home to a Teheran in which his supporters had tried to reerect the toppled statues of his father. He told Kim Roosevelt of the CIA, "I owe my throne to God, my people—and to you."

Many of his opponents considered that the role of the CIA was

---

* One eyewitness described the scene as a "grotesque procession. . . . There were tumblers turning handsprings, weightlifters twirling iron bars, and wrestlers flexing their biceps. As spectators grew in number, the bizarre assortment of performers began shouting pro-Shah slogans in unison. The crowd took up the chant and there, after one precarious moment, the balance of public psychology swung against Mossadeq."

Mohammed Mossadeq on trial

more crucial than that of the Almighty. It is certainly true that the actions of the CIA and MI6 were important. But alone they could not have removed Mossadeq. The demonstrations were indeed provoked and begun with MI6 and CIA money—no one knows how much was spent—but money alone could not adequately explain the way in which the protests rushed so fast through the city. The costs of Mossadeq's policies had come to seem too high to too many people and there was already widespread dissatisfaction with his rule. The CIA and MI6 provided a spark, but the dry tinder was Iranian. Nonetheless, to many Iranians the events proved the Shah was an American if not a British puppet.

Immediately after the coup, Prime Minister Zahedi and his son Ardeshir, who had helped round up the demonstrators, met with their American advisers. Zahedi said he intended to settle the oil dispute with Britain as fast as he could, and the United States at once promised the loans that it had refused Mossadeq. The first money was the remainder of the CIA's coup fund in Roosevelt's safe. Then, to meet the deficit in Iran's operating budget, the United States extended aid of $60 million in fiscal 1954, $53 million in 1955, and $35 million in 1956.

Many of Mossadeq's supporters were jailed and his foreign minister was executed. But there was no bloodbath. Mossadeq was put on trial and blamed a British plot for his downfall. He called upon Iranians to throw off foreign influence. He was sentenced to three years' house arrest, was released in August 1956, and lived till his death in 1967, under guard on his estate.

This drama and first brush with exile seems to have taught the Shah several things. First, that while British influence in Iran remained enormous, the Americans were becoming ever more influential in the world. He subsequently began to abandon Iran's long tradition of playing off East against West and turned increasingly toward the United States for the support of his regime.

Throughout the second half of the fifties, the Shah did little to reform the essentially feudal structures of his country. He was more interested in increasing his military power, as his father had done, and he incessantly demanded more military aid from the United States and his other allies.

At the same time, he determined never to allow anyone to develop power independent of the throne as Mossadeq had done. From now on he would strive to develop a government of courtiers. In order to destroy all domestic opposition, he began, with the help of the CIA and the Israeli secret service Mossad, to build a formidable secret police, which became known by the acronym SAVAK (from its Iranian name, Sazeman-e Ettela't va Amniyat-e Keshvar, which means National Intelligence and Security Organization). SAVAK was to develop a fearsome reputation both at home and abroad—indeed, it eventually came to symbolize the excesses of all secret-police societies.

His experience with Mossadeq also convinced the Shah that he needed his own money, and outside the country. He began to allow members of his family to amass fortunes.

Finally, and perhaps most dangerously, he came to believe that his restoration was evidence of some sort of divinely inspired relationship between him and the Iranian people. "I knew that they loved me," he had declared with emotion in Rome. His good fortune in surviving subsequent assassination attempts increased his belief in his divine protection. In his last memoirs, written in his second exile, he wrote that before 1953, "I had been no more than a hereditary sovereign, but now I had truly been elected by the people." Even after he had left the country once more, in January 1979, this remained his conviction—and the root of his tragedy.

On the afternoon of January 16, as his blue-and-white 707 neared Aswan airport, the Shah walked back into the cockpit to rejoin Captain Moezzi. He landed the plane himself and taxied it over to where President and Mrs. Sadat were waiting with a guard of honor, a twenty-one-gun salute, a military band to play the national anthems of Iran and Egypt, and a red carpet. Nowhere else in the world would he ever again be accorded such honors.

CHAPTER FOUR

The Host

It was an exquisitely warm afternoon in Aswan—just the sort of day for which the swallows fly so far. When the Shah walked slowly down from the plane, looking drawn and exhausted, Sadat stepped forward to kiss him on both cheeks—despite advice from his officials that he should be more circumspect with the fallen King. "Rest assured, Mohammed, you are in your country and with your people and brothers," he said to the Shah, whose eyes filled with tears.

Egypt had not always been so welcoming. After the Shah's former brother-in-law, King Farouk, was overthrown in a military coup in 1952, Egypt became the Shah's leading opponent in the region. Farouk's successor, Gamal Abdel Nasser, a Socialist and a revolutionary, attempted to unite the Arab world. He was fiercely opposed not only to the Shah's monarchism but also to his foreign policy.

After Anwar Sadat succeeded Nasser as president of Egypt in 1970, he began to transform the direction of Egyptian policy. Rapprochement with Iran was one result. Sadat and the Shah had become friends the previous year, after first quarreling at an Islamic summit in Rabat, about the measures needed to protect Islamic shrines under Israeli occupation. This was after the el-Aqse mosque had been burned by a deranged tourist. Sadat found the Shah's response too weak and said so. But after the Shah responded angrily, Sadat told him in Persian, "There can be no love except after enmity." He also liked to remind him that the first time he had seen him was during the military parade in Cairo to celebrate Mohammed Reza's marriage to Princess Fawzia in 1939. "You were on a raised platform and I passed before you in the parade." Sadat laughed. "The distance between us was very small, yet in reality it was great. You were the heir to a throne and I was a minor officer from a village you had never heard of."

Sadat visited the Shah in Teheran in October 1971, and each man impressed the other with his friendship and strategic views. The Shah told one of his ministers, "We have a lot to learn from Sadat. He's a man with wide horizons who knows what he wants." Subsequently, wrote Mrs. Sadat, they felt a special kinship for they led the two most ancient civilizations in the Middle East—"the Iranian Empire dating back 2500 years and Egypt's civilization going back seven thousand."

Since the mid-seventies the Shah had extended substantial financial aid to Egypt. Mrs. Sadat and the Queen had become friends after an official visit the Sadats had made to Iran in 1976. During that trip, Jehan Sadat had been impressed by the progress made by Iran under the Shah, but she said later that she was also appalled at the extravagant opulence that the rich displayed. A government official gave a party for the Shah, the Queen, and the Sadats. The steps of his house seemed to Mrs. Sadat to be made of crystal, kilos of caviar were laid out on tables in the garden, fruits were woven into the trees, chocolate mousse was presented in swans made of spun sugar, orchestras played, fountains splashed, and the plates were made of gold. She had never in all the world seen such overindulgence. "There will be a revolution, I feel it," she said to her husband when they left. She said she wanted to warn the Shah, but her husband forbade her to do any such thing.

Like the Shah, Sadat identified himself with the state. (The critics of each of them would say "confused" rather than "identified.") Each man had grandiose visions. Neither was able to turn them into reality but, for better or for worse, they had a lasting impact on the Middle East.

Sadat, perhaps more than any other Middle Eastern leader in the seventies and eighties, attempted to come to terms with one of the most extraordinary acts of modern times—the creation and development of the state of Israel. His visit to Jerusalem in 1977 did not, as he hoped, bring peace, but it was an astonishing, moving tribute to the ideal of reconciliation.

In the fall of 1978, while the Shah's power was draining away from him in Teheran and riots against his rule dominated the U.S. television news, Sadat was closeted with Menachem Begin and Jimmy Carter in the Maryland hills working out the interstices of what became known as the Camp David Agreement. This was hailed as historic at the time—as a giant contribution toward a peaceful settlement of the Middle East. In fact it served to isolate Anwar Sadat and Egypt from most other Arab leaders and governments. While Sadat was praised in the West as a saintly figure prepared to make great sacrifices in order to end the strife between Muslim and Jew, in the Middle East he was widely denounced as a traitor and a knave.

During those last months of the Shah's regime, Jehan Sadat was constantly on the telephone to the Shah's wife, Farah. In January 1979, when the revolution was well under way, Mrs. Sadat invited the Queen and the Shah to visit Cairo. At first they refused; the Shah thought that the Americans were using Sadat to get him out of the country. But after he had agreed to leave Iran, he accepted the invitation to pause in Aswan on the way to the United States.

Amir Aslan Afshar, the grand master of ceremonies, felt there was a conspiracy behind this decision. "I think it was an American plot not to have the Shah come to the U.S.," he said later. "Just before we left Iran, the Shah asked me to call Sadat, but the telephone was on strike, the telex also. Even the Egyptian ambassador could not get in touch with Cairo. The Shah said, 'Find a solution.' About ten or eleven at night I got a call from the U.S. embassy . . . 'We have got in touch with [Vice President Hosni] Mubarak by radio and Mr. Sadat is expecting the Shah the day after tomorrow at two P.M. in Aswan.' So you see, the Americans prepared everyone."

From the White House, the view was different. Gary Sick, the aide to Zbigniew Brzezinski on Iranian affairs, has written that the Shah's last-minute decision to visit Egypt completely disrupted the complex arrangements made for his arrival in the U.S. "and gave rise to concern about the Shah's real intentions." Reports reached Washington that the Shah was hoping for a restoration similar to that which occurred in 1953.

From the airport the Sadats and the Pahlavis drove to the Oberoi Hotel, which is secluded on a man-made island in the Nile. Sadat had ordered photographs of the Shah, left over from an earlier state visit, to be mounted along the route. The Shah sat in the car and wept. He told Sadat that his officers had cried at Teheran airport and begged him not to leave. "I feel like a leader who has deserted the battlefield."

According to Mrs. Sadat, her husband then offered to provide sanctuary for the Iranian Air Force and navy. "Egypt will host them until the conditions stabilize in Iran," he said. But the Shah replied, "The Americans will not allow it. They forced me to leave." He went on to tell Sadat that the U.S. ambassador kept looking at his watch at the airport, "saying that every minute I delayed was not in my interests nor in the interest of Iran." (In fact, the ambassador, William Sullivan, had been nowhere near the airport.)

Sadat was shocked; later he told his wife that he could not believe that the Shah would have allowed any foreign power such influence over his country's affairs.

The Shah and his party spent five days in Aswan. There were not many visitors. One person who called by telephone was ex-King Constantine of Greece, a great favorite of Queen Farah. He found both her and the Shah in a state of shock, quite confused and uncertain what to do.

The arrival in Aswan

One man who came to Aswan, at the Queen's request, was a youthful-looking Frenchman with a shock of curly hair and a slightly puzzled expression behind his glasses. He and an Iranian doctor flew from Paris as discreetly as they could. The Frenchman had made many such trips to Teheran before the fall and he understood the need for absolute secrecy. His name was Dr. Georges Flandrin and for five years he had been treating the Shah for cancer. But not even the Shah really understood the extent of his illness.

When they arrived in Aswan, they found problems in getting to the Oberoi; the river was patrolled and few people were allowed across. From a café beside the Nile, the Frenchman called the Oberoi and asked for the Queen. Somewhat to his surprise, he was put through to her at once. *"Majesté, c'est moi,"* he said simply.

She recognized his voice and sent a boat for him. Dr. Flandrin had seen the Shah only two weeks before, ill at ease and nervous in the palace. Now he seemed rather calmer and appeared pleased to see his doctor. Flandrin examined the Shah, took a blood test, and went away. No one else in the Shah's entourage knew who he was or why he had come.

There was another visitor, who was just as discreet—and just as vital to the Shah as Dr. Flandrin. Mohammed Behbehanian was seventy-eight years old. He came now from his haut-bourgeois villa in Basel, the banking capital of Switzerland, and he was frightened by the forces that the uprising in Iran had unleashed.

Behbehanian looks like a pleasant, well-to-do Swiss grandfather —a retired dentist perhaps, round, with a small gray mustache and a fine smile. He had been the administrator of the Royal Estates and head of finance at the court. He was the man who held the drawstrings to the Shah's own private fortune, amassed at home and abroad since the Shah had found himself penniless in his first exile in 1953.

Behbehanian had not fled the turmoil early in 1978, like so many of the Shah's nearest and dearest. On the contrary, through much of the year, he was, he said later, an intermediary between the Shah and one of the principal mullahs in Iran, Ayatollah Shariatmadari, who was less radical than Ayatollah Khomeini and who maintained contact with the Shah through 1978. Eventually Behbehanian left Teheran for his home in Basel just before Christmas 1978.

"On January 16, 1979, I heard on the radio the Shah had left for Egypt. I called him in Aswan that afternoon. I said, 'Majesty, do you want me to come?' He said, 'Come at once.' "

When Behbehanian arrived at the hotel in Aswan, he was shown into the Shah's suite. The Shah told him, "I want to control everything now." Behbehanian was to write to all the foreign banks that held the Shah's funds to inform them that from now on His Imperial Majesty would be dealing with them direct and that he, Mohammed Behbehanian, would no longer be acting on the Shah's behalf.

Behbehanian was not just a money man. He also had very firm ideas on what had gone wrong in Iran and how things should be righted. Like many Iranians, particularly of the older generation, he was convinced that the British were behind much of the upheaval in the country. He thought the British were angered by the extent to which the Shah had criticized British sloth in recent years. (The Shah had indeed been strident in his denunciations of Western decadence and corruption.) "The Shah had given a press conference in which he insulted British workers, saying they were not as good as Iranians," said Behbehanian later. As a result the British had deposed him. He now believed that if only the Shah apologized, then the British would restore him. So he put forward a plan of action to the Shah.

"I said, 'Let's get up and go to Mecca. You can worship there and the nation will understand that you are a Muslim. We will get a loan from King Khalid [of Saudi Arabia] and then we will go to Britain and settle affairs with the British government. We can apologize for insulting British workers and then, with British support, we can go back to Teheran.' "

Behbehanian sincerely and deeply believed this would do the trick. Six years later, when he talked about it in his house in Basel, he still believed it, and with absolute conviction. Everyone knew how influential the British had always been in Iran. Moreover, there was the queen of England's interest. "I am a banker not a politician. But I had noticed the sincerity of the British queen toward the Shah. I had lunched at Buckingham Palace and then met with her at Ascot. She was so interested in the Shah and his family." (The queen had been due to visit Iran on the royal yacht *Britannia* in January 1979; at the last minute the trip was canceled because of the turmoil in Iran and the queen sent the Shah a gracious and sympathetic handwritten note of regrets.)

The Shah shared much of Behbehanian's suspicion of the British. But now, in Aswan, he did not seem to be greatly in favor of Behbehanian's suggestion that he throw himself on their mercy. Wearily, he waved his financial adviser away.

Queen Farah seemed to like the idea even less. After Behbehanian left the room, he paused outside with Amir Aslan Afshar, Colonel Jahanbini, and others. According to Behbehanian, the Queen rushed out and declared that the Shah would go along with such a plan "over my dead body." She was very angry, and Behbehanian felt humiliated. Like some others of his generation around the Shah, he did not much like the Queen.

In Behbehanian's proposal one can detect elements of the fantastic, almost surrealist path the Shah had been destined to try to follow throughout his life. Constantly, he had been torn by contradictory forces. There was the towering image of his father—to whom almost no son could be equal. There was the justified belief in external manipulation—and yet there was dependence on those same manipulators. There was the impetus, coming mostly from the West, but also from within himself and his own Western education, toward the modernization and reform of his country. There were similar demands for reform from the people—and there was a corresponding conservatism. Conspiring against almost everything (one can say in retrospect) were his exaggerated notions of his own divinely inspired relationship with the Iranian people. The combination of Cyrus the Great, the Great Satan, and the schisms in the Middle East that followed the creation of the state of Israel was almost intolerable—as the events after his restoration by the CIA and MI6 in 1953 were to show.

Almost alone among Middle Eastern states, Iran pursued, from the start, a policy of discreet cooperation with Israel. Indeed, its relations with Israel provide one key to its relations with all its neighbors.

Persian tolerance of Jews is a long and honorable tradition. The Book of Ezra records that when Cyrus captured Babylon in 539 B.C., he freed the Jews captured in the city and allowed them to return to Jerusalem, whence they had been exiled by their Babylonian conquerors.

After this the Jewish community began to spread into Persia, and by the mid-twentieth century there were probably about 100,000 Jews in Iran. Until Reza Khan seized power they were required to live in ghettos, but as part of his policy of diminishing the power of the traditional landowning classes, he decreed in 1927 that they could own land, vote, and live outside the ghettos.

In 1948, when Israel was created, Iran allowed Iraqi Jews who, unlike Iranian Jews, were being persecuted, to flee to Israel through Iran. At this time one of the principal tasks of Mossad, the Israeli secret service, was to facilitate Jewish emigration to Israel; the Iranian government allowed Mossad agents to operate in Teheran. Right from the start of the Israeli state, in other words, Iran gave rhetorical support to the Arabs and covert assistance to the Israelis. It was an enduring pattern.*

In July 1949 the various armistice agreements between Israel and the Arab states formally ended the 1948 war and established Israel's territorial position. Israel's principal foreign-policy objective now became to break the walls of its political isolation in the region. Its first success was full diplomatic recognition by Turkey in 1949; the second was de facto recognition by Iran in 1950.

From documents in Israeli archives, it has since become clear that it was not the Shah's personal decision to grant de facto recognition to Israel. (The Shah at this time did not have much authority.) Israel in fact obtained de facto recognition from Iran by paying a substantial bribe to the then Iranian prime minister, Muhammad Saed.

The negotiations were conducted on Israel's behalf by an American still known only as "Adam," who was close to Mossad and also knew an Iranian merchant who was the friend and "silent business partner" of the prime minister. Through him Prime Minister Saed asked for $400,000 to stack the Cabinet and to persuade the Shah that de facto recognition of Israel was in Iran's national interest. This request led to agonized debate within the Israeli Foreign Ministry. Not only was it a vast amount of money for the fledgling state to raise, but many Israeli officials felt passionately that Israel should not begin its life by seeking to extend its reach and influence through such obvious corruption. But then Adam, on his own initiative, paid a first installment of some $12,400 to

---

* The Jewish Agency representative in Teheran, who was in fact an Iranian, reported in 1948: "Action is being taken . . . to excite and incite the Muslims against the Jews in general and the Jewish population in Israel. Thousands of 'Soldiers of the Faith' have already enlisted and the populace and the parliament are vociferous. [But] there is no doubt that [not even] a few tens from among them will cross the borders. There is thus not much to fear from these descendants of Cyrus, the real Aryans of yesterday, who have become blood brothers of the Arabs. . . ."

the merchant for the prime minister. There were immediate results. The prime minister began to talk to the ayatollahs about the need to distinguish between global politics and religion, he made some changes in his Cabinet to assure a favorable vote, and he talked to the Shah.

The Shah was reported to the Israelis as having said, "If the prime minister and the foreign minister were in favor of recognizing Israel, I have no objections." So the $400,000 was paid. These initial contacts and bribes led to almost thirty years of close political, military, and developmental cooperation between Israel and Iran.

Their common interests were obvious. First of all, Iran could provide Israel with oil, and in return Israel could, eventually, provide Iran with manufactured products, including arms, and all sorts of experts. Mossad, together with the CIA, played an important part in the creation of SAVAK in the mid-fifties.

After the overthrow of Mossadeq in 1953, the United States began to replace Britain as the dominant external power in Iran—though many older Iranians (like Mohammed Behbehanian) continued to believe for decades that it was the British who really still called the shots and that the Americans were only British stooges.

The Shah realized that his Western friends wanted above all a stable, friendly Iran. As the fifties proceeded, a succession of coups, countercoups, wars, revolutions, and civil disorders made the Middle East one of the most volatile areas on earth, a place that in the words of one historian, "reverberated with the sound of crashing thrones." First Farouk had been deposed. Then Egypt tried to overthrow King Hussein of Jordan. In Iraq, Iran's neighbor, the Hashemite royal family was murdered in a coup in 1958 and was replaced by a pro-Soviet dictatorship.

The Shah saw himself surrounded by enemies. Quite apart from the new radical Arab regimes, the Soviet Union remained a bellicose, threatening neighbor—as Russia almost always had been to Persia. This was the context in which the Shah determined to do as his father had done—to destroy all possible Iranian opposition, and to build up the armed forces as the basis of his power.

That might have been thought to be in tune with the Cold War music of the era. However, U.S. government papers, released under the Freedom of Information Act, show that President Eisenhower, his secretary of state, John Foster Dulles, and, later,

The Shah and Soraya with Mr. and Mrs. John Foster Dulles

Presidents Kennedy and Johnson, all had misgivings about the Shah's abilities. They doubted his capacity to rule Iran effectively, and they constantly tried to limit his apparently insatiable appetite for military hardware.

For example, when the Shah met Dulles in March 1956, he told Dulles that he thought Iran was "the most critical spot in the world today." Dulles replied that a good many countries in the world saw themselves the same way. If the U.S. responded to each accordingly, the total amount of aid it would have to disburse would be "astronomical." The Shah asked for $75 million a year in military aid for the next three years, but Dulles thought this was excessive.*

The Shah said that he thought the U.S. was "perhaps spending too much in other countries such as Vietnam although he recognized that that was important. He said that was because we had come in too late. He did not want to see us make the same mistake in Iran as it might cost us much more if we did not move now."

* According to Dulles's own account to Eisenhower of the conversation, "I said I had been told that by Pakistan and now I was going to India where Nehru would undoubtedly say the same thing and then on through my trip where at each place the demands would be tremendous on the ground that their support was necessary to prevent a critical breakthrough of Communism. I said that trip only covered a small part of the world, but that wherever I went, I found a similar point of view. I said if all these things were added up, the total would be of astronomical proportions." Dulles then gave the Shah a civics lesson, explaining that under the U.S. system the Executive could not just make decisions and then "extract the money from the people. I said that could be done in Russia where a decision of the Kremlin could automatically be reflected in turning the screw down a bit tighter on the Russian people. . . ."

The Shah continued, every year, to ask for increased aid, and constantly threatened that unless the U.S. provided it, he would turn neutralist or even move toward the Russians.* In January 1958, Dulles talked with him again, in Teheran, and immediately cabled Eisenhower in exasperation, saying that the Shah "considers himself a military genius," and his ministers were unable to cope with Iran's pressing economic problems "in the face of the Shah's military obsessions." He suggested that Eisenhower "flatter the Shah with the prospect of an exchange of views with you on modern military problems." Eisenhower subsequently did so at a meeting with the Shah in Washington. He reminded the Shah that "maintenance of too much force for limited war could be self-defeating economically."

Notwithstanding Eisenhower's record as a military man and a statesman, the Shah was still unsatisfied, and in 1959 he flirted with the idea of signing a nonaggression pact with the U.S.S.R. unless he was given more U.S. military aid.† Dulles said he thought the Shah's behavior "in some instances seems to border on blackmail tactics." Eisenhower and Dulles both believed that since no Iranian Army could ever resist an actual Soviet invasion, the Shah should not build up a vast Army but should depend on U.S. guarantees. Were such an invasion ever to happen, it would inevitably lead to a wider war involving the U.S. anyway.

By the end of the fifties, Washington had agreed to help improve the Iranian armed forces more rapidly, but American military aid was still far less than the Shah wanted. In his memoirs he complained that in the fifties the U.S. gave twice as much aid to Yugoslavia, three times to Turkey, and four times to Taiwan.

In March 1958, after seven years of marriage, the Shah and Queen Soraya were divorced, largely because of their inability to have a child together. They had sought professional advice. On

---

* One telegram from the U.S. ambassador to the State Department in 1957 noted that the Shah was "far more interested in military hardware and installations" than in economic aid. "Shah personally appears under psychological compulsions which lead him to desire military forces well over and above what might be objectively required for internal security, prestige, or a rational contribution to regional collective security."

† In 1959, Nikita Khrushchev told the Iranian ambassador to Moscow that a neutral Iran would be able to obtain "ten times" as much aid from the U.S.A., and Soviet aid as well. He also warned that Iran's ties to Washington might lead the U.S.S.R. to invoke a forty-year-old treaty that would permit the Soviets to move against foreign bases in Iran. This threat caused alarm in Teheran.

one occasion, Soraya saw a gynecologist who was said to have been sent by Kim Roosevelt. "Four times a night and twice every afternoon," she said. "Still I don't have a baby." The doctor explained to her how hard it sometimes was for the sperm to coincide with the egg; she just had to continue to keep the Shah interested.

"Doctor," she replied, "all I'm asking you to do is find something to break my eggs. I'll see the Shah goes on making the omelettes."

The question of succession had been made more urgent because in 1954 the Shah's only full brother, Ali Reza, who was next in line to the throne, was killed in an air crash. Their mother, who was still a dominant influence in the court, was rumored to have believed that Ali Reza would have been a stronger Shah and should succeed (if not replace) Mohammed Reza. Indeed, one CIA report claimed that she had contempt for her elder son, that she felt he was unworthy of his father, and that she had actually plotted to put Ali Reza on the throne. After Ali Reza's death, she insisted that the Shah must produce a son and heir.

The Shah announced the divorce on the radio; in many ways it was reminiscent of King Edward VIII's speech to the British people when he announced he had decided to marry Mrs. Simpson. Edward declared he could not continue to be king without the woman he loved. The Shah said that he loved Soraya but the demands of monarchy meant that he must have an heir and so he had to sacrifice his love.

After the divorce, Soraya was dispatched with her pension to Europe where, in Lesley Blanch's memorable phrase, she became "the cynosure of all eyes about the empty halls of international pleasure." The Shah was said to have remained very fond of her.

He played around again. His tastes, the CIA later noted in one of its profiles of him, were "ecumenical": he liked all races. Soraya wrote in her memoirs that "the European type appealed to him most," but that he had too much common sense to marry one of them. The European he was said to be the most fond of was Princess Maria Gabriella de Savoia, but her father, the former King Umberto of Italy, would have insisted on a Catholic wedding. That would have been impossible for the Shah. (Gabriella's family would retain close links with Iran; her brother Vittorio Emanuele represented Bell helicopters and other companies in the days of the great boom.) In 1959 the Shah married for the third time, to Farah Diba, a twenty-one-year-old Iranian student of architecture.

John Kennedy was even more ambivalent about the Shah than Eisenhower had been. When Kennedy became president in January 1961, the state of Iran was not encouraging. The Shah had built up his armed forces and had begun to create a nationwide secret police, but he had done almost nothing to meet the disparate but urgent demands of his people.

He was behaving more and more as an autocrat. The state of emergency inherited from Mossadeq had been lifted only in 1956. The National Front, where most leading opponents had grouped, could not operate at home, but it re-formed abroad. The Communist Tudeh Party also began to organize abroad, chiefly in Eastern Europe. The 1960s opened with student demonstrations and teachers' strikes against the Shah. There was religious dissension in the holy city of Qom and disaffection in many of the tribal areas. The peasantry still had virtually no rights whatsoever. After the Shah publicly endorsed Iran's links with Israel, Nasser cut off diplomatic relations with Iran and increased Egyptian propaganda attacks against the Shah. Syria and Iraq and other Arab states supported a "liberation movement" in Iran's oil-producing province of Khuzistan, and Iraq began to menace Kuwait. The Arabs began to describe the Persian Gulf as the Arabian Gulf and Khuzistan as Arabistan—its old name under the Qajar Shahs.

When President Kennedy met Nikita Khrushchev in Vienna in 1961, the Soviet leader scoffed at the Shah. The Shah, he said, claimed that his power was given to him by God, but everyone knew that the throne had been seized by his father. And his father was not God but a sergeant. Khrushchev warned that Iran would undergo political upheaval. It would fall like a rotten fruit into Soviet hands. No doubt Moscow would be blamed, but it would not be responsible.

Kennedy was alarmed. Back from Vienna, he ordered a report on Iran from the State Department; it concurred with Khrushchev's assessment. A 1961 National Intelligence Estimate on Iran concluded that "profound political and social change in one form or another is virtually inevitable." It reckoned that such change was likely to be revolutionary. From then on, Kennedy's attitude to Iran was unashamedly interventionist. The Shah resented this and subsequently noted that during Kennedy's presidency there was "increased U.S. intrigue against our country."

Kennedy encouraged the Shah to undertake reforms and was pleased when the Shah appointed Ali Amini, the former Iranian ambassador to Washington, prime minister of Iran. Amini came from one of the great landowning families of Iran and had the distinction of serving in the Cabinets of both Mossadeq (with whom he broke) and General Zahedi. But as minister of finance under Zahedi he had become too well known for negotiating the new agreement with the oil companies, and so the Shah had exiled him to the Washington embassy. Amini had concluded that the Shah's choice was to divide his lands or face revolution—and perhaps death. This view impressed Kennedy.

Although the Shah appointed Amini prime minister, he disliked U.S. interference. He also feared the growth of Amini's influence and began to think that the reforms his prime minister proposed were too extensive. The Kennedy administration was not pleased. One State Department cable to the U.S. ambassador in Teheran asked him to remind the Shah that reforms were necessary "because it is generally agreed that without some reforms Iran was likely as Khrushchev predicted to fall to Soviets like ripe plum."

Washington was not confident about how to deal with the Shah. The 1961 Presidential Task Force on Iran noted that "the Shah is a highly complex personality: intelligent and forceful on occasion, but often moody, erratic, and indecisive. He is constantly haunted by the fear that the U.S. might abandon him for one reason or another and has been particularly uneasy over the new U.S. Administration's attitude toward him."

In April 1962 the Shah came to Washington. He told Kennedy that many of his officers were worried that other countries received more military aid than Iran did. Kennedy replied that the United States felt that the main problems in Iran were internal and, thanks to the new reforms, things were improving. He rhapsodized about Franklin Roosevelt who, he said, was still regarded "almost as a god in places like West Virginia," because, although rich, he had worked for the common people.

The Shah agreed, and said that this was his great goal. But he repeated that what Iran needed was "an honest first-class Army with a decent standard of living. With such an Army Iran can resist Communist pressures and build the country into a showcase so that other peoples can see that it is possible to work with the West and get more effective support than countries such as Egypt receive." (Egypt, under Nasser, was then being armed and under-written by the U.S.S.R.)

Kennedy was alarmed at the "showcase" notion, which he thought unrealistic. The Shah then said, "[I am] not by nature a dictator. But if Iran is to succeed, its government [will] have to act firmly for a time." He said he knew that "the United States would not insist that Iran do everything in an absolutely legal way."

This was not then a popular view in Washington. The Justice Department, under Robert Kennedy, was resisting Iranian requests that the U.S. extradite Iranian students to Iran on the grounds they were "Communists."* John Kennedy replied, "There [are] always special factors that have to be taken into account in different countries. We are aware that the Shah is the keystone to the arch in Iran." But Kennedy also praised Amini, the reformer.

The Shah returned to Iran and three months later he dismissed Prime Minister Amini. After his experience with Mossadeq, he was not prepared to allow any other Iranian to develop a following either at home or in Washington. Moreover, the Shah thought that Amini's reforms were altogether too radical.

And so, like so many other politicians of merit, Amini was excluded from any positions of responsibility in Iran from the early sixties onward. The Shah appropriated the idea of reform to himself and launched what he called his "White Revolution"—white because it was meant to be bloodless. In fact the measures were rather less "revolutionary" than those that Amini had sought to implement.

There were six principal areas to the White Revolution. It provided for nationalization of forests, the sale of some state-owned industries to provide money for agricultural development, some worker participation in profit sharing, revision of electoral laws (including significant rights for women), the formation of a Lit-

---

* On one occasion the Iranian ambassador to Washington asked Dean Rusk, the secretary of state, to send back twenty such "Communists." Rusk informed Robert Kennedy, who asked the opinion of Justice William O. Douglas, who knew Iran well. Douglas said, "I told him that that meant the Shah was making up lists for firing squads"; the students should not be sent back "unless the FBI can prove conclusively that they actually are Communists." A few weeks later Robert Kennedy called Douglas to say, "The FBI report is in, and not a bloody one of these kids is a Communist, so I just told Rusk to go chase himself."

eracy Corps in an attempt to take education to the countryside, and, above all, land reform.

The Shah had already given away some of the land that had been seized by his father after 1925. But in the early sixties Iran's agriculture was still dominated by vast estates owned by rich private landlords and by Muslim clerics. Both resisted the Shah's decrees, and the clerics encouraged protest riots in the holy city of Qom at the end of 1962 and more serious riots in Teheran in June 1963. These were suppressed with force.

For the next few years, the White Revolution achieved marked successes. Some lands were redistributed to landless peasants, literacy was raised, industrialization proceeded, women became freer than ever before, health care improved in many parts of the country. The achievements were considerable; the economy grew. But as all opposition and criticism were suppressed, it was hard to make real judgments as to how popular these measures made the Shah's regime outside of the new, growing middle class which benefited most.

As a result of his reforms, the Shah enjoyed an excellent public image in the West by the second half of the sixties. He was seen as an enlightened despot pursuing liberal policies in the face of dogmatic reaction from priests and landlords. *The New York Times* declared that in his White Revolution he had "aligned himself directly with the workers and peasants against conservatives and traditionalists." Policy makers in Washington and London were sometimes privately more skeptical about the Shah's intentions, the viability of his economic policies, the growing corruption of his court, his apparently insatiable appetite for arms, and even his personality.* But such doubts rarely appeared in print. More important was the fact that the Shah was an important ally of the West (and of Israel) in an increasingly vital and turbulent part of the world—particularly after Israel's momentous victory over its Arab neighbors in the Six-Day War of 1967.

---

* For example, when the Shah visited Washington in June 1964, the U.S. ambassador cabled that he was no longer as "depressed and insecure" as he had been during his 1962 visit; indeed he was "buoyant" in the belief that his reforms were working. "But he is gravely disturbed by recent trends in the Arab world. He still requires reassurance that we are with him, that we admire him, and that we understand his current concerns." As usual, more weapons was his principal concern. The ambassador stated that "in repeated and intensive discussions with him, we have tried here during the past weeks to bring his current requests down to the level where they are reasonable both from the military and from the economic-political points of view, and it now appears that we have had some measure of success."

There was no more humiliating defeat for Egypt and for Nasser's policies. The Shah subsequently told the Israeli foreign minister, Abba Eban, that he had jumped for joy at Nasser's humiliation and distributed gold coins to his friends as a token of the Israeli victory. When Nasser died, three years later, Anwar Sadat told his wife, Jehan, "He did not die on September 28, 1970. He died the morning of June 5, 1967."

Now, in January 1979, as he fled Teheran for the second time in his life, the Shah had intended to fly on to America after just a few days in Egypt. During his visit, he and Sadat prayed together in the Nasr (Victory) mosque and they went on a cruise around the islands of the Nile. A picture of the Shah at the ruined temple on Philae shows him in a blazer and tie, wearing tinted glasses and looking very gaunt as a guide earnestly explains it all to him.

Just before he was due to leave for the States, there arrived in Aswan a herald from another king. It was the Moroccan ambassador to Egypt, who had flown from Cairo to extend an invitation to the Shah from His Majesty King Hassan, an old ally. Like Sadat, Hassan had received considerable funds from the Shah. Now, Mrs. Sadat recalled, the Moroccan king felt that he too should make a gesture to his fallen brother king. Would His Imperial Majesty the Shah be so good as to pause in Marrakesh on his way to the U.S.? He would.

In Washington, President Carter was delighted that the Shah's arrival in the States would be further delayed. He reckoned that it was better for the new Iranian prime minister, Shapour Bakhtiar, that the Shah stayed in Muslim country and he thought that Hassan's influence would help "keep Khomeini under control."

It would not be long before Jimmy Carter and much of the world realized that there was very little, perhaps nothing, that could "keep Khomeini under control"—not, that is, from a liberal Western point of view. In his diary, on January 20, Carter added, oddly for a man who had rather recently praised the Shah, "And I believe the taint of the Shah being in our country is not good for either us or him."

The Shah's enemies saw the move differently. The fact that he was now lingering in the area, first in Egypt and now Morocco, rather than proceeding straight to the United States as announced, inevitably aroused the suspicion that he was hoping for some sort of repeat of 1953. No one knew.

On January 22, just six days after they had left Teheran, the

Shah, Queen Farah, and the entourage, including now Mr. Beh-behanian, left for Morocco in the style that Anwar Sadat wished to accord them. A red carpet was laid out on the runway by soldiers—they only just had it straight when the official parties arrived. There was a guard of honor for the Shah to inspect—more than one hundred troops. As when he arrived, cannons fired a salute. They all said their emotional farewells, Sadat begged the Shah to return whenever he wished, the Shah and the Queen boarded, the doors were closed, and the Shah walked forward to sit beside Captain Moezzi in the cockpit.

The formality of the occasion was slightly spoiled as Sadat and about thirty Egyptian officials waved good-bye; the Shah turned the 707 too soon and his hosts were exposed to the full blast of its taxiing engines. The Sadats crouched low, clasping their heads as the red carpet and the wooden poles holding red and blue ropes flew into the air around them.

CHAPTER FIVE

The Queen and a King

The most formidable personality on the flight out of Egypt was not the Shah. It was his third wife and Queen, Farah Diba.

One CIA report in the mid-seventies noted:

> The Shah's own household has provided him with one of the major problems of his reign. The court was at one time a center of licentiousness and depravity, of corruption and influence peddling. The image may have softened somewhat, or is less the subject of common gossip, but the old picture remains in the public mind and some of the derelictions continue but with more discretion.

Some courtiers were intelligent, some had the leisure to educate themselves, but on the whole these people had little interest in politics, beyond a vapid enthusiasm for the status quo which treated them so well, and an unthinking conservatism, which led them to dismiss anyone with views to the left of their own as "Communists." The same CIA report labeled many of them "drones, sycophants, and timeservers." Another U.S. embassy study remarked, "Several members of the Royal Family are thought to be, in varying degrees, corrupt, immoral and largely uninterested in Iran and the Iranian people."

The only section of the court that had a reputation for some seriousness and probity was that around the Queen. Indeed, she accumulated considerable power in a society dominated more than most by men. Many of her associates were intellectuals and artists; some were thought to be liberals, even leftists. Inevitably, many of the men around the Shah blame the Queen and her circle for the debacle that befell the monarchy in 1978. This was a view ascribed to Princess Ashraf, who was not enamored of the Queen and the way in which her political star rose as Ashraf's waned.

The Queen had had very mixed feelings about their leaving the country. She agreed with the Shah that they could not and should not use massive bloodshed to keep the throne. At one stage she had suggested that he leave for a vacation and she stay behind, heading a Regency Council. This seemed like a grab for power to some, but she saw it differently. "I said to my husband, 'If we all leave, there's no hope for those who believe in us.' I wanted to stay just to be present physically and symbolically without any involvement in politics." The Shah dismissed the notion. So did Bakhtiar.

"Nobody can tell what would have happened if he had stayed, if he'd reacted more strongly," she said later. "Hindsight is always easy, but I don't think it would have worked. There would have been more bloodshed, more killing, but of the people in the streets, not of the people responsible. My husband didn't want bloodshed."

By the time of their exile, Farah had been married to the Shah for nineteen years. She had been studying architecture in Paris when he first met her in 1958. They met again in Iran in 1959, the year they were married.

Farah's mother, Faridah Ghotbi, came from a family of provincial gentry on the Caspian. Her father's family, the Dibas, had served the shahs for generations. They had a reputation for honorable conduct. Her father himself had been an army officer trained first in St. Petersburg and then in France. He became one of those Persians for whom Paris was a second home, and Farah later shared that enthusiasm. He died when she was ten. For a long time his death was concealed from her; her mother and others told her he had gone to Europe to be cured. "But presently I began to wonder, to notice that everything was changed . . . they would stop talking when I came into the room, or there were

hush-hush whispers . . . and my mother crying so dreadfully. . . . Of course I began to suspect—it was terrible, and at last I asked why my father didn't write to me. In my heart I knew he was dead, but I wanted to hear what she would say. . . . From that time on, I never spoke to my mother of my father—never again, till I was eighteen and leaving for France, to study there. . . . It was all locked up inside me, all my sadness."

Marriage to the Shah was, said Farah later, something of an unexpected challenge. "To marry a king—my king—the man for whom I and my friends felt such unbounded admiration, and whom we had so often watched, passing in some procession, while we cheered and waved flags. . . . He was a sort of god to us. . . . And then, suddenly, I had to see him as a MAN—my husband! Yes, it was a great challenge."

She was sent back to Paris to be plucked, groomed, coiffed, gowned, *à la mode*, hair by Carita, dresses by Dior, shoes, jewelry, gloves, and lingerie from all the best houses. "I was like a little doll then," she said later. "I did what I was told, wore things others chose for me. . . . I really was a little doll, being dressed up and arranged and ornamented." She had become, like the Shah's friends the Grimaldis of Monaco, a *Paris Match* person presented to massed readers as a fairy tale, a pretty commoner raised to royalty and yet retaining her human touch.

Back in Teheran they were married regally, on December 21, 1959. The honeymoon was spent in the bosom of the Pahlavi family, on the windswept shores of the Caspian. Farah was to learn that her husband's siblings and mother were an ineluctable part of almost every day. Dinner almost every night was at one or another of the relations' palaces.

With equal grace and dispatch she produced the son and heir the Shah craved. Crown Prince Reza was born on October 31, 1960. Then came a daughter, Farahnaz; another son, Ali Reza; and finally another daughter, Leila. No queen could have performed her dynastic duty with more aplomb.

The wedding of the Shah and Farah Diba

But then Farah did everything with style and with courtesy. Born outside the pompous circumstance of the court, she was relaxed and convivial and far less snobbish than most of the Shah's family. Through the sixties she began to emerge as a warmhearted, rather cultured figure who was much easier with her role than the Shah with his. She was visibly interested in social programs, in women's affairs, in medicine, in leper colonies, and she managed to develop a reputation for compassion. In many ways she became a symbol of the White Revolution during the sixties.

After a second attempt on the Shah's life, in 1965, he decided (and the U.S. embassy concurred) that the Queen should have the power to become regent in the event of his death while their son was still a minor. In 1967, the Shah arranged his own coronation and, having crowned himself, like Bonaparte and his father before him, he crowned Farah too. Her crown, designed by Arpels of Paris, had at its center an emerald the size of a tangerine.

She retained something that the Shah had never had—an ability to appear spontaneous and in touch. Sometimes on progresses through the country she would depart from her official schedule and visit some village that had not been sanitized in advance. She would be enraged if her security guards tried to force people away from her; surrounded by crowds of ordinary people she glowed. She attracted real affection, while the Shah himself aroused fear or, at best, respect. Inevitably there was a lot of sycophantic nonsense around her too. Thus when she made a blood donation, the director of the clinic declared that the room would remain a shrine forever and anyone who now had a transfusion would insist that it was her divine blood that flowed miraculously and potently into his veins.

She had tried to alter the manner in which the Persepolis celebrations were conducted. She said she had disapproved of their reliance on French rather than Iranian products and people. She knew the press would seize on the food from Maxim's, the tents by Jansen, and so on. Before the party, she had suggested that it be delayed. "We have waited twenty-five hundred years," she said, "why not wait another three years to do things more Iranian? It will be more interesting for everybody; it will please the Iranians."

She was not heeded and later she argued that the party provided an extraordinary, unparalleled forum for kings and Communists, dictators and democrats, and that the attention given around the world to Iranian history and culture was invaluable. Nonetheless, she agreed that the "details"—the French connections—"ruined the whole thing. People in Iran were unhappy, and there were enough people to incite them, and then there was so much fuss in the press outside. . . ."

During the 1970s, her relationship with the Shah became complicated. As the Queen had matured, and perhaps become more politically aware, so on the Teheran rumor mill it was reliably asserted that there was a rift between her and the Shah. There were rumors that the Shah's womanizing had now become intolerable.

Call girls from Madame Claude's establishment in Paris, and other services, were one thing. Hundreds passed through Teheran for the Shah and for other members of the court. All this was taken for granted; it was part of the Pahlavi style. But then something more serious happened.

In the early seventies the court (and the bazaar) buzzed with stories that the Shah had fallen in love, not with a European but with a nineteen-year-old Iranian girl with dyed blond hair. Her name was said to be Gilda. Not only was he being fearfully indiscreet, but it was said that he had been foolish enough actually to marry her and to install her in a cottage in the palace grounds.

The Queen apparently lost her patience. At the end of 1972 she left Iran abruptly for Europe. As the CIA later noted, "This sparked rumors of a rift between the Shah and Farah. Although there were suggestions that Ashraf may have had a hand in the affair it seems more likely that the Shah's dalliance with another woman was the real cause."

The Queen returned, but it was said that she insisted that the Shah get rid of Gilda. The Shah was rescued by his brother-in-law, General Khatami, the rich, "affairist" husband of Princess Fatimeh; Khatami took Gilda as his own mistress. The Shah was very grateful at the time, according to the minister of the court Assadollah Alam.

As in many of the high-level intrigues of the Persian court, documentary proof of this story is hard to come by. But such gossip was often well-founded. In many ways, the court was the sum of the stories which circulated around and about it. All courts thrive upon gossip and innuendo. At the end of 1973 the Shah was asked by the intrepid Italian jounalist Oriana Fallaci if it was true he had taken another wife.

"A stupid, vile, disgusting libel," he replied.

"But, Your Majesty, you're a Moslem. Your religion allows you to take another wife without repudiating Empress Farah Diba."

"Yes, certainly. According to my religion, I could, so long as my wife grants her consent. And, to be honest, one must admit there are cases where . . . when a wife is ill, for instance, or when she refuses to perform her wifely duties, thereby causing her husband unhappiness. . . . Let's face it! One has to be a hypocrite or an innocent to believe that a husband will tolerate that kind of thing. In your society, when something like that occurs, doesn't a man take a mistress, or even more than one? Well, in our society, instead, a man can take another wife. . . ."

But there was another side to Farah, one that was perhaps more problematic for the Shah. As well as being an ideal wife and mother, and a symbol of social reform, she also represented a strong Western influence, an influence which was anathema to the Shiite clergy and to many ordinary, conservative Iranians. This was particularly true in her patronage of the arts.

Much of her work was beyond reproach. She rescued old houses from the juggernaut of industrialization, restored them, and opened them to the public. She had the state collect paintings, carpets, silver, jewelry, and ceramics, and display them in museums created especially by her. Some of the objets d'art were bought on her orders, at home and abroad; others she prised out of rich Iranians who often found her acquisitiveness on behalf of the country irksome but impossible to resist. It was a good deal more attractive than the usual Pahlavi type of greed.

Although she started out a creature of Parisian tastes in the sixties, by the seventies she had turned toward Iranian fabrics and designs; where she went, her court and many others followed. She encouraged the rich to take holidays within Iran, and so tried to foster a sense of Iranian culture and a national pride among a people notoriously liable to succumb to self-pity and paranoia.

Nonetheless, sometimes her enthusiasms seemed to jar. Although she was determined to preserve Iran's past, her contemporary tastes were often too avant-garde, too cosmopolitan, for most of her countrymen. Andy Warhol, Stockhausen, Peter Brook, appealed to her and to some of the intellectuals and artists around her, but they were lost on most Iranians. "We were only just beginning to listen to Bach," said one Iranian businessman. "Stockhausen was impossible." And those few Iranians who liked Stockhausen certainly did not like the Shah.

The Queen was a patron also of the Shiraz international arts festival. By the mid-seventies this had become one of the most controversial cultural events in the country. Among its most notorious performances was one by a Brazilian troupe whose members bit the heads off live chickens in the course of the action. It reached a climax in 1977 when another troupe of actors took over a shop in the main street of Shiraz, hard by the mosque, and performed in the shop and on the pavement a play that involved a full frontal rape and lewd acts between naked, consenting actors. Such a performance would have led to scandal (and the arrest of the actors) in any English or American provincial street. Performed in Shiraz it aroused enormous anger and offense.

Such excesses were no doubt the responsibility of her courtiers or producers rather than of the Queen herself, but they became associated with her. Later, in exile, she defended the festival, saying that it brought to Iran purist, traditional art from all over the world. She had been unaware of every detail of performances, and one or two offensive productions had crept in. "In any art festival it is difficult to have free expression by the artists and expect it to appeal to all the different social groups."

During the seventies her court became known, at least to both the friends of the Shah and to his conservative critics, as a den of avant-garde liberalism. She was one of the few people in Iran who dared speak her mind to him (perhaps the sole person), but what was on her mind was not to everyone's liking.

She was always perhaps a bit too trusting. Now in exile, her faith in other people was becoming somewhat tried. In Cairo, exhausted by the traumas of recent weeks, she had been concerned not only about the Shah and his morale, but also about their four children, who had gone ahead of them to the States. Where, for example, would they now go to school? "Even that would make me burst into tears, because all the simple things in life had become a problem for me."

"I used to have so much illusion," she said later. "So much belief in everything. But so many things happened, and you lose those illusions, ideas. Thank God, I've not lost them altogether. It's true we [saw] a lot of the negative side of human behavior, but there [was] also a lot of the positive side. So putting them in balance, I still want to hope that the light will overcome the darkness."

It was in Morocco that the twilight began to fall.

King Hassan II was at the airport to welcome the Shah and Queen when their Boeing touched down at Marrakesh on January 22, 1979. But he gave them none of the honors accorded by Anwar Sadat.

Tourists and journalists, including, to their chagrin, the three American networks, were detained in a hotel on the airport road and were not even allowed to watch the cars pass by. Publicity in the local press was discouraged by the regime; officials insisted that this was "a strictly private visit," to take place "in absolute discretion," and that the Shah himself had "expressed no desire to see the press."

He was taken to the Jinan el Kabir palace, set in an oasis outside Marrakesh, with a splended view over the Atlas Mountains. Palace sources told foreign journalists that Hassan had invited the Shah "as a gesture of friendship."

Monarchs share understandable interests. Theirs is, after all, a smallish society in international terms. Whether they be Asian, African, or European, they have a great deal more in common than most of their respective citizens would have with one another. Since the community appears to be forever shrinking, some of those in power tend to be understanding of those who have lost it—if, that is, they are still sufficiently powerful in their own states to be able to override the diplomatic problems involved. Thus the Shah himself had supported several fallen royals, including the former kings of Afghanistan and Albania, as well as Constantine of Greece. Umberto, the former king of Italy, and his family had lucrative contracts with Iranian agencies, and the onetime King Simeon of Bulgaria, now a Spanish car dealer, had a food contract with Iran. Simeon was on Hassan's list as well. He was often invited to Hassan's birthday party, and since he was usually the only other monarch there, he took precedence in the receiving line over almost everyone else in the room.

It was in this spirit that Hassan had now asked the Shah to Morocco. But he meant him to come for only a few days, not for an indefinite stay. Hassan wanted to demonstrate royal loyalty. But he did not wish to jeopardize Morocco's relations with the new authorities in Teheran, or with those radical Arab states that rejoiced in the fall of the Shah. Still less did he wish to disrupt his carefully crafted relationship with the mullahs in Morocco.

Moreover, King Hassan was reported to be ambivalent about the Shah. It was widely said that he had long resented the Shah's great oil wealth and the independence that it gave him. Morocco had no oil and Hassan by contrast was dependent on support from the Saudis and, until rather recently, from the Shah himself. There must therefore have been a certain piquancy for him in now extending hospitality to the fallen monarch. From Hassan there was to be none of the commitment already expressed—and to be expressed ever more passionately as the Shah's journey continued— by Anwar Sadat.

In his last memoirs, completed just before he died in exile, the Shah described King Hassan II as "a sovereign with a rare intellectual elegance . . . a perfect incarnation of two cultures, the Koranic and the European." There is a poignancy in this remark. It was true that Hassan had managed to balance the often conflicting pressures of secular Westernism with his country's religious traditions far more successfully than had the Shah. Indeed, the Shah's failure to do so had caused this downfall.

Like Iran, Morocco was (and still is) governed by an educated but often corrupt elite gathered around the person of the King. But Hassan was more cunning than the Shah. His family has ruled Morocco since the seventeenth century. The French imposed a protectorate at the beginning of this century; in the 1940s and fifties Hassan's father, King Mohammed V, emerged as leader of the struggle for independence, which was won in 1956. Hassan became king on his father's death in 1961. Since then, unlike the Shah, he has managed to remain the spiritual leader of his people. Whereas the Shah came to be seen in Iran as doorman to the Great Satan, pushing Western goods and notions, Hassan had cleverly portrayed himself as resisting both Morocco's former colonizers, the French, and, more recently, the American intrusion. Indeed, he frequently managed both to play the French and the Americans off against each other and then to blame them when anything went wrong. And while the Shah despised and fought against the mullahs, Hassan had his own representatives in almost all the brotherhoods and mosques. The church was not an enemy for Hassan, it was an accomplice.

Like the Shah, Hassan used financial favors to keep the loyalty of his courtiers. Like the Shah, Hassan had survived several assassination attempts. In 1971 rebels attacked his birthday party; the King hid in a lavatory. The story goes that a young rebel opened the door—precisely why is not known—and the King held out his hand, declaring, "I am the Commander of the Faithful." The boy dutifully fell to his knees, kissed the hand, and the King lived.

In 1972 his own principal aide, General Oufkir, who ruled the country in the King's name, attempted a coup. Till now Oufkir had controlled the secret police and pursued the King's enemies ruthlessly. By 1972, however, he had apparently tired of the court's corruption and his own subordination to the King. He ordered fighters to shoot down Hassan's Boeing. But even he had underestimated the King's nerve. While his plane was under attack, Hassan grabbed the radio operator's microphone and shouted words to this effect: "This is the navigator. The King is dead."

The fighters paused and the King escaped again. It was later announced that General Oufkir had committed suicide by shooting himself in the head—three times.

Marrakesh has long been a winter watering hole for the rich, the chic, and the famous, and the Shah had arrived at the height of the tourist season. There was not much room for all the Iranian courtiers who flew in to see him. Some of them offered help, but more usually they were there to ask for favors—which nearly always meant money. They almost all wanted to stay at the fabulous old Hotel Mamounia, a place of wonderful gardens and lakes that had achieved fame when Winston Churchill came to paint there in the fifties. Other patrons in those days had included Barbara Hutton and some of the relatives of J. Paul Getty. More recently Marrakesh had been taken over by some of the biggest names in haute couture. Pierre Balmain, Yves St. Laurent, and Pierre Cardin had bought old palaces in the town and renovated them elegantly.

Among the guests at the Mamounia while the Shah was settling in were Henri, Count of Paris, the pretender to the French crown, who was finishing his memoirs there; the Reverend Ndabaningi Sithole, then a member of the coalition government of Rhodesia, but soon, like the Shah, to be swept away by revolution; and Hassan's friend, former King Simeon of Bulgaria, who was reported to be there on some business. Also in residence was General Vernon Walters, who, since his trip with Harriman to see

Mossadeq, had been one of the more redoubtable and mysterious figures in the American military-intelligence complex. He was a discreet consultant to King Hassan, whom he had first met when Hassan was a young prince. The details of his work were not well known within the U.S. Embassy in Rabat. Now he was reported to be at the Mamounia in order to work on a book entitled *The Mighty and the Meek*. The American ambassador sent his CIA station chief to ask Walters what he was really doing in Morocco at this of all times. Walters insisted that his visit had nothing to do with the Shah.

When the Shah arrived, Moroccan officials evidently did not know how long he planned to stay. But they made it clear they hoped he would soon be on his way to the United States. The Shah, however, now wished to wait a little longer before he went on to America.

On January 26 his seclusion was broken for what is called a "photo opportunity" at King Hassan's winter palace outside Marrakesh. The place was surrounded by troops as the journalists were ushered in. The Shah was, as often, wearing a dark jacket, lighter trousers, and a striped tie; the Empress, a smart patterned suit. They both looked tense and uncomfortable, and seemed to be searching the journalists for faces they knew. Pierre Salinger of ABC News managed to get past the Moroccan security officials. The Shah said that he was staying on for a while, not flying immediately to either the States or back to Egypt.

A few days later the Shah sought assurances from the U.S. Embassy that he was still welcome in the United States. The State Department cabled Rabat to say, "We assured the Shah publicly as well as in private messages that he would be welcome in the U.S.A. should he choose to go there, and that there should be no doubt whatsoever as to our willingness to receive [him] and provide him with appropriate protection."

When he conveyed this message to the Shah's entourage, the U.S. ambassador, Richard Parker, warned that as the situation in Iran changed so might the attitude in Washington. The Shah should therefore proceed with dispatch.

He did not.

One of the people who advised him to remain in Morocco was the legendary Ardeshir Zahedi, son of the Shah's prime minister in 1953, and till recently the Iranian ambassador in Washington.

Perle Mesta, "the hostess with the mostest," once declared that if you hang a lamb chop in the window the whole town will come running. Ardeshir Zahedi had done far better than that. The windows of the Iranian embassy in Washington were forever hung with pots of caviar and magnums of Dom Pérignon, and the whole town was at his feet—until they were swept by the revolution from under him. Then the influence that he exercised, rather than his generosity, became the talk of the town.

In Washington in the seventies Ardeshir Zahedi played the part of a fun-loving playboy, shoveling edible and liquid gold down the throats of the powerful, of the rich, and of the merely famous. He had a personality as big as the Ritz. He was a fabulous showman, the Cecil B. De Mille of the dinner party trail, equally happy embracing Henry Kissinger or Liza Minnelli or Andy Warhol or Elizabeth Taylor—who was one of the more celebrated of his many lovers. *Le tout* Washington adored him; no other place was so lavish as the Iranian embassy on Massachusetts Avenue, with its mirror-domed ceilings, its drapes and its silks, all dominated by two full-length portraits of His and Her Imperial Majesties and brought alive by the bounding, capacious personality of Zahedi, the ultimate host. Gold watches, caviar, champagne, and beautiful women—all these became associated with Zahedi's munificence.

He was tall, aquiline, and dashing. But behind his large smiles and large cigars, his eyes often seemed to brim with regret. While Iran was undergoing fundamental changes in the seventies he was on the outside, instead of in a position of authority at home.

In a court in which obsequious obedience to the monarch was the rule, Ardeshir Zahedi had always been different. Most of the men around the Shah were tied to him by fear, by devotion, or by the tentacles of corruption. Zahedi was one of the few men in the court with his own standing. During the 1953 crisis he had operated, literally, as the strong arm of his father, General Zahedi. He had been one of the principal Iranian liaisons with Kim Roosevelt and he had helped to organize the demonstrations in support of the Shah. As a result, he was later dogged by the claim that he had continuing CIA links, a claim he always denied.

In 1957 Zahedi married the Shah's daughter by Fawzia, Princess Shahnaz. It was they who introduced the Shah to Farah Diba. Soon afterward the Shah appointed him, for the first time, ambassador to Washington. He liked America; he had studied agriculture at the University of Utah after the Second World War. As ambassador he tried without overwhelming success to convince radical Iranian students that they should support rather than demonstrate against the Shah. (One story, which entered his official State Department biography, has it that he told several students that his own rise to the position of ambassador showed what great opportunities there were for the young in Iran. To which one of the students replied, "Yes, but the Shah has only one daughter.")

In 1962 he became ambassador to Britain. London was then

supposed to be swinging. Zahedi enhanced this reputation, and London society had a taste of the party giving that was to hit Washington ten years later. His princess enjoyed herself less; they were divorced in 1964.

In 1967 Zahedi returned to Teheran to become foreign minister. He was energetic and in many ways successful. A U.S. Embassy profile commented, "Partly in order to counteract his playboy image, Zahedi drove himself and his staff extremely hard and achieved a reputation as a leader with impressive knowledge. Zahedi clearly had the Shah's ear and often made policy suggestions outside the foreign-policy area, a tactic which resulted in rather strained relations with Prime Minister Hoveyda."

In fact, by the end of the sixties Zahedi's relationship with Amir Abbas Hoveyda had degenerated into utter dislike, which Zahedi, impetuous and frank, took less and less trouble to conceal. In 1971 he was also angered by a visit made by the Shah's sister Princess Ashraf to China, which he felt was an intrusion on his turf. On her return, Ashraf reported directly to her brother and did not even send the foreign minister a copy of her conclusions. After further disagreements with Hoveyda, Zahedi left the Foreign Ministry and took himself off to his father's house in Switzerland.

Ardeshir Zahedi and Farah Diba

This was not the way in which people usually behaved toward the Shah. No one was allowed to resign; people served until the Shah dismissed or moved them. By the early seventies, Teheran was littered with forgotten men who had worked in the government or the court and had once—once was too often—dared to question a decision or a policy and had thenceforth been frozen out of all official life. Zahedi was different, first because of his and his father's roles in 1953, and secondly because of his absolute and unflinching loyalty to the Shah. Eventually the Shah asked Zahedi to leave Switzerland and become ambassador to Washington again.

Aside from the society pages, Zahedi was a successful envoy in the Nixon-Ford era. Nixon liked him. He was closer to William Rogers, Nixon's first secretary of state, than to Henry Kissinger, though the press showed him more frequently embracing the latter. He spent much time visiting most states of the Union and acting as a supersalesman for Iran. He invited scores of congressmen and journalists, civic officials and academics to visit Iran and made sure they were lavishly received and entertained. All such activities paid dividends in the sense that, until the second half of the seventies, there was almost no questioning of the Shah's priorities or stability in the American press or Congress.

When Jimmy Carter took office in January 1977, Zahedi found it harder to be close to senior officials. Under Carter's human rights program, the State Department began to pressure the Shah to restrain his secret police, and Zahedi's opulent flamboyance was ill suited for Carter's desire for a less pretentious style of government. Nonetheless, Zahedi had easy access to Zbigniew Brzezinski, Carter's national security adviser.

As the Shah crumbled toward collapse, Zahedi shed the mantle of bon vivant and became, in partnership with Brzezinski, a controversial player in the drama of the final days. He returned twice to Teheran. Before his second visit, in November 1978, Brzezinski asked him to come to the White House to meet Carter, Secretary of State Cyrus Vance, and Stansfield Turner, the director of the CIA. Carter made a rather remarkable commitment to him, saying, "Don't worry about Washington. I will be ambassador for Iran here."

In Teheran, Zahedi was one of the protagonists of a military solution to the crisis. His view was echoed by Brzezinski but not by the Shah. Zahedi was also opposed to the Shah leaving Iran. Here again he failed to convince his liege. He returned to Washington and then went to Switzerland.

Soon after the Shah left Teheran, the Iranian embassy in Washington was taken over by militants and by members of Zahedi's staff who had hitherto seemed loyal to him and the Shah. Zahedi's Château Lafite and other vintages were poured into the embassy fountain, and he was publicly denounced as having bribed congressmen and journalists with drugs and call girls. (Such charges were investigated by Congress and the Justice Department and were dismissed.)

By the time Zahedi rejoined his king in Morocco at the end of January 1979, he had decided that by refusing to give the Shah unequivocal support, the United States had betrayed him. He now thought that the Shah should keep his distance from Washington. Moreover, once the King went to the States there was no way he could ever return to Iran except as a parcel from the CIA.

Zahedi advised the Shah to stay in Morocco. At the same time he and some of the Shah's entourage, including Colonel Jahanbini, hatched a simple and dramatic plot. The Israeli commando unit at Entebbe was the model to which they aspired.

The idea was that a group of them should take back the second of the Shah's planes to Teheran, contact those military commanders known to be most loyal to the Shah, and convince them to hijack Khomeini's plane when, as they assumed he would, he flew back to Teheran from Paris.

What then? One possibility was to force it to land at an army base remote from Teheran. What would then be done to contain the rage of the millions of people waiting to greet the Imam in the streets of Teheran? Their proposal was that Teheran radio should announce that the plane had technical problems and that Khomeini was safe at another airport. There they would force Khomeini to negotiate a deal and to broadcast it to the people. If he did not? They would kill him.

The other alternatives were to shoot the plane down before it landed or blow it up on the ground at Teheran airport when all the Imam's followers had come forward to welcome him.

Of these three schemes, the conspirators preferred the first—the diversion of the plane. The other two were messier; for one thing, each would have involved killing anyone else who was flying back with Khomeini. (In the event, the plane was filled with journalists whose tickets financed the cost of the charter from Air France.) But in Morocco even that was not seen as totally out of the question.

Years later, when they told this story, those who had conceived the plan insisted that they would have carried out the attack in their own names, as rebels, and not under the Shah's authority. The Shah could then have denounced them and ordered their arrest and execution.

They did substantial planning and then they took the idea to the Shah. His reaction, they say, was disappointing. He said, "You must be mad. If you carry on like this I will ask Hassan to put you behind bars."

But even while the Shah shrugged off such schemes, saying that this was not 1953, he also seemed to feel that the allies who had saved him then had somehow betrayed him now. Where was Kim Roosevelt or his successors, come to tell him how to fight? Not in Marrakesh. Nor even, it seemed, in Teheran.

With or without the help of the CIA and the participation of the Shah, some of his commanders left behind in Iran were still attempting to organize a coup.

Before Christmas the Shah had constantly refused to approve such efforts, saying that the King could not secure his throne by massive bloodshed. Just before the Shah had left Iran, Admiral Habib Olahi and other commanders had gone to him one last time and asked his permission to undertake a coup. This time the Shah had seemed ambiguous. "But it seemed he didn't want any responsibility for any military action, even while out of the country," said Habib Olahi later. "He didn't want blood on his hands but on ours. If it worked, he could return. If not, we would be tried and executed," Habib Olahi recalled. Obliquely the Shah had agreed to let them start some planning; it began just as he left for Egypt.

By January, the Navy had already taken over the oil fields from striking oil workers and was producing just under a third of normal output. The Navy also controlled the ports. Under the coup plan, Habib Olahi would be responsible for running the country's whole electric grid, taking over key factories if necessary.

It took nearly two weeks of detailed discussion by planning officers of all three services to work out the details. They had virtually no contact with the Shah.

His absence made their planning almost impossible. This was because the Shah, always nervous of a military coup against him, had structured the armed forces in such a way that lateral collaboration between the services was very hard to arrange. Until now the commanders had all reported upward to the Shah, who himself made all decisions. Now that the apex of the pyramid was gone, there was no obvious way for decisions to be reached. Eventually, however, those commanders still loyal to the Shah (or still hoping to resist the imposition of Islamic government) produced a series of plans for a military takeover.

But they had not had time to implement them when, on February 1, 1979, the ayatollah returned to Teheran in triumph, like Lenin to the Finland Station.

CHAPTER SIX

The Priest

Since early 1979, Ayatollah Sayyed Ruhollah Mousavi Khomeini has preoccupied the Western world he so despises. He has been its implacable scourge, its unbending critic, preaching and practicing austerity and revenge. To many in the West he has seemed an utterly ruthless and even deranged enemy, a terrifying symbol of an anger and hatred that we had not expected, could not understand, and had no hope of controlling. At the very least he has made the subject of Islam one of widespread fascination in the West. As the historian Edward Mortimer has pointed out, before the Islamic revolution in Iran there was comparatively little Western interest in the spiritual aspects of the Islamic world. The Arabs were seen in terms of oil, the Palestinian problem, and terrorism. The Iranians were symbolized by the Shah. Only with the rise of Khomeini did the politics and spirituality of Islam become a burning issue among strategists, conversationalists, politicians, and writers.

Yet the faith that Khomeini represents, Shiism, is radically different from the Sunni faith practiced by most Muslims. The Koran is common to the two, but the Shiites and the Sunnis have distinct interpretations of the legacy of the prophet Mohammed.

All of Mohammed's sons died and only his daughter, Fatima,

who was married to his chosen successor, Ali, had children. So all his descendants are through Fatima. After Mohammed's death a schism developed between those (who became known as Sunnis) and the followers of Ali (the Shiites, from Shi'a Ali, or party of Ali).

The followers of Ali were defeated after his own death and the deaths of his sons. Shiism became a sect distinct from the mainstream of Muslim thought. It came in a sense to represent opposition rather than power, which was assumed by the mainstream Sunnis. Shiism was imposed on Iran under the Safavid dynasty in the sixteenth century. For Iranians it was always a political as well as a religious creed, and a way of differentiating themselves from the Arabs.

The importance of the Imams as spiritual leaders is at the heart of Shiite doctrine. The Imams do not have the authority to change anything in the divine revelation of the Koran, but they are able to interpret it, through the divine guidance with which they are endowed. Shiites believe that there were eleven Imams after Ali and that the twelfth Imam disappeared from human view around the ninth century but still exists in spirit. This hidden Imam will one day reappear, and when he does so, all the wrongs of the world will be righted.

When the Afghans overthrew the Safavid dynasty and tried to reimpose Sunnism on Iran in the eighteenth century, the principal Shiite mullahs and teachers (ulama) fled to Iraq. There they were able to be independent of the Iranian state authorities—a tradition that has continued since.

During the nineteenth century, the ulama became increasingly critical of the Qajar dynasty and found themselves acting in effect as guardians of the people against the government; but they did not seek to govern themselves. They allied themselves with Western-influenced opponents of the Qajars and were influential in the revolution of 1906 which further weakened the authority of the Shah by creating a constitutional monarchy, similar to that of Belgium—and which remained nominally in force until 1979.

As far as the Shiite ulama were concerned, any Shah ruling before the return of the hidden Imam does so unlawfully, unless he has been licensed by the chief priests, the ayatollahs. Thus the mullahs can legitimately incite revolution, and since the seventh century they have done so. Over the centuries, Iranians have become used to having their religious leaders denounce the Shah's policies on the grounds they were contrary to Islam. Indeed, as Barry Rubin has pointed out in his seminal history *Paved with Good Intentions*, "Tens of millions of Iranians, particularly those living in the rural villages and even the many peasants who had recently migrated to the cities, accepted these clerical proclamations as guides to proper behavior toward their king." At first, Reza Shah had the mullahs' support when he crowned himself king in 1926. At that time, the mullahs were the country's principal teachers, and in many rural areas they had become considerable men of property, taxing the people and buying land for themselves. But Reza Shah's introduction of new civil, commercial, and penal codes, which diminished the power of the ulama, his expansion of the secular school system, and many more of his attempts to create a modern, centralized state, weakened and therefore infuriated them. By 1941, when Reza Shah abdicated, the mullahs had lost much of their former influence.

They began to regain lost ground in the first years of Mohammed Reza's reign, were probably involved in his attempted assassination in 1949, succeeded in killing the prime minister in 1951, and initially allied themselves with Dr. Mossadeq's campaign to nationalize the Anglo-Iranian Oil Company. The mullahs' next great battle with the Shah came over his White Revolution in the early 1960s. It was then that Khomeini first came to prominence.

Khomeini was born at the turn of the century, to a family of mullahs who liked to trace their ancestry back to the prophet Mohammed. His father was killed while Khomeini was a baby, apparently on the orders of a powerful landlord. He was brought up by his mother and an aunt and then, after their deaths, by his elder brother.

Both brothers followed the family tradition and became mullahs. Until the early sixties Khomeini spent his life in the holy city of Qom, where he taught law, philosophy, and ethics, insisting that Islam had a commitment to social and political causes and that Iran had to be independent of both Eastern and Western colonialism. He was a splendid teacher and his lectures drew large crowds from the 1940s onward.

His views were always stern. He believed that there was either good or evil, with no gray area in between. Thus corruption cannot be reformed but must be destroyed. He used to recount a parable of a clean spring and a stagnant pond. The spring can pour into the pond, but the pond will remain stagnant unless it is drained.

It was inevitable that Khomeini would loathe the attacks that Reza Shah made on the power of the mullahs. After Reza Shah's abdication, Khomeini wrote a book in which he described the King as a usurper who had ignored Islamic precepts and had run a corrupt, cruel, and illegitimate state. His later declarations were filled with similar anger at the way in which Mohammed Reza was substituting Western values for the Islamic tradition in Iran.

In the 1940s Khomeini published his view that the clergy must ensure that secular rule is limited by the laws of Islam. Later he declared, "From the beginning Islam represented a political power, not limiting itself to problems of religious practice. In fact, if one refers to the practice of Mohammed, which are the main Muslim texts, one sees that they deal as much with politics, government, the struggle against tyrants, as with prayers."

In the fifties Khomeini attempted, vainly, to obtain clemency for members of the Islamic fedayeen (the precursors of Islamic Jehad and Hezbollah which came to prominence in Lebanon in the 1980s), who had been sentenced to death for assassinating prominent members of the Shah's regime. He abhorred the Shah's relationship with Israel. In the sixties he saw the White Revolution as an attack upon the remaining powers of the clergy and the place of religion in Iranian society. That was accurate enough.

Khomeini described the Shah's attempt to enfranchise women as an effort "to corrupt our chaste women." The Shah's Literacy Corps, under which young army conscripts spent their national service as teachers in poor villages, threatened the monopoly of the mullahs as teachers. Land reform endangered their financial independence. Khomeini asserted that many of the reforms were "perhaps drawn up by the spies of the Jews and the Zionists. . . . The Koran and Islam are in danger." On some issues he managed to force changes in government policy. It gave him a sense of his power.

When the land reform began to take effect in 1963, the Shah himself denounced the religious opposition as "black reaction" and dismissed the clerics as "lice-ridden mullahs." Land reform was popular and the National Front politicians, what remained of them, could hardly oppose it. But Khomeini again insisted that it was all being done for foreign enemies. "In the interest of the

Ayatollah Khomeini arrives in Tehran

Jews, America, and Israel, we must be jailed and killed; we must be sacrificed to the evil intentions of foreigners."

In June 1963, Khomeini denounced the Shah particularly harshly as a Zionist agent, and was arrested. This caused widespread riots that the government suppressed with brutality. Estimates of the number of people who were killed by the military varied from several hundred to several thousand.

Significantly, the key decisions in containing these disturbances were afterwards said to have been made not so much by the Shah as by his prime minister, Assadollah Alam, a vital figure in the development of Iran in the sixties and seventies. Alam came from a great landowning family in Birjand, in northeastern Iran. He remained by the Shah's side first as prime minister and then as minister of court until his death from cancer in 1977. He was said to be one of the very few senior officials who ever dared to question, if not contradict, the Shah.

Mohammed Behbehanian, the Shah's personal financier, was with Alam at the time of the 1963 riots. He later recalled that the Shah had told Alam not to kill anyone. Alam had replied, "You are the Shah. I am the prime minister. I am responsible for security. I will quiet the people any way I can. If I succeed, you will still be Shah. If I fail, you can hang me and you will still be Shah."

It was rumored that Alam wanted Khomeini executed in 1963

but other religious leaders prevailed upon the Shah not even to put him on trial.

In spring 1964 Khomeini was released. Various emissaries of the Shah tried to persuade the ayatollah to leave politics to the politicians. "All of Islam is politics," he replied.

The final breaking point between Khomeini and the Shah came over relations with the United States. In July 1964 the government introduced a bill that allowed American military advisers and their families to be subject to American, not Iranian, courts. Such agreements on extraterritoriality are common where American forces or advisers are stationed abroad, but in Iran it aroused memories of the humiliating capitulations demanded by the British and the Russians in the nineteenth and early twentieth centuries.*

The act was only narrowly passed by the parliament and Khomeini denounced it as "a document for the enslavement of Iran." The parliament, he said, had "acknowledged that Iran is a colony; it has given America a document attesting that the nation of Muslims is barbarous." If only Islam was still predominant it would not be possible for Iran to be the prisoner of England at one moment and of America the next. He demanded that the Army rise up against the government.

Khomeini's denunciation was widely reproduced and popular. The Shah rejected more advice to kill him, but Khomeini was arrested and banished to Turkey. In 1965 he moved to the Shia shrine in Najaf, in Iraq, where he stayed until 1978. His bitterness against the Shah grew; he constantly denounced the crimes and the tyrannies of the Iranian government and derided the Shah as "a servant of the dollar." He upheld the rights of students imprisoned by SAVAK, of intellectuals and the poor. He saw the Shah's reform movement as designed to sell out the country to foreign powers, especially Israel and the United States, and he exhorted the mullahs to resist.

From Najaf Khomeini denounced the Persepolis celebrations

---

* Russia was the first country to obtain extraterritorial rights in Persia under a treaty of 1828. Between 1855 and 1890, fifteen other countries obtained such rights. In the first two decades of the twentieth century, the cancellation of such rights was one of the principal demands of nationalist politicians and intellectuals. In 1927 Reza Shah declared that all such treaties were void—including the 1856 agreement that gave extraterritorial rights to Americans. He dismissed all Western objections and said that his government was drafting new laws that were based on Western principles and would more than adequately safeguard the interests of foreigners. That was how matters stood until the late 1950s.

absolutely. "Anyone who organizes or participates in these festivals is a traitor to Islam and the Iranian nation," he declared. Despite the fact that the mullahs had originally urged Reza Shah to accept kingship, he stated that the title King of Kings "is the most hated of all titles in the sight of God. . . . Islam is fundamentally opposed to the whole notion of monarchy. . . . Monarchy is one of the most shameful and disgraceful reactionary manifestations."

For a long time it seemed as if these were merely the rantings of a bitter exile. Certainly few people in the West, even the intelligence agencies whose job it is to monitor such dissidence, had much idea of the latent forces that this voice in the wilderness represented in Iran itself. It was a scurrilous attack on Khomeini that the Shah allowed to be published in an Iranian paper early in 1978 that led to the beginning of the apparently endless cycle of protest and suppression that undermined and destroyed the Shah.

In October 1978, the Iraqis expelled Khomeini from Najaf at Iran's request. He was refused entry to Kuwait and asked for asylum in France. President Giscard d'Estaing asked the Shah his views and the Shah made one of the worst mistakes in his reign by agreeing that Khomeini should go to France. He assumed that the obstreperous priest would be less of a threat to him in distant, Christian France than in a neighboring, radical, Islamic country.

The Shah had reckoned without the power of modern communications. From France, Khomeini's aides would dial Teheran direct and the ayatollah could read his sermons straight into Iranian tape recorders for instant distribution throughout the country. And for the first time all the world's press had unfettered access to him. His pronouncements were published and broadcast almost daily, and his young, Western-educated aides acted as brilliant propagandists. The BBC, in particular, gave full coverage to his views. By the end of 1978, the ayatollah had come to be seen, by many of these Western intellectuals interested in Iran, as a saintly old man who was determined to establish a far more just, democratic, and "spiritual" regime than that run by the cruel, corrupt, and despotic Shah.

About three million people thronged the airport and the streets of Teheran to greet Khomeini when he flew home on February 1, 1979. The crowds were delirious and impassable. The ayatollah had to be flown by helicopter to his chosen headquarters—symbolically, a school in the poor part of South Teheran, far from the villas and the palaces of the northern sector, which had till now dominated the lives of the masses.

There were still those among the Shah's military who believed that a coup against Khomeini was possible. They tried to persuade Shapour Bakhtiar, who was still prime minister, to agree to it. He was reluctant, because he believed that he personally had ejected the Shah and that his standing was now so great that he could face down Khomeini alone. "For fifty years, never has the Army been so obedient to a prime minister," he declared the day after Khomeini returned.

Bakhtiar now offered to head a government of "national unity" which would include Khomeini's followers. The ayatollah simply ignored him, urged all government officials to resign, and set up his own alternative government under Mehdi Bazargan, a long-time member of the National Front, a lawyer, and a campaigner for human rights under the Shah. He had spent five years in prison in the early sixties for his opposition to the Shah.

By the seventh of February, followers of Khomeini had taken control of the administrative, police, and judicial functions in several cities. Millions of people demonstrated in favor of the ayatollah and an Islamic government. Bakhtiar denounced Khomeini's plans as "archaic and medieval."

As the Shah sat in the palace at Marrakesh, listening to Radio Teheran, the Army he had so carefully nurtured began to fall apart. Soldiers deserted in droves. SAVAK agents were either fleeing for their lives, being murdered, or, the lucky ones, being allowed to rally to Khomeini. A pro-Khomeini mutiny began among Air Force technicians (known as *homafars*) and then spread to other ranks; by February 10 the Air Force was fighting against the Imperial Guard. "I never thought the Army would collapse so quickly," said Habib Olahi later.

Thousands of civilians swarmed over several military garrisons, seizing the weapons and "liberating" the bases. Bakhtiar gave a broadcast in which he declared these actions would have "no effect on me."

The coup de grace for this unrealistic man of reason attempting to rationalize revolution came on February 11. Armed civilians, Islamic militiamen, and pro-Khomeini troops took to the streets to take control of other military installations. Those army commanders who had still been hoping for a coup realized that all such hope was now lost. The armed forces would not even support Bakhtiar let alone the Shah. The Army's Supreme Council ordered troops back to barracks and assured Bazargan, Khomeini's prime minister, that the military was now prepared to support his provisional government.

Bakhtiar finally understood that his own cause was lost. While machine-gun fire raked the streets around his office, he walked down a back staircase and managed to slip away into hiding. He eventually contrived to smuggle himself, heavily disguised, onto a commercial flight out of Iran and to exile in Paris.

Admiral Habib Olahi and some others finally escaped on foot across the mountains into Turkey. (Some of them had crucial help from the Israeli secret service, Mossad.) Those army commanders who did not immediately hide were not so lucky. Some were dragged out of their cars and butchered by angry crowds in the street. Others were executed after swift show trials.

The Queen remembers that day, February 11, 1979, well. "I was passing through a corridor [of the palace in Marrakesh]. We had the radio on all the time to Radio Teheran, and I heard: 'The revolution has won, the bastion or something has fallen.' For a few seconds I wasn't sure which side had won. For me, we were the good guys and they were the bad guys. Unfortunately it was the other side."

When news of some of the executions reached Morocco, the Shah was on a new golf course built for King Hassan by Robert Trent Jones, a celebrated designer of golf courses. Jones said later that the reports from Teheran had left the Shah rather distracted.

In Washington not everyone understood at once how complete Khomeini's revolution was. As the Army collapsed in turmoil on February 11, the White House Situation Room put through several calls to the U.S. ambassador in Teheran, William Sullivan, saying that Zbigniew Brzezinski wanted to know what were the chances of a coup d'état. Since he had already told Washington that the Army had disintegrated and as he was trying to rescue American officers from a mob, Sullivan dealt with these calls impatiently. He suggested that Brzezinski should "get stuffed" and then asked if he should translate this into Polish.

In the end the American officers were rescued by the intervention of one of Khomeini's closest associates, Ibrahim Yazdi, who had been with him in exile and who became foreign minister. The next day the Iranian military unit that had been guarding the

American embassy was ordered to return to its barracks. With tears pouring down his face, the young captain in charge drew up his men, kissed the U.S. Army attaché good-bye on both cheeks, and drove away. Khomeini's new prime minister, Mehdi Bazargan, assured Sullivan that the embassy would be helped in case of attack, and gave him his direct telephone number in case of trouble. But Sullivan immediately made his own plans for repulsing an assault on the embassy.

It came on St. Valentine's Day, February 14, 1979. That morning, just after Sullivan had received a cable from Washington telling him to inform the new government that the United States would continue diplomatic relations with Iran, machine guns mounted on the surrounding buildings all opened up in a prearranged barrage. Windows shattered and lead flew around the offices. Ambassador Sullivan dived for the floor.

Sullivan ordered his staff to try to reach Prime Minister Bazargan on the "hot lines" he had been given. Eventually the new authorities dispatched a rescue mission. But before it arrived, the residence had been captured and the chancery was under assault by more than a hundred militants. Many of them wore the checkered scarves of the Palestinian fedayeen, which Sullivan took to mean that they had been trained by George Habash, the leader of the Popular Front for the Liberation of Palestine.

Sullivan crawled to the relative security of the chancery's central corridor and on his walkie-talkie ordered the U.S. marines guarding the compound not to resist, still less to shoot anyone. He reckoned that if a U.S. soldier killed an Iranian, such rage would be unleashed that all the Americans would be torn limb from limb. He sent most of his staff into the embassy vault where they set about burning and shredding the classified papers that remained (he had had most shipped out of the country already), destroying the cryptographic equipment, and dismantling the controlling element in the satellite communications station.

Sullivan then surrendered the embassy and opened the steel doors to the second floor of the chancery, which the attackers had been trying to batter down. Armed and unarmed Iranians streamed in—along with gusts of tear gas that the U.S. marines had laid down around the doors. It gradually became clear that some of the intruders were attackers and some were rescuers dispatched by Bazargan and Yazdi.

Then Yazdi himself arrived, apologized profusely to the Americans, and, with the help of a senior mullah, exhorted all the attackers and onlookers to leave. He agreed to station Iranian guards both inside and outside the walls of the compound in the future. In the next few days nearly all Sullivan's diplomatic colleagues came to offer their condolences and to marvel at the fact that no one had been killed.

Despite the assault, the U.S. government announced that it would maintain normal diplomatic relations with the new Iranian regime. One reason, which Secretary of State Cyrus Vance has mentioned, was the protection of American lives, and another was to prevent "sensitive military and intelligence equipment from falling into unfriendly hands."

On February 21, Sullivan called on Prime Minister Bazargan to assure him, and through him Khomeini, that the U.S. accepted the revolution and would not interfere in Iran's internal affairs. He even offered to continue to supply arms—though at this time the new regime was trying to get the United States to buy back some of the more expensive equipment that the Shah had purchased.

Sullivan also persuaded Bazargan to help obtain the release of a number of Americans who had been taken hostage in the listening posts that the U.S. had manned along the Soviet border. The men were being held not by militants but by Iranian Air Force personnel who feared that they would no longer be paid. He told Bazargan that the posts were useful for Iranian security, since they provided information on Soviet troop movements. The prime minister agreed, and the embassy air attaché and the prime minister's assistant flew up to northern Iran carrying the payroll. Given Khomeini's constant anti-American rhetoric, this was quite a success for the United States and it led Ambassador Sullivan to hope that he could develop a viable relationship with the new regime.

But he and his staff were now convinced of one thing—that that would be impossible if the Shah proceeded to the States. Moreover, after the attack on the embassy, they were also persuaded that their own lives would be seriously threatened if the Shah arrived in America. They began to cable Washington to this effect. If the Shah went to the United States, they said, American diplomats would be coming home in pine boxes.

CHAPTER SEVEN

The Royal Farewell

With the spectacular success of Khomeini's revolution in Iran, opposition within Morocco to the Shah's stay increased. The sudden apparition of the avenging, victorious ayatollah not only astounded the West, it also gave an immense, immediate surge of pride in their culture and in the political power of their religion to other Muslims. Moroccans opposed to the monarchy, or to Hassan's tilts away from either fundamentalism or the PLO, began to protest.

In Marrakesh there were work stoppages by post office and junior government clerks, many of them members of the Islamic Youth Movement. Wall posters denounced Hassan with a clever play on words: *"LE CHIEN REÇOIT LE CHAT"* (The dog welcomes the cat—*chat* sounding very like Shah). Another slogan read, "The King is the Shah's dog."

It was embarrassing for the king. Morocco had recognized the new Bazargan government and Hassan had no interest in continuing to display hospitality to his fallen brother. He was too clever not to realize that harboring the Shah increased the danger of Muslim fundamentalism gaining ground in the kingdom. In recent years he had made a point of appeasing the fundamentalists at the

same time as co-opting left-wing opposition. He was not about to
see the Shah's prolonged stay upset that.

There was also the danger of assassination squads being sent to
Morocco; Iranian officials had begun to say such things as that the
Shah and his family would be "hunted down like Eichmann."
There were other stories that a group of terrorists was planning to
kidnap Hassan's family and hold them hostage against the Shah's
return to stand trial in Iran.

By the middle of February, when the Shah had been in Morocco
more than a month, it had become common gossip in the diplomatic corps that Hassan was giving him the cold shoulder. His
officials were talking about "the man who came to dinner" and
making it clear that he would just have to go before the Islamic
summit that was scheduled to meet in Morocco in April.

The Shah himself could not believe that Hassan would throw
him out. He would never himself have done such a thing to a
brother king in trouble. When Mohammed Behbehanian, who
was still in Morocco writing to all the Shah's bankers, told him
that he had heard Hassan wanted him out as quickly as possible,
he refused to accept it.

He spent his days listening to the radio, wandering around the
garden of the palace talking to Amir Aslan Afshar or to the Iranian
ambassador, Farhad Sepabhodi, or reading in the library. He still
found it impossible to understand what had happened and why.

Twice during February, the White House dispatched a CIA
official to see him. This man was selected not because of his
knowledge of Iran but because he exuded a certain gravitas. Farhad Sepabhodi was told by the Americans that the official's visit
to the Shah must be kept absolutely secret. So the ambassador
recorded in his log merely the man's most obvious physical characteristic—"Moustachio."

The Shah told "Moustachio" that he had avoided a bloodbath
and he hoped that this would mean that one day the monarchy
could again play a part in Iranian life. He said he was not now in
touch with the military leaders in Iran; in fact most of them were
either dead, arrested, or in hiding.

"Moustachio" was shocked by the Shah's appearance and de-
meanor. Vanished was the cold, proud, and arrogant leader; in his
place was "virtually a broken man." The Shah seemed traumatized
and to have no plans. He did not mention that he was now thinking of taking up his invitation to the U.S.

The Shah's confusion was evident in an interview he gave to one of the journalists whom he had known the longest, Clare Hollingworth of the *Daily Telegraph* of London. (This was a paper that had consistently supported him.) He talked to her on condition she quote only "court sources," not him directly.*

He blamed the Communist Tudeh Party for his overthrow; the Communists were far more powerful than the mullahs, he said. He believed that hundreds of the "veiled women" demonstrating in the streets of Teheran in favor of an Islamic Republic were actually militant Communists dressed up.

The Shah acknowledged to Hollingworth that he had perhaps become too remote from his people and that his courtiers had not always reported adverse criticisms to him. And he said that although he had earlier hoped that his stay abroad would be brief, he knew now that he would die in exile. But he was horrified by what was happening to his country. He thought that members of the new regime were "Marxists, terrorists, lunatics, and criminals."

He could not understand how the West could have allowed it all to take place. A vital barrier against Russian expansionism was now lost. It was "far worse than the giveaway at Yalta," he said. The United States was above all to blame. He left her with the impression that he would soon be proceeding to the States.

He also talked in Morocco to Barbara Walters of ABC News. Walters was among those Western journalists with whom the Shah was on good terms and who could expect exclusive interviews when they came to Teheran, as well as personal attention from the Iranian ambassador in their own countries.

The Shah had always placed more importance on prominent American and European journalists than on contact with Iranian journalists. This was a characteristic he shared with Anwar Sadat. At the same time, he was often outraged by critical press coverage in the West. His ambassador in London, Parviz Radji, constantly received demands from His Imperial Majesty to do something to curb the satirical British magazine *Private Eye*, which referred to

---

* Hollingworth was one of Britain's most redoubtable reporters. In 1939 she was the only journalist to witness and to report the Nazi invasion of Poland and her career had taken her to almost every country and every war since then. In 1943 she had interviewed the Shah. She had found him charming and modest—except in his confidence in his own military knowledge. "He was a bit pompous about that," Hollingworth recalled. She had seen him several times since, during the White Revolution and the heady days of the empire.

the Shah as "The Shit of Persia." Radji was disinclined to protest as the Shah wished. *

The Shah told Walters that he had no intention of abdicating. "Why should I abdicate? I left my country to help straighten things out. It obviously has had the opposite effect. . . . If only I'd had three more years. All my programs would have been working and people would have seen what I was trying to do."

Since he believed that he personified Iran, it was not surprising that he saw almost everything in terms of personal betrayal. Thus, as ambassadors who had till recently expressed total loyalty to him "rallied" across the world to Khomeini, he expressed bewilderment. "Why has this man turned on me?" he would ask. "I was nice to him."

One ambassador who did not turn was Farhad Sepabhodi in Morocco. Because he was serving the Shah, he received a telegram from the Foreign Ministry in Teheran ordering him to pack his bags and come home at once. He replied that he could not come right away, to which the foreign minister, Ibrahim Yazdi, replied, "Mr. Farhad Sepabhodi, I cannot listen to your statements. If you do not come back immediately, very serious action will be taken against you." In those days that was a substantial threat, but Sepabhodi took the risk. (Later Princess Ashraf gave him work in New York.)

There were others among the Shah's immediate entourage who had to decide what would be the best of several uncertain futures for them.

First, the backup plane flew back to Iran. The grand master of ceremonies, Amir Aslan Afshar, was all for the Shah's keeping or selling his personal plane. "It must be worth twenty million dollars," he says he told the Shah.

According to Afshar, the Shah refused. "Are you mad?" he asked. "It belongs to the air force. We have to send it back."

---

* There were other journalists in Britain who were much more appreciative of the Shah. Amongst his supporters was Lord Chalfont, a former Labour minister. In one article in 1976 he dismissed such criticisms as *Private Eye* made. "It is not simply that the Shah, like most Iranians, is heartily sick of the strident and repetitious vilification of Iran by the Marxists of the West and their hangers-on among the extreme left and devotees of radical chic," he was also offended by the schadenfreude displayed. "The survival of Western industrial society is a matter in which Iran, like Brazil and South Africa, may yet have an important part to play. If we alienate such countries by the application of double standards and irrelevant criteria to their internal political systems, we shall have only ourselves and our own feebleminded hypocrisy to blame." Chalfont remained loyal to the end. In 1978 he inquired of the Iranian ambassador, Parviz Radji, about the possibilities of writing a biography of Princess Ashraf. Radji felt the time was inappropriate.

In the middle of February, the pilot of this plane, Captain Moezzi, and the crew came to the palace to talk to the Shah and the Queen. The Shah had said, "We don't know when we will return and you need to be with your families. We can get a plane from our friends if necessary." There was weeping. The Shah had had Amir Aslan Afshar find among the Iranians in Morocco some Iranian currency for those who were returning home—they went back with more than $50,000. At Teheran airport they came down from the plane with Korans in their hands. Captain Moezzi declared how glad they all were to be back in Teheran and how much he had hated flying for the Shah.*

Others of the Shah's courtiers fell away, not for Iran, but for the West. Each had his or her own reason—a dying father, an urgent operation, sick children, financial problems—whatever seemed most plausible or appropriate. Behbehanian, the money man, fled into hiding, terrified. The new govenment in Iran had announced that he was the key to the millions or billions of dollars that the Shah had plundered fom Iran and was therefore one of their most wanted men. To elude Khomeini's avenging angels, Behbehanian went underground and for the next few years lived incognito at the homes of various friends, particularly in Switzerland. He avoided traveling, and if he had to fly, he went only on charter flights, for fear that on a scheduled airline his name would show up on computers that could be tapped by Iran Air officials. He was pursued also by an unsubstantiated rumor (put about by others in the Shah's entourage) that he had stolen millions of dollars from the Shah. This he denied categorically.

Kambiz Atabai, the master of the horse, left but later returned to the journey. Amir Aslan Afshar, the grand master of ceremonies, retired to Europe. Ardeshir Zahedi also went, but only temporarily, to Switzerland. Zahedi was almost the only former senior official who stayed closely in touch with the Shah throughout his exile.

---

* There was a story, published in a book by Michael Ledeen and William Lewis, writers on national security affairs who were critical of the Carter administration's handling of the Iran crisis, that the mullahs broke Captain Moezzi's hands to punish him and prevent him from ever flying again. It was not so. Indeed, in July 1981, when Abolhassan Bani-Sadr, one of Khomeini's most devoted disciples and the first president of the Islamic Republic, was impeached and was about to be devoured by the revolution, it was Captain Moezzi who secretly flew him out to safety. Thus did one pilot spirit two leaders of Iran out of the country in the space of some thirty months. Subsequently Moezzi joined the left wing Mujaheddin opposition to Khomeini in Paris.

Within a few weeks after his arrival in Morocco, only a handful of servants, bodyguards, and Dr. Pirnia, the pediatrician, remained with the Shah and the Queen. It has to be said that the Shah was not totally displeased by this exodus. For, like many rich men, he was worried about money. He had never before had any control over his own finances and he was finding the many demands on his purse upsetting and worrying. "We are in exile now and we have no money," he would tell people who came to Morocco and asked to be paid for past services to the crown. It was not quite true, but he certainly no longer disposed of the sort of funds as he had done when he was in power.

On February 22, the Shah sent a message to the American ambassador in Morocco, Richard Parker, saying that he would now like to proceed to the States. He had finally realized that there was now absolutely no chance of returning home.

This news caused a flurry of concern in Washington. It was only a week since the attack on the embassy, and there were still thousands of Americans in Iran. They were in obvious danger from the revolutionary "komitehs" that had sprung up throughout the country to enforce radical change. On February 23, a committee of the National Security Council, chaired by Zbigniew Brzezinski, met at the White House and decided that the Shah should be told that while the invitation remained open, the delicate situation in Iran meant that it would be very awkward for the United States if he arrived right now.

Among senior American officials, Zbigniew Brzezinski was least happy with this decision. Indeed, in the account of his aide, Captain Gary Sick, he found it "repugnant." He accepted that some delay in the Shah's arrival might now be needed, but he felt that the United States owed him refuge. On February 26, Ardeshir Zahedi called Brzezinski from his home in Switzerland. Zahedi asked whether the Shah could come to the States in the next few days. Brzezinski said the invitation remained open but it was difficult at the moment; someone would go and explain things to the Shah very soon. Next day Brzezinski suggested to Carter that the decision to keep the Shah out be reconsidered. Carter angrily said no; he did not want the Shah playing tennis in the States while Americans in Iran were kidnapped or killed.

Jimmy Carter's relationship with and feelings toward the Shah were, it must be said, ambiguous. The Shah had always preferred

Republicans to Democrats and he had felt that Carter's human rights program was in some senses directed against him. He was in part correct. But on the two occasions they had met, the president had given the Shah reason to believe he valued him. Those meetings are cameos of the perplexities of international relations, and they help explain the Shah's own confusion.

The Shah had visited Washington in November 1977, toward the end of Carter's first year. He was worried by Carter's election, and the new administration had impressed upon him that although the United States still regarded him as an important ally, the days of unrestricted arms sales, while arrest and torture by SAVAK were ignored by the U.S., were over. In fact, the Shah had already moderated SAVAK, released some political prisoners, and allowed a little more criticism of his government to be expressed, even before Carter's inauguration.

Nonetheless, when he arrived in Washington, the Shah learned that hundreds of Iranian students had gathered to demonstrate against him. Many of them were masked to prevent identification by SAVAK. There were pro-Shah demonstrators out on the streets as well, many of whom had been produced by the Iranian embassy. As the Shah arrived at the White House to be officially welcomed by President Carter, the two groups shouted abuse at each other just beyond police railings. Then they started beating each other with clubs and sticks. The Washington police fired tear gas at them and the gas was blown at once across the White House garden. There stood the King of Kings and the president, choking and weeping as they tried to praise each other, their wives by their sides.

The Shah and President Carter in Washington choking on tear gas.

Teheran, New Year's Eve, 1978

Inside the White House, the Shah behaved impeccably. He made no mention of the demonstrations and the tear gas, although many Iranians, including some of his own supporters, would be convinced that the episode had been planned by the U.S. government as a deliberate insult to him. Instead, he gave Carter and his advisers a long talk on how he saw the international situation. He spoke without notes, and his ability to relate economic changes in one part of the world to political rivalries in another left Carter and his staff greatly impressed. Here was a leader of both stature and vision who understood the power politics of the contemporary world and who eschewed the vague rhetorical generalizations favored by many Third World leaders.

That evening Carter gave a warm toast to the Shah in which he spoke of the great importance of Iran's relationship to the United States. As the Shah listened, his eyes glistened with tears. The next day at lunch he referred to the previous day as bringing "tears in the morning and tears at night."

As Gary Sick has recorded, another aspect of the Shah's personality emerged that night. The Carters had laid on a jazz evening, featuring Sarah Vaughan and Dizzy Gillespie. At the end of the performance, Jimmy and Rosalynn Carter leaped onto the stage to congratulate them. The Shah remained stiffly seated. His wife whispered to him to go on stage. He did not. Eventually she literally dragged him up to shake hands. He was visibly uncomfortable.

Carter and the Shah met again for the second and final time only a few weeks later. It was New Year's Eve in Teheran. Carter was on a hectic world swing and Teheran was a convenient resting place between Warsaw and New Delhi.

The Shah suggested, and the White House agreed, that the visit would provide a good chance for Carter to talk to King Hussein, whom both men wanted to encourage into the Israeli-Egyptian peace process. But the king could not be asked to the dinner because protocol would demand that he be seated above Carter. He was invited to come to Teheran to talk to Carter after dinner.

The dinner was a typically lush, typically Pahlavi affair. After the Carters, the most important guests were Pahlavi relations—half brothers, sisters, half sisters, cousins. Cyrus Vance, the U.S. secretary of state, the Iranian foreign minister, and other senior officials were well below the salt. This caused some comment among the Americans.

The meal was of course splendid. Dom Pérignon, caviar, kebabs, a pilaf of diced partridge, fruit salad, fabulous wines, and, the pièce de résistance, flaming ice cream in honor of which the lights were lowered.

The Shah made a gracious speech, but the high point of the evening was Carter's toast. The President with eloquence evoked his concern for human rights in Iran by quoting lines from Saadi, one of Iran's best-loved poets:

> *Human beings are like parts of a body,*
> *created from the same essence,*
>
> *When one part is hurt and in pain, others*
> *cannot remain in peace and be quiet.*
>
> *If the misery of others leaves you indifferent*
> *and with no feelings of sorrow, then you*
> *cannot be called a human being.*

This reference was encouraging to many of the Shah's Iranian opponents who interpreted it as the president's support for their struggle against the Shah. But Carter went out of his way to underwrite the Shah himself as well. He declared that he had asked Rosalynn with whom she would like to spend New Year's Eve, "And she said, 'Above all others, I think, with the Shah and Empress Farah.' So we arranged the trip accordingly and came to be with you." He talked of a picture book on Iran that the Empress had given him, *Bridge of Turquoise*. This was one of the dozens of expensive Pahlavi public-relations productions commissioned by the Ministry of the Court. Some of them were garish, some absurd propaganda, and some, like this one—beautiful but marked above all by a pseudomysticism. These tended to suggest that Iran was a magical, fairy-tale land where only justice prevailed and where progress was assured by an omniscient king.

"One night," said Carter, "I started to thumb through its pages, and I called my wife, Rosalynn, and I called my daughter, Amy, who climbed into my lap, and we spent several hours studying the beautiful history that this book portrays of Persia, of Iran, of its people. . . ."

Then Carter went on to add a phrase that was to haunt him as, only a few weeks later, riots and disaffection began to unfold across the country and within twelve months led to the fall of the Shah.

"Iran," he declared, "because of the great leadership of the Shah, is an island of stability in one of the more troubled areas of the world. This is a great tribute to you, Your Majesty, and to your leadership and to the respect and the admiration and the love which your people give to you. . . . There is no leader with whom I have a deeper sense of personal friendship and gratitude."*

Some American officials at the banquet were dumbfounded by this testament. Princess Ashraf later wrote that as Carter spoke, "I looked at his pale face. I thought his smile was artificial, his eyes icy—and I hoped I could trust him." (Over the course of the next year she decided she could not.) The Shah was naturally

---

* Gary Sick has pointed out that this ringing tribute "did not appear in the original draft of the toast as prepared by the State Department and the National Security Council staff for inclusion in the President's briefing book. The text was redrafted in the forward cabin of *Air Force One* between Warsaw and Teheran. Perhaps not surprisingly, the author has proved to be unusually diffident in taking credit for his or her work."

delighted, and led the diners in clapping enthusiastically and smiling brilliantly at Jimmy Carter. Never before had any American president, not even his greatest friend and admirer, Richard Nixon, paid tribute to him in terms quite as fulsome as that.

After dinner, the Shah and Carter retired to a study to talk about the Middle East with King Hussein, whom Crown Prince Reza and Ardeshir Zahedi had just welcomed at the door. Then the Shah persuaded the Carters to see in the New Year at the palace and the Queen sent the Crown Prince into the library to organize a smaller party.

Once more the liveried waiters appeared with the Dom Pérignon, while the teenage Crown Prince acted as disc jockey on the balcony. The Shah asked Mrs. Carter to dance, Carter danced with the Queen, while Princess Ashraf and King Hussein, each of them only about five feet high, shuffled around like two little mechanical dolls, staring distractedly over each other's tiny shoulders. Lesser mortals stepped out as best they could.

At times the Crown Prince swapped the staid dance music for rather more lively rock and roll. The Shah would gesticulate to him to stop it, but finally the Prince and his younger sister were allowed to perform a spirited disco dance while everyone below watched and then applauded.

Next morning Carter flew off to India, leaving behind an elated Shah. A group of American businessmen and their families had been invited to the airport for the president to pump their hands. After *Air Force One* left, Ambassador Sullivan asked the Shah if he would like to meet them too. Nervous at first, by the time the Shah reached the end of the line, he was obviously enjoying himself. He turned to Sullivan with a glow on his face and a slight mist in his eyes and said, "You Americans are really very nice people."

Emboldened by Carter's support, the Shah ordered the publication of the scurrilous attack on Khomeini which precipitated the first of the riots against him and, within a year, had led to his fall. By early 1979, after what he saw as U.S. failure to support him, and as he now looked for a refuge from Morocco, he was less certain.

By the end of the first week in March 1979, King Hassan was even more anxious for the Shah to move on. But views in Washington were hardening. On March 6, David Aaron of the NSC warned President Carter that American hostages might be captured in Iran if the Shah was allowed into the States. Carter authorized the State Department to try to find another asylum.

Ardeshir Zahedi was searching also. Among the possible destinations there was Switzerland, where the Shah had spent a lot of time (and a lot of money) on his ski holidays. He had his famous chalet, the Villa Suvretta at St. Moritz, where during the oil crisis of 1973–74 treasury ministers from around the world had come to kiss his hand and pay homage, and he had a house on Lake Geneva. But the Swiss, like all other mercantile nations, were now frightened of their relationship with such a vital Middle East country as Iran. They were not about to destroy their commercial prospects in that huge market, still less to jeopardize their oil supplies, for a misplaced sense of loyalty to a fallen friend. When Ardeshir Zahedi inquired, it was made clear to him, indirectly, that it might be wiser to postpone a formal request. The security problems would be immense, murmured Swiss officials with apologetic sighs.

There was Britain—the country with which Iran had had the longest association and with which many Iranians had an almost neurotic relationship. Mr. Behbehanian, his banker, who believed that the British controlled every event in Iran, was still pressing him to repair there and to apologize to the British for insulting them in recent years. The Shah was not very keen, even though he had a house in southern England. Nor was the British Labour government, despite its previous support for him. Still, word came to Morocco that Mrs. Margaret Thatcher, the leader of the Conservative Party, had promised informally that if she won the general election, which was expected soon in Britain, she would welcome Britain's old ally and friend.

But that was in the future. For now, France might be a possibility. He did not have a house there, but Princess Ashraf did and so did many other members of the family. Emotional, cultural ties between Iran and France have always been strong. Many Iranians have seen France as neutral and with fewer designs upon them than Britain.

And France owed the Shah a good deal. Years before, when Valéry Giscard d'Estaing was minister of finance, he had been among those to call on the Shah at the Villa Suvretta in St. Moritz. It appeared that he was anxious to make amends for President Pompidou's lèse-majesté in refusing to attend the Persepolis party, and also to request special help for France. "He stood there meekly smiling, with his hands clasped across his balls," said Ardeshir Zahedi later, "ingratiating himself." There were stories that the Shah had kept Giscard waiting in an anteroom while he finished a game of cards with his cronies, but Zahedi said later, "The Shah was always too polite to do that."

In following years France had indeed benefited from the financial bonanza unleashed in Iran by the oil price rise. But by the end of 1978 the French had decided that the sooner the Shah left Iran the better. In the first week of January 1979, President Giscard d'Estaing expounded his view when he met for a summit conference with Jimmy Carter, Helmut Schmidt, the West German chancellor, and James Callaghan, the British prime minister, on the French West Indian island of Guadeloupe.*

By the time they had reached Morocco, the Shah and the Queen both believed that Giscard had betrayed them personally at Guadeloupe. It was something they talked about frequently. Once Giscard called the Shah in Morocco. The Shah was in the garden. Amir Aslan Afshar asked the French president to call back. At lunch the Shah said, "I have nothing to say to him. We were so nice to France and we did so much for them. Now they have changed their minds. What can I say?"

Afshar suggested, "Your Majesty, time will tell, but you could say to him, 'If you try to sit on two stools, you will fall between.' "

By now, early March 1979, the French were concerned that the Shah's prolonged stay in Morocco was endangering their ally, King Hassan. The head of the French secret service, the Comte de

---

* In his memoirs, Jimmy Carter later revealed that at Guadeloupe, "I found little support for the Shah among the other three leaders. They all thought . . . that the Shah ought to leave as soon as possible." Carter's wife, Rosalynn, was rather more explicit in her own memoirs. She quoted Helmut Schmidt as saying at Guadeloupe, "We all knew how weak [the Shah] was, but I'm surprised that he's going under before the Saudis." According to Mrs. Carter, James Callaghan declared, "Everyone is of the same opinion . . . very weak. Nobody has been willing to tell the Shah the truth. We haven't told him the truth about the disintegrating situation in ten years." Schmidt: "There was absolutely no dissent around him. The only one ever to disagree with him was his wife." Mrs. Carter found it interesting that "after the fact" everyone claimed to have known what was going to happen.

According to another account of Guadeloupe, Giscard spoke last and most forcefully, saying that if the Shah stayed, Iran faced civil war and immense bloodshed. The Communists would grow in strength. American officers stationed in Iran would be drawn into the fighting and this would give a pretext for Soviet intervention. Europe needed Iranian stability and Iranian oil. While Khomeini had been in France, the French had come to think he might not be so unreasonable. Washington should reconcile itself to the change.

Marenches, who had visited the Shah just before he left Teheran, flew from Paris to express his own concerns to both kings.

According to Marenches, he and the Shah had long had an excellent relationship. "He asked me to meet him several times a year. I tried to advise him, to tell him how I saw things in the world." More than that, Marenches said later that the Shah had told him, "I count on you always to tell me the disagreeable things that other people won't say."

As far as Marenches was concerned, the most important thing for a Western intelligence agency was to stop the spread of Communism. In his Paris office he had maps showing Communist encroachment in red. He handed them out. He considered the Shah an autocrat, not a dictator; a dictator would have crushed the clerical unrest as soon as it began to appear, and the Shah had not. He suppressed political opposition perhaps, but Marenches argued that by the standards of the Orient, SAVAK was not that brutal.

Marenches had strong views on the reasons for the Shah's fall. He blamed President Carter.

Later Marenches said that he had told the Shah to beware of the mullahs, and the merchants in the bazaar, but above all to beware of Jimmy Carter. "I told him that this national and international disaster, President Carter, had decided to replace him." Marenches thought that Carter knew absolutely nothing about the Middle East. "In the narrow mind of this Boy Scout person, with his doll's face [poupin], who only just knew where Iran was, the Shah was a dictator who put people in prison and so had to be replaced as soon as possible with a democracy like the U.S.A."

Now, in Morocco in March 1979, Marenches first saw Hassan, whom he had known since the king was a twenty-five-year-old prince. He would later describe the king as "one of the most brilliant statesmen I have ever been privileged to meet, with a fantastic memory and a third eye which gives him great sensitivity and extraordinary perception." Marenches considered it most unfortunate that Morocco did not have oil, for Hassan was "one of the rare statesmen of our time."

Now Marenches informed the king that the continued presence of the Shah would cause him grave problems. Marenches claimed later that the king replied that the Shah was his guest and that was that. Then, Marenches says, he had to convince the king that his other duties, including guarding the Straits of Gibraltar, which was "so vital for the camp of liberty," must take precedence over hospitality. When he realized that Hassan himself would not tell the Shah to go, Marenches offered to do it himself. The king agreed. (Other accounts suggest that Marenches probably had much less difficulty in obtaining the monarch's agreement than he maintains.)

When the Shah and Empress received Marenches, he told them that the ayatollah had sent kidnappers to sieze Hassan's family and bargain them for the Shah. The danger was terrifying, he said. When the Shah realized that his host's family was at such risk, said Marenches, he agreed to leave within three weeks.

For all his admiration of the Shah and his disdain for President Carter, Marenches did not suggest France as a possible destination. Nor did President Giscard d'Estaing offer it.

By now there was almost no one in the U.S. government, save Brzezinski, who wanted the Shah in the States. Previously Cyrus Vance had been in favor of his admission; indeed, in January he had asked Henry Kissinger to help find the King a home. Now the State Department argued that both America's interest in a good relationship with Iran and the safety of Americans there demanded his exclusion.

In the middle of March, Vance made what he later called "one of the most distasteful recommendations I ever had to make to the president." It was that the Shah should be told formally that it was no longer appropriate for him to come to the U.S.A.

President Carter thought the same. In his memoirs he said that on March 15 he learned that Hassan was pressing Washington to admit the Shah. But because of the growth of anti-Americanism in Iran, "I decided that it would be better for the Shah to live elsewhere." And so, wrote Jimmy Carter, rather casually, "I asked Cy to scout around to help him find a place to stay." In fact, by this stage, the State Department knew that there was almost no country prepared to accept the Shah.

An immediate and embarrassing problem was: Who should tell the Shah?

Cyrus Vance turned to two of the Shah's American associates, David Rockefeller, the chairman of Chase Manhattan, and again to Henry Kissinger. (David Rockefeller's older brother Nelson, who had recently died, had been almost a friend of the Shah.) Would either of them fly to Morocco and tell the Shah that the

U.S. government preferred that he not come to America right now? Neither accepted this chalice. Indeed, each man refused it with some indignation; Kissinger in particular thought it outrageous that such an old friend and ally as the Shah should not be allowed into the States.

In the end, several people, apart from Alexandre de Marenches, told the Shah to leave. "Moustachio," the U.S. intelligence agent who had already visited him in February, returned. He met with the Shah in the palace in Rabat and told him of all the dangers that the U.S. system would pose for him—lawsuits to find his money, congressional subpoenas, and demonstrations. The Shah took the news with his usual appearance of calm.

To make sure that the Shah understood, Cyrus Vance sent Ambassador Richard Parker to see him as well. Parker was a career State Department official, tall, balding, with a cautious, academic mien. He believed the Shah should be allowed into the U.S. He did not enjoy this mission.

He was received by the Shah in the library of the Dar Salaam palace. The Shah was wearing a sports jacket and looked well. He motioned Parker to sit down. The ambassador began by saying, "Your Majesty, you are always welcome in the United States, but it would be very inconvenient right now. There could be legal problems for you, and problems of security."

The Shah, said Parker later, took the news "like a man. He was very dignified." He did not complain about a friendship betrayed. He simply nodded his head and made some neutral comment.

Parker went on to say, "I am authorized to tell Your Majesty that both Paraguay and South Africa will be glad to receive you." These were the only two countries in the world that, at this stage, the State Department had found prepared to take the Shah.

The Shah replied that he had sad associations with South Africa, because his father had died there. And he did not wish to go to Paraguay. "I would prefer to go to Mexico," he said. That would be close to his mother, who was living in the Beverly Hills house of his sister Princess Shams, and who was very ill. Perhaps she could visit him in Mexico. Parker told him that the State Department had asked Mexico, but there had been no reply as yet.

There was nothing more to say on that and so the Shah started talking quietly about Iran. He did not know how "these people" thought they were going to run the country. They could not control the Army, let alone the various tribes. No one understood the Army as he did. Iran would now fall apart.

When Parker took his leave, he was, he said later, ashamed. His country, he thought, was treating the Shah abysmally.

Another emissary was an American lobbyist retained by King Hassan. This was Don Agger, a cheerful, puckish man with a narrow beard, a former assistant secretary of transportation under Lyndon Johnson. Since 1977 Agger and his associate, former New York Senator Charles Goodell, had represented Morocco in Washington. Early in March 1979 they were summoned to Rabat. "We saw the King at once," said Agger later. "It was clear he had a problem. The Shah was the man who came to dinner. . . . There was an Arab summit coming up. How could he tell his Muslim brother to *fiche le camp?* He couldn't. He just had to get the Shah's butt outta there."

Agger realized that the Carter administration would not now accept the Shah. "We didn't have the balls." He and Goodell met several times with the Shah to discuss other possible destinations. Agger was struck by the Pahlavi dogs, particularly the Great Dane, Beno, a vast animal that had a habit of nuzzling people's laps. There go the family jewels, thought Agger to himself more than once.

The worst meeting they had with the Shah was the last. There was no country in sight, at least none that the Shah liked the sound of. Nowhere in Europe would take him. Nor would King Hussein of Jordan, a man whom the Shah had constantly supported. King Khalid of Saudi Arabia had also said no. Yet Hassan was at the very end of his patience. He told Agger that he must inform the Shah that the visit was over, that the king's plane was at his disposal, and that he must use it—very soon.

So, on Saturday, March 24, Don Agger and Charlie Goodell went back to the palace library to offer the Shah Hassan's own plane. Former Senator Goodell tried to cheer up the Shah. He said that he too had lost an election; he had felt very bad when the people of New York rejected him, and he could empathize with what the Shah now felt. The Shah nodded. Agger thought these kind remarks helpful, but he knew also that they could hardly sweeten the bitter pill he was about to force the Shah to swallow.

Finally he presented it. Without any sweeteners. "Your Majesty, the aircraft has been arranged for Friday. So please tell us where you want to go. We are at your disposal."

"I'm sure if I ask my Muslim brother for another ten days it will be all right," the Shah replied stiffly.

"Your Majesty," replied Agger quietly and formally, "I'm only authorized to say that the aircraft has been prepared for Friday."

The Shah stood up and left the room without a word.

Early in the morning of March 30, the Shah and the Queen and their entourage drove to Rabat airport to board Hassan's own 747, which had been loaded with their baggage—368 pieces in all.

Until a few hours before, they had had no idea where they would be going. South Africa seemed the most likely place; Hassan had dismissed the Shah's opposition. If that was the only place that would take him, that was where he would go, said the king.

The State Department had still failed to find anywhere else. But by now Princess Ashraf had asked David Rockefeller to take a much closer interest in the Shah's predicament and he was discussing it constantly with Henry Kissinger.

Literally hours before the Shah was about to be bundled off to South Africa, the Rockefeller-Kissinger connection had finally found him at least a temporary haven—the Bahamas. It was not entirely satisfactory; the arrangements were complicated. "Even at one or two A.M. the night before, we were not sure we could go there," said the Queen later. But at the last moment, the Bahamian government agreed (there were rumors that a good deal of money changed hands), and a new flight plan was drawn up for Hassan's 747.

The plane crossed the wine-dark ocean with very few passengers aboard. Apart from the Shah and the Queen, there were Colonel Jahanbini, the Shah's principal bodyguard; a few other guards; his valet, Pourshoja; the faithful Dr. Lucy Pirnia, the family doctor; and the dogs. Expelled by a cunning king, they flew again toward the west on the next leg of their ride through a world that all the time was changing and shifting against them. "When you think of the relations we had with most countries," said the Queen later, "and suddenly they don't care to talk to you, or write to you, ask you to come and stay in their country . . . That was very sad. It's a sad human experience to go through."

CHAPTER EIGHT

The Spear-Carrier

On the tarmac at the airport of Nassau was a slim, slight, well-turned-out young man. He had a narrow face dominated by an aquiline nose and carefully styled dark hair. He bowed graciously when he met the Shah and Shahbanou. He looked very like one of the many courtiers with whom the royal couple had been surrounded in Teheran. His name was Robert Armao and from now on he would be closely, even intimately involved in the developing drama of the Shah's exile. In some ways he was well equipped—for he had long been part of another great empire, that of the Rockefellers.

Some years before his fall, the Shah insisted to one of his biographers that, like his father, he had no friends. In Iran he had cronies, men at whose luxurious villas in the suburbs of North Teheran he played cards and whored. He had, of course, advisers —few of whom dared advise—and he had courtiers. But his concept of his own dignity and imperial majesty did not allow him to have Iranian friends.

Outside Iran there were other kings and ex-kings—Hussein, Hassan, Constantine—with whom he sometimes relaxed, and who used to come and frolic on the Caspian or in the Persian

Gulf.* And among the uncrowned, Nelson Rockefeller was one of the people whose company he most enjoyed. That was understandable; Nelson was, quite simply, more like a shah than anyone else. One biography of him was called *The Imperial Rockefeller.* He too had his court and it stretched through New York City, Albany, and the labor unions.

Like the Shah, Rockefeller had immense patronage. Both men were fabulously ambitious for their countries and for themselves. Both men were divorced and remarried and each was attracted to young women. Neither had many intimates but each admired Henry Kissinger.

Both the Shah and Rockefeller frequently published self-congratulatory books that appeared under their own names but were ghosted by hacks or teams of aides. (An exception was the Shah's last memoir, which he wrote in French in the early part of his exile. But even that was rewritten by his staff for the American edition.) Each had huge family foundations, though the Pahlavi Foundation attracted rather more stringent criticism than that of the Rockefellers. Both men had strong family ties. There was a whiff of excess fraternalism when Governor Nelson Rockefeller had the State of New York occupy brother David's empty World Trade Center on a forty-year lease. That was the sort of good turn the Pahlavis were infamous for doing for each other, though usually on a more astonishing scale.

An important difference between the two men was of personality. Rockefeller was a gregarious, backslapping type of man. "Hi ya, fella" was his habitual greeting. The Shah was aloof and shy. Rockefeller also had a sense of humor that was quite lacking in the Shah. When, as vice president of the United States, he and his wife, Happy, had visited the Shah in 1975, they asked to look at the bazaar in Isfahan. The place was cleared of all other shoppers —not in itself a very popular move. Still, the Rockefellers enjoyed themselves, moving from stall to stall, inspecting much of the more exotic merchandise, and buying some. Suddenly Richard Helms, the U.S. ambassador, noticed a Secret Service man stag-

---

* One of the games that the family and their friends enjoyed at the Caspian was jumping out of a helicopter over the water. The Shah used to pilot it while everyone else jumped, from about twenty feet; he then handed over to the copilot for his own jump. The problem was that the copilot would invariably be frightened of allowing His Imperial Majesty to jump from any height, so by the time the Shah reached the door, the helicopter would be hovering only a couple of feet above the water and all he could do was step out daintily. It was very irritating.

gering under the weight of an ordinary iron anvil. The vice president, he gasped, had just bought it. Helms asked Rockefeller what on earth he wanted it for. Rockefeller grinned. "I'll say it was sculpted by Max Ernst and get thirty-five thousand dollars for it."

Nelson made his last visit to Teheran in May 1978. There had already been several rounds of rioting against the Shah. And a few weeks before, a Soviet-sponsored coup in Afghanistan had turned the government over to the Communists. The Shah asked Rockefeller, "point-blank" (as he himself later described it), whether this meant that "the Americans and the Russians have divided the world between them." It was a genuine fear on his part, one that was shared by many other Iranians who believed that the turmoil in Iran was a monstrous international conspiracy against their country.

As the Shah's predicament worsened through the second half of 1978, Nelson Rockefeller remained in touch by telephone, and sent offers of help. He also sent Robert Armao.

In the past the Shah had depended on American presidents, secretaries of state, national security advisers, as well as CIA station chiefs. Now his crutch was to be an assiduous young public-relations man who had started his career as Nelson Rockefeller's gofer.

After Robert Armao emerged as the spokesman and protector of the Shah, it was easy for the press to portray him as some sort of stage villain. This was particularly tempting when the wanderings of the Shah provoked crisis and humiliation for the United States. Much of the criticism was undoubtedly unfair.

Only thirty years old in 1979, Armao was something of a dandy. He dressed exquisitely and kept trim by constant visits to the New York Athletic Club. He was a man who gave the impression of being on the way up and up and up—into the world of power and glitz, where maître d's hover and chauffeurs of black-glassed stretch limos dash to open doors. A *New York Times* profile of him began, "Without asking, you know that as a young man he was polite to adults."

Others described Armao as a "mystery man" or "an enigma." He used to say that he did not understand why this was. But even his former colleagues on the Rockefeller staff had been surprised by how such a young man managed to live in quite such a lordly style. When Nelson had been vice president and the Rockefeller entourage flew into New York City, Nelson would bound into his chauffeur-driven limousine, and Armao, still in his twenties, would climb into his, while the rest of the staff boarded government-issue cars.

In 1979 there were rumors, which Armao denied, that he worked for the CIA. Journalists noted that the telephone of his small public-relations firm, Armao and Company, in Rockefeller Center, was unlisted. "I don't deal with off-the-street business. Nobody looks in the phone book for our kind of firm," he explained. He liked to work behind the scenes, with "a low profile," he would say. "Anonymity is bliss."

His family had come originally from Portugal. His father had been medical director for the longshoremen's union and was the personal doctor of Teddy Gleason, the union president. So Armao grew up knowing many senior labor officials on a first-name basis. It was this that had brought him into the orbit of Nelson Rockefeller.

While still a teenager, he had begun to work as a volunteer in Governor Rockefeller's labor office. His ability to get along with union leaders apparently made an impression and he was brought closer into the family circle. He went into public relations and took other jobs, including working for Peter Brennan, who was secretary of labor at the beginning of Nixon's second administration; but always he returned to Nelson. "He inspired me, that's all. From Nelson Rockefeller, I learned the great responsibility to your fellow man. He was a man of great dignity," said Armao later.

But he had contacts with some important Democrats as well. In 1978 Mayor Koch had appointed him New York City's official greeter—the man who, for a salary of $1 a year, stands on the tarmac or at the gate at Kennedy Airport to bow, smile, and make very important people feel that they are indeed just that. Koch thought Armao was ideal for the job. "He could be a count, a baron," said the mayor. But after Armao started to work for the Shah, he relinquished the post of greeter; Koch became concerned lest even "perceptions" of a conflict of interest arise. After all, the greeter just might have to welcome the ayatollah one day to New York. Then there was the little matter that Armao and Company now represented, among others, the New York State Coalition for Casino Gambling, a lobby group in favor of a referendum on legalized gambling in the state.

It was through Nelson Rockefeller that Armao went to work for the Shah. As he tells it, he was visiting Nelson in August 1978 and Nelson was on the telephone. "In his inimitable way he covered the phone speaker and winked, 'It's the Shah.' So then I heard Rockefeller's side of the conversation. After he hung up, he said the Shah had told him that the people who were closest to him were all gone. He was all alone, he wasn't feeling well, and that's when Rockefeller said that it was very sad to see him alone."

After Princess Ashraf was sent by her brother into exile, she asked the Rockefellers if they could do anything to counter "the propaganda campaign" against the Shah. Armao saw Ardeshir Zahedi and Ashraf in New York. Zahedi did not warm to him, but Princess Ashraf took him seriously. At the end of 1978, when the Shah's collapse was imminent, Rockefeller had asked Armao to take a letter to the Shah, to see if he could help with a propaganda campaign in Iran. The notion that a young Republican PR man from New York could enable the Shah to rescue his throne says a good deal for the self-confidence of both the public-relations industry and of the Rockefellers. Ardeshir Zahedi says that he prevented Armao from seeing the Shah in Teheran.

While the Shah was in Morocco, Nelson Rockefeller died. His staff first put out the story that he had been alone at his desk, working on his latest book. James Reston wrote how the manner of his death befitted his great public service. It soon emerged that in fact he had died in the arms of a young mistress. After that, his brother David assumed the Rockefeller family responsibility for the Shah.*

Now that the U.S. government was attempting to distance itself from the Shah and his fate, in order to preserve its links with the new and ever-changing regime in Iran, the Rockefellers and Chase Manhattan began to provide him services that the CIA and the British MI6 had provided in the past. Throughout his exile the Shah would now be associated with the Rockefeller machine in ways that brought joy to the complicated hearts of conspiracy theorists.

---

* David Rockefeller had visited Sadat in Egypt soon after the Shah was there. He had then written to the Shah in Morocco saying that he shared Sadat's view that he should remain in the Middle East rather than fly on to America. But a few weeks later, when Cyrus Vance asked him to go to Morocco to tell the Shah he should not now come to the U.S., Rockefeller had refused. Instead he had helped arrange the Bahamas.

It was at Ashraf's request that Armao flew to the Bahamas to help make the arrangements for the Shah's arrival. Over the next few months he and his staff gradually took over the running of the Shah and his family in exile. This did not please all the Shah's friends and relations. There were many, Ardeshir Zahedi among them, who felt that the Shah should have either Iranians as his spokesmen and advisers, or at least Americans with some gravitas and standing—a retired ambassador or two, perhaps. Zahedi later described Armao as "Ashraf's ears and eyes" in the Shah's little exiled court. Armao, by contrast, saw himself as one of the few people in the world prepared to help the Shah on a selfless basis. (Naturally his company was also recompensed by the Pahlavis.)

Armao was convinced that the Carter administration had betrayed the Shah. He became *plus royaliste que le roi* and in dealing with U.S. officials he was often openly hostile. This attitude would play an important part in the development of the drama ahead. President Carter said later that Armao was "a troublemaker . . . who made damaging statements to the news media and, I think, caused the Shah a lot of grief." Gary Sick, Zbigniew Brzezinski's aide, wrote that "Armao's suspicions and lack of cooperativeness severely complicated relations and communications between Washington and the Shah during the course of the hostage crisis."

Later, after the death of the Shah, Armao told one interviewer, "For two years I absolutely lived for the Shah. I was running all over the globe trying to secure a home. I would go to Paris on the Concorde for dinner, come back home the next morning and immediately get on a plane to where he was. When he was in exile, there wasn't an hour I wasn't with him. I was with him in the morning when he woke up, and in the evening when we went to sleep."

Armao did indeed work hard and single-mindedly on the Shah's behalf. But the role of inseparable shadow was undertaken by a quiet, blond young man named Mark Morse. Morse had worked with Armao on Nelson Rockefeller's staff and he had also consulted with the Office of Secretary of Defense. Now Armao invited him to become a vice president of Armao and Company and to come to the Bahamas. It was meant to be just for a few days, but while Armao flew back and forth to New York and elsewhere, scouting possible refuges, arranging the children's schools, Morse remained with the Shah throughout his exile; he became quite close to both the Shah and the Queen, as well as to their shrinking Iranian entourage.

At the "21" Club in New York, where Armao likes to take guests to lunch, he is treated by waiters with great respect. In an interview with one writer, he laid an elegant black cigarette case on the table. It bore a crest of a lion with a scimitar—the Pahlavi emblem. The Shah's own cigarette case. "He gave it to me," said the right-hand man.

When King Hassan's 747 landed at Nassau airport, the Bahamian ground crew was reluctant to approach—scared, it seemed, of bombs. While Robert Armao flew by helicopter with the Shah and the Empress to the new home they had been assigned, Mark Morse was left standing under the vast bulk of the plane in his blue suit, wondering how to get the luggage out. Eventually he managed to pay airport workers to load all the effects onto flatbed trucks and had it all driven through Nassau to Paradise Island.

There are seven hundred islands and cays in the Bahamas, but the Bahamian government had insisted that there was only one place in the entire chain where the Shah could stay—in the private home of James Crosby, chairman of Resorts International, on Paradise Island.

Crosby was a bizarre figure, who is now almost crippled by emphysema. His lifetime interest in both aviation and gambling, his reclusiveness and his business acumen had led to his being compared with Howard Hughes. He and his family owned 60 percent of Resorts, a gambling business. He had bought Paradise Island, which is linked to Nassau by a bridge, in 1966. It was then little more than beach, but by the end of the seventies Resorts had developed a multimillion-dollar casino hotel and owned hundreds of acres of beachfront property. In 1978, when Resorts opened the first casino in Atlantic City, New Jersey, officials charged that a Resorts official had flown Bahamian customs officials to Las Vegas where he had procured women for them. The company said its employee was "acting on his own" and disavowed his initiative. New Jersey officials also charged that Resorts had paid off Bahamian officials and therefore should not be granted a permanent license in New Jersey. Resorts won that battle.

The Bahamas have long reeked of corruption. So close to Florida, they have always attracted organized crime from the United States. During Prohibition, bootleggers established themselves there. After Fidel Castro took over Cuba, organized crime syndicates that had controlled the gambling in Havana moved a few miles north to Nassau and other Bahamian islands. After the islands gained independence of Britain in 1973, they became major drug-running centers—they lie directly en route from Colombia to Florida and are thus ideal for smuggling cocaine and marijuana to the world's largest market. On deserted beaches and isolated airstrips, mother ships and cargo planes transfer contraband to smaller carriers or to individuals for its onward passage to the United States.

In recent years a whole service industry has been built up in the Bahamas around the drug trade. Lowly officials are handsomely bribed, suave lawyers and bankers represent smugglers and launder money, senior civil servants and politicians accept huge payoffs. At the center of the miasma has been Sir Lynden O. Pindling, who has been prime minister since 1967 and who did much to win the islands' independence in 1973.

Pindling in many ways appears a pleasant, modest man, who eschews the trappings of leadership and has kept the Bahamas a democracy. (He was reelected once again in 1987.) But he has always seemed to need money. In the seventies he enjoyed the sponsorship of the fugitive financier Robert Vesco. He allowed Vesco sanctuary in the Bahamas. He was later accused of taking money from Resorts International.*

Crosby's house was open to the beach and tiny. Only the Shah and the Queen and one servant could actually sleep there. The Shah's staff discovered more suitable accommodation on another island in the Bahamas. But the Shah and his wife were not allowed to move from Paradise Island. They tried to negotiate with Crosby's agent, said Colonel Jahanbini, the Shah's bodyguard. "But we were told, 'It's not negotiable. This is where you have to stay.' We heard that they were sharing everything with government ministers. There were so many Mafia and casino interests." Subsequently, *The New York Times* reported that both David Rocke-

---

* In 1984 a commission of inquiry in Nassau found that the prime minister had accepted $2.8 million in gifts and loans between 1977 and 1983. He denied that he had received any drug money. He said he was a victim of overzealous officials from the U.S. Drug Enforcement Agency who wanted to be able to operate more freely in the Bahamas. But neither he nor his associates were able to explain the large sums of money that appeared to have been made over to him. According to evidence given to an official inquiry in New Jersey, $425,000 was provided by Resorts International. As a result of this disclosure, Resorts nearly lost its Atlantic City license.

feller and some State Department officials dealing with the Shah believed the prime minister was profiting from the Shah's stay in the Bahamas. Pindling himself has denied it. But someone made a lot of money out of the Shah's ten-week stay in the Bahamas. It cost him $1.2 million. He was not pleased.

Most of the entourage were found rooms in the nearby Ocean Club, at $250 a day. Since it was the Easter season, the place was full, and about twenty of the guests had to be moved out or have their reservations changed. This was not popular. The manager of the Ocean Club, who was given only a few hours' notice of the Shah's arrival, pointed out, "The type of guest we have is not here for a handout. You can't appease them with a free steak dinner."

The worst problem was security. In Teheran summary trials and executions of senior military offficers and of SAVAK agents were continuing. The ayatollah had demanded the return of the Shah to face trial for treason. Yasser Arafat had visited Teheran in

triumph, the new regime had repudiated the Shah's close relations
with Israel, and Arafat had taken over the former Israeli Mission.
(Although Israeli intelligence about Iran had been better than that
of most other countries, even the Israelis were taken by surprise
by the speed of the revolution. Thirty-two Israeli officials were
trapped in Teheran in mid-February. The Israeli Mission had
asked the U.S. ambassador, William Sullivan, for help in evac-
uating these people. Sullivan judged that they were in greater
danger than Americans in Iran and so he bumped thirty-two
Americans off one of the evacuation flights he had arranged for
U.S. nationals.)

Arafat had declared that he would send a PLO team to kidnap
or kill the Shah. The Bahamian police chief commented, "We
know that Arafat doesn't fool around." The Bahamians provided
extra police. Armao hired thirty security men from an American
firm and they set up an elaborate security system around the
Crosby house. Everyone had to be identified by plastic badges.
At night the place was wired by a series of electronic devices
designed to detect intruders. *Paris Match* enthused about the place
being like a James Bond set, or Cape Kennedy.

The worst strain was on Colonel Jahanbini; ultimately he felt
responsible for the safety of the Shah and the Queen. He still had
half a dozen of his men. But several of these were assigned to the
Shah's children, who flew from the United States to visit their
parents on Paradise Island. When they returned to their schools
in the States, the guards went too.

"It was the roughest time of my life. It was terrible," said
Jahanbini later. He was not impressed with the hired guards. It
was not possible to keep away tourists on the beach, and in fact
the Shah seemed to enjoy meeting them. Most of them were rich
Americans who told him he was terrific. For the first time he
became quite adept at pressing the flesh.

He did it carefully watched by Jahanbini and his men, who
walked along the beach looking nervous and carrying their submachine guns in brief cases. It was an incongruous sight by the
sea, slightly reminiscent of violin cases on the streets of Prohibition Chicago.

At this stage it was the Queen who seemed to be suffering most.
She was chain-smoking, and looked both hunted and exhausted.
The press was kept away from her and the Shah—one photograph

taken with a powerful zoom lens showed her looking like a fawn at bay—but she did talk to a journalist from *Paris Match* who had known them for years and who followed them everywhere in their exile.

She had just heard that she and her mother and Ashraf had all been condemned to death in Teheran. "And they have even asked foreign governments not to arrest or punish our assassins, but to assist them."

She talked of a great French pastry chef who had created a magnificent cake topped with a crown for the Persepolis celebrations. "While it was being moved, it collapsed. He was devastated. All his work, his art, in crumbs. That's a bit how I feel today. Everything we tried to create, all our work in crumbs!"

In Morocco the Queen had begun to realize that former friends no longer wanted them. To most states, Iran was Iran; it was not the Shah. And Iran was just too powerful to offend. Heads of state who had previously embraced them now denounced them publicly—even if sometimes they also made discreet and apologetic private phone calls. Businessmen and financiers who had begged for invitations to the palace and who boasted of their intimate connections with the Pahlavis were no longer around. She found it very disillusioning. "Everyone has these kinds of problems in life, at a different level. But the higher you are, the wider things are around you. . . . Each time something happened, I said, 'My God, it's not possible.' But it was possible. . . . Sometimes I felt the whole world behaved as if we were the biggest criminals. Inside myself I knew what I was and what my husband was, but the Islamic government wanted us to appear in public opinion as something else. The way we were treated, tossed from one place to another. Now that I am out of it, I think how could you survive it?"

She later said that for the Shah as well this was the worst part of the exile. (Not that it became any easier later.) She found Crosby's house tiny, humid, and claustrophobic, with all the security men around and all the baggage piled in a little courtyard. "All of us in three rooms, we having our meals in one room, the others staying outside. A terrible ambience."

Even the dogs were not allowed out of the house; when one of them ran on the beach there was an official letter of complaint. Everyone was exploiting them for as much cash as possible. Worst of all, the Bahamian government forbade them to make any comments on what was happening in Iran, where the waves of executions were continuing. This infuriated the Queen. "What foreign policy have they got to forbid us to say a word?" she asked later. "I said, 'Let's get a boat, go into international waters, and from there speak.' "

That was a measure of how powerless they had, in the space of only weeks, become.

CHAPTER NINE

The Dream Merchants

On April 7, 1979, Henry Kissinger called Zbigniew Brzezinski to give him a piece of his mind. Kissinger can be harsher than many to people he considers his inferiors, and Brzezinski noted later in his memoirs that Kissinger had castigated him "in rather sharp terms" for the administration's failure to allow the Shah into the United States.

With the revolutionary terror in Iran at its height, Kissinger and the Shah's other friends in the States were beginning a long campaign first privately with the Carter administration and then also publicly for the admission of the Shah.

Among the prominent personalities who felt the same was John McCloy, one of the perpetual "wise men" of the American foreign-policy Establishment. McCloy was one of those great American fixtures who, at least until the end of the 1960s, was in and out of rich private law or banking firms and high public office, and whose advice and consent were constantly sought in the clans of power of Washington and Wall Street.* Now he summoned all his energies to the defense of the exiled Shah. "John is a very

---

* McCloy was a poor boy from Philadelphia who put himself through Harvard Law School. His charm, his tact, and his intelligence marked him as a high flier almost before he had taken his degree. During the war Roosevelt made him assistant secretary of war under Stimson, and after the war he had been made head of the World Bank to be followed by high commissioner for Germany, and then chairman of Chase Manhattan. He was a senior partner in the law firm of Milbank, Tweed, Hadley and McCloy, and when President Kennedy took office, McCloy advised on almost everything. He also came to represent both Chase Manhattan and the major oil companies, the Seven Sisters, and their anti-trust-busting actions. "My job," he told the writer Anthony Sampson, "was to keep 'em out of jail." Through the sixties and the seventies he made it his business to visit each new attorney general and tell him of the danger implicit in OPEC's banding together and the need therefore for the antitrust laws to be applied flexibly to the oil companies. It always worked.

The Shah and Henry Kissinger—Zurich, 1975

prolific letter writer. The morning mail often contained something from him about the Shah," lamented Cy Vance later.

Then there was of course David Rockefeller, whose staff was now handling most of the Shah's affairs. Not only were Robert Armao and his people in the Bahamas with the Shah, but one of the bank's vice presidents, Joseph Reed, was now helping look after the Shah's finances. Most contact with the State Department was now being done by Reed.

But the undisputed leader of the campaign was Henry Kissinger who, in those days, still commanded enormous attention within the Washington–New York foreign-policy community. His relationship with the Shah was much newer, but in recent years it had been more significant than most. Now, the White House felt, he was mounting a strong campaign against Jimmy Carter on the theme "Who lost Iran?"

Kissinger argued publicly that the Shah should have been given much firmer support by the United States in standing up to the revolutionary forces. "One of the reasons for the Shah's progressive demoralization was his very real doubt whether we were actually supporting him. He certainly had the means at his disposal to resist more strenuously than he did. And he chose not to exercise them because he must have had doubts about our real intentions." Kissinger thought it absurd for Washington to argue for a coalition in face of revolution. Such a form of government was not even practiced in the United States, so there was no reason to suppose it could work in a less-developed and more turbulent polity.

Now that the Shah had fallen, Kissinger insisted that the United States owed him a debt for his thirty-seven years of friendship and that, therefore, he should be admitted to the country forthwith. Kissinger also argued that unless the Shah was well treated in his hour of need, then other rulers would be discouraged from placing trust in the United States.

There is no reason to doubt the sincerity or, indeed, the internal logic of Kissinger's views. Moreover, he showed deep and consistent loyalty to the Shah. But for the Carter administration there was another dimension to his campaign. The White House was about to complete the second Strategic Arms Limitation Treaty with the U.S.S.R. Senate ratification was bound to be difficult. Indeed, just as Camp David had been the White House's overriding obsession in the fall of 1978, so was SALT II in the spring and summer of 1979. Carter's strategists reckoned that Henry Kissinger's support of the treaty was essential to convince doubting senators when the treaty was submitted for ratification. They feared that he might impose some linkage to the Shah's admission.

When Kissinger called Brzezinski on April 7 about the Shah, Carter's national security adviser was sympathetic. He too believed that the credibility of the United States with its other allies would be badly damaged if it now refused to succor the Shah. He thought that the issue should never have risen at all. "We should make it unambiguously clear that the Shah was welcome whenever he wanted to come. Our mistake was to ever let it become an issue in the first place." He suggested that Kissinger call President Carter.

Kissinger did so, a few days before David Rockefeller was due to visit the president. According to his account, he told the president that "I was behind whatever Rockefeller would raise with him [about the Shah]. I said I felt very strongly about this."

Accounts differ as to what Carter said. According to Kissinger, the president replied that he personally was not against it, but that Cy Vance was adamantly opposed and he could not overrule him. But Carter later insisted that this was not true, and that in April he too was against admitting the Shah. Other accounts confirm Carter's recollection, not Kissinger's. Carter's chief of staff, Hamilton Jordan, quotes him as saying, "As long as there is a country where the Shah can live safely and comfortably, it makes no sense to bring him here and destroy whatever slim chance we have of rebuilding a relationship with Iran. It boils down to a choice between the Shah's preferences as to where he lives and the interests of our country."

It was those interests short term and long term, that were so difficult to determine. Kissinger wrote in his memoirs, "America and its allies shamed themselves by their later behavior toward him, abandoning a friend not only politically—which can result from the brutal dictates of national interest—but also humanly, when he was adrift without a refuge and required succor. History is written by the victors; in this case they have been cruel."

That may well have been true, but the problem was seen to be more complicated by many in the Carter administration. There seemed to be often conflicting moral and pragmatic questions. It was an issue on which different members of the administration took strongly opposing views, though they were views that wavered and were subject to change. It might well be true that friends need to be well treated, if only for the pragmatic reason of encouraging others. Kissinger's view was shared by many officials. Several U.S. ambassadors had already been told by friendly foreign governments that they were watching with dismay the way in which the Shah was being shuffled off now that he had fallen.

However, all the advice from the embassy in Teheran and from State was still that the Shah's entry to America would provoke another and much more ferocious attack on the embassy in Teheran. When Brzezinski brought up the matter with Carter himself, the president was "visibly irritated . . . and asked me quite flatly, 'What would you do if you were president?' " To which Brzezinski replied that he thought it was not only a question of pragmatism, in which the impact on rulers like King Hassan and President Sadat needed to be weighed, but above all a matter of principle. "We simply had to stand by those who had been our friends."

Brzezinski says that Carter did not like this reply and "was torn by the political and human dilemma with which he was now confronted." On April 9, he was troubled by a visit from David Rockefeller. At the end of the conversation, as he rose to leave, Rockefeller mentioned the Shah. "I told him of my concern that a friend of the United States should be treated in such a way and said I felt he should be admitted and we should take whatever steps were necessary to deal with the threats [to the embassy]. I didn't tell him how to deal with it, but I said it seemed to me that a great power such as ours should not submit to blackmail."

Carter's reaction was "stiff and formal," according to Rockefeller. "I got the impression the president didn't want to hear about it."

Carter noted in his diary: "The main purpose of this visit, apparently, is to try to induce me to let the Shah come into our country. Rockefeller, Kissinger, and Brzezinski seem to be adopting this as a joint project." He was determined to resist the appeals. "Circumstances had changed since I had offered the Shah a haven. Now many Americans would be threatened, and there was no urgent need for the Shah to come here."

As a result of Rockefeller's failure to sway the president, Henry Kissinger went public with his concern that night. It was then that he declared that it was quite wrong for the U.S. to treat the Shah, a friend for thirty-seven years, "like a Flying Dutchman looking for a port of call."* *The New York Times* declared itself not "much impressed" by Kissinger's intervention. "The former secretary of state once refused even to lunch with the exiled Aleksandr Solzhenitsyn lest he offend the Soviet leaders." Nonetheless the *Times* felt that the Shah should come. "Americans should welcome the unwanted, proudly."

Kissinger was certainly expressing his view of the nation's responsibility, but perhaps his call also reflected his own sense of responsibility to the Shah. No one had emphasized the importance of Iran's relationship with the United States more than Henry Kissinger and Richard Nixon. The Shah had been an ally of the United States since the 1940s, but all American presidents before Nixon had expressed at least some skepticism of him and his ambitions. Richard Nixon by contrast threw himself into the Shah's cause with enthusiasm.

In tracing the cause of a revolution, it is not possible to isolate factors from one another, still less to rate them neatly in order of importance. But almost all accounts of the Shah's own psychological development, the overheating and then the degeneration of the Iranian economy in the 1970s, the growth in the cruelty of SAVAK, and the spread of opposition to his rule, stress the im-

---

* This critical decision was made in a haphazard, almost careless manner. In November 1967 the British government had assured the rulers of the Gulf that Britain had no plans to leave. Then came one of Britain's recurring financial crises during the winter of 1967–68 and only months later, the Gulf rulers were told that the British would, after all, be withdrawing by the end of 1971. The financial saving to Britain was marginal; it was above all a political decision. The effects on the Gulf were vast.

portance of the day that Richard Nixon and Henry Kissinger had
come to call in May 1972.

This was a fine time for Richard Nixon; he was at the apogee of
his power. The Democrats seemed determined to select George
McGovern as their presidential candidate—and he was the man
whom Nixon's strategists considered the easiest to beat. At the
same time, Nixon had recently won two foreign-policy triumphs.

He had just become the first American president ever to visit
the People's Republic of China and had been extensively, if not
exhaustively, filmed talking with Mao Tse-tung, exchanging toasts
with Chou En-lai, gazing from the Great Wall. It was a spectacular, even moving occasion, splendid television, and magnificent
electioneering.

The North Vietnamese had responded to this reconciliation between one of their two principal allies and their main enemy by
launching a massive Easter offensive against South Vietnam. It was
checked only by a similarly massive increase in the use of American bombing and the mining of North Vietnamese ports.

This further escalation of the war came only just before Nixon
was about to embark on his second triumphant voyage—to be
the first American president to visit Moscow and there to sign the
first SALT agreements. Many of Nixon's advisers feared that the
new attacks on North Vietnam would lead the Soviets to cancel
the trip. But, like the Chinese, the Soviets deemed détente more
significant than solidarity, and ignored the predicament of their
Vietnamese ally. Nixon and Leonid Brezhnev signed the SALT I
treaty and an agreement on "Basic Principles of Relations" between the superpowers.

On May 30, when Nixon took off from the Soviet Union to fly
to Teheran, he was apparently in a mood of exhilaration. His
ambitions for a new world order seemed to be close to realization.
Now he was on his way to meet a ruler whom he had known and
admired since the early 1950s.*

On the flight to Teheran, Nixon had time to read the briefing
paper prepared for him by the State Department. This began with

---

* Richard Nixon and the Shah had first met in 1953 when Vice President Nixon was on an
international tour. Nixon was impressed by the Shah and later wrote, "I sensed an inner
strength in [the Shah] and I felt that in the years ahead he would be a strong leader." He
returned to the United States with the belief that the Shah would be built into a powerful
ally. He remained in touch with the Shah and visited Iran again in the sixties.

the words, "The Shah is highly gratified over your prospective visit to Teheran and the recognition it will bring him as an important world figure." This was absolutely right. Like Nixon, in May 1972 the Shah was at the pinnacle of his power.

In the last few years, the White Revolution had appeared to be achieving success; steady increases in oil revenues meant that Iran was no longer dependent on U.S. aid. Instead the Shah was able to buy more and more arms.

With Nixon's election in 1968, the Shah could at last feel that he had a friend in the White House. When Dwight Eisenhower died, early in 1969, the Shah did not ignore his funeral as he had Kennedy's; he came in person. He was welcomed by Vice President Agnew, he found himself the senior chief of state among the mourners and so he was given top protocol ranking at the official ceremonies. He called on Mrs. Eisenhower; he had a forty-five-minute private meeting with President Nixon, and longer sessions with Henry Kissinger; William Rogers, the secretary of state; Melvin Laird, the secretary of defense; and other officials. He impressed many of them—including Kissinger, who went to talk to him at the Iranian embassy on Massachusetts Avenue—by his ability to make a cogent *tour d'horizon*, examining the problems and interrelations of the world. American officials needed briefing books; the Shah could speak at length, extemporaneously and with great authority. He stressed the U.S. interest in Iran's self-reliance and referred frequently to the U.S. and Iran as "natural allies." He pictured Iran as a bastion of stability and progress in an unstable area. He stressed, as always, his need for more arms. He was told that arms sales policy was currently being reviewed. The State Department cabled the embassy in Teheran that "he came across as an intelligent, experienced, and determined leader."

There was an essential new element to Iran's situation. In 1968 the British Labour government had decided to end its military commitments east of Suez by the end of 1971. In July 1969 Kissinger had commissioned a National Security Study Memorandum on how the U.S. should respond to the vacuum thus created in the Gulf. In July 1969 Nixon enunciated on Guam the thoughts that were later to be enshrined as the "Nixon Doctrine." Their essence was that in future, America would not supply military manpower to its friends in Asia but would provide them the arms with which to defend themselves against Communism.

In the Gulf, the United States, and Britain as well, concluded that only Iran could possibly replace the British military commitment. The Shah would have to become the policeman of the Gulf. The Shah was not unhappy; in a complicated deal with the British he agreed not to seize Bahrain, which Iran claimed and the British had protected. However, he was allowed to take three islands in the Strait of Hormuz, islands that had been under British control and that the Arab sheikhdoms now wished to take over. This proved a momentous event. On one island there was resistance, and a few casualties on both sides. Iran offered compensation to the former owners of the three islands and the sheikh of Sharjah accepted; he was later assassinated in reprisal. At the same time, Colonel Qaddafi of Libya used the Iranian takeover as an excuse to expropriate British Petroleum within Libya, and Iraq broke relations with both Britain and Iran.

In Washington, attitudes toward arming the Shah changed completely. Gone was the caution of the Eisenhower, Kennedy, and even Johnson administrations. Between 1950 and 1971, aggregate U.S. arms sales to Iran had been $1.8 billion. Within weeks of Nixon's taking office, restrictions began to be eased. Orders rose from $86 million in 1968 to $184 million in 1969. At last the Shah was beginning to acquire arms in the quantities he had always craved.

There was opposition to this policy from the State Department. The Bureau of Intelligence and Research concluded in a June 1970 study that despite the Shah's request,

> There is no immediate military threat to Iran that would justify new inputs of military equipment. . . . Moreover Iran could not afford extensive new arms purchases and still maintain the level of economic development that the Shah considers necessary for political stability without substantial amounts of concessionary financing. Increased military spending could thus lessen rather than enhance Iranian security.

This was not the White House view. Indeed, the U.S. now began to develop a policy of benign neglect toward internal developments in Iran. Previous U.S. administrations had urged domestic reforms upon the Shah and had used U.S. aid as a lever. Now the White House argued that the United States should not instruct the Shah how to run his country, though the evidence was that his government was becoming more autocratic and less able to meet the challenges of rapid development.

As he flew from Moscow to Teheran on May 30, 1972, Nixon's briefing paper did not mention the fact, but some of the Shah's reforming zeal, apparent in the sixties, seemed by now to have been extinguished. There was now no one of independent thought around him. Surrounded by courtiers and sycophants and the pomp he insisted upon, he was apparently coming to believe only in himself and his own divine mission for Iran. His methods of government were very much those that, according to Herodotus, Cyrus and Darius used to control their empires.

The core of the system was fear and distrust. Fear of the Shah, from whom all authority flowed, and distrust of everyone else. At every level of government, an individual, be he a minister or a clerk, would see himself surrounded not by colleagues but by rivals, each of whom was competing with him for their superior's grace and favor. Thus in every ministry or government organization, senior officials would compete for access to the Shah, and below the leadership would descend myriad different rivalries, deriving from and reinforcing the competition and insecurity at the summit.

No one could see himself or others as independent. On the contrary, everyone was in a closely defined slot in a pyramid of which the Shah was the apex. This was recognized even (or perhaps especially) by those closest to the Shah himself. One example noted by U.S. diplomats had occurred in 1971 when the Shah honored his able minister of finance, Jamshid Amouzegar, with Iran's highest decoration, the Order of the Taj (First Class), as a reward for his success in negotiating the Teheran Oil Price Agreement of that year. The agreement had indeed been a substantial triumph for Amouzegar himself. But instead of accepting the award as a personal tribute, he arranged that the televised signing ceremony focus on the Shah and that the head of each OPEC delegation make a speech praising the Shah as architect of the agreement. Moreover, immediately after he had received the award, Amouzegar deliberately disappeared from view to avoid the great dangers implicit, in the words of the Persian proverb, of being "the tallest flower in the Shah's garden."

Just as senior officials must give credit for their own successes to the Shah, so they had to shoulder personal blame for mistakes made by the all-powerful and omniscient monarch. It would be hard to call a system based on the competition of thousands of insecure rivals stable. But for many years it did function—thanks to the Shah's own manipulative skills. One U.S. diplomat suggested that it showed true genius on the Shah's part. To work the system, the Shah

> must keep the details of more than a hundred personalities and their shifting relationships with one another in mind. He has to insure that not only men but organizations remain in mutual competition so that cooperation between men not competing in the same ministry will not threaten him. At the same time, these men and organizations must be manipulated so that while distrusting one another and cynical about themselves and their compatriots, they nonetheless work long and hard to achieve the common goals the Shah has set the country.

But even before the massive oil boom and bust of the mid-seventies, it was becoming clear that the development and increasing sophistication of Iran were overloading the capacity of this personal, private system of government. Good management is not compatible with highly centralized dictatorship. More and more use had to be made of coercion and control. The state became increasingly dependent upon the work of its secret police, SAVAK.

SAVAK, the National Intelligence and Security Organization, was founded in 1957 "for the purpose of the security of the country and prevention of any kind of conspiracy detrimental to public interests." In American terms, SAVAK was supposed to be a combination of the CIA, FBI, and National Security Agency. Its powers were very broad, like the organization that served Darius as "the eyes and ears of the King." Its principal duties were to protect the Shah by discovering and rooting out individuals opposing his government, and to inform him on the mood of the people. Its agents had been trained by Mossad, by the CIA, and by the U.S. Agency for International Development.

The first head of SAVAK was General Teimur Bakhtiar, a man who had the reputation of a brutal sadist. He was not a loyal brute. In 1958 he visited Washington and met with Kim Roosevelt, who had helped reinstall the Shah in 1953, and with Allen Dulles, the director of the CIA. According to Roosevelt, he told them that he wanted to depose the Shah, and he wanted their support. Dulles said at once that the United States would give no such help and immediately called his brother, John Foster, the secretary of state, to warn him not to allow Bakhtiar to say anything of his plans when they met. So John Foster Dulles started talking nonstop the moment Bakhtiar was ushered into his office, and did not cease until he was ushered out.

The CIA told the Shah about the treachery of his secret police-man. The Shah waited until 1961, when Bakhtiar organized dem-onstrations against reforms that the Shah had authorized, and then removed him. For some years Bakhtiar directed anti-Shah activi-ties from Switzerland but then moved to Iraq, whence more ag-gressive actions could be mounted. He was arrested in Beirut for possessing arms, and when the Lebanese refused to extradite him, the Shah broke off relations with Lebanon. In 1971 he died in a hunting accident in Iraq which was widely believed to have been arranged by SAVAK.

SAVAK then passed through various hands, including those of one general who was described as far too mild and intellectual for the job. During the late fifties and early sixties, SAVAK had con-centrated on following, intimidating, and sometimes arresting those connected with Mossadeq, his National Front party, or the illegal Communist Tudeh Party. By the seventies, when these people had been either exiled or neutralized, SAVAK began to stretch its arms abroad among both exiled politicians and students. Every Iranian embassy had its SAVAK men, just as every Soviet embassy has its KGB. Most groups of students, at home and abroad, were thought to have at least one SAVAK informer aboard.

By the time Nixon and Kissinger visited, in May 1972, violent dissidence and its corollary, violent repression, were increasing in Iran. For example, in 1970 a mullah had been arrested and tor-tured to death for having objected to a conference on increased American investment in Iran. The government was trying to curb the movement of pilgrims between Iran and the Shiite shrine of Najaf, in Iraq, where the Ayatollah Khomeini was based. In the course of 1971, there had been a number of demonstrations against the Shah, and samizdat leaflets had protested against the expense of Persepolis at a time of starvation in several provinces. Thirteen people were tried and executed for killing two gendarmes in the Elburz Mountains. In January 1972, the government announced the trial of 120 people on various subversive and antistate activi-ties. Thirty-two of them were sentenced to death amid foreign charges, especially in Western Europe, that their guilt was prede-termined and that they had been tortured. Nineteen of them were known to have been executed. Just before Nixon's visit another

five young Iranians were executed as terrorists; there had been
thirty-eight such executions in the past sixteen months.

The nature of this growing crisis was already becoming evident
to some of the more astute U.S. diplomats in Teheran when Nixon
and Kissinger arrived. But the president's briefing paper, prepared
by State, made no mention of dissidence. He and his national
security adviser were more concerned with the development of
Iran as a powerful military ally of the United States than with the
internal stresses that the Shah's dictatorship was causing.

The Shah had prepared minutely for the visit, with more attention to detail than even Nixon's advance men. He insisted that the
motorcade from the airport be rehearsed not once but twice—and
at night, so as not to disrupt traffic. It seemed that *le tout* Teheran,
including the prime minister, the minister of court and U.S. embassy officials, and excluding only the Shah and the Empress
themselves, spent two nights driving out to the airport, standing
on the tarmac, shaking hands with stand-ins for the Nixons,
climbing in and out of limousines, roaring into town.

The Shah gave a state dinner for the president and his entourage.
A typical, smallish court affair, 140 guests, including many Pahlavis, lashings of caviar, vodka, fine wines and champagne. In the
glare of television lights, Nixon made a characteristically awkward
toast, ending with a joke that quoted President Eisenhower as
saying that all successful political leaders had "the ability to marry
above themselves." Kissinger later recorded that at this the Shah
"looked off into the distance with melancholy."

After dinner Kissinger went with Prime Minister Hoveyda to a
cabaret. The press was in attendance and a belly dancer sat on
Kissinger's lap. SAVAK officials prevented photographs of this
friendly gesture.

Nixon and Kissinger had two working sessions with the Shah
during their twenty-four-hour stopover. No written records of
their talks have been released. But people who have seen the internal memoranda of the conversations—among them George Ball,
a former under secretary of state who was asked by President
Carter to review the files—have been surprised by them.

During their talks Nixon stressed that what the Shah was doing
was right, and he should do more of it. He encouraged him to be
a tough ruler and urged him to take control of the Persian Gulf
and never to shut off oil as that "crazy man" Mossadeq had done.

The United States depended on him and he embodied the Nixon Doctrine. According to one account, Nixon actually said to the Shah, "Protect me."

Perhaps more unexpected, from the leader of the world's largest democracy, was that Nixon complimented the Shah on the way he ran Iran itself. He apparently urged him to pay no attention to "our liberals' griping" about human rights. Thus, Nixon must have seemed to the Shah to be endorsing SAVAK. Certainly he made no objections to its methods.*

The Shah was understandably delighted that at long last his statesmanship and his stature were being recognized. He was more than happy to undertake the role of policeman of the Gulf. He asked three things in return: that the CIA help him to help the Kurdish people in their long-standing insurgency against Iraq; that the United States send him a large number of military technicians; and that, most important of all, he not only be armed but also be given carte blanche to buy all the most sophisticated weapons in the U.S. armory. He was particularly insistent on this point because the Pentagon had been delaying on his request for F-14 and F-15 fighters.

The U.S. often ties up its military aid in strings that the recipient country finds unacceptable. Some embassy officials in Teheran agreed with the Shah that the Pentagon was too slow in meeting his requests for arms. On the other hand, for years the Pentagon's own studies had concluded that the threats to Iran's northern and western borders were best met by the slow but consistent development and training of its armed forces—not by the sudden transfer of the latest American military technology.†

Now Nixon and Kissinger overrode all such concerns. They agreed that, short of nuclear weapons, the Shah should have everything he wanted. From now on he, not the Pentagon, would decide what Iran needed.

Nixon also offered the Shah a U.S. naval presence in the Gulf.

* Gary Sick, Zbigniew Brzezinski's aide on Iran, who reviewed the files on the May 1972 visit, later recorded that when SAVAK attacked the opposition during the seventies, "the Shah had reason to believe that a crackdown on opposition elements would be welcome in Washington and that his methods would be regarded with a considerable measure of tolerance."

† In the case of the F-14 and F-15 fighters, the Pentagon had till now argued that they were still in an early stage of development and by the time they could be delivered it might no longer be in the U.S. interest to supply them to Iran. Furthermore, Melvin Laird had been reluctant to send technical assistance teams. There was also a concern that sophisticated weaponry could fall into Soviet hands.

This the Shah turned down, saying that he could defend the area himself. The Shah thanked Nixon for his advice on dissidents; he would put them in jail. He agreed with Nixon that the students must be stopped from being infected with "subversive" tendencies.

The second day in Teheran was marred by anti-American violence, which, at least in retrospect, seemed a warning against the intimate relationship that the Shah and Nixon and Kissinger were set on forging. Two sticks of dynamite exploded near the office of the United States Information Service, then an American Air Force general advising the Iranian Air Force was seriously injured in an explosion, and finally a bomb went off at the tomb of Reza Shah just forty-five minutes before Nixon was due to lay a wreath there. Ronald Ziegler, the White House press secretary, said that "there is no indication whatsoever that the reported incidents today were aimed at the well-being of the president or any members of his party."

Before leaving, Nixon had another conversation with the Shah reaffirming the United States commitment to Iran's new role as policeman of the Gulf. Then he gave a modest lunch party for the Shah and about twenty other Iranian and American officials. Afterward the motorcade set off for the airport. To avoid demonstrations, it skirted Teheran and went instead through unpopulated hills north of the town. But even there students were waiting; the limousines were pelted with stones. Hundreds of students were subsequently rounded up and imprisoned in the spirit of Nixon's advice.

After the Americans had left, the Iranian ambassador to Washington, Amir Aslan Afshar, asked the Shah if the talks had gone well. "Yes, very good," replied his monarch.

"Did you get what you wanted, Majesty?"

"Yes, more than I wanted, more than I expected."

A few weeks later, an Intelligence Note from the State Department's Bureau of Intelligence and Research pointed out that the bombings during Nixon's visit and previous attacks

> show that a violence inclined "youth underground" has taken root in Iran with possibly serious long-term consequences for the country's long-term stability. . . . At a minimum, several hundred, mainly middle-class Iranian young people, educated overseas or at

home, are sufficiently alienated from their government and society to accept the hardships of long-term clandestinity and personal danger in pursuit of radical change, frequently no more than "revolution for the sake of the revolution."

The memoranda that Kissinger began to fire into the bureaucracy were different; they implemented Nixon's promises to the Shah. The CIA was ordered to start arming the Kurds. The CIA station chief in Teheran protested, predicting disaster. The new policy did indeed prove disastrous for the Kurdish people, for the Shah discarded them when they had served his purpose.*

In July 1972, Kissinger issued what must be one of the more remarkable memoranda ever written by a national security adviser. In the name of the president, he ordered the secretaries of defense and state to give the Shah all the weapons he wanted. If the Shah wanted F-14s, he should have them. If he wanted F-15s, he should have them. "The President has told the Shah that the U.S. is willing in principle to sell these aircraft as soon as we are satisfied as to their operational effectiveness. Within that context, decisions on purchases and their timing should be left to the government of Iran." If he wanted laser-guided smart bombs, he should have them too. If he wanted more American military technicians, he should have them. And that was not all.

---

* Nixon and Kissinger's decision to have the CIA run an extensive arms program to the Kurds was opposed by the U.S. ambassador to Teheran as well as by the CIA station chief there. In Washington, the Forty Committee, the key oversight group for covert operations, was given no opportunity to discuss and approve the policy; members were simply hand-carried a one-paragraph synopsis of the project to sign, after John Connally had been sent to Iran to assure the Shah that the program was under way.

Neither the White House nor the Shah wished to enable the Kurds to win the autonomy for which they were fighting; they were to be used to tie down Iraqi troops so long as that was how the Shah perceived Iranian interests. The Kurds did not understand this. Their leader, Mustafa Barzani, frequently told CIA officials that he distrusted the Shah but fully believed in the United States. If his cause succeeded, he was "ready to become the fifty-first state."

In March 1975, the Shah reached an accommodation with Iraq; he cut off aid to the Kurds and closed the frontier while Iraq launched an offensive against them. Barzani sent desperate cables to the CIA station in Teheran, begging for help. The station sent them to Washington, underlining its own concern at the situation. Barzani also wrote Kissinger: "Our movement and people are being destroyed in an unbelievable way with silence from everyone. We feel, your excellency, that the United States has a moral and political responsibility toward our people, who have committed themselves to your country's policy."

Further pleas were sent by the CIA station. There was no reply from Washington. The Iraqi offensive destroyed Barzani's movement. Two hundred thousand refugees fled to Iran. Humanitarian assistance was inadequate. Iran forcibly repatriated 40,000 Kurds. Kissinger was quoted as saying of this, "Covert action should not be confused with missionary work."

The President has also reiterated [wrote Kissinger] that, in general, decisions on the acquisition of military equipment should be left primarily to the government of Iran. If the Government of Iran has decided to buy certain equipment, the purchase of U.S. equipment should be encouraged tactfully where appropriate, and technical advice on the capabilities of the equipment in question should be provided.

The generosity in itself was notable. But most extraordinary of all were Kissinger's instructions that the Shah and the Shah alone would determine what Iran needed. He, and not the U.S. government, would decide what and how many American weapons were to be sent to Teheran. As Kissinger summed it up in a subsequent memorandum to Nixon himself, "We adopted a policy which provides, in effect, that we will accede to any of the Shah's requests for arms purchases from us (other than some sophisticated advanced technology requirements and with the very important exception, of course, of any nuclear weapons capability . . .)."

These orders were greeted with some dismay in the Pentagon, at least among the civilians in the office of International Security Affairs who were supposed to regulate U.S. arms sales in the national interest. They were not opposed to the notion of the Shah taking the place of the British in the Gulf—few American or British policy makers saw any alternative to that. But they questioned whether it was really in the U.S. interest that professional American judgments as to Iran's needs and capacities be suspended in order for the Shah alone to make decisions.

In many ways the Shah was a simple man; or at least he was a military man at heart. He once said that if he had not been Shah he would have liked to be an Air Force general. His wife once said, "One of the only things my husband likes in life is flying, driving, driving boats—speed!" All his life he had been delighted if not obsessed by military machinery. Now there were no restrictions to that obsession. That same year, 1972, he said, "Today, speaking geographically and strategically, it is no exaggeration to dub Iran 'the center of CENTO.' And since CENTO is the center of NATO-CENTO-SEATO, my country is in a way the keystone of the whole structure."

George Ball, the former under secretary of state and "wise man" of American foreign policy, subsequently reviewed the files on Iran for President Carter. He called the Kissinger memoranda

ARNING

"the most extraordinary I have ever seen." In his memoirs, Ball wrote that by selling Iran whatever the Shah wanted, regardless of views in Washington, Kissinger "drastically broke with past American practice." Moreover, "I think it clear that in anointing the Shah as the guardian of Western interests in the whole Gulf area, Nixon inadvertently encouraged the megalomania that ultimately contributed to the Shah's downfall."

Ball had known the Shah since the early sixties, and visited Iran almost every year in the late sixties and seventies. In his view, giving the Shah free access to the most advanced American military hardware "was like giving the keys of the world's largest liquor store to a confirmed alcoholic." American approbation, unrestricted arms sales, and inflated oil revenues persuaded the Shah he was "commissioned by Allah to transform Iran into what he now boasted would become the fifth most powerful nation in the world. . . . In trying to fulfill his Messianic mission, he isolated himself from his people and lost his sense of proportion, thus encouraging the destructive forces that proved his undoing."

Henry Kissinger's view was, naturally, different. In the first volume of his memoirs, *White House Years*, he wrote that it was necessary to help arm the Shah and that

the specific decision facing Nixon was the Shah's wish for the F-14 and F-15 aircraft and associated equipment. There had been opposition: some Defense Department reluctance to part with advanced technology and State Department fears that the sale might be provocative. The Shah's alternative was to purchase the slightly less advanced French Mirage plane. Nixon overrode the objections and added a proviso that in the future Iranian requests should not be second-guessed. To call this an "open ended" commitment is hyperbole, considering the readiness and skill with which our bureaucracy is capable of emasculating directives it is reluctant to implement—a quality repeatedly demonstrated in the Nixon Administration (as during the India-Pakistan crisis) and soon compounded by the erosion of Nixon's authority as a result of Watergate.

By contrast, Captain Gary Sick, Zbigniew Brzezinski's aide on Iran, has written, "The President's order was unequivocal and comprehensive. It afforded not the smallest loophole for those who questioned the wisdom of a blank check to the Shah. . . . The order was implemented, with a vengeance." U.S. military contracts with Iran grew from about $500 million in 1972 to $2.5 billion in 1973 alone.

In his second volume of memoirs, *Years of Upheaval,* Kissinger took a different approach. He wrote that "there was no blank check" and that "I doubt that Presidents Ford and Carter were even aware of the directive—as I had forgotten it." Yet, when the Shah visited Washington in 1975, Kissinger had sent President Ford a briefing memorandum in which he wrote, "After President Nixon visited Teheran in May 1972, we adopted a policy which provides, in effect, that we will accede to any of the Shah's requests for arms purchases from us." The only exceptions, wrote Kissinger, were some sophisticated advanced technology armaments and nuclear weapons. Thus, not only was President Ford made aware of the policy by Kissinger himself, but, as Sick points out, "the directive remained the object of hotly contested debate at the highest levels of government through the very last days of the Ford administration, with Kissinger consistently supporting it against opposition within the government." Never before in American history had the president ordered the national security bureaucracy to accept the demands and judgment of a foreign leader on arms transfers. The implications were to be catastrophic —for the Shah himself, for Iran and for U.S. policy.

CHAPTER TEN

The Noble Resource

Life in the Bahamas very quickly became almost insupportable for the Shah and his entourage. He had begun to feel ill. His French doctor, Dr. Flandrin, had secretly come and, with the help of the Queen and Dr. Pirnia, had attempted to treat him. But it was not adequate.

The beach house was claustrophobic. With tourists, journalists, autograph hunters, and other hucksters all over the beach, most of the day had to be spent in a minute courtyard of the house, with the trunks and cases piled along one wall. There were very few things to laugh about. One was a letter from an American women's group offering to marry all the Shah's aides so as to enable them to get U.S. visas. Another was a letter from Madame Chiang Kai-shek, who wrote how familiar it all seemed to her.

Yasser Arafat was still threatening to send a PLO team to capture the Shah and drag him home. Then another PLO official in Teheran announced that had the Shah remained in Morocco he would have been seized. The press began to report that Palestinians were now en route to the Bahamas. Anyone on the beach, save perhaps a few of the elderly blue-rinsed female tourists, could have been an assassin.

In Teheran, Sadeq Khalkhali, the head of the revolutionary

courts, announced that the Shah and other members of his court had been sentenced to death and that anyone who assassinated them would be carrying out the courts' order. "I have signed many execution orders and am proud of it," said Khalkhali. "I want the Shah's blood in return for all the blood shed in this country."

Later Khalkhali declared that he had sent a squad of gunmen after the Shah—and that the notorious international guerrilla Carlos was also under contract. Furthermore, there was now a reward of $70,000 for whoever killed the Shah. Khalkhali announced that the Empress and Princess Ashraf were also on the hit list, but they would be reprieved if they killed the Shah instead. Moreover, "if Farah killed the Shah she would not only get the money but a pardon as well and she could return to Iran." Security in Paradise could never be strict enough.

At the same time, the cost of staying there was becoming fantastic. "The Shah was being taken for such a ride and so outrageously overcharged and treated in the Bahamas that he very quickly wanted to find an alternative place," said David Rockefeller later.

President Carter's reaction was less sympathetic. "Despite his great wealth," Carter wrote in his diary, "he seemed obsessed with the belief that people were trying to cheat him."

Meanwhile there was growing criticism within the Bahamas at the Shah's extended stay. Opposition parties condemned his presence as "a blot and disgrace." The Socialist Party said it was the price the Bahamas must pay for being "the backyard playground of the Western world."

Under all this pressure, the Shah tried to start writing a new memoir, one intended to justify his rule and, inter alia, to explain the madness that had gripped Iran since the oil price rise of 1973.

Oil runs through the history of modern Iran like blood through a body—except that it has not been merely life-giving. Indeed, oil was a curse to the Shah himself, in much the same way as was gold to King Midas.

Throughout the first half of the twentieth century, the Iranian oil industry was dominated by the British. One of Mossadeq's most effective arguments against them was that after fifty years there were still no Iranian technicians in the industry and most workers of the Anglo-Iranian Oil Company remained unhoused.

After the British and Americans conspired to overthrow Mossadeq and the Shah was restored to the throne in 1953, an international oil consortium was formed for the exploitation of Iranian oil. It consisted of the Anglo-Iranian Oil Company (renamed British Petroleum), Royal Dutch Shell, Compagnie Française des Petroles, Standard Oil, Gulf Oil, Texas Oil, and Socony-Mobil. In 1954 they reached an agreement with the Iranian government for 50–50 profit sharing, which was then the norm in the Middle East. The Iranians did not discover, until much later, a secret agreement among the members of the consortium to limit Iranian production and income.

OPEC—the Organization of Petroleum Exporting Countries —was formed in 1960 and at first the Shah feared that it might be "an instrument of Arab imperialism." He continued to suspect that the oil companies would not favor Iran adequately. In both 1966 and 1968 he managed to force the consortium into increasing production rates for Iran. (The oil companies had been reluctant but had acceded to U.S. government pressure "not to antagonize the Shah.") The Shah had warned that if they did not do as he wished, he would seize the oil fields.

The Shah then concentrated on making Iran a dominant member of OPEC; in February 1971 the producers, under Iranian pressure, managed to force the first of the large-scale price increases from the oil companies. Large, that is to say, by previous standards, not by what was to follow. It was not until the Yom Kippur war of 1973 that the Western world understood for the first time the power of the cartel—and of the Shah.

The Arabs imposed an oil embargo, but the Shah continued to supply the United States, Israel's principal ally, despite Arab pressure on him. Notwithstanding his friendship with Sadat, he considered Israel's survival essential to the area. To placate his neighbors, he called for Israel's withdrawal from the lands it had occupied in 1967, sent medical supplies to Jordan and logistical assistance to Saudi Arabia, and permitted Soviet supply planes to overfly Iran.

After the war was over, the Shah declared that the National Iranian Oil Company was now taking control of Iranian production away from the consortium. In a real sense he was finally implementing Mossadeq's ambition.

In the aftermath of the war, OPEC hoisted prices by some 400 percent. The Shah played one of the most belligerent and public parts in this achievement. The United States, whose dependence on foreign oil had increased annually since it became a net importer in 1970, protested. The Shah was dismissive. "No one can dictate to us. No one can wave a finger at us, because we will wave a finger back."

The Shah's position was simple, and logical. Oil was "a noble resource." Iranian oil belonged to Iran. Yet foreigners (particularly the British) had sought to steal it from Iran ever since it had been discovered—indeed, even before its discovery. The oil companies' profits were "excessive." Western demand for cheap oil was a paramount example of Western greed—and Western waste. Oil had many excellent properties and uses; how grotesque that it should be squandered in gas-guzzling automobiles. The prices of other commodities had already risen much faster than that of oil.

Furthermore, Iranian oil would last for only about twenty more years. A high price was essential for Iran's future. "Why should we cut it?" he asked in 1974. "This is what Iran is using to improve the lives of 32 million people. By development. We do not want to sell our oil for fuel. Anyhow, oil is more beneficial to mankind in other forms. There are 70,000 things to be had from oil, including very valuable petrochemicals and pharmaceutical products." The new high price was "just and reasonable" because it was based on the cost of replacing oil with alternative energy sources—in particular nuclear power.

All of this was arguable and much of it was incontestable. But the oil price rise, coming so soon after his own celebration of himself in Persepolis, suddenly began to give the Shah a kind of demonological status in the West.

Until now he had been of marginal interest to newspaper readers and television viewers in most of the countries where such publics exist. He had had favorable but by no means extensive coverage in the sixties—an enlightened despot was the sum of it. During his party at Persepolis, he had emerged, briefly, to shine with a certain Ruritanian luster. He had been treated by much of the press as the star of an *opéra bouffe* and some questions were asked. But then he had been consigned again to the inside pages.

Now, suddenly, after manipulating the oil price rises, the Shah was everywhere—on front pages, on television documentaries, the hero or antihero of mass market fiction like Paul Erdman's *The Crash of '79*. All at once he, his fantastical court, his secret police, and his apparently imperial ambitions began to become part of popular contemporary mythology, as columnists, novelists, and filmmakers struggled to comprehend what was happening. Many people found it hard to understand why the man whom Henry Kissinger later called an "unconditional ally" was one of the most aggressive of the OPEC leaders in pushing a revolution that seriously disrupted the entire world. Suddenly the Shah became an object of fear and skepticism.

Nor was the change just in Western perceptions. Even to those around him, the Shah appeared to alter. His ambitions seemed to become increasingly detached from the object of his obsessions. One of his courtiers later used another image. "Persepolis was his blast-off into the heavens. After that he was refueled by Nixon and by oil. He never came back to earth."

The Shah seemed to see the OPEC price rises as unalloyed good. From now on there was, he said, and many of his ministers parroted after him, no problem that could not be solved by throwing money at it. He seemed quite oblivious of the distortions, both internal and external, that the price rises would cause. He appeared convinced that the industrial countries would go on buying oil, at whatever the price, and he ignored the fantastic inflationary effect that the price rises would have on the capital and consumer goods that Iran needed to purchase. Indeed, he later used that very inflation to justify the oil price that had caused it.*

Before the vast new oil revenues had been mooted, Iran had embarked on a new and relatively modest five-year plan for 1973–78. When the oil money began to arrive in 1974, the Shah decided to double, at a stroke, the expenditure on public-sector investment. He announced this decision to a Cabinet meeting; some of his ministers were astonished, some appalled, but none dared to try to dissuade him. The prime minister, Amir Abbas Hoveyda, asked if this would not strain the country's infrastructure. The Shah ignored him, asked if there were any other questions, and declared that it would be done. Such an enormous increase in expenditure by decree smacked, in retrospect at least, of alchemy. One com-

---

* Inflation, the Shah declared, should be beaten "by working harder and wasting less." Americans worked hard enough, he told an American magazine, "but not the others—not the Europeans. The Germans—yes. The French—well, maybe pretty well. But the others—no, not enough. Americans yes, still—you have people working. That's one answer to inflation —work. . . . The other is the waste of the affluent societies. You go to an American restaurant or a home and you see immense amounts of butter and other foods being wasted, thrown away, because the consumer has taken a little and left a lot—and this is thrown away. You waste paper—everything, everything."

mentator, Robert Graham, later pointed out, a "hyperboom" had been arranged.

A kind of frenzied insanity developed. The dream of "a second Japan" became more and more of a fixation for the Shah and those around him. Prime Minister Hoveyda gave it as his considered view that in thirty years Iran's living standards "will overtake Japan's" and that Iran would be producing more steel than all Europe and the U.S.S.R. before 1983. (Where the market would be found was not clear.) The Shah declared time and again that he would turn Iran into "one of the five industrial powers before the end of the century," a model not only for the Third World but also for the West, whose "decadence," sloth, and waste he now constantly attacked. He was particularly dismissive of the British. In just a decade, Iran would be the equivalent of West Germany. "Oh, yes, we can do that," he asserted to one journalist, as he calmly sipped tea on the porch of the palace. "And in twenty-five years, we can OVERTAKE the European countries."

The Great Civilization was only just around the corner, the Shah insisted. "No other state in the world, I think, gives its workers, farmers, and other groups as many benefits as Iran does." And much more was to come. Free elementary education, free milk for students, national health care, housing loans for workers. All this and more could be achieved, because Iranians were capable of extraordinary effort. "There is that difference beween us and the blasé societies" where people "demand more and more money but work less," he told a writer from *Fortune*. It was all too much for this correspondent, who decided that the Shah had "a reality problem."

But that was a problem exacerbated by his allies, all of whom were now desperate to share in the fabulous new riches of Iran. Western embassies in Iran, never long on analysis, became dedicated export missions, above all intent on making sales.

And why not? After all, Iran's new wealth was money taken directly from the industrialized countries and other oil consumers. The oil price rises for which the Shah had fought were an unprecedented shock for the developed world (a "*shokku*" to the Japanese). In 1974, the British government, faced with a coal miners' strike as well as the massive increase in oil prices, instituted a three-day work week in order to conserve energy. Almost everywhere, inflation galloped ahead, businesses were foreclosed, and employment fell. It was inevitable that every nation affected should attempt to claw back some of the vast transfers it had been compelled to make by increasing its exports to the oil producers.

The British were among the most eager to court the newly enriched monarch. In January 1974 the chancellor of the exchequer, Anthony Barber, and the secretary of trade and industry, Peter Walker, dashed to see the Shah on the ski slopes of St. Moritz to ask for money. They came away with a one-year barter agreement by which Iran sold Britain five million extra tons of crude oil in return for £110 million worth of industrial goods.

This new, indeed reversed relationship with Iran induced some dismay in Britain. The *Guardian's* diplomatic correspondent complained, "The Shah has snapped an imperial finger and two senior members of the British cabinet are to come a-running." The *Daily Express*, a more populist paper, editorialized bitterly that whereas London was once the world's financial center and sterling its currency, now British ministers had to humiliate themselves to "crave an audience with the Shah of Persia." The paper declared that it was a grim prospect that Britain should be dependent on the Shah. "How incredible, how ignominious that the chancellor of the exchequer should take to the slippery slopes of St. Moritz. After all, if he wants to talk money why didn't he send a Rothschild?"

Not everyone took such a chauvinistic view. The day after the British ministers left, the West German economic minister arrived in St. Moritz to discuss supplies of natural gas with the Shah. The French came. And so did many others.

In spring 1974 Henry Kissinger cabled the Shah to suggest that the U.S. and Iran "broaden and deepen our relations." Theirs was to be "an equal partnership." He proposed a Joint Economic Commission at the Cabinet level, to be headed by the U.S. secretary of the treasury. One of its first tasks might be collaboration on expanding Iran's nuclear power program. He was also keen to transfer more U.S. technological skills and know-how to Iran so as to develop a research or manufacturing capability in other selected areas it considered of high priority. "We have in mind such areas as water desalinization, solar power, and certain fields of mechanical and electronic engineering, including solid state electronics and production of selected military end items." The U.S. would also help the Shah develop his petrochemical industry and Iran's radar and communications systems, including satellites and ground systems. At the same time, political and security ties should be expanded still further by frequent visits back and forth by senior U.S. and Iranian officials. If the Shah thought a Joint Commission on Security Affairs should also be set up, then "we are prepared to respond to his wishes."

The Shah was delighted with Kissinger's proposals and accepted almost all of them with alacrity. He suggested also that under the label of technology transfer the U.S. should allow Iran to manufacture missiles in Iran; they would be cheaper than those produced in the States and he would then sell them back to the U.S. government. Indeed, he attached great significance to this notion. Kissinger also approved it. In the months to come he urged that such coproduction of missiles be speedily implemented.

On Kissinger's proposal that U.S. and Iranian officials fly back and forth between Teheran and Washington, the Shah commented that it would be better for most meetings to take place in Teheran because "I take the decisions and it is easier for me to do that in Teheran."

The Joint Commission was formally unveiled when Kissinger visited Teheran in November 1974, soon after Gerald Ford succeeded Richard Nixon as president of the United States. Nuclear cooperation was among its first tasks. For its future meetings Kissinger was to represent the U.S. Hushang Ansary, Iran's minister of economic affairs, and one of the richest men in the country, represented Iran. Early in 1975 the commission announced that it would promote $15 billion in non-oil trade over the next five years. Iran would spend another billion on U.S. nuclear power plants and technology. Kissinger declared that it was "the largest agreement of this kind that has been signed by two countries."

There were then fewer than ten nuclear technicians in Iran.

No one profited more from the oil bonanza than the Western arms merchants, who had already been unleashed by the Nixon-Kissinger May 1972 decision to "give the Shah everything he wants." After the price rises, he wanted—and could have—so very much more. Former CIA station chiefs, heads of the U.S. Military Assistance and Advisory Group, and dozens of other former officials succumbed to the lure of lucrative contracts from members of the industrial-military complex. Even the newly retired chairman of the Joint Chiefs of Staff, Admiral Thomas Moorer, turned up on a corporate sales job in Teheran. So did

British, French, German, and Scandinavian salesmen.

All the companies that had been big in Vietnam and now found their order books collapsing after the 1973 Paris Peace Agreement came to praise the Shah, their glossy brochures and expert sales talks well prepared. They constituted a new court, and one riven with just as many jealousies as that which revolved around the Shah and his family. Many of the men who became better known during the "Irangate" hearings of 1987—Richard Secord, Manucher Ghorbanifar, Albert Hakim—were involved one way or another in the arms business to Iran at this time.

Some of the purchases were justified by the nature of the Soviet threat to Iran and the instability of the area. The Shah himself felt that the 1973 Arab-Israeli war alone more than explained his need. "There is no economic power without military power," he would say. For at least two years there was no restraint at all. By 1976 the Shah had ordered more than $11 billion worth of the most sophisticated weapons in the American armory, and still more from America's European competitors. The major U.S. weapons systems to which the Shah committed the country included battery upon battery of Hawk missiles, more than five hundred military helicopters, 240 F-14 and F-15 fighter aircraft, four destroyers, and three submarines, not to mention the airborne radar warning system known as AWACS. The number of American military technicians to service all these systems grew three times, from just over three hundred in 1972 to more than a thousand in 1977. At the same time American corporations sent more than five thousand civilians to work in Iran on the arms sales program by the mid-seventies.

The Americans became a catalyst for the revolution.

One of the main reasons for the break between Khomeini and the Pahlavi regime in 1964 had been the extralegal rights granted to the American military in Iran. Now, instead of a few hundred, there were thousands of Americans stationed in Iran. They tended to conglomerate in their own little suburbias, with their own dollar shops, pizzerias, hamburger joints and their large cars and their alien customs. Their behavior was as infuriating to many Iranians as was Washington's unquestioning support for the Shah.

One of the worst places in this context was Isfahan. There the Bell Helicopter company had a contract to train Iranian servicemen to run the Shah's huge new helicopter fleet, one of the biggest in the world. Many of Bell's employees were Vietnam veterans whose only previous experience outside the United States was as part of an army of occupation where the natives were trying either to kill or to service them. The intricacies of the Shiite faith were, not surprisingly, lost on most of these men. During religious holidays of mourning, the Americans would have large parties with stereos blaring and drunken revelers staggering from place to place. Their bars were closed to Iranians. Several of them featured Vietnamese bar girls.

Inevitably, American workers became the symbol of an increasingly unpopular alliance. As the boom of 1973 turned to slump, discontent among peasants who had crowded to the cities to find work, and who now had neither work nor homes, turned to fury. For many people that fury was easily directed at the United States. A few Americans were murdered.

For a time the Shah's new wealth allowed him to improve his relations with some of his Arab neighbors. He continued his close relations with Israel. But he also gave large amounts of aid to Egypt and rather less to Syria, neither of which have oil. In March 1975 he and Sadam Hussein, the Iraqi leader, even settled, with a disdainful kiss, the principal border disputes between their two countries. The immediate consequence was that the Shah dropped his support for the Kurdish rebels fighting Iraq, with the consequences already noted.

Despite such mercantile rapprochements, many Arab leaders— not least the Saudis—remained wary of the Shah. There was a widespread, if usually silent, fear that he was not to be relied upon and could actually be a threat to their own integrity. At one level they may have appreciated his dispatch of Iranian troops to help the sultan of Oman put down a left-wing guerrilla movement in 1973. (This was the first example of the Shah carrying out the dictates of the Nixon Doctrine, whereby the U.S. provided the arms and a regional power provided the men to fight Communist encroachment in a given area.) But some Arabs saw the foray into Oman also as a trial run for Iranian interference in their own affairs. Sheikh Yamani, the Saudi petroleum minister, frequently complained about the nature of the Shah's ambitions. Yamani consistently tried to limit the rises in oil prices; the Shah almost always tried to push them as high as possible. Iran had a far larger population than Saudi Arabia and the Shah wanted to maximize revenues at once; the Saudis had no sense of urgency. The Shah would publicly describe the Saudi petroleum minister as "that fellow Yamani."

In August 1975 Yamani told the U.S. ambassador to Riyadh, James Akins, that the Saudis believed the U.S. was encouraging the Shah to take over the entire Arab littoral of the Persian Gulf. According to Akins, Yamani declared that "the talk of eternal friendship between Iran and the United States was nauseating to him and other Saudis. They knew the Shah was a megalomaniac, that he was highly unstable mentally, and that if we didn't recognize this there must be something wrong with our powers of observation." (At this time Akins was dismissed by Secretary Kissinger, in good part because he failed absolutely to endorse Kissinger's wholehearted support for the Shah.)

Yamani also warned that "if the Shah departs from the stage we could have a violent, anti-American regime in Teheran." He could not understand why almost all American officials were "totally taken in by the Shah."

One of those who was not taken in was the U.S. treasury secretary, William Simon. Indeed, he publicly called the Shah "a nut." This caused some unhappiness in the Niavaran Palace—*The Washington Post* reported that the Shah's government had even considered breaking diplomatic relations over the incident.

On another occasion, Simon advised President Ford that Iran "is the dominant force in OPEC for higher world prices" and that "the Shah's bogus economic arguments . . . should not go unchallenged." He suggested Ford "take a tough private line with Iran," threatening U.S. counteractions "if their stance is not altered." This is what the Saudis were also urging on Washington.

James Schlesinger, who became secretary of defense in 1973, was also skeptical of the Shah. He was alarmed by the corruption and chaos of the area free-for-all that had developed in Teheran and tried to bring order to the procurement process. After Nixon's resignation, Schlesinger had voiced his doubts about "giving the Shah everything he wants" to President Ford and suggested an interagency review. But Henry Kissinger was still secretary of state and he delayed the proposal within the bureaucracy.

When the Shah visited Washington in 1975, Kissinger's briefing memo for President Ford praised the Shah highly—"a man of extraordinary ability and knowledge"—and advised that Ford say nothing about high oil prices. "I see little point in your trying to argue with the Shah that prices were raised too fast and too much, inasmuch as he is utterly convinced of the correctness of what he has done and easily takes umbrage at suggestions to the contrary."

Such silence on the most important issue of the time for much of the world could only have assured the Shah that the United States supported him, or was at least relatively unconcerned by his oil policy. In fact Ford did intervene and did thereby gain a brief respite in price rises.

The charge was later made that Kissinger actually encouraged the Shah's oil price rise so that he be better able to arm himself. Kissinger has vigorously denied it. At the very least, however, it is clear that the massive increase in the Shah's wealth after 1973 did not lead Kissinger to rewrite the "blank check" on arms purchases the Shah had been given in May 1972.

By 1976, Gerald Ford's last year in office, the Shah himself had concluded that much of the procurement counsel he was given by U.S. officials was tainted by the fact that they were inextricably entwined with various arms manufacturers. Americans were so self-righteous about corruption, he said. They were always complaining about it in Iran, but there was so much in the U.S. as well. He had also become exasperated by the delays, cost overruns, and ineffectiveness of many of the arms he had bought. He had his chief procurement officer, General Toufanian, take a six-page letter to Secretary of Defense Donald Rumsfeld complaining about U.S. "malfeasance" and "crude deception" in hiding from him deficiencies in a radar system that Westinghouse was trying to sell him. There was a furious row over lunch; according to the Iranian version of events, Rumsfeld said that the problem was that Iranians were corrupt. He accepted no responsibility for Americans' conduct. Subsequently the Shah asserted that "the chicanery of Pentagon officials and their military and civilian representatives here was intolerable."

In August 1976 the Senate Foreign Relations Committee published a critical review of the entire arms sale program in Iran. The White House decision of May 1972 came in for special scrutiny. Despite his own growing misgivings about the plethora of arms salesmen, advice, corruption, and doubtful systems involved, the Shah was not pleased by this attack. Kissinger flew at once to Teheran. The Shah denounced the congressional report to the world's press. "We are a sovereign country looking after our defense. . . . We are the only judge of what we need," said the Shah, with the U.S. secretary of state sitting by his side.

The Shah also made an implicit threat. "Can the United States, can the non-Communist world, afford to lose Iran?" he asked. "What will you do if Iran is in danger of collapse? If you do not pursue a policy of standing by your own friends, who are spending their own money and are ready to spend their own blood, the alternative is nuclear holocaust or more Vietnams." The logic was perhaps not unassailable, but the warning was heard; a few days later Kissinger announced that the U.S. intended to sell the Shah 160 F-16 aircraft at a cost of $3.4 billion.*

After Jimmy Carter became president in January 1977, he ordered an immediate review of the whole range of U.S. arms sales policies. In May 1977 he issued a directive completely reversing the trend of the Kissinger years. "I have concluded," wrote Carter, "that we must restrain the transfer of conventional arms by recognizing that arms transfers are an exceptional foreign-policy implement, to be used only in instances where it can clearly be demonstrated that the transfers contribute to our national security interests."

So many of the Shah's plans were dreams. Not all of them ignoble, but dreams nonetheless. For him to have had any chance of realizing his ambitions, Iran would have had to go for massive and immediate capital investment so that it could switch from oil to industrial exports. In fact Iran's exports other than oil fell after the 1973 price rise, and most of what was still exported consisted of traditional goods such as farm products, cotton, and carpets. At the same time, imports doubled—to a staggering 30 percent of GNP. And less than a third of these imports were of capital goods —the bulk of them were armaments and consumer or luxury products. Iran was buying guns and butter—and champagne. In the 1960s Iran had been able to feed itself. Not in the 1970s.

By 1975 the economy was careening out of control. Credit had been expanded much too rapidly and the banks were now in the position of having to apply for international loans—despite the gigantic oil income of the country. Imported goods were left stuck in docks which could not possibly handle the new volume. Cus-

---

* Henry Kissinger does not often appear to have attempted to restrain the Shah; the two men were fulsome with each other. When the Shah sent Kissinger a message congratulating him on a South African initiative in 1976, Kissinger replied, "It is always a pleasure to be congratulated for one's efforts, but when it comes from a man of your vision and wisdom, it is indeed an honor."

toms procedures were quite unsuited to the boom; over twenty signatures were needed to clear goods. By mid-1975 there were over two hundred ships waiting off the port of Khoramshah to unload. Immense bribes usually had to be paid to obtain priority to discharge cargoes.

Two thousand trucks were ordered to help shift the other new imports. But there were not enough drivers. Korean and Pakistani drivers were brought in. But they did not like their conditions, and most of them soon left. The trucks, like other goods, stayed in the docks and rotted.

There was a desperate shortage of skilled and unskilled labor of all sorts. Sixty percent of Iranians were still illiterate and so Iran now had to rely more and more on foreign technicians at all levels of the economy.

Despite many such problems, the Shah did not waver. One British writer, Gavin Young, who had remarked on his unpretentious informality in the sixties, found a very different monarch in the mid-seventies. Surrounded by the enfolding trappings of the court, the Shah still seemed at times gentle, soft, even humorous. But when he began to talk of his vision of the future, "he moves perceptibly into a sort of emotional overdrive, and his words blend into an alarming monotone, almost as if he were programmed. 'We Iranians are entering a great era,' he says, staring at a point rather high up on the wall. 'My country will become the second most sophisticated nation in Asia after Japan. My people's cultural maturity and intelligence is going to put this country up with yours. Iran will be one of the SERIOUS countries in the world. . . . Everything you can dream of can be achieved here. . . .' "

In some ways Iran did indeed become a place of fantasy. In 1976 on the celebration of the fiftieth anniversary of Pahlavi rule, the diplomatic corps were required to attend ceremonies at Reza Shah's mausoleum. The Shah and Empress arrived, as they did everywhere, by air, landing in a helicopter about two hundred yards away. The diplomats, among them Britain's Anthony Parsons and his wife, heard a burst of applause and then the royal couple came into sight and walked up the steps of the mausoleum.

After the show was over, as they drove back to Teheran, Parsons noticed four horses' heads peering out of what looked like an enormous police van. "SAVAK have started arresting horses, it seems," said Parsons to his wife. Then they passed a tank transporter carrying a state coach in a plastic sheet. "How odd," said Parsons.

That night the whole ceremony appeared on television. The Shah and Empress were seen driving in an open coach drawn by horses for what seemed miles and miles, with cheering crowds massing along the route. In reality, Parsons surmised, they must have driven about fifty yards through a bunch of extras; on television it looked like a triumphal progress. Such were the illusions in which the Shah would bathe.

As the oil money poured in, the Shah's centralized, personal dictatorship had become less and less effective. Since almost all important decisions could be made by him alone, many were inexorably, sometimes fatally delayed. The problems became acute in organizations like the Ministry of Planning. Senior officials of the National Iranian Oil Company found that modern management was impossible unless they hived off many of NIOC's operational functions into separate enterprises, while the parent company remained part of the Shah's personal domain.

Attempting to reconcile good management with the demands of highly centralized monarchical dictatorship was particularly frustrating for executives trained in Western business-school methods. They found that their new, expensive skills were far less useful than the ancient arts of intrigue and obedience. A further complaint was that almost all government servants were grossly underpaid, and could merely watch as they saw grotesquely huge fortunes being made in the private sector, by none more easily than the relatives and courtiers of the Shah.

CHAPTER ELEVEN

The Great Civilization

The little beach house refuge in the Bahamas and his new staff had been found for the Shah after the intervention of his twin sister, Princess Ashraf, with the help of David Rockefeller and Henry Kissinger.

Throughout his exile, the Shah had no more passionate propagandist than Ashraf. A tiny, beautiful, fiery woman, she had always been one of the most powerful and controversial figures in the Pahlavi pageant.

It seems that in many stories of contemporary dictatorships there is a character whom the popular press likes to call the Dragon Lady. Almost always she is the wife or a close relation of the dictator. In Vietnam there was Madame Nhu, the sister-in-law of President Diem; in Haiti, Michelle Duvalier, wife of Baby Doc; and in the Philippines, Imelda Marcos, the queen of footwear. In the land where the dragons originally had their lairs, there have been two Dragon Ladies, Madame Chiang Kai-shek and then Madame Mao Tse-tung. (The original Dragon Lady first appeared in a 1930s comic strip called *Terry and the Pirates.* She was Asian, wore long, slinky dresses, and was quite clearly evil.)

In the case of Iran, the Dragon Lady was not the Shah's third wife, Farah Diba. Rather it was Ashraf, who liked to consider herself far closer to him than any of his wives. She was known in

At the coronation, 1967, from right: Princess Ashraf, Princess Shahnaz, the Shah, Empress Farah, and Princess Shams. In front are Crown Prince Reza and his sister Princess Farahnaz.

court circles as SAIPA, Son Altesse Impériale la Princesse Ashraf, and the stories about her are legion, and often no doubt untrue or at least exaggerated. She was said to have enjoyed a remarkable series of amorous adventures. She was alleged to have been connected with the drug trade; she successfully sued *Le Monde; The Washington Post* retracted its version of this allegation, saying "*The Post* has no substantive evidence that these reports are true, and regrets their inclusion." She was thought to have made scores of millions of dollars in her multifarious business deals. Apocryphal many of these stories may have been, but it surely says something of the bizarre, frantic, almost hysterical nature of Iranian society in the seventies that they were even alleged about her. She herself later remarked with rue, "Even if you win [libel] suits, people always say there must be something to it. The same way with the charge you have heard that the revolutionaries have photographs of me naked with senators or congressmen. I only know senators Percy and Javits. Which one was it supposed to be?"

Ashraf was feared, she was hated, she was admired. She was rarely ignored.

In the formal portraits of the family before their fall, the men stand stiffly and, at least in the case of the Shah, tautly nervous in dark uniforms emblazoned like Christmas trees with miles of gold braid and garnishings of medals. The women are in long, white gowns slashed by imperial sashes. It is the tiny Princess who seems to tower above the rest—in gall, in fury, in chutzpah, in sexuality (and this among a crowd well known for its sexual appetites), and in imperiousness.

Many of the recent histories insist, and there is no reason to doubt them, that in several of the crises of the Shah's reign she acted "to stiffen the Shah's backbone." It was commonly said among Iranians that Reza Shah's genes had become mixed up and that Ashraf should have been the boy twin and become ruler of Iran. Subsequently she acknowledged that she was indeed both more stubborn and more robust than her brother. "I always felt that I had to look after him and protect him. Even as a little girl, I never left his side." All the evidence suggests that she would have made a far more determined ruler than the Shah himself; had she been on the throne in 1978, the palace's response to the disturbances would have been far more ruthless and might, for a time at least, have halted the people's enraged march toward revolution. But she, of course, was one of the causes of that rage.

She was born a few hours after her brother, and it was he, the male heir, who gave the joy, as Ashraf came early in life to recognize. "To say that I was unwanted might be harsh, but not altogether far from the truth," she wrote on the first page of her autobiography. "I realized very early that I was an outsider, that I would have to create a place for myself. In later years my critics would say I had overdone this somewhat, that my presence was everywhere. But as a child I was scarcely noticed at all." Her memoirs contain a classic photograph taken when she was about three years old; it shows her father holding her twin brother on his knee and embracing their half sister Shams, while little Ashraf stands to the side, alone, her mouth tentatively open.

She found all her sense of family in an obsessive love for her twin. One of her lovers later wrote, with no exaggeration, that her brother "was the light of her life, the apple of her eye, the blood that flowed in her veins. She loved him with a passion that was both possessive and unsharing. [He] was one half of the symbiotic whole of which the Princess was the other." Once, strangely for a Muslim, Ashraf compared her brother to Jesus Christ and said, "Some people worship God and I worship my brother." After his death she wrote of their relationship:

> No matter how I would reach out in the years to come—sometimes even desperately—to find an identity and a purpose of my own, I would remain inextricably tied to my twin brother. I would marry more than once. I would have children of my own. I would work for my country in ways unheard of for a woman of my generation. . . . But always the center of my existence was, and is, Mohammed Reza Pahlavi.

When he was sent away to school in Switzerland, "I felt as if I had been separated from a part of myself." She believed that the two of them were "like faces in a mirror." Two years later she and her mother visited him in Switzerland; a photograph of her and her brother taken there shows her elegantly, petulantly, but seriously pouting at the camera. He, as often, has a more hesitant appearance. He has slicked-back hair and is wrapped in a double-breasted jacket that is rather too grown-up for him. Together they look more like runaway lovers than teenage brother and sister. She cabled her father to ask if she could stay with Mohammed Reza in Europe, which she found fabulous. He sent a harsh cable back: "Stop this nonsense and come home at once." She was very upset. When Mohammed Reza returned in 1936 to Iran, it was, says Ashraf, "one of the happiest days of my life."

Ashraf had a miserable first marriage; "I was so sexually naïve and so repelled by my husband that I had to take what we would now call a tranquilizer before I could bring myself to share his bed." She divorced him and fell in love with someone else. But her brother thought him unsuitable and forbade the marriage. She was later grateful to him, she claims, because she came to realize that "I could never embrace any future course at the cost of cutting myself off from my brother."

At around this time, the end of the Second World War, her sex life became a matter of widespread gossip. This, she insisted later, was because many Iranian men were outraged that she should broach their exclusive preserve of politics. They therefore spread stories about her. Her brother suggested she squelch the rumors by taking another husband. So she married an Egyptian friend, Ahmad Shafiq—but the stories continued.

She became known as "the Black Panther." After the war, when the Soviets were refusing to leave the Iranian province of Azerbaijan, she visited Stalin and, she says, greatly impressed him by the force of her arguments and style—their scheduled ten-minute meeting lasted for two and a half hours and then Stalin invited her to a sports stadium with him. He called her "*ana pravda* patriot," a true patriot, and told her to tell her brother "that if he had ten like you, he would have no worries at all." Then the great dictator gave the beautiful little Princess a magnificent sable coat.

Such compliments emboldened her to intervene even more forcefully in domestic politics; in 1948 she decided that the then prime minister was becoming too powerful and so, she wrote later, instructed him to resign. On a visit to the United States to study the work of the American Red Cross in 1947, she talked of her brother's commitment to democracy; she was praised for her clothes but was asked by a man from the State Department to keep quiet when she spoke favorably about the Soviet welfare system. She later claimed that she was greatly impressed by the informality of Harry Truman's White House; it was quite a contrast to the awesome majesty of the Kremlin.

When the United States pitted itself against Mossadeq, her mettle was seen by Washington to have its uses. One U.S. embassy report from 1951 noted, "Her motives have been improper and her actions often maladroit. But she has an instinct for decision which is badly needed in the Shah's close entourage. Her forceful character, her sharp insistence for action, can push her brother from passivity." The embassy reckoned that while the Shah had inherited his father's "dream of national progress," Ashraf had been granted Reza Shah's "merciless determination." Mossadeq also understood this and first had her exiled and then removed very fast when, with U.S. and British support, she flew back to encourage her brother to act against him.

As the Shah became more powerful and somewhat more self-confident through the fifties and sixties he seemed disinclined to allow Ashraf political power at home. So her energies were channeled into a variety of other interests—such as the rights of women and the United Nations.

Princess Ashraf and
Premier Chou En Lai in
Peking, 1975

Under the Shah, women's rights did indeed improve dramatically in Iran—they were allowed more freedoms than in most countries of the Middle East. Ashraf was Iran's delegate to the U.N. Human Rights Commission in the late sixties. With a sense of timing and unintended irony that is perhaps possible only in the United Nations, she became the chairman of the Human Rights Commission in 1970—just before SAVAK began to become an international byword for the cruel abuse of such rights.

The Shah sent her to China in 1970; it was a successful visit, and eventually Iran and China restored full diplomatic relations. When China won its seat at the United Nations in 1971, one of the first invitations its delegation accepted was to a glittering lunch with Ashraf at the house of the Iranian ambassador to the U.N.

Her China visit was followed by others to India, Pakistan, North Korea, and several African countries. By the mid-seventies Ashraf was leading the Iranian delegation to the U.N. for at least part of the General Assembly sessions. She accomplished these international missions with some distinction. Yet at the same time she was becoming at home the symbol of all that was most unattractive in the Pahlavi family.

A CIA report of 1976 declared that the Princess had "a near legendary reputation for financial corruption and for successfully pursuing young men." Her relationships with these swains often ended amicably and many of them went on to rise in government service—among them Parviz Radji, who was the Shah's last ambassador to London and who, after the fall, published his revealing and gossipy diary of his service to the Peacock Throne. He wrote in September 1978 of the quandary in which the gathering revolution placed him. Wondering whether the Shah's hands were now so bloody that he was no longer "worth saving," he asked,

> And yet, and yet—shouldn't I be ashamed of ever entertaining
> such thoughts? Would I dare look [Princess Ashraf] in the eyes if
> ever she should read these lines? I, who have shared with her so
> many moments of tender affection; I, who owe her so enormous a
> debt of gratitude, for the office that I hold, for the munificent
> generosity with which she has treated me!

The same CIA report described her business entanglements as
"often verging on if not completely illegal." The governor of an
Iranian bank apparently once told the U.S. embassy that her activities would land other people in jail for ten years but that the Shah
just shrugged them off.

Ashraf always vigorously denied any wrongdoing on her part.
In 1976 her car was ambushed by gunmen near her home in Juan-
les-Pins in the south of France. It was raked with bullets. The
driver managed to ram the attackers' car and rush Ashraf away.
But a woman friend with her was killed in the assault. "No arrests
were made," she said later. "Some people said it was a mafia-type
thing, connected with what they called my drug traffic. I doubt
experienced assassins would have bungled it."

When the unfavorable CIA report on her was released, Ashraf
angrily denied its allegations and demanded that the agency produce its evidence, if any. She insisted that such fortune as she had
was based entirely on the sale of lands she had inherited from her
father. (These were lands that Reza Shah had seized.) In *The New
York Times* she declared that she would use every possible method
to combat such calumnies.

She had another claim to make. The CIA attacks, she asserted,

> show that the CIA surely plotted against my brother. Before seeing
> them I would never have thought it so. But the CIA made contact
> with Khomeini as early as 1977. The West thought that by Islam-
> izing the whole region—Iran, Afghanistan, Pakistan—it would
> serve as a barrier against Communism. They feared that if my
> brother stayed in power, the country would wind up going Com-
> munist because so many people were being educated.

She also insisted that the West had destroyed the Shah because
it feared the economic power of the new Iran. In her view the

U.S. and Europe could not tolerate the rise of a "second Japan" in the Middle East.

Ashraf had two sons and a daughter. The younger son, Shahriar, was a model naval officer. In the late seventies he graduated first from Dartmouth Naval College in Britain. He was then stationed with his family at Iran's Bandar Abbas naval base where he commanded the Hovercraft fleet—Hovercraft were one of the Shah's obsessions.

Her elder son, Shahram, had inherited more of his mother's business talents. The CIA noted once:

> He is widely, and unfavorably, known in Teheran as a wheeler-dealer with holdings in some 20 companies, including transportation, night clubs, construction, advertising, and distributorships. Some of these apparently provide a cover for some of Ashraf's quasi-legal business ventures.

In September 1978, a few months before her brother fell, Ashraf returned to Teheran from a trip to the Soviet Union. The streets were clogged with demonstrators; she flew to her palace by helicopter and was appalled by the massive crowds she saw below. She was horrified particularly by the fact that the women had thrown away the emancipation the Pahlavis had granted them and were all wearing "the mournful black *chador* their grandmothers had worn. My God, I thought, is this how it ends? To me it was like seeing a child you had nurtured suddenly sicken and die." To her dismay, her own brother no longer sought her advice; indeed, he is said to have considered her presence in the country an embarrassment, and he asked her to leave again. She packed up her goods and chattels and fled westward.

Soon after the Shah flew into exile, Ashraf joined him in Marrakesh. There she had encouraged him in her belief that he really had been betrayed by his allies, above all by the United States in general and by Jimmy Carter in particular. Certainly she was being treated differently herself by the U.S. government. When she applied to have her U.S. visa renewed in early 1979, Harold Saunders, assistant secretary of state, wrote that this was a special problem because she was "probably regarded in a worse light by Iranians than the Shah himself. Ashraf's unsavory past may possibly render her ineligible for a U.S. visa." She had been coming

to the United States, without question, for thirty years. Her visa
was in fact renewed.

Ashraf was not unique. In the 1970s, the whole country became
a wonderland for businessmen and -women. Kickbacks, bribes,
agents' fees, secret understandings between princes and PR men,
princesses and CIA agents, Samsonite briefcases packed with
hundred-dollar bills hand carried on executive jets, companies
with P.O. box addresses in the Caribbean and Liechtenstein, secret orders and counterorders conveyed in private meetings with
the Shah—this was the stuff of which business was made from
1973 onward.

Everyone was cashing in. The Shah's own cronies got themselves appointed "agents" for different foreign corporations, insisting that without their services nothing would be achieved, no
contracts won. Indeed, some five or six "superagents" together
with between twenty-five to thirty subagents literally began to
dictate the economic direction of the country. The Council of
Ministers and the High Economic Council took due note of their
wishes and commands. One of the key ministers—who later
safely fled abroad with much of his wealth—devoted much time
and great effort toward making sure that the various princes and
princesses were getting everything they said they had to have. One
of the Pahlavis openly stole and exported for his personal gain part
of Iran's national art treasures, in particular gold artifacts
unearthed at the prehistoric archaeological site at Marlik. In 1971,
in 1974, and then in 1978, when it was too late, the Shah made
attempts to curb this sort of corruption. But he was always
halfhearted. His underlying attitude was that if common Iranian
businessmen were making mountains of money from his policies,
there was no reason why his family should not also profit from
the benefits he was conferring on Iran.

In any court there are courts within the court. In Teheran the
satellite courts swirled jealously around the Shah's relations, who,
through their birth, controlled so much patronage in the land.
Each of the siblings had his or her own gallery of hangers-on and
cronies, the men and women who fixed contracts and commis-
sions on behalf of the princelings.

There was also a children's court—or children of courtiers.
Some of them lived pretty wildly in the seventies. They used to
bring large amounts of drugs, particularly cocaine, into Iran; their

parents' positions meant that they were never searched at customs. There was a Colombian dealer whom many of them used; he came so often that they called him "Concorde." Any child of the court could get him through the airport by simply threatening officials there: "If you give me shit, I'll give your name to X."

Court corruption was increased immeasurably by the fact that ambitious Iranians could achieve no political power. They could serve the Shah as his agents, no more. Such authority as they had, as ministers, governors, university chancellors, all derived from him. It was not so much a gift as a loan, which they knew could at any time be recalled. But they could become rich—that was the alternative to becoming powerful. Moreover, wealth had to be displayed, as competitively as possible. Never in a Third World country have European and American dressmakers, luxury car manufacturers, executive jet salesmen, art brokers, wine merchants, furriers, jewelers, done so well as in Teheran in the seventies.

To the poor, there was just the ostentation of the rich. But among the rich, there were the old rich and the nouveaux riches. The old rich liked to say they came from the "Thousand Families," the great landowners who had owned and governed large tracts of Iran for centuries. Some of them had lost land to Reza Shah and many had seen their influence curbed by Mohammed Reza and his reforms, though most also increased their fortunes enormously. Some of them saw the Pahlavis as vulgar parvenus. But their real loathing was for the thousands of fixers who prospered in the hyperboom of the seventies and who displayed their cars, their clothes, their jewels, their mansions even more ostentatiously than the old rich. One such man built a home modeled exactly on the Petit Trianon in Paris.

Subsequently Madame Afshar, the wife of the grand master of ceremonies and herself from an old family, complained, "After the White Revolution, the Thousand Families were swept away. You didn't know who anyone's father was. A woman would go into the hairdresser in a Dior mink and hang it up with the label outside. It was the nouveaux riches who threw sparklers in the faces of the people, not us."

There was no more blatant symbol of the excesses of the Pahlavi court than Kish.

Kish is a small, low, sandy spit of island that lies close to the

Strait of Hormuz and just southeast of the Persian Gulf.

Some said it was Sinbad the Sailor's island. In any case, the Persian Gulf has always been one of the world's major trade routes, and in many centuries Kish was a pirate base that lived off vast fortunes of gold and pearls looted from passing ships. It was not until the 1850s that the British fleet finally managed to clear the Gulf of pirates (and Arab competitors of the British East India Trading Company) and the people of Kish began a more prosaic life; date farmers and pearl divers lived off its soil and shoreline. By the mid-twentieth century, pearling had collapsed, and until the Pahlavis alighted on Kish, not much happened there. Then its silence was interrupted.

At the beginning of the seventies, the Shah decided to make Kish into one of his country homes. He built himself a small palace on the beach. Large contingents of the royal household were flown back and forth for weekends. Even horses were shuttled to and fro. The Shah insisted on being able to ride there, but the intense heat of the Gulf did not allow the thoroughbreds to remain for any length of time.

The palace, white walls, sharply gabled blue roofs, was right on the sea. The royal family spent most of their time on the beach; when any one of them swam, lifeguards swam farther out, in order to protect their highnesses against sharks. The children had their own separate quarters two miles down the beach. The Pahlavi dogs were all over the place. Lesley Blanch, the Queen's official biographer, wrote that their presence around the dining-room table gave "an agreeable sense of family living to the feast. Even the servants, though doubtless dreading a canine trip-up, have learned that in the royal family's private life all animals are welcome and all to be treated well everywhere. It is in such slight, indirect ways, that the lesson the royal family wish to spread, goes out." For most Muslims, dogs are unclean.

But Kish did not provide only a palace for the Shah. In the mid-seventies it was also being developed as a winter playground for the very rich of Iran, for European jet-setters, and for Arab gamblers.

It was not the best of ideas. Considerable local fury was aroused when the bazaar was pulled down to make way for the development. Because of the heat, Kish was suitable as a resort for only six months of the year. Absolutely everything had to be imported. The golf courses needed watering twenty-four hours a day.

Millions of dollars were spent on private villas, luxury hotels, a casino and duty-free shops (Kish was a free port), and golf courses. It was not quite clear at the time where the money was coming from. Some said it was the Shah's private money; others, that it was stolen from the government. Documents released later by the revolutionaries showed the government had indeed paid for most of the scheme. SAVAK owned 80 percent of it. Other money had come from various banks, including the Bank Omran, which was closely associated with the royal family. According to internal documents released after the revolution, there were serious irregularities in the funding of the development.

Kish was meant to be the ultimate in chic, the Monte Carlo of the Middle East, a modern-day Xanadu. Girls from Madame Claude's—the most sophisticated call-girl service of the time—were to be flown out on Concorde from Paris. (And some British girls too, the British ambassador was assured.) Croupiers from South Africa; boutiques from Rome; hi-fis, motorbikes, cameras, and beach buggies from Japan. And clients from all over the Middle East. That was the fantasy. One small problem was that most rich Arabs preferred to go to Europe for the gambling and their whoring; few of them wished to do either under the keen eyes of the landlords, SAVAK.

The new Kish was officially opened in January 1978. The cream of Parisian café society was flown in. Many of the buildings were still incomplete, but one hotel—where a girl was said to come with every room key—was finished, and so was the casino.

At almost exactly the same time, the first rumbling of fury against the Shah burst onto the streets. Within a few months of Kish's opening, the Shah, in one of his attempts to appease the people, had ordered all the casinos in Iran—even those owned by his family—closed. The man in charge of the development was reported to have fled at the time of the revolution with a case filled with hundreds of hundred-dollar bills.

For everyone but the rich, life in Teheran became more and more unpleasant during the seventies. Land prices soared—to the benefit of those who, like the royal family, already had large landholdings, and to the detriment of everyone else. Rents in Teheran became prohibitive even for the new middle class that was supposed to be the heart of the Great Civilization. People had to pay up to 70 percent of their incomes to landlords.

For the poor, life was much worse. Thousands upon thousands of illiterate peasants had fled the countryside in the hope (nearly always vain) of making fortunes in the city. The land reform of the White Revolution had now begun to fail the peasants it was supposed to help.

By now it seemed that one of the principal purposes of land reform was not simply to enfranchise peasants but also to extend central government control over their lives. Furthermore, the Shah was encouraging agribusiness ventures by European and American banks and multinational companies. Between 1970 and 1976 more than fifty thousand villagers were dispossessed, and to no avail. All the agribusinesses failed.

Those displaced and the other peasants who fled to Teheran helped build houses and hotels and other facilities for the rich and the foreigners in North Teheran. At night they themselves slept in crowded shacks or in holes in the ground, by which ran the open sewers. In the mid-seventies, Teheran became one of the nastier capitals of a world in which capital cities were being degraded faster than most assets. Cars were imported by the tens of thousands; traffic jammed to a halt. Power cuts were frequent. Tempers became uncontrollable. Envy was everywhere. Disappointment was the norm.

Everyone was affected. One night in 1977 Parviz Radji, the Shah's urbane ambassador to London, was back in Teheran for an audience with H.I.M. After visiting and bowing to the Shah, kissing his hand, and trying in vain to persuade him to compliment rather than insult the British, Radji returned to the Hilton, and noted later:

> There is a complete power cut, beginning at 6:30 and lasting four hours. Looking out of my hotel window toward South Teheran, I see a forest of cranes standing idle in the dusk. With the air-conditioning off, the heat becomes oppressive in less than an hour, and there is no radio or television either. From my balcony I can see an endless queue of cars stuck in a colossal traffic jam, their taillights shimmering in the evening heat, their horns sounding in protest against the extinction of all traffic lights. One can't even read. The ice has melted, so I sip warm vodka and try not to lose my temper.

Radji and most of his class loathed the mullahs. (A few of the court found in Islam a solace from the frenzy of Iran by the mid-seventies. The Shah's daughter by Fawzia, Princess Shahnaz, was one of them.) Radji wrote of the mullahs in September 1978:

[Their] demands for strict literal adherence to everything the Koran says, their degrading primitiveness and misplaced self-righteousness, their nauseating bigotry and sanctimonious hypocrisy, have only served to confirm my contempt for the values they claim to represent and uphold. . . . [If] they should ever come to power [the] country will be set back a hundred years, and, initially at least, there will be violence, lawlessness, vandalism, and, worst of all, the ugly vengeance that inevitably accompanies the overthrow of an authoritarian regime.

That may well have been true, but in the upheavals of the Great Civilization, the only certainty and the only solace for millions of people was that offered by their traditional teachers, the mullahs.

The Shah himself gave little balm. Indeed, he seemed to become continually more certain of his own wisdom, and more detached from the life of the people he probably genuinely thought he cared for. In 1975 he eliminated the last pretense of political freedom by abolishing (without consulting any of his advisers) the token opposition party and introducing a one-party system. From now on Iran was to have only the Rastakhiz (National Resurgence) Party, which he would head. Those who refused to support it, he said, could either leave the country or go to prison. A few months later, he said of those who did not join the Great Civilization, "we shall take them by the tail and throw them out like mice."

In 1976, to celebrate the fiftieth anniversary of the Pahlavi dynasty, the Shah changed Iran's calendar, bypassing the prophet Mohammed once again. Instead of basing its calendar on the flight of Mohammed from Mecca to Medina, from now on Iran was to fix its dates on the reign of Cyrus the Great. For the clergy it was another affront; for almost everyone else it was at least infuriating, yet another example of the Shah's grandiose flights of fancy. Such arrogance was insulting and humiliating for very many Iranians.

No ruler could have imposed such rapid, vast, and often capricious changes as the Shah sought to effect without the use of force. Iran in the seventies was a country in turmoil. To control it, the Shah came to rely more and more on SAVAK.

By the mid-seventies, SAVAK was nominally run by General Nassiri, a man who was distinguished only by his total obedience to the Shah. It was he who had delivered the Shah's *firman* dismissing Mossadeq in August 1953, and whom Mossadeq had arrested. He was not a clever man and he had little to do with the collection of intelligence or of political prisoners. He was principally concerned with SAVAK's other interest—real estate, like Kish. SAVAK's intelligence operations were controlled by a man who wore Yves St. Laurent suits and ties, Parviz Sabeti. His duties were broad.

SAVAK was responsible for gathering intelligence on foreign powers. On this it cooperated closely with the CIA; indeed, successive U.S. administrations considered the information that they gathered on the Soviet Union from Iran to be vital. At home, SAVAK was able to overrule ministers when it saw threats to the state. It could deny visas that the Ministry of Foreign Affairs had planned to grant; it constantly interfered with the release of films and the publication of books. It also seized books at customs and opened letters with brazen contempt for discretion; often envelopes would merely be stapled together again. Iranians took this as evidence that SAVAK was so powerful that it had no need to pretend.

SAVAK operated through thousands upon thousands of informers at every level of society. That very knowledge created an atmosphere of fear and distrust among large sections of the population. No one knew for sure which of his acquaintances, even friends, was SAVAK.

Many SAVAK agents were not thugs but smooth, well-educated young men who dressed, like Sabeti himself, in designer suits with wide ties and heavy gold cuff links. They were undistinguishable from thousands of other ambitious young men to be seen around town in the seventies. They glided through the corridors of power and the universities, attempting to entice and to entrance others. These men did not bully or threaten; instead they sympathized with the frustration of their peers, but pointed out suavely, over coffee and cognac at the Royal Hilton, how much, how very much, was on offer and how wise it was to grab it. The system might not be perfect, but where in the world could perfection be found? And even if there was no political freedom in Teheran, and even if the family left some things to be desired, were there not far more opportunities for advancement here than elsewhere in the Middle East?

But, as with all secret police forces, SAVAK's principal object was to gather intelligence and to sow fear. It did not function only at home; every embassy had its SAVAK agents and among every group of Iranian students abroad there was thought to be at least one SAVAK informer. There were reported to be SAVAK assassination squads on the prowl. Often students were arrested when they returned home on the basis of their alleged opposition to the Shah abroad. One Iranian journalist, Parviz Raein, told the U.S. embassy how even he, a correspondent for the Associated Press, had been swooped upon by SAVAK. He sent a brief story to New York about heavy snow which had isolated several Iranian villages. The desk in New York decided to jazz the story up a little; an editor added the sentence: "And while several Iranian villages struggled to dig their way out of heavy snows, the Shah was enjoying himself on the ski slopes of St. Moritz."

As soon as this story went out on the wires, SAVAK men pounced on Raein and threw him into prison. In the end he was released after an urgent phone call from Ambassador Zahedi in Washington to the Shah, confirming that the offending line had indeed been added in New York.

As far as the Shah was concerned, all those who opposed his rule were "Marxists," "terrorists," or "Islamic Marxists," who derived from what he called "the unholy alliance of the Red and the Black."

Until 1972 foreign observers and sometimes journalists had been allowed to attend political trials and so there was some scrutiny of procedures. After 1972 every trial of people arrested on political grounds was held *in camera*. Because of such secrecy it is impossible to say accurately how many people were arrested and tried.

Once a person fell into the arms of SAVAK there was nowhere to turn. SAVAK was empowered to act as the sole investigator of all alleged political crimes and also to bring charges. Suspects had no right to choose an independent lawyer, and usually were able to make contact with no one outside the prison. Once in SAVAK hands, people could simply disappear.

According to the testimony of former prisoners, SAVAK's instruments of torture allegedly included whipping and beating, electric shocks, pulling out nails and teeth, pumping boiling water into the rectum, hanging heavy weights on the testicles, tying the prisoner to a bed frame that was slowly heated, inserting broken bottles into the anus, and rape.

SAVAK was entirely its own master, answerable only to the

Shah. The accused had no right to call witnesses or to cross-examine anyone. The prosecution merely read out the evidence obtained by SAVAK, including confessions, if any. In practice the defendant was assumed guilty, and the only way he or she could hope for leniency was to confess and recant. But often torture was said to continue after trial and conviction.

In an interview in *Le Monde,* the Shah said of the allegations of torture, "Why should we not employ the same methods as you Europeans? We have learned sophisticated methods of torture from you. You use psychological methods to extract the truth: we do the same." In another interview, with CBS in 1975, he said that SAVAK used the same "methods" as any other secret service. Asked about allegations that SAVAK tore out fingernails, shoved bottles up rectums, or raped women in front of their husbands, the Shah replied that such claims were "ridiculous . . . disgusting. . . . Not that I accept the fingernails, the pulling of the fingernails, but the others are really disgusting. I don't like it at all." Asked why he needed a secret police, he replied, "Why? Everybody has. Who hasn't got a secret police?"

By the mid-seventies, fear of SAVAK extended even into the elite. Almost everyone with higher education knew someone who had disappeared, or whose death was thought, perhaps wrongly, to be the work of SAVAK. Even members of the court were afraid.

There are still disputes about the numbers who suffered from the evils of the secret police under the Shah. Khomeini claimed at the time and later that the Shah held up to 350,000 political prisoners and had killed 100,000 opponents. The Shah himself said there were about three thousand political prisoners in 1976. According to Amnesty International, the regime admitted to sixty-two executions for political offenses between 1972 and 1976; Amnesty reckoned the true number in excess of three hundred.

The International Commission of Jurists stated that between 1971 and 1976, 424 people were known to have been arrested and imprisoned on charges relating to state security. Of these, seventy-five were executed, fifty-five were given life sentences, thirty-three were given sentences between ten and fifteen years in prison, and others were given lesser sentences. Fifty more were killed in skirmishes with the police, nine were killed in prison, presumably while trying to escape, and sixteen had been named in the exiled opposition press as having been killed under torture.

When researchers for David Frost, the British television interviewer, tried in 1979 to calculate the numbers, they reckoned up
to fifteen hundred "political" deaths between 1963 and 1977. The
Shah's defenders could point out that during the seventies Idi
Amin was held responsible for at least 300,000 deaths in Uganda
and the Khmer Rouge for well over a million in Cambodia.

In 1976, when economic disappointment and political disaffection were greater than ever—and liberalization therefore the more
dangerous to any regime—the Shah began to restrain SAVAK. He
ordered the practice of torture to cease. Extra-judicial executions
were ended. Early in 1977, the Shah received delegations from
Amnesty International, the International Commission of Jurists,
and the International Committee of the Red Cross. He allowed
the Red Cross to make the first of three visits to political prisoners. Red Cross delegates were able to see whomsoever they
wished; some prisoners found it difficult to believe that they were
not SAVAK officials attempting to provoke them. Subsequently,
the International Committee released reports that showed "a substantial and significant improvement" in the treatment of prisoners
during the last two years of the Shah's reign.

This improvement was later associated with the 1976 election of
Jimmy Carter. Undoubtedly Carter's human rights program had
an impact on the Shah; he had always wanted to be friendly with
the man in the White House, and he had always found this more
difficult with Democrats than Republicans. In fact, however, the
Shah's softening actually began before Carter's election. It was
perhaps also due to his realization that repression had not secured
a successful society, and that if the Great Civilization was to
succeed and to be handed over to his son, yet another method
should be tried. He began to talk about the success of King Juan
Carlos in shepherding Spain from dictatorship to democracy. Perhaps such an attempt should be made in Iran, he would say.
Undoubtedly, one of the most important influences on him in this
regard was the Empress. She was probably the only person around
him who consistently complained about SAVAK.

There was a famous, talented, and left-wing film director named
Ebrahim Golestan. He was invited to a party for Jacques Chirac,
and Amir Abbas Hoveyda, the prime minister, introduced him to
Chirac, saying, "He is our foremost writer and director, but we
ban all his works in Iran." A few nights later he was seized by the

police and carted off to the Central Police Station. Next morning his wife called the Empress, and she managed to have him not only released but also invited to the palace on the Caspian. The Shah remarked on his suntan and said with a half smile, "I didn't know sunbathing was allowed where you've just come from."

As the Shah made himself more remote and surrounded himself only by courtiers who would not question him, the Queen became about the only channel to him that people with a grievance could use. This infuriated many of the Shah's men and the policemen from SAVAK. In exile the Queen recalled an occasion when an industrialist had come to her with a complaint that he hoped she would pass on to the Shah. The next thing she heard was that the man had been arrested. "I said to my husband, 'It's not possible. An Iranian comes to your house, sits with me, has tea, and opens his heart to me, and the next day there is someone from SAVAK arresting him. It's very wrong. I see these people in order to report to you, and lighten your burden.' " The Shah had this man released. But the Queen often felt that SAVAK, resenting her influence, tried to undermine her. Hence the rumors that people with whom she was associated were "Communists" or "terrorists."

The Shah did not always appreciate the Queen's views. She was often rudely ignored. The Italian journalist Oriana Fallaci had elicited from him the claim that not a single woman had ever influenced him.

> In a man's life women count only if they're beautiful and graceful and know how to stay feminine. This Women's Lib business, for instance. What do these feminists want? What do you want? Equality, you say? Indeed! I don't want to seem rude, but . . . You may be equal in the eyes of the law, but not, I beg your pardon for saying so, in ability. . . . You've never produced a Michelangelo or a Bach. You've never even produced a great cook. . . . Women, when they are in power, are much harsher than men. Much more cruel, much more bloodthirsty. I'm quoting facts, not opinions. You're heartless when you're rulers. Think of Caterina de'Medici, Catherine of Russia, Elizabeth I of England. Not to mention your Lucrezia Borgia, with her poisons and intrigues. You're schemers, you're evil. Every one of you.

In 1975, the Queen poured out her problems to Sally Quinn, a formidable reporter of *The Washington Post*. "I try to talk to him, not as a queen talking to a king but as a wife talks to her husband.

Sometimes though, I care so much about something, I get so excited that I can't breathe. But I have to be so careful, because if I'm not and I start raising my voice, he will think I'm blaming him for what's wrong and he'll get angry."

Later, in exile, Farah Diba said, "Sometimes he would listen, sometimes not. You don't want your wife always giving you bad news." She wondered whether she had too often taken the side of people with a grievance. "I feel that that's what I was there for, to be on the side of the people, not the administration. My husband would say, 'Oh, for you it's always a question of life and death.' Which is true. I would get very involved and emotional."

Unlike most other members of the Shah's family, there was little stain of corruption around her. But, in time-honored style, her family gradually acquired more and more positions of influence or power. Some were avaricious. Some were able. One of her able cousins was the head of National Iranian Radio Television since the mid-sixties. He was one of the alleged "leftists" whose views and activities so aroused the dislike of some of the people around the Shah.

It was true that by 1978 many of the Queen's circle were openly and sometimes astonishingly critical of the Shah. Some of them even went so far as to declare that the Shah's "Revolution," like any other revolution, had suppressed dissent and thus prevented many able and patriotic Iranians from serving their country. This was not the sort of thing that those around the Shah liked to hear.

In the chaos of the last weeks of 1978, when everyone was giving the Shah contradictory advice, the Queen was the one constant in the palace. But like everyone else, she was confused. She too felt there was a well-organized conspiracy against the Shah. Even though there was martial law, the press was becoming wildly critical. In the parliament everyone started his speech with a quote from the Koran, which she saw as giving in to the religious leaders. Those who were in favor of the regime stayed at home, frightened. Those against were out in the streets, superbly well drilled, all organized, she thought. "All the brainwashing, the political program. Among the schoolchildren, the teachers, among the oil workers, in the ministries, the strikes—all organized long before. You can't just suddenly have people infiltrated everywhere, who know when the King or prime minister is giving a speech, or to organize strikes in the oil fields—rumors, rumors all the time. They were cutting the head off sheep and throwing the blood in the streets of Teheran, saying that these are people who have been killed."

She thought all this careful planning must have been made by Communists. "It was their sort of organization. Because we are not a disciplined people."

She did not consider that the regime was blameless. She said later that perhaps the changes in Iran had been too fast and that expectations had been raised far beyond anything the government could provide. That made everyone unhappy. But she was certain that the basic principles of the White Revolution were a matter of pride. "I loved my country, wanted to work hard for an Iran whose social values I could understand, where there could be some justice. The land reform, emancipation of women, nationalization of some of our natural resources, and many other things made me proud to be part of the country."

Sitting in her mother's apartment in the Sixteenth Arrondissement of Paris years later, she said, "Nobody really studied the differences between Iran thirty-seven years ago and when the Shah left. The good things that were done, and what was not done well. It's not that we didn't have problems, difficulties, and shortcomings, but it is worth comparing Iran with [other] countries in our own situation, in the Middle East, among the Third World. . . . My husband had a vision as head of state—a vision of the world, a vision of Iran. We were friendly with most countries of the world, East and West. We had economic and cultural relations with all of them. . . . Iran was a country with a lot of capacity. Of course we had not only a great civilization, which we were proud of, but we had natural wealth and we had human wealth. . . . It is so sad when one thinks what is happening today."

CHAPTER TWELVE

The Scapegoat

The news came to Paradise Island on a high-powered radio set given to them by King Hassan. The Shah, the Queen, and the staff listened every day to Radio Teheran.

On April 7 they heard that after a rushed sentence of death, Amir Abbas Hoveyda, the Shah's prime minister, and then minister of court throughout the rise of imperial Iran and into its decline, had been executed. "I shut myself up for a whole day and prayed," said the Shah later. He had cause for remorse; Hoveyda died because the Shah had allowed him to be used as a scapegoat.

Hoveyda's grandfather was a Baha'i, a religion that developed in the mid-nineteenth century. It is non-Muslim; indeed, it is an ecumenical religion that looks to all the other religions of the world for inspiration. It is intensely disliked by the Shiite clergy, partly because its initial followers were Muslim apostates (a capital offense under Islamic law) and partly because it believes in a new revelation coming after and superseding the Koran. In the past many of its followers had been educated in the West and were employed by Westerners, particularly the British. The mullahs therefore often saw them as British agents. The Shah had more Baha'is in his entourage than many Muslims thought appropriate. (After the revolution there was a purge of the Baha'is in Iran and thousands were murdered.)

Hoveyda's father had left the Baha'is and Hoveyda was brought up within Islam by his mother, who was from the family of the Qajar shahs. His father became minister to Saudi Arabia.

Hoveyda himself was educated in Beirut, and later took a degree in political science at the University of Brussels before taking classes at the Sorbonne where France and French literature became abiding loves of his life. He became a diplomat and then joined the National Iranian Oil Company in 1956.*

Hoveyda was minister of finance in the Mansur government in 1964 and the Shah made him prime minister after Mansur was assassinated in 1965. For a time he was an effective prime minister. The best years of the Shah's reign were the mid-sixties, and Hoveyda presided over them.

He was a Freemason, member of a French lodge, and, as such, close to many French politicians and businessmen. He was round and balding, and looked rather like a caricature of an Italian friar. He was as jolly as such caricatures are supposed to be. Unlike many of those in the Pahlavi court, he was not thought to be greatly interested in women and was divorced from his wife, a pretty, vivacious and outspoken woman named Leila, who came from an old and distinguished family, with mullahs on her father's side. She had a profitable orchid business; she and Hoveyda remained on close terms and every day Leila sent her former husband an orchid for his buttonhole. He was nothing if not elegant, even though he often dressed informally in leather jackets and casual trousers from Lanvin. Following a car accident he walked always with a stick and a slight limp.

He was cultivated, well read, and also witty. Among the celebrated stories about him was one concerning Richard Helms, the former director of the CIA, who was appointed ambassador to Teheran in 1973. The Soviet ambassador, Vladimir Yerofeyev, went up to Hoveyda at a party at the prime minister's residence and said with a sneer, "We hear that the Americans are sending their Number One spy to Iran." Hoveyda looked at him calmly and replied, "The Americans are our friends. At least they don't send us their Number Ten spy."

In a nation of either courtiers or internal exiles, Hoveyda was

---

* Hoveyda's last diplomatic posting was to the embassy in Ankara; the ambassador was General Hassan Arfa, who had had a distinguished military career since the beginning of the century. (He called his autobiography *Under Five Shahs*.) Unfortunately, by the second half of the fifties General Arfa was not as effective an ambassador as he had been a soldier. One of his customs was to have his staff report to him every day standing in a line in order of their height. Hoveyda found the ambassador intolerable.

one of the very few politicians. He had an ability to make easy friendships; Canadian Prime Minister Pierre Trudeau liked him at once, and so did Alexei Kosygin. Anthony Parsons, the British ambassador, considered him one of his closest friends. So also did many European writers, particularly French.

Corrupt? In one sense everyone intimately involved with the Shah was corrupt, or corrupted—that was the nature of the system. The corruption took many forms, and desire to be close to the King was perhaps the most powerful. Hoveyda wanted that, to be sure. But many of his peers wanted fortunes as well. He was one of the few in positions of great authority who was thought to be financially honest on his own account. He had the use of a lavish prime minister's residence, but he lived modestly enough himself. Still, he was skeptical to the point of cynicism and (like the Shah himself) he appreciated the use of graft. At least in the more moderately corrupt sixties, he waved a limp dismissal at the payoffs and the percentages in which so many courtiers and officials were immersed. "Ah well, it keeps the boys happy," he would say, with a little sigh or an amused smile. Like other ministers, he had a secret budget—it was said to be over $100 million —with which he could reward lavishly those whom he chose.

In the seventies, Hoveyda described himself as managing director of Iran, to the Shah's chairman of the board. Many of his Cabinet ministers were gifted. Indeed, Anthony Parsons, the British ambassador, remarked that, "Never in my career had I encountered such a glittering array of talent" as in the Iranian government. Some senior officials were women—which was a remarkable leap forward in an Islamic country. (The minister of education, Mrs. Farrokhrou Parsa, was executed after the revolution.) There were some areas in which Hoveyda and his Cabinet could make decisions on their own. But such was the nature of the monarchy that it was generally thought more appropriate to ascribe all Cabinet decisions to the Shah himself. Indeed, almost every order was signed by "His Imperial Majesty," rather than by the prime minister, still less by individual ministers. Moreover, there were vast areas of government that the Shah arrogated to himself. SAVAK, defense, and foreign affairs were outside the prime minister's control.*

---

* This is not to say that Hoveyda ignored everything to do with SAVAK. In 1973 he responded to an appeal from Jerzy Kosinski, president of American PEN, and secured the release from prison of a group of Iranian intellectuals. But in 1976, when the whole Pahlavi experiment

He was not one of those few counselors of the Shah who occasionally dared question him. On the contrary, he wished away the problems caused by the forced march toward the Great Civilization in the mid-seventies. Puffing contentedly on his Dunhill pipe, he told one incredulous American writer, "In Western countries, you talk too much about things, take them from committee to committee. Here we just go to the Shah and then act." He insisted that even though there weren't enough teachers, students could teach elementary school and within two years Iran's own satellite would be broadcasting televised lessons to all schools. The fact that most villages were still without electricity was not a problem —"We'll use batteries." Milk would be distributed to every school child in the country. So what if there were only ten thousand doctors? Medical care could still be made widely available by hiring foreigners and purchasing fully staffed hospitals from the U.S. and Europe. "We don't mind if the nurses are blond."

However, as the years went by, Hoveyda knew he was running an increasingly rotten system. While publicly embracing the Shah's development dreams, he was privately opposed to the massive arms purchases, and he realized that after the oil price rises of 1973–74, corruption became grotesque. At one dinner he pointed across the room to a fabulously rich Iranian businessman and said, "This gentleman has just earned six hundred times my salary in one deal." On several occasions among friends, he pounded the table and cursed the corruption of the Shah's family. During one such dinner in 1978, the telephone rang for him. He apparently heard that one of the princesses had just had the Imperial Guard arrest one of her foreign business partners. She was aggrieved with the man, and to secure his release, the man had to pay the Princess a million dollars. Hoveyda returned to his companions and said, "The regime is dying inside."

In 1978, Hoveyda finally persuaded the Shah to agree to set up a code of business conduct for his family. But it was so late as to be meaningless; it merely won Hoveyda more hatred in the family. "They considered Iran a business, not a country," says Leila, Hoveyda's widow. Now the family, ranged with many of the

---

was beginning to fall apart, Hoveyda took a much stronger public line in defense of SAVAK. When the International Commission of Jurists issued a report accusing SAVAK of systematic torture of prisoners, Hoveyda accused the ICJ of being financed by the CIA. This was an unusual complaint coming from the head of a government that had been installed by the CIA.

Amir Abbas Hoveyda on trial

generals, whose greed and fantastic military ambitions he mocked, were against him.

Perhaps because of his distance from the family, and because of his reputation for modest living, he retained considerable popularity in the country. One evening in early 1978, just after the riots in Qom, which were the first of the serious assaults upon the throne, Hoveyda drove the British ambassador Anthony Parsons to South Teheran, the poor part of town. They were stuck in a traffic jam and people recognized Hoveyda, crowding around the car, kissing him, patting him through the window. Parsons said what a pleasure it was to be driven by so popular a politician and asked why the Shah did not have a dialogue with his critics.

Hoveyda replied that he had always tried to keep in touch with the people. But as for the Shah, "Well, Tony, you know His Majesty's definition of a dialogue. It is, 'I speak, you listen.' He will not change."

Hoveyda's many friends found him a man of immense charm and friendliness. He was not arrogant and, unlike most of those around the Pahlavis, he could laugh at himself—and (in private) at the Family. One of his protégés, Parviz Radji, wrote that he was cunning as well as clever, and would sometimes argue ruthlessly, but that he tried to be kind to his colleagues. Radji recalled one occasion on which Hoveyda lost his composure and reduced a subordinate to tears. Then the prime minister called the aide back "and threw the curved handle of his ubiquitous walking stick around the man's neck, pulling him gently forward. He then kissed him on both cheeks, expressing regret for his excessive harshness."

But Hoveyda's critics were fierce. Some, like Ardeshir Zahedi, blamed him for many of the ills which befell the regime. Others could argue that by lending his intellect and culture to the Pahlavis, he gave them a respectability—especially in Europe—which they did not deserve. He was also subsequently rebuked for the fact that he never contradicted the Shah. Bur nor did any other minister or senior official. When Assadollah Alam, the minister of court, did offer some unwelcome advice in the mid-seventies, the Shah said to the other officials, "Alam is becoming senile." Still, some thought that Hoveyda went further than obedience. He understood the Shah so well, that he was able to anticipate his wishes. He pandered to his need for reassurance, he flattered him by comparing him with his hero, de Gaulle. And thus he, like other counselors, helped increase the Shah's estrangement from the real people and the real problems of Iran.

By the summer of 1978, the religious leaders in Qom, many leading politicians, and his personal enemies were urging the Shah to arrest Hoveyda. At first the Shah resisted, telling his associates that this would be tantamount to putting himself on trial. At one point in August 1978, he suggested Hoveyda leave Iran and become ambassador to Belgium; Hoveyda refused.

But as summer turned to autumn the Shah seems to have become more persuaded that scapegoats might save him. In early November 1978, he forced General Nassiri, the former head of SAVAK, to fly back from Pakistan, where he was now ambassador. He was arrested in Teheran. General Khademi, the former head of Iran Air, committed suicide when he learned he too was about to be arrested. The Shah told Anthony Parsons that he was under pressure from his generals to arrest Hoveyda as well.

Parsons was appalled. He declared to the Shah that Hoveyda had been his friend of twenty years, but quite apart from that, to arrest him would be to arrest the Shah, to try him and condemn him would be to try and condemn the Shah himself. Parsons thought it was almost a suicidal act.

The Shah was silent at the end of Parsons' outburst and then muttered something about not liking political vendettas. Parsons, rather surprised by his own boldness, pushed on, and told the Shah what he thought about the corruption of the royal family.

The Shah asked him to be specific, so Parsons listed the rumors concerning the business activities of all the princes, princesses, and their hangers-on. The Shah took no offense and two days later announced that an investigation into the family's dealings would begin.

Alarmed by what the Shah had said, Parsons called Hoveyda to warn him that his former master might be about to betray him. He suggested that Hoveyda flee while he could. Hoveyda laughed into the telephone and said, "My dear Tony, I am an Iranian and I have done nothing that I am ashamed of. I have absolutely no intention of running away. If it comes to a trial I shall have plenty to say. In any case, I have a lot of detective stories to read and must stay where I am to finish them!"

Then the Shah himself called Hoveyda and said, "For your own safety, I am asking you to place yourself under house arrest." Hoveyda telephoned Leila, his ex-wife, and asked her to come over.

On the evening of November 8, three officers, one of whom was also later executed, came to arrest him. Hoveyda was not only polite but asked them to have a drink and then dinner with him. Leila was not so hospitable and told the officers they had destroyed the country.

"You shat on Iran. And through a funnel to make sure that none of it should be wasted," she declared. After dinner, they took him away.

Cartoons ridiculing and abusing Hoveyda immediately began to appear in the press. For the next two and a half months he lived reasonably comfortably; he was not in prison, but in three different places of detention, the last of them a SAVAK house in a park. Leila and Hoveyda's niece, Dr. Fereshteh Razavi, were able to bring him food.

On Christmas Eve, Anthony Parsons went to bid formal farewell to the Queen before his recall to London in mid-January. It was a surreal occasion. Iran was in revolutionary ferment, a senior American oil official had just been shot, expatriate workers were being pulled out, oil production was almost at a standstill, gangs of demonstrators were roaming the streets. Yet there was the British ambassador in frock coat and top hat and his wife in a hat and long gloves on their way to a palace that was empty now of all but illusions.

The Queen was calm but detached. Parsons asked her how he

could get in touch with Hoveyda. He knew he could not help him, but he wrote later, "I owed it to my long friendship at least to say good-bye, and I knew that he had always been very close to the Empress." He was shocked by her response. "She appeared uninterested and scarcely concerned about Hoveyda's fate."

A few weeks later, just before the Queen herself left the country, another of Hoveyda's friends went to her to ask her to try to have Hoveyda released. "It's out of our hands," she replied. By this time, the Shah and Queen felt they had no authority in the country the Shah had ruled absolutely until so recently. When they flew out, they made no move to take Hoveyda with them.

On February 11, 1979, ten days after Khomeini returned to Teheran, the Army collapsed and the streets filled with exultant and sometimes vengeful crowds. Prisons were attacked and several of the Shah's imprisoned ministers escaped. The military guards at the house where Hoveyda and other prisoners were being kept disappeared. For the second time, Hoveyda refused to run away.

He called his friend Manoucher Shahgoli, the former minister of health, who offered to pick him up and spirit him off at once. But Hoveyda insisted, "I can't escape while my ministers are in jail." He did want assurances that he would be properly tried and eventually just such a promise was given to him.

He called Leila, who had by now left for Paris. She too told him to flee. He refused. "He was foolish," she said later in her apartment on the Avenue Foch. "He didn't think like an Iranian. He was more European. So much time abroad; he spoke better French and Arabic than Farsi. But why didn't he remember the French Revolution, of which he had read so much? He thought he was clean. And he would have been very unhappy if he had run away and then seen all his ministers killed while he was safe."

His niece, Fereshteh Razavi, arranged with the new authorities that she and a lawyer and a mullah and a soldier should all go to pick him up to take him to prison. They went in an ambulance. Immediately after Hoveyda was led on board, the mullah asked him why he had allowed the sale of alcohol and other crimes against Muslim law. Hoveyda replied that he was not yet before a tribunal and would not answer. They asked him to lie on a stretcher to escape detection. He refused.

The ambulance, with the mullah in a car in front to clear the crowds, drove to the school where Khomeini had his headquarters. There Hoveyda was searched by a soldier who refused to let him talk. He was then transferred to Qasr prison.

The revolution was producing turmoil in Iran. Throughout the countryside thousands of revolutionary committees, known as komitehs, sprang up. They were extensions of the neighborhood committees that had been formed throughout 1978 to encourage the revolution, but suddenly they were much more numerous and much more powerful and, in many cases, well armed. They served as the terroristic arm of the revolution, stopping people associated with the ancien régime, searching homes, dragging people off to prison. They were quite outside the control of the Bazargan government.

Alongside the komitehs, and much more closely controlled by the new government, were the revolutionary courts. It was always Khomeini's intention to put members of the Shah's regime on trial. He could hardly do otherwise given the accusations of murder and plunder that had been so vociferously hurled against the Shah and his associates. But the nature of the justice to come was not something that had ever been spelled out.

The day after Hoveyda surrendered himself he was displayed in Khomeini's schoolhouse, along with three of the Shah's generals, including General Rabii, the air force commander till the day before. They were introduced to the foreign press as "some of the honorable thieves who have run this country for the last ten years."

Hoveyda was leaning on his cane and looked tired, but he attempted some of his old joviality. He said he expected a fair trial and was eager to face it. "I take responsibility for my actions and I am not afraid because I believe in God."

They were interrogated, on television, by one of Khomeini's associates, Ibrahim Yazdi, who was an American citizen who had previously been teaching chemistry at Baylor University in Texas. "The principal Jacobin interrogator," the U.S. embassy called him in a cable to Washington. When Yazdi told Hoveyda that he was being held because of the "crimes he and his henchmen committed against the nation," Hoveyda responded that the prosecution "should be made in court."

Unlike Hoveyda, General Nassiri, the former head of SAVAK, looked terrified. He was interrogated for about two hours on television. His head and his neck were wrapped in blood-soaked bandages. His face was bloody from scalp wounds. His voice croaked through an obviously crushed thorax. He said he knew nothing of torture by SAVAK agents; he had to answer only to the Shah, whom he saw twice a week. Hoveyda also denied he knew anything of torture. He cautioned one Iranian journalist, "Don't forget, we all lived under the same system."

A few days later Nassiri and three other generals were given summary trials in the schoolhouse. They were found guilty of "torture, killing the people, treason to the country, spreading sedition on earth." The death sentences were pronounced by Sadeq Khalkhali, a middle-level cleric and enthusiastic follower of Khomeini who seems to have been distinguished by his sadism. Until 1979 he was known, if at all, for the pleasure he took in strangling cats.

As soon as the sentences were pronounced, the generals were led onto the roof of Khomeini's headquarters, ordered to lie spread-eagled, and were shot. A few days later another four senior officers of the Shah were summarily tried and executed. All these executions were carried out without the authority of the prime minister, Mehdi Bazargan, by a new, secret organization, the Islamic Revolutionary Council. By the middle of March about seventy people, most of them members of SAVAK or the Army, had been put to death after secret and in most cases very hurried trials. It was done partly out of revenge, partly out of a blood lust, partly to ensure that there really could be no counterrevolution by senior army officers.

Bazargan, who had been a civil rights activist under the Shah, described the procedures as "shameful," as did several of the more moderate clerics. Bazargan went so far as to denounce the summary executions as a disgrace that tarnished the image of the revolution and brought protests from just those human rights organizations that had protested the abuses of the Shah's regime. In mid-March, Bazargan managed to persuade Khomeini to stop the process until proper regulations could be drawn up.

Then the revolutionary prosecutor journeyed to see Khomeini in Qom to ask him to restore the executions. "If you don't do it, we will kill all the prisoners without any form of trial," he said. The ayatollah himself believed that any insistence on normal judicial procedures reflected "the Western sickness among us," that those on trial were criminals, and "criminals should not be tried; they should be killed."

By this time the trial of Hoveyda had been announced. The

prosecution demanded the death sentence for his crimes, which were said to have included corruption, antireligious activity, following the dictates of the United States and Britain, surrendering Iran's resources to foreigners, spying "for the West and Zionism," "direct participation" in smuggling heroin into France, and turning the country into a consumer market for foreign goods. He was not accused of causing bloodshed.

Posing as his doctor, his niece was able to visit him twice in prison. The first time was the day that the first four generals were shot. "It's a dangerous illness," he said to her. She then sent him a Koran with verses that might be useful for his defense underlined. This he received.

Next time she saw him, he was huddled on the cold, damp floor of a tiny cell without a lavatory. He managed to slip her a letter which she smuggled out of prison. In it he wrote that he now knew he would be condemned and executed, but it was better than staying in prison.

Fereshteh Razavi left for Paris to try to help raise an international appeal. This was not hard. Almost every prime minister and foreign minister in Europe was a friend of Hoveyda and there was widespread outrage against the treatment he was receiving. Kurt Waldheim, the UN secretary general, asked for clemency. Edgar Faure, the French politician and lawyer, offered to defend him.

In fact Hoveyda was denied any form of legal assistance. But shortly before he was actually put on trial in early April, he was visited by a French television crew. The interview was conducted by a French television reporter, Christine Ockrent.

Ockrent had seen Abolhassan Bani-Sadr, an aide to Khomeini. Although he was a rival of Prime Minister Bazargan, he agreed with Bazargan that Hoveyda's trial should be "exemplary" in order to help "legitimize" or "legalize" the revolution. He arranged for Ockrent to see the public prosecutor, Mahdi Hadavi, whom she later described as the Fouquier-Tinville of the Iranian revolution.*

---

* Antoine Fouquier-Tinville was the French public prosecutor during the French revolutionary Terror. He presided over the trial of Georges Danton and Camille Desmoulins in April 1794. Fouquier-Tinville was "pale and rather stout, with thick black hair, thin lips, a pockmarked nose, jutting chin and small glittering eyes." He was widely dreaded, for it was known that he was more than ready to enable the authorities to destroy whom they wished through his courts, whatever the actual burden of evidence.

The night before Danton was arrested, his friends urged him to flee. Like Hoveyda, two

Mr. Hadavi had a pale, narrow, ill-shaven face. He picked at a bowl of rice and at his teeth while abstractedly looking over the supplicants who had come to beg him for news of or access to their loved ones. One woman, completely robed in the new fashion of black, complained, "They've arrested my brother." "Well, he was SAVAK, of course," came the reply from Hadavi. She bent to kiss his hand as she left.

With Hadavi's permission, Ockrent and her crew were driven to Qasr prison. The gates were surrounded by people clamoring for news. "Are you going in? Could you see if my brother, my father is there?" A young man in a silk scarf and designer glasses said, "My father is a general. He has disappeared. I think he is in there."

They were hustled through the gates and were marched through dark passages to Hoveyda's cell. He was lying on a cot in the corner, wearing a velvet cap and white socks. Ockrent scarcely recognized him, without the orchids, the charm, the luster.

"We are from French Television, sir, France Three," said Ockrent. "Sir, we have permission to talk to you. So many people are anxious for news of you."

Hoveyda was not happy. "It's not worth asking me questions. A scapegoat should be allowed to keep silent, it's better that way."

Ockrent sat on the end of Hoveyda's cot. He asked her, "Tell me, the press conference the other night, was that the beginning of my trial or not?" She thought he had no clue what was happening to him and so she began to ask him the questions that she said all the world wanted to hear answered.

"Did you know what tortures were being inflicted in your prisons?"

Hoveyda said he did not.

"How could the prime minister not be aware of what was happening?"

---

centuries later, he refused. "A man," he responded, "cannot carry his country away with him on the soles of his shoes." At his trial he conducted himself with great courage and bravado, quite intimidating Fouquier-Tinville by his defiance. "The Court now knows Danton. Tomorrow he hopes to sleep in the bosom of glory. He has never asked for pardon and you will see him go to the scaffold with the calm of a clear conscience. . . . I demand that the Convention establish a commission to hear my denunciation of the present dictatorship. Yes, I, Danton, will unmask the dictatorship which is now revealing itself in its true colors. . . . You say I have sold myself. A man such as me has no price. . . ." In vain did Fouquier-Tinville try to quiet him.

In response to her questions, he replied, "I am not guilty. There was a *domaine réservé.*" The crimes of the Shah were the Shah's alone.

Ockrent thanked him for his time and he had replied with a smile, "Oh, you know, my program is very full! You have brought me a little of the atmosphere of France and I thank you. Forgive my poor hospitality. I have nothing else to offer." Off camera, he said he had confidence in Iran's judicial system and was certain he would be acquitted.*

On April 5 new regulations governing the revolutionary courts were promulgated. Crimes were loosely defined as "crimes against the people," "crimes against the revolution," "ruining the economy," and "violation of the people's honor." Defendants were given very few rights. Hoveyda was immediately taken from his cell to be tried.

He sat in casual clothes on a white wooden chair before two small tables in a courtroom crowded with about one hundred men, mostly Islamic guards.

Full records of the trial have not been released and it is not known how Hoveyda defended his record. According to such partial official accounts of the trial that were released, he declared, "I was a link in the system and I had no interest in politics but I was drawn into it." He said the policies of his government were not wrong, but they needed more time to achieve results. He had not acted differently from other prime ministers; like them he had accepted the Shah "as one who did not have to account for his deeds." He said his hands were stained with neither blood nor

---

* When the film was shown in France two weeks later, it caused an outcry. One columnist in *Figaro* declared, "This affair is revolting. A journalist does not have the right to take part in such a masquerade. One does not interrogate a political prisoner in his cell with his enemies sitting by. One does not demand if he is or is not guilty. One does not try to extort from him declarations which can be used against him to send him to the place of execution. . . . The question is not whether Hoveyda is guilty or not. The question is that it is not for Madame Ockrent to decide and that in asking questions on torture, she is behaving as an accuser, worse, a provocateur, not to say a prison spy."

In her own defense, Ockrent wrote a long account of the macabre nature of the Teheran judicial system; she said that she had told Hoveyda of the efforts being made on his behalf by his French friends. He had been moved.

Ockrent pointed out also that she was bringing to the world the voice and the look of a man whom the world needed to remember. "We were neither his prosecutors nor his advocates. We were his echo." He had been kept silent since the Shah had arrested him; the press did not have the right to be part of that conspiracy of silence, nor to allow political prisoners "to stagnate in arbitrary isolation."

money. According to Radio Teheran, Hoveyda "asked forgiveness from the youths who were arrested, jailed, and tortured by the people under his power." He also asked God to forgive his sins and said he accepted the verdict of the court because it was a just Islamic court.

The court found Hoveyda a "doer of mischief on earth" and a traitor to the Iranian nation. "Hoveyda was the symbol of thirteen of the darkest years in the life of the Iranian nation," declared Radio Teheran. "Hoveyda was a player who sat at the opposite side of a chessboard to the crowned murderer and watched the murder of the Islamic masses. . . . He carried out the program of the American plunderers and other plundering countries in our country. . . . What else could there be except death for the one who dragged our nation to its death?"

Immediately after the death sentence was pronounced, Sadeq Khalkhali rushed around the prison ordering all the doors to be locked and the telephones disconnected. He knew the scale of international concern and he knew also that Prime Minister Bazargan and other senior officials wanted no summary trial and execution.

Within minutes, Hoveyda was dragged into the prison yard. He was tied to a metal ladder and shot. The first bullets hit him in the neck but did not kill him. He was ordered by his executioner, a mullah, to hold up his head. The next bullet hit him in the head and he died. His body was then trucked to the city morgue.

His niece Fereshteh was asked to identify his corpse. In the morgue she was shown first the bodies of all the others killed that day. They were filled with bullets. Then they opened a drawer to show her Hoveyda.

Paris Match published a picture of the body watched by three militants, one of whom was carrying a machine gun and smiling. *Match* published alongside it a photograph of the royal family swimming on Paradise Island.

The Shah made no immediate statement, because the Bahamian authorities had enjoined him to silence on political matters. Later he wrote an article in *Le Monde* insisting he had tried to save his prime minister. Later still he wrote in his memoirs that he wanted "to make some clarifications which seem to me to be necessary. During the fall of 1978, the most diverse methods were employed to accuse the administration. Amir Abbas Hoveyda served as the scapegoat."

Afterward Sadeq Khalkhali, the cat strangler, frequently related, with pride, and often with giggles, how he executed Hoveyda. Khalkhali was a small, fat man whose clothes looked a mess and whose eyes seemed frantic behind their glasses.

He told one Teheran newspaper that he had "probably" sentenced four hundred people to death in Teheran by summer 1979. "On some nights, he said, bodies of thirty or more people would be sent out in trucks from the prison." He said there had been a plot, hatched in the South Korean embassy, to rescue Hoveyda and others. As soon as he heard of it he decided to deal a blow to the CIA and Zionism by bringing forward their cases and executing them in one evening.

In August 1979 Khalkhali told the writer V. S. Naipaul, who had an interview with him in front of some of his disciples in Qom, "I am very clever, very intelligent. . . . The mullahs are going to rule now. We are going to have ten thousand years of the Islamic Republic. The Marxists will go on with their Lenin. We will go on in the way of Khomeini."

He then said gravely, "I killed Hoveyda, you know." He said this with a straight face, but Naipaul recorded that the Iranians around him "threw themselves about with laughter."

Naipaul asked him if he had killed Hoveyda himself. The answer was no. "But I have the gun," Khalkhali said, as though it was the next best thing. According to Naipaul, everyone again rolled about the carpet with laughter.

CHAPTER THIRTEEN

The Ambassador

For a few weeks in the Bahamas, the Shah had hoped that he might find refuge in the country with which his relations—and his father's relations—had always been most tortured: Great Britain. That hope was fostered, for a short time, by the election on May 3, 1979, of Margaret Thatcher as prime minister of Great Britain.

Several years before, Mohammed Behbehanian, the Shah's personal financier, had bought for the Shah a large equestrian estate called Stilemans in the stockbroker belt of Surrey, south of London. In early 1979, while he was in Morocco, the British press had been filled with rumors that he might want to come and settle in Surrey. There was talk of tank traps being dug in the gardens.

The Shah made no formal application to come to Britain, but a number of his British friends and supporters quietly approached the British government to ask for such permission.*

According to well-founded rumors on the diplomatic circuit,

---

* It would have been hard for the Shah himself to make an approach. His feelings about Britain were equivocal. On one occasion in 1977 when his ambassador to London suggested he should stop abusing the British in interviews and should compliment them instead, the Shah had replied with anger in his voice, "Compliments? I can't pay them compliments if I don't believe in what I say. . . . I can't . . . praise a people who twice invaded my country and jeopardized its integrity." He hesitated a moment, and then, as if he had suddenly found the solution, he said, "You pay them compliments. That's right—you sing their praises. That's what ambassadors are for."

the most discreet and perhaps the most tantalizing of these suggestions came from the sovereign, Queen Elizabeth II. Her constitutional position did not allow her to instruct the government on
how it should act in any matter. But at the beginning of 1979 she
was said to have expressed the view that she felt Britain should
show the Shah loyalty for the long years in which he had supported British interests in the Middle East. It was said she believed
that states must recognize personal as well as national obligations.

In taking this view, the Queen would have been reacting very
differently from her grandfather, King George V, who had urged
the British government not to give refuge to his cousin, Czar
Nicholas II, when he was under threat during the Russian Revolution. The king had been afraid that such a gesture might spread
the contagion of bolshevism in Britain.*

In spring 1979, the British Labour government found itself in a
quandary. When the Shah was still clinging to power, the foreign
secretary, David Owen, had publicly supported him, saying,
"Real friends are those who stand by you when you are under
attack." Now, after the Shah's fall, Owen still defended Britain's
stated commitment to him, despite much scoffing from Conservative members of Parliament and abuse from his own left wing.

"Maybe we made mistakes," he had acknowledged in Parliament in early 1979, but he justified British support because of the
economic consequences that the Shah's fall would have for Britain.
Loss of Iranian orders would mean a rise in British unemployment
and a fall in the British standard of living. In any case, Owen

* In March 1917, the Provisional Government in Russia asked that the czar be granted asylum
in Britain. The British prime minister, David Lloyd George, agreed and the British government formally offered asylum to the czar and his family. But the king objected strongly,
despite the fact that he considered Nicholas a beloved cousin and close ally. He had his
private secretary write several letters to the government asking that the invitation be withdrawn. In one such letter the secretary, Sir Arthur Bigge Stamfordham, wrote to the foreign
secretary, "He must beg you to represent to the Prime Minister that from all he hears and
reads in the press, the residence in this country of the ex-Emperor and Empress would be
strongly resented by the public, and would undoubtedly compromise the position of the
King and Queen. [The Russian government should be told] that the opposition to the Emperor and Empress coming here is so strong that we must be allowed to withdraw from the
consent previously given to the Russian government's proposal." At the king's insistence the
invitation was quietly dropped. In April 1918, the czar and his family were taken to Ekater-
inburg where, in July, they were shot. George V's biographer, Kenneth Rose, wrote that
"the King, by persuading his government to withdraw their original offer of asylum, deprived
the Imperial family of their best, perhaps their only, means of escape."

declared, he was "prepared to be justified by history." This remark aroused some mirth for its grandeur. "History may have other things on its mind," said one Conservative member of Parliament.

But when it became clear that the Shah needed an asylum, the government's notions of "real friendship" had begun to change. The queen's views, expressed only privately, were discounted. Whitehall began to make it clear that the Shah would be better placed elsewhere. The difficulty of providing adequate security was cited.

In early March 1979 the government insisted in Parliament that it had received no formal request for a visa from the Shah. This was true. But informal soundings had been made. Among those who had made representations were ex-King Constantine of Greece, who had himself been given refuge in Britain, and Sir Shapoor Reporter, a shadowy British agent and businessman who had lived most of his life in Teheran.*

Another intermediary was a British television journalist named Alan Hart, who had made films in Iran in the mid-seventies. Hart had visited the Shah and the Queen in Morocco. The Queen, he said later, had just received an unpleasant letter from Princess Ashraf in which Ashraf blamed the Queen for everything that had befallen Iran. The Queen told him she had no idea where they could go next. Hart said he would try to persuade the Irish government to take them. Dublin said no.

Hart had access to a more important contact—Margaret Thatcher, the leader of the Conservative Party in Britain. The general election was imminent and, after months of strikes and industrial action already known as "the winter of discontent," it seemed likely that the Labour government would be thrown out of office in favor of the Conservatives.

Mrs. Thatcher had already been dubbed "The Iron Lady" by

---

* Sir Shapoor Reporter, KBE, secret agent and businessman extraordinaire, symbolized well the bizarre and confusing relationship between Britain and Iran.

There used to be a tradition in the British secret service, MI6, for jobs to be handed down from father to son. Shapoor's father was a Parsi Indian who came from Bombay to Teheran in 1893 as the agent of the Parsis. He developed friendships in the British Legation and then began to work for the British. It was he who introduced General Ironside to Reza Khan, and it was Ironside who encouraged Reza Khan to seize power. Subsequently, Shapoor Reporter inherited his father's position as a British agent. He then became a middleman as well, selling British arms to the Shah. He made a fortune. In a 1976 bribes trial in London, he was described as "Mr. Fixit" and he was said to have received £1 million commission on one arms deal.

the Russians for her hard-line criticisms of Soviet policy. She rejoiced in this sobriquet and liked to present herself as a much stauncher supporter of British and Western interests than her socialist opponents. When Hart visited her at Scotney Castle, then her weekend home in Kent, she was receptive. She had visited Iran, had been impressed by the appearance of progress, and considered the Shah an important ally. Now she told Hart, "I would be ashamed to be British if we could not give the Shah refuge." They arranged that Hart should call her at home a week after the election, if she won.

Hart conveyed this promise to the Shah in Morocco. The Shah had two questions: Will she win, and will she keep her word? Hart said he thought the answer was yes to both. The Shah and Queen were delighted. Then, on May 3, 1979, Margaret Thatcher was elected prime minister. On Paradise Island they drank a toast; their expectations were high. Queen Farah subsequently recalled that Hart had told her, "Mrs. Thatcher said, 'When I come to power I give you my word I will let you come.' " Robert Armao said later, "I believe Mrs. T. put her hand on her heart and said, 'On my word.' "

At last, they thought, their peregrinations were over. No more being shuffled around the world on the cusp of power, the guest of uneasy princes or unscrupulous entrepreneurs. Instead they could settle into one of their own homes, Stilemans. Robert Armao was sent to England. He thought the house ideal.

A week after the election, Hart called Mrs. Thatcher as arranged. She was cooking breakfast for her husband Denis. According to Hart, she said she was sure it would be all right. But soon, hesitant whispers came via third parties to the Bahamas from London; Mrs. Thatcher was not as resolute as she had declared. And then there arrived a most unexpected visitor, a former senior British diplomat whom the Shah knew well. But the strange thing was that he was traveling in disguise, without a wig but with a funny name and a false passport. Sir Denis Wright, GCMG, had flown into the Bahamas.

Mrs. Thatcher's promise to the Shah had been referred to the Foreign Office soon after her election. One of the deputy under secretaries was now Sir Anthony Parsons, who had returned from Teheran earlier in the year and was even now mourning the murder of his friend Hoveyda. The Foreign Office objected to the

Shah's entering Britain. It put forward three reasons.

The first was security. Officials argued that it would be very hard to protect the Shah against the anger of many of the twenty thousand or so Iranian students in Britain. Not all were revolutionaries, but some undoubtedly were. Moreover, the Shah had his own heavily armed security guards. Sensible enough, perhaps, but not quite the sort of private army that Britain appreciated. The press stories of tank traps at Stilemans were unsettling to the neighbors. (In fact, according to Alan Hart, the Shah had agreed that he would accept British police protection as adequate.)

The second objection was economic. Britain's relations with Iran had once been based on the superiority of British power but were now dominated by Britain's need to compete for the vastly profitable trade that had developed. Indeed, Parsons himself acknowledged that pushing British exports had played a disproportionate part in the work of his embassy—so that he and his staff had paid too little attention to the clouds of dissent looming over the horizon. Until 1978, the embassy had been unashamedly gung ho about the Shah, and the prospects for British sales.

Now that the Shah was gone, some of the deals might not survive, and economic relations might be cut back. But these were early days in the new government and its import needs would continue to be great. If Britain were to admit the Shah, the Iranians would react by blocking all British trade, including oil. The financial losses and the loss of jobs in Britain would be great.

Mrs. Thatcher was inclined to reject both these objections. She shared the opinion of Henry Kissinger that friends were to be stood by.

But the Foreign Office still had objection number three. This was that if the Shah came to Britain, Iran was in such revolutionary turmoil that the British embassy would be seized. Then the ambassador and his staff would be held hostage and the Iranians would demand that the Shah be traded for them.

The Iron Lady bent.

The question now was how to tell the Shah. Since Mrs. Thatcher had pledged herself to welcoming him, Britain had now to make some sort of official response. Sir Anthony Parsons called Sir Denis Wright at his cottage in Buckinghamshire.

Sir Denis was the mid-twentieth-century embodiment of that two-hundred-year-old phenomenon, the Englishman among the Persians. He was a diplomat who had served in Iran in the fifties and had been ambassador there from 1963 to 1971—throughout the White Revolution. He was also a distinguished student of the relationship between the two countries. (He later published two books on the subject—*The English Amongst the Persians* and *The Persians Amongst the English*.)*

Wright's feelings about the Shah were ambiguous. By 1971 he had felt that the Shah was "beginning to get too big for his boots" and he had advised that Queen Elizabeth not attend the Persepolis celebrations. After his retirement from the diplomatic service that year, Wright paid three brief visits to Iran. He increasingly disliked what he saw and heard. Corruption seemed worse than ever. On his last visit, in 1977, he said later, he was amazed to hear denunciations of the Shah from some of his most senior, and previously docile, servants. Like many British officials, Wright was also irritated by the Shah's role in the oil price rises and by his increasingly strident denunciations of British idleness. However, in 1977 he dedicated his book, *The English Amongst the Persians*, "to my Iranian friends with the sincere wish that the progress and prosperity which have marked the first half century of Pahlavi rule will long continue."†

In spring 1979, he was dead against the idea of the Shah coming to Britain and had already publicly said so in a letter to the *Daily Telegraph*. (The *Times*, to which the former ambassador would normally have written was at that time closed by an industrial dispute.) He argued that the Iranians were so suspicious of Britain that his arrival would be taken as proof that the British government was conspiring to restore him, as in 1953. He willingly agreed to Parsons' request that he fly to Paradise with the bad news for the Shah. But he was now a director of the Shell oil company; he did not want Shell's interests in Iran to be damaged

---

* One critic, Cyrus Ghani, noted that in this second book, Wright portrayed most nineteenth-century Persian notables as venal, unscrupulous, greedy, and very cunning. "That may have been the case," noted Ghani, "but Britain as the leading parliamentary democracy in the world was not exactly pursuing a policy of liberty, justice, and freedom for the Persians, nor could its motives be equated with altruism, charity, or straightforwardness."

† After the Shah's death, Wright wrote a harsh obituary. He stated that "the Shah lived too long. Had he died in 1972 or 1973, he would have gone down in history as one of the greater post–World War II leaders . . . but he will be remembered as the king who failed, the despot who brushed aside all the unpalatable advice, surrounded himself with sycophants and undesirables, tolerated massive corruption amongst those closest to him, and flouted human rights to such an extent that he was eventually rejected by his own people and forced to abandon a country all but ruined by policies of his own making."

by his visiting with the Shah. So he said he did not want to go to Paradise as Denis Wright, GCMG. He wanted a new identity.

"Edward Wilson" arrived in dark glasses at the Ocean Club, where some of the Shah's people were staying, and asked to see Kambiz Atabai, the master of the horse, whom he knew well. Atabai recalls, "He behaved in a very cloak-and-dagger way and said that no one must know his true identity." So Atabai called him Edward.

Atabai went to tell the Shah of the unexpected visitor. "The Shah smiled meaningfully."

The Shah received "Mr. Wilson" in his open-necked shirt at 6 P.M. on the evening of May 20. "Wilson" noticed the plethora of American security guards patrolling the place. He was frisked.

"Wilson" had tea in the little house on the beach, while the Shah drank mineral water. After a brief exchange of courtesies, "Wilson" explained to the Shah that "Her Majesty's government has decided that for so long as the Iranian authorities do not exercise effective control over the country, it cannot offer asylum to you or your family." He said he hoped the Shah would accept and understand this.

They had a rambling talk, much of it reminiscences about the state of Iran in the fifties and sixties. As for the present crisis, the Shah blamed the West for making him first liberalize and then leave the country.

After about an hour, "Wilson" returned to the business in hand. He said to the Shah, "My government wants to be able to say if asked that you accept and understand the decision not to grant you asylum." The Shah demurred.

"Wilson" persisted. He said that the new foreign secretary (Lord Carrington, an old supporter of the Shah) needed to be able to say, if asked, that the Shah both understood and accepted the decision. "Understand and accept" were the key words. Again the Shah demurred. "Wilson" persisted.

Eventually, and with considerable dignity, the Shah agreed to "accept" the British decision—but only on condition that the British acknowledge that he had never formally asked to come to Britain anyway. This was true—the requests for asylum had indeed all been unofficial. On behalf of Her Majesty's government, "Edward Wilson" accepted this formulation. He stood up, shook hands and left the Shah sitting in his poky room with no view.

From the British High Commission, "Wilson" cabled the Foreign Office to say "Mission accomplished."

The Shah's reaction to all this, according to Robert Armao, was one of disbelief. "He shook his head and said, 'Would you believe it, after what I've done for my friends in the U.K., that it would come to this?' "

He also said that he understood national interests gave no place for past allegiances or friendships. But he thought it was very shortsighted of the British to see it as in their interest "to humor terrorists."

Among others in the Shah's entourage, the incident encouraged a new conspiracy theory about the British. It was that the British now sought to prolong the turmoil in Iran. There were several reasons. First, they wanted the price of oil pushed up so that their own North Sea oil would increase in value. (As a result of the huge 1979 oil price rise, the pound did indeed rise to its highest level for years against the dollar.) But more importantly, the British were angry with the Shah for listening more to the Americans (and buying more from them) in recent years. So they had undermined the Shah both to punish him and to humiliate the Americans. They were certainly not now prepared to resolve America's predicament by giving the Shah asylum. Indeed, some of those around the Shah even believed that the British had told the Iranian revolutionaries that if the Shah did go to the United States, they should capture the U.S. embassy to humiliate the U.S. even further. Thus Britain could regain its dominant influence in Iran.

Shortly after "Wilson's" visit, the Bahamian government told the Shah's entourage that their visas would not be renewed. Inevitably the Shah saw this as the result of British pressure. "I have a long-standing suspicion of British intent and British policy which I have never found reason to alter," he wrote in the memoirs that he had begun during exile. In the face of American indifference and perennial British hostility, he thought the Bahamians just wanted him out—"despite the enormous sums I spent there. . . ."

Just as in Morocco, now in the Bahamas there was a rush to find a new refuge. The Bahamian visas were good for only another ten days.

The United States still would not take him. Despite the pressure from Henry Kissinger and the Shah's other friends outside the

White House, and despite Brzezinski's arguments from within, President Carter remained adamant.

From Egypt, Anwar Sadat once again repeated that he was only too willing to give the Shah a home. He said he was "deeply sad for those who are too scared to give asylum." He thought the situation in Iran was very tragic. "Moslem revolutions never use blood as a means of power. It is against Islam."

But the U.S. government did not want the Shah to return to Egypt. President Carter and most of his advisers felt that Sadat was already in enough trouble with the Arab world as a result of the Camp David Agreement. The Shah would be a new and quite unnecessary burden.

Apart from Egypt, there was just one invitation outstanding. It came from Panama. But the Shah knew nothing of the place and, although he was pleased to be asked, he preferred to go elsewhere.

David Rockefeller tried Austria, and the chancellor, Bruno Kreisky, seemed sympathetic. A playboy member of the Krupp family offered his castle near Salzburg. But while Kreisky never actually said no, it became evident that he thought the Shah's arrival would cause him considerable political problems. No official invitation was extended.

The Shah still thought the best place was Mexico. He had liked the place when he had made a state visit there and he had gotten to know the then finance minister and now president, José López Portillo. Furthermore, his mother was relatively nearby, in Los Angeles.

Ardeshir Zahedi flew with Colonel Jahanbini to Mexico City and received permission from the president. Henry Kissinger also contacted López Portillo and the president repeated the invitation. The State Department had already intervened on the Shah's behalf. The Mexican Foreign Ministry objected on the grounds that Mexico was being required to take a risk that the United States was unprepared to assume. López Portillo overrode their objections.

The Shah sent Robert Armao and Colonel Jahanbini to Mexico to find a house and make all other arrangements. Foreign Ministry officials told Armao that they were opposed to the visit but must accept their president's wishes. The police were very cooperative.

Armao found a pair of houses belonging to a wealthy Palm Beach socialite, in the rich resort of Cuernavaca. (There was quite a large American community there; indeed, the U.S. ambassador to Iran, William Sullivan, had just bought himself a property.) The Villa des Roses was at the end of a cul-de-sac in the middle of a large garden, and surrounded by a wall. It was easily protected and far more suitable than James Crosby's beach villa in the Bahamas. With the help of American residents in the neighborhood, the place was furnished and equipped within forty-eight hours.

On June 10, 1979, the Shah, the Queen, their dogs, their few remaining Iranian servants, and their new American aides bundled themselves onto a chartered executive jet and flew out of the Bahamas and on to their fourth country of exile.

When they arrived in the Villa des Roses, the Shah looked around the pretty house and garden and seemed relieved. "At least we can live again," he said.

But it was not true. He might now have a home, but it was his life that was about to be called into the question. In the Bahamas he had become quite sick. In Mexico he came close to dying, as a result of his best-kept secret, his cancer, and his failure to treat it properly.

CHAPTER FOURTEEN

The Private Patient

There is an almost surreal quality about the Shah's cancer. In a sense the disease, his reaction to it, the way in which it was treated, and its eventual impact on his own country, the United States, and his other allies, create a metaphor for his rule. It is a story of obsessive secrecy degenerating into macabre farce. Altogether eight teams of doctors looked after the Shah. They did not all perform brilliantly.

On a Parisian spring morning in April 1974, Professor Jean Bernard, the sixty-seven-year-old pope of French hematology, received a call from Teheran. On the telephone was a young Iranian doctor, Abbas Safavian, who had trained under Bernard in Paris. The Iranian simply asked him to fly to Teheran as a matter of some urgency. Bernard was used to such covert requests; his patients often demanded not just confidentiality but also anonymity. He packed his bags, and he asked his pupil Georges Flandrin to go with him.

"It might be one of the children in the royal family," said Bernard to Flandrin as they boarded the Air Force flight to Teheran.

"Oh perhaps it's a joke," suggested Flandrin.

"In my experience, jokes don't usually involve first-class tickets," replied Bernard.

Several hours later they were met at Teheran's Mehrabad Airport by Abbas Safavian. He told them that he was taking them to see one of his patients, Assadollah Alam, the Shah's minister of court, who had cancer. Alam gave them a good lunch and then told them that he wanted them to see the Shah.

The Shah was with his Great Dane and his personal doctor, Abdol Karim Ayadi, a small man who had dyed hair and wore a military uniform. (Ayadi, like many of the people closest to the Shah, was not a Muslim but a Baha'i. He was reported to have used his position to embezzle very large sums of money for himself.) The Shah told the two doctors, in French, that he had felt a swelling under his left rib cage while on the beach at Kish. He knew that it was his spleen. Sometimes it swelled and then it went down again, he said. He did not seem to be unduly concerned.

The Frenchmen examined him and talked about his previous medical history. They learned that he had once had malaria and that, a few years before, he had had a nephritic crisis. For several years he had had several allergic reactions to various foods. He could not eat fish—which meant no "pearls of the Caspian" for the Shah. Generally he was in good health, complaining of a discreet asthenia, which was probably a result of his tiring life. His appetite was good, his weight stable. (He exercised every day; his wife later said that "he had a fantastic body for a man of his age.") His blood pressure and pulse rate were normal. He slept well, though he took continual small doses of Valium every day.

With some difficulty they aspirated a sample of bone marrow and took a blood sample and Flandrin asked for a microscope. There was none at hand; Dr. Ayadi sent out for one. From then on it never left the Shah's side.

Flandrin examined a smear. The Shah's white cell count was slightly high. He had too many lymphocytes and too few granulocytes. His platelet count—150,000—was low normal. His red cell count was normal. It did not seem a dangerous condition. A doctor might well say, "You've got a slight infection. Come back next week." But the bone marrow showed 55 percent lymphoid cells, where 10 percent or less would have been normal. *

* To understand the implications of this and the nature of the Shah's treatment, it is helpful to understand a little about leukemia. Blood contains red cells, white cells, and platelets. Their concentrations are very different. There are about 5 million red cells to every 250,000 platelets and 5,000 white cells. But all are essential. The red cells carry oxygen, the platelets are for clotting, and there are two forms of white cells. The granulocytes ingest and kill bacteria, and the lymphocytes create immunities by making antibodies against different infections.

The Frenchmen told Dr. Ayadi that they thought the Shah had chronic lymphocytic leukemia. Naturally, Dr. Ayadi was concerned. And, just as in many matters of state, when the Shah's advisers were reluctant to tell him the truth, Dr. Ayadi asked the French doctors not to mention the words "cancer" or "leukemia" to the Shah.

So his doctors told the Shah that he had a blood complaint called Waldenström's disease. This was what Georges Pompidou suffered from and is in fact a mild form of lymphoma or leukemia, with a less frightening name. They said that no treatment was necessary now and that they would wait to see the progress of the condition.

Subsequently, Bernard and Flandrin were criticized for not having made a more complete examination on this first visit. But it was not possible. The Shah would not allow any intrusive examination or an X ray, let alone surgery, for any of these would have been impossible to conceal from those around him, and he wanted no hint of any illness to be noised abroad.

In any case, the Frenchmen's advice was not necessarily wrong. Leukemia of the type which they had diagnosed is often divided into five levels (zero to IV) of seriousness. They thought the Shah was now at Stage II. Specific treatment can be delayed until Stage III or Stage IV of the disease.

More problematic is whether the French doctors should have specifically told him that he had cancer. This is a decision that doctors tend to make on a case-by-case basis. Since the Shah's own physician asked them not to tell him the truth, they felt they could not act otherwise. One may speculate whether, if the Shah

---

Under the left diaphragm in the upper abdomen there is the spleen, a small organ that acts like a garbage disposal. It filters out old or abnormal blood cells and gets rid of them. Before a child is born, the spleen actually makes blood cells. It is not supposed to do so in a normal healthy human being, but because it is related to the bone marrow, patients with malignancy of either the lymphoid tissue or the bone marrow tissue often find their spleens are involved.

All cells in the body reproduce themselves. Cancer is a loss of control over that reproduction process. Moreover, most cells begin as immature and then mature over a given period of hours, days, or weeks. Only mature cells function—thus only a mature white cell will kill bacteria. In cancer the maturing process often goes wild. If the malignancy is in the bone marrow, and the marrow is not producing enough white cells, or enough platelets, but only young immature cells, then obviously serious deficiencies will arise.

Lymphoma means tumors of the lymph cells. There is lymph tissue throughout the body; the spleen, lymph nodes, and thymus are lymphoid organs that produce and store infection-fighting cells. Lymphoma can be in just the lymphoid tissue or in the marrow. In leukemia there are abnormal cells in the peripheral blood.

had known he had cancer, he would have cooperated more fully.

In September 1974 they were called again to Teheran. The Shah's spleen was still enlarged and they recommended that he start to take the least aggressive anticancer drug available—chlorambucil. At that time this was the preferred treatment for the Shah's condition.

In fact the Shah did not take the pills as prescribed, and in February 1975 the two Frenchmen were summoned again, this time to Zurich where the Shah was meeting those statesmen who were paying court to him to press their countries' cases for a greater share of his new oil wealth. The doctors took a taxi to Dolder Grand Hotel. A court official led them through the camera crews littering the lobby with their lights, their parkas, and their cables, and took them upstairs to the Shah's suite. There they found him again with Dr. Ayadi, and his dog.

At once, they found that the spleen was very much enlarged. Indeed, the condition was dangerous, but to their alarm the Shah said that he was skiing a lot and that he felt fine. This was clearly rash because if he fell he could rupture his spleen and bleed to death. They insisted that he must take three tablets of chlorambucil a day.

The problem was how to monitor the response of his blood and spleen to the drug. They told the Shah that he would have to be examined again in a week and then again every four to six weeks. The Shah asked Flandrin if he would be prepared to come back in a week's time.

"Why not?" said Jean Bernard.

At this point, said Flandrin later, "My fate was decided."

When Flandrin returned to the Dolder, he was concerned that the white blood cells might have fallen too much under the chlorambucil; to his relief they had not. The spleen had gone down already and the blood count was near to normal. He told the Shah to continue taking his daily pills and said his blood count would have to be checked in one month's time. The Shah asked him to come to Teheran. By now, Flandrin knew, he was becoming trapped.

Subsequently, in Teheran, Flandrin suggested to Dr. Safavian that it was not really necessary for him to fly from Paris just to take a blood sample. He, Safavian, could do it, and then send it along to a Teheran lab for analysis—under a false name if necessary. Or could not Dr. Ayadi do it?

Dr. Georges Flandrin

The two doctors looked at Flandrin and shook their heads. Out of the question, they said. The Shah had asked for French doctors and French doctors he must have. No Iranian doctor would assume the responsibility for treating the Shah's cancer. Furthermore, the mortal illness of the King was far too great a secret for any of his subjects to bear alone.

The Shah had chosen French doctors for a particular reason. He had confidence in their discretion. His distrust of the British was such that he was sure that somehow they would profit from whatever illness he might have. And he thought that if he saw a top American specialist, then there would be a memo on the desk of the secretary of state or the director of Central Intelligence within days. If Washington knew he was ill, he could no longer expect the same unqualified American support he now enjoyed. He would be deserted by his allies. The Great Civilization would crumble. (When his cancer was finally revealed in 1979, American officials did indeed say that had it been known before, American support for him would have been much less absolute.) And so it was that every five or six weeks for the next four years, Dr. Flandrin of the Hôpital St. Louis secretly flew to Teheran to take care of the King. He made thirty-five such trips before the Shah left Teheran in January 1979.

Georges Flandrin was forty-one years old in 1975, but he could easily pass for thirty. Tall, mild-mannered, with curly hair, spectacles, and a diffident smile, he was often thought to be far too young to be a senior physician. In fact he was an associate professor. He and his wife, Monique, a nurse, lived in a small apartment filled with splendid paintings by his uncle Flandrin—a noted if not first-rate Impressionist painter—in an anonymous block in a southwest suburb of Paris. Before he started to care for the Shah, they had spent much of their spare time visiting auctions and salesrooms in the provinces in search of more paintings or of their other interest, crucifixes of different styles and epochs.

Once he started treating the Shah, Flandrin developed a ritual. Every few weeks, he would take the Saturday Air France flight out of Paris. Dr. Safavian would meet him at Teheran airport and drive him to the same house in Teheran to stay the night. He tended to stay indoors, reading; he was frightened that if he became too visible in Teheran, his identity would be discovered and the Shah's secret would be out. On Sunday morning he was taken to see the Shah, who always treated him with great courtesy, even humor. "Are you really a doctor or just a medical student?" he asked once, referring to Flandrin's boyishness. Usually Flandrin would spend about fifteen minutes with him, examining him and taking a blood sample. Flandrin liked the Shah. He remembers Assadollah Alam telling him how extraordinary it was that such a powerful man could be so naive in certain respects.

The Shah responded well to the treatment. By June 1975 his spleen had decreased substantially and his cell count was better. Flandrin reduced the dosage of chlorambucil.

Once, in early 1976, Flandrin panicked. He found that the Shah's spleen had grown again and the abnormal cells had increased. He was horrified; it could mean only that the disease was becoming resistant to treatment.

But then Dr. Safavian did some detective work and learned that for the sake of secrecy Flandrin provided the Shah his chlorambucil tablets in a bottle with a different, anodyne label; his valet had noticed they were running out, so he had had the bottle refilled according to its label. Inevitably, the spleen had enlarged again and the atypical lymphoid cells had grown apace.

Both disturbed and relieved, Flandrin gave the Shah a new supply of chlorambucil. By the time he next visited Teheran, the spleen had shrunk again and the blood count had returned to near normal.

Although the Shah still did not know that he had cancer—and probably did not wish to know—this incident apparently gave him great confidence in his French doctor and in the prescription. His condition remained stable.

Even so, it was a taxing assignment for Flandrin, especially because of the absolute secrecy that the Shah demanded. Only Flandrin's wife knew where he was really going on these covert weekends. For more than four years he lied to his colleagues about his constant trips out of Paris and his tiredness on Mondays. To make it easier to get his tongue around the lie he would say that he was going duck shooting in Ireland: in French, the names "Ireland" and "Iran" sound very similar. Some of his colleagues felt sorry for his wife.

Sometimes he recognized people on the plane and then he would spend the entire trip behind his newspaper. He always tried to take what he hoped was the least conspicuous seat—next to the window at the back of First Class, just in front of the bulkhead separating the sections. He traveled light, carrying only a little bag of falsely labeled drugs. Once he was horrified to meet a doctor friend of his at the airport. He was taking the same flight as Flandrin but traveling beyond Teheran to Southeast Asia. Flandrin dissembled, but it was impossible; he had to admit he was going to Teheran. *"Aha, Jean Bernard et les grands malades,"* said his friend, and that was all he ever said about the incident.

Testing the Shah's blood samples in Paris was also difficult. In France, samples have to have not only names but also social security numbers on the label. He used the name and number of an elderly relation. To keep the Shah's secret, he was forced to lie all the time. Not just singly, but in complicated series of lies that had to be internally consistent. And it was not as if he were part of a conspiracy or a secret police force in which lies could be devised and shared by the group. He had to free-associate, to make up his own falsehoods and then try to lure them into a logical pattern.

He clearly did well. In retrospect, it is extraordinary that so many visits by a fairly well-known physician to a ruler of such importance should have remained so secret so long. There is no evidence that the CIA, for all its myriad assets in Iran, nor MI6, for all its longevity there, ever discovered that the Shah had cancer. Even more remarkable, it seems that the Israelis, whose Mossad was well placed inside SAVAK, had no idea. As for the French secret service, Flandrin is convinced that they did not know, either. If they did know, the French never told their allies.

In Teheran there were constant rumors that the Shah was ill, but that tends to happen in any society where the health of one man is so vital. In 1978, an American diplomat, John Stempel, was warned by his Soviet counterpart, with whom he regularly lunched at one of the city's better restaurants, that the Shah had cancer. But the embassy dismissed this information with the comment, "This rumor has abounded in many quarters and may be of Soviet inspiration."

Over the years, the circle of people known to be aware of the Shah's condition grew, but only slightly. In 1977 Flandrin and Bernard decided that it was time that the Queen was informed. They were more frank with her than with her husband; they used the word "cancer." It put her, she said later, in a terrible position; she now knew more about her husband's illness than he did himself. She decided that this was wrong and that he should be told more. "I said, 'We have to tell him for two reasons. On the human side, he is feeling well. It's not as if he were very sick. And he is not a child. He is strong, and he can take it. There is also the political side. He's the king of a country, has responsibilities. You can't just hide something like that from him.'"

But even then it seems that the fearful word "cancer" did not pass between the Shah and his doctors nor between the Shah and his wife. As far as the Shah was concerned, he was still suffering from Waldenström's syndrome. But he understood it was more serious than he had first realized.

"For me it was a really hard period, because I didn't know whether he knew or not," the Queen said later. "The doctors would talk to him, but without mentioning 'cancer.' They would say 'sarcoma' or 'lymphoma' instead. In the evening my husband would talk to me and mention some phrases. Then I would go to the doctors and ask, 'What have you told him? They said, 'We have told him everything but we haven't mentioned the word 'cancer.' So all my answers accorded with what he was telling me. Sometimes I thought, Maybe he knows and doesn't want me to know. For a long time it was just this act. My husband said we mustn't tell anybody. Then again the doctors would talk to me and then he would say, 'Why do you think they're giving me all these pills?' I would tell him, 'Well, it's because your blood is not making platelets or something.' So for a long period it went like this, not mentioning it to each other. It was strange for me. . . . I thought, How come I've mentioned Waldenström's to him and he's not curious? Or lymphoma?"

It was inevitable that after the cancer was revealed publicly, many commentators would see it as explaining much about what

went wrong with the Shan and Iran in the seventies—in particular
the haste with which he sought to transform the country. But if
the Shah did not know that he was critically ill, his malady may
not have had a crucial impact on his decisions. His disease would
have caused tiredness. But the chlorambucil was easy to take and
without side effects. For most of the time, says Flandrin, the Shah
felt very well.

Flandrin continued his visits to Teheran through the crisis of
1978. Then, after seeing the Shah in Aswan, he made several visits
to Morocco. There, both the Shah and the Queen seemed very
tense about their future. The Queen said that she did not know
where they would end up. Perhaps in a banana republic. She was
disgusted that Giscard d'Estaing had given asylum to Khomeini
but not to the Shah.

At the end of April 1979 in the Bahamas, the Shah found a
swollen gland or lymph node in his neck. The Queen asked Dr.
Pirnia, the Iranian pediatrician traveling with them, to look at it;
Pirnia knew nothing of his cancer. Flandrin was called. He was
alarmed; a lymph node meant that the lymphoma was accelerat-
ing. He flew to the Bahamas and was met by Mark Morse. Morse
thought he might be a French journalist, or perhaps a gynecologist
come to see the Queen.

Flandrin found the Shah quite depressed. The terror was at its
height in Iran; his officials who had remained were being executed, and daily threats were being made against him. He was
forced to keep silent in what he and the Queen considered conditions of acute and expensive discomfort.

With the help of the Queen and Dr. Pirnia, Flandrin aspirated
one of the swollen lymph nodes in the neck, and took a bone
marrow sample. A biopsy back in Paris showed very large, abnormal lymphoid cells (immunoblasts). However, his blood and bone
marrow were still fairly normal.

The French doctor returned to the Bahamas. He was now in a
difficult position. He explained to the Shah that his chronic condition had now become acute and that he therefore needed much
more aggressive treatment. Medical logic would have demanded
that the Shah go into a hospital so that his doctors could establish
exactly just what "stage" the disease had now reached. They
might take out the spleen and then begin intensive chemotherapy
to be followed by radiation.

But that would have meant telling the world that the Shah had

Former President Richard M. Nixon with the Shah in Cuernevaca

cancer. Although he now knew that he was seriously ill, the Shah still did not want to reveal the truth. He evidently thought he could still influence the course of events in Iran; he told Flandrin that if those still loyal to him learned he was ill, their morale would suffer. Could he not continue with secret treatment?

Reluctantly, Flandrin agreed to try this for another three months, but said it would then be necessary to start radiotherapy —which would be impossible to keep secret. The Shah agreed.

Flandrin now started much more intensive chemotherapy. He put the Shah on four drugs: Nitrogen-mustard, Vincristine, Procarbazine, and Prednisolone. They had to be administered through a drip, which he applied with the help of the Queen and Dr. Pirnia. It was a painful and debilitating process, which had to be done every seven days. So Flandrin started shuttling between Paris and the Bahamas and then Paris and Mexico.

At first, the sojourn in Mexico went well. The house at Cuernavaca was far more pleasant than the beach house on Paradise Island, though the Queen said later that she thought "it was a place for retired people and I must say it was rather depressing." Security was both easier and less obtrusive. The Shah finished writing the French version of his final memoirs. During the summer holidays, the children flew from their schools in the States. The Shah's elder son, Reza, later said that he had never really known his father before the exile.

In Cuernavaca, the Shah also received a number of old friends, including members of the Iranian court and, from the United States, Henry Kissinger and Richard Nixon.

William Safire described the meeting between Nixon and the Shah as one of "two fallen non-angels." Nixon told Safire that the

Shah "is not sorry for himself. He is sorry for his country. He is grief-stricken by the execution of his friends and the suffering of his people under the new regime." According to Nixon, the Shah gave him a "breathtaking and wise" *tour d'horizon* about the consequences of the retreat of U.S. power. He was bitter about the way the United States had let him down.

During his stay in Cuernavaca, a Mexican paper published a claim from the Iranian embassy in Mexico City that 365,995 Iranians had been killed during his reign. He immediately issued a statement saying that this did not contain a grain of truth. "During my absence from Iran I have watched in anguish as the country has slipped from the edge of the twenty-first century into the abyss of medieval leadership and mentality."

The threat to himself remained. In Iran, Sadeq Khalkhali announced once more with relish that gunmen were on the way to Mexico. "I have told them they must carry out the sentence to take revenge from that traitor on behalf of the Iranian nation." Then Iran revoked the Shah's passport, in order, according to Foreign Minister Ibrahim Yazdi, to force him to return to Teheran and stand trial.

Asked about such threats and about the possibility of ever returning home, the Shah said, "I believe in Providence. All depends on that. I do not fear being assassinated. I am a religious man."

On June 23, Anwar Sadat once again underlined his own wish to succor his friend. He asked the Egyptian parliament to adopt a resolution that would allow the Shah to take refuge in Egypt. He was making his proposal, he said, in the name of Islam, Christianity, and civilization. It was greeted in the parliament with loud applause.

In the United States the debate over the Shah's homelessness continued throughout the summer, at least within the administration. John McCloy continued to bombard Secretary of State Vance with letters of reproach; Henry Kissinger made fairly frequent criticisms of the Carter administration, and announced that only he had done anything about getting the Shah a Mexican visa.

Carter himself became increasingly exasperated. Vice President Walter Mondale oscillated over the summer as the reports of chaos and revanchism from Teheran made the Shah's regime seem mild by comparison. On one occasion, Brzezinski, who had always argued for letting the Shah in, told Kissinger that Mondale was tilting that way, so Kissinger called him to push him further.

Toward the end of July, Mondale sent Carter a memorandum in which he said he now favored letting the Shah come. At a breakfast meeting Mondale and Brzezinski both pressed Carter to relent. Carter exploded.

"Fuck the Shah!" he said. "I'm not going to welcome him here when he has other places to go where he'll be safe." (When he later told the story, Carter deleted the expletive and used the phrase "Blank the Shah.") Toward the end of July, Kissinger called Brzezinski again. This time, according to Brzezinski, "Kissinger in his subtle fashion linked his willingness to support us on SALT to a more forthcoming attitude on our part regarding the Shah." Carter was apparently not pleased when told of this implied threat. It was at another breakfast that he complained rather bitterly about the Kissinger-Rockefeller-McCloy campaign and said that he did not want "the Shah to be here playing tennis while Americans in Teheran were being kidnapped or were even being killed."

Brzezinski complained that the United States was being bullied by "a third-rate regime." As far as he was concerned, American traditions and national honor were at stake. His attitude did not please Carter and Vance. Even so, Vance asked State to work out how the Shah could be admitted with the least harm done to the U.S. relationship with Iran and the least risk to the embassy in Teheran. The embassy in Teheran remained strongly opposed to allowing the Shah entry.

Then Princess Ashraf, who was living in New York, sent President Carter an emotional letter on her brother's behalf but without his knowledge. She wrote of "the increasing difficulty and traumatic situation in which my brother, his wife, and their son find themselves in their search for a relatively stable place where they could find some continuity in their family life." (All four children were at school in the States at this time.) She said also that there had been a "quite noticeable impairment of his health in Mexico" (she did not know about his cancer) and asked that he be given asylum in the States at once.

For many years State Department officials had considered Princess Ashraf to be utterly corrupt. But she was treated as a princess and would have received a most courteous reply to any communication. Now she was sent only a curt letter from Warren Christopher, deputy secretary of state, writing "on behalf of the President who is on vacation." (Brzezinski says the original draft was even colder and was actually addressed to "Ms. Pahlavi." "I felt this was uncalled for, and redrafted it in a somewhat warmer fashion, with a more appropriate salutation.")

Some four weeks after his arrival in Mexico, the Shah's health began to deteriorate again. His staff called in Mexican doctors and they diagnosed malaria. That was not unreasonable; he had had malaria before, and there were mosquitoes in Cuernavaca. But he did not respond to the treatment. "We were very worried," said the Queen later. "Was it because of the disease, or was it malaria, or typhoid?" Members of his entourage thought that hepatitis was a possibility; they all had shots of gamma globulin.

Georges Flandrin visited his patient on July 12 and 19. The Shah's white cell count had fallen, so Flandrin reduced the chemotherapy. By August 20 the blood count had improved, so Flandrin resumed the treatment. By the middle of September he found the Shah jaundiced.

At the end of September, Mark Morse called his employer, Robert Armao, in New York. He told him the Shah seemed seriously ill. Armao decided that the Shah needed to have the advice of an American consultant. He assumed that malaria might well be the problem. He spoke to Joseph Reed, David Rockefeller's assistant, who was now helping to administer the Shah's finances and liaising with the State Department. Reed called Dr. Ben Kean, who was an old friend of the Reed family and who had recently treated both Armao and Morse for diarrhea, and asked him to go to see the Shah.

Benjamin H. Kean is a large man with a large, some would say overwhelming, personality. He is a parasitologist and pathologist and is proud to relate that he comes from socialist English stock. He has a square head topped with closely cropped gray hair. He chomps cigars, spins a terrific yarn, and wears a suntan with his three-piece suits. He has been described as "a boulevardier [who] has traveled the world over many times and squired—and married —some of the world's most beautiful women."

Kean is a physician who inspires passion. The writer David Halberstam says, "He is a wonderful man. A great, old-fashioned doctor who really cares about his patients." But he sometimes seems like a pocket steamroller, and within the medical profession —where egos are frequently vast and clashing—there are those

Dr. Ben Kean

who speak less fondly of what they see as his tendency to flatten those who disagree with him.

Ben Kean then had a fashionable private practice on Park Avenue and an office and lab at Cornell University Medical College, New York Hospital. He has written a standard work on Mexican "turista," but although parasitology is his principal concern, he has also worked as an internist with patients whose illnesses covered the whole panorama of medical problems.

When Reed called, he said the problem had to do with "Peter Smith."

"What, not again?" said Kean.

"No," said Reed, "this is a different Peter Smith."

Some years before, Kean had been called in as a consultant to a Marcus Wallenberg, a leading Swedish industrialist (and cousin of the war hero, Raoul Wallenberg), who had developed a rare lung infection. When Kean examined him, he was close to death and Kean told his Swedish physicians, "this man cannot be treated according to the status of his real identity. He must be treated as an ordinary patient, as a 'Peter Smith' if he is to survive." In other words, he should not be privately coddled by nervous consultants hired for the occasion, but be given the best public medical team in the country. It was done as Kean advised, and "Peter Smith" lived, Kean told Dennis L. Breo of *American Medical News*.

Now there was a new "Peter Smith," said Reed. It was the Shah, he was in Mexico, and he was suffering from malaria and jaundice. Please, would Kean get down there.

Thus did "Peter Smith" become the first of many medical aliases in the coming months. (Or perhaps the second, if one includes the false name that Flandrin had, for years, applied to his blood samples in Paris.) But Kean had made a significant if paradoxical point. The rich and powerful are not always able to obtain the best medical care; their very importance denies it to them. Private facilities are often not so well equipped to deal with the most serious illnesses as are public teaching hospitals, and doctors are often more frightened of taking necessary risks if their patient is someone of consequence. In the event, the Shah's condition would be aggravated by the fact that it proved impossible to treat him as a Peter Smith. "He should have received the best of care. In fact he got near the worst," Kean told Breo later.

After arranging Kean's trip to Mexico, Reed called the State Department to speak to David Newsom, the under secretary of state who had been the U.S. government's link to the Rockefeller-Pahlavi entourage all year. Reed told him that the Shah had fallen ill in Mexico and might need to come to the U.S. for treatment. Newsom had always been opposed to the Shah's admission. He reacted cautiously and said "a substantial medical case" would have to be made.

By chance Secretary of State Vance had just outlined to the Council on Foreign Relations in New York the reasons why the Shah was still being refused entry. The embassy in Teheran was still advising that his arrival in the U.S. would be very dangerous for Americans there. After Reed's call, State checked with the embassy again; the view was the same.

Kean arrived in Mexico on September 29. Dr. Pirnia told him a little about the Shah's problems, but made no mention of cancer. He found the Shah was indeed sick—he was deeply jaundiced and had lost about thirty pounds. After examining him, Kean decided that he probably did not have malaria, or hepatitis, but rather obstructive jaundice, which could be caused by either gallstones or pancreatic cancer. He told the Shah he wanted to take some blood samples.

But this the Shah declined. He had not asked Kean to come to Mexico; that was Robert Armao's idea. He trusted Georges Flandrin, who had been to give him his chemotherapy only a week before. He still did not want anyone else to see the state of his blood. He said that his French doctors had recommended cortisone for his hepatitis and that he had taken a large dose that very morning.

Kean said that cortisone could be dangerous and he urged the Shah to get his French doctors back to make a new diagnosis. "I told him my 'Peter Smith' story and said, 'You must change your name to Peter Smith.' "

The Shah replied, "Ah, but do not forget, I am a Muslim. I cannot change my name." Kean thought that was quite a good joke.

It was clear to Kean that the Shah was determined to control his medical care and to trust only his French doctors. In which case they should be in Mexico. "You require much more sophisticated care than you are now receiving," said Kean. Then he flew back to New York, puzzled and angry at the Shah's refusal to let him take any blood samples. He was not used to being dismissed in such a way even by famous men. "I thought that my advice was either not needed or not welcome. I did not expect to hear from him again."

The Queen summoned Flandrin from Paris. When he arrived in Cuernavaca in early October he realized at once that his patient was very ill and was no longer responding to the chemotherapy; the lymph nodes in his neck had begun to swell again. He knew that the local doctors' diagnosis of malaria was incorrect and that the Shah was in fact suffering from jaundice caused either by gallstones or by his cancer. "I decided he must go into a hospital at once," said Flandrin later. A full examination had been postponed for more than five years; it could be delayed no longer.

The Shah accepted his doctor's advice but said, "Not in the United States. After what they did to me, I would not go there even if they begged me on their knees." So Flandrin went with Dr. Pirnia to Mexico City to try to find the best place for the Shah to be hospitalized there. They decided that the facilities at the University Hospital, where the cancer consultant had been trained in France, would do well.

In mid-October, Robert Armao flew in from New York. He had not seen the Shah for more than a month. He went into his bedroom and was horrified by his appearance. The Shah's face looked black. He said he had terrible pains in his stomach and was nauseous. He could barely eat a thing. Armao thought he was dying.

Outside the bedroom, Flandrin and Armao met for the first time. Flandrin was struck by Armao's impeccable appearance. He revealed to the young American PR man that he and his superior,

Jean Bernard, had been treating the Shah for years.

Their names meant nothing to Armao. But when he called Kean to ask him to return, Kean understood. The name Jean Bernard is to leukemia and lymphoma as Christiaan Barnard is to heart surgery. Now the disputes that were to bedevil and jeopardize the Shah's last year of life began in earnest.

On October 17, Joseph Reed called David Newsom at the State Department again. He said that the Shah's condition had worsened and that he might have cancer. Newsom asked that Dr. Kean contact the State Department's medical officer, Dr. Eben Dustin. Kean did so. Next day Kean arrived in Cuernavaca and Flandrin handed him a thirty-page memorandum outlining the treatment he and Jean Bernard had given the Shah since 1974.

According to Kean, Flandrin was "almost apologetic about the care the Shah had received." The Shah had allowed them to do so little.

Flandrin's recollection is somewhat different. He said later that he had thought Armao was going to summon an oncologist from New York, not an expert in tropical diseases. He thought that Kean might be a fine fellow, but he could not know enough about the Shah's real problems. "Medicine has become a very specialized business. One knows nothing of what is going on next door to oneself." Kean had another view; he believed that a good doctor called in the appropriate specialists.

Kean, Flandrin, and his Mexican doctors then went in to see the Shah. It was the first of many international (and to some extent internecine) cabals around his body. He looked appalling. Kean was convinced he had obstructive jaundice and thought the cause was gallstones. The chemotherapy was clearly not working anymore; his spleen was swollen again and so were the lymph nodes in his neck. Flandrin agreed.

According to Kean, the Shah apologized to him for not telling him the truth before, saying that "reasons of state" precluded it.

Now Kean's formidable personality began to assert itself. Georges Flandrin was the Shah's physician, and had been for years. But Ben Kean began to take charge. As Flandrin had already done, Kean informed the Shah that he had to go into a hospital at once. Obstructive jaundice should be operated on within forty-eight hours, yet the Shah had had it for seven weeks. The cause was probably cancer of the head of the pancreas, or gallstones, and it would have to be removed. After that the doctors would have to consider what to do about his spleen, his lymph nodes, and his blood condition.

The Shah asked whether all this could be done in Mexico, where Flandrin had already made arrangements. Kean replied in his rambunctious manner—which was to be central to the developing drama—"Your Imperial Majesty, of course you can have your operation in Mexico, or in Dacca, or even in Timbuktu in a tent."

The Shah's preference was still Mexico. He had confidence in Flandrin and Flandrin thought the Mexican facilities were good. But even Flandrin had to agree, when asked, that American facilities were superior. Moreover, rich Mexicans were telling the Shah's entourage that when they were sick they went to the States. Armao said to Flandrin, "For a man like him only the best will do, and the best is only in America."

There was another concern—security. Armao was worried that in a Mexican hospital it would prove impossible to protect the Shah from the emissaries of the Ayatollah. Any hospital porter, any man in a mask and gown could be an assassin from Teheran. For that reason as well, Armao wanted him to go to the U.S.

But the Shah himself was still very reluctant. "I am not welcome there," he kept saying.

Later Dr. Kean stated that by this stage, "Dr. Flandrin had withdrawn as chief of the case, although he would stay to the end. I was now the Shah's physician." He began to plan to take him to New York.

Flandrin saw it rather differently. As far as he was concerned, he had not withdrawn; Kean had taken over. There is often tension between doctors of different nationalities, and although Flandrin speaks reasonable English, he was not bilingual. He pointed out later that some Americans get irritated by people who do not speak their language fluently. "They are not very gentle."

Flandrin later said that he became agitated. "I made a scandal. I said I did not want to hand over my responsibilities to a cheerful parasitologist. It was rather painful [assez pénible]." He felt his point was logical enough. He was the oncologist in charge of a cancer patient whose illness had become critical. Why should he be replaced by an expert in tropical medicine? By his own account, Kean did not remark on Flandrin's dismay.

Flandrin says he was calmed by assurances that Dr. Kean would not remain in charge of the case but would hand the Shah over to an oncologist at Memorial Hospital of whom Flandrin approved. But as the discussion around the bedside continued, it came out that Dr. Kean intended to take the Shah to New York Hospital. Flandrin started. That was where Assadollah Alam, the Shah's minister of court, had died after being treated at the American Hospital in Paris. Flandrin and other French doctors had flown to New York with Alam; they had had a dreadful experience with the staff at New York Hospital. Now he went over to the Queen to whisper, "It's a catastrophe. The worst thing that could happen."

Flandrin says the Queen repeated this to the Shah, who told Kean and the others that Flandrin did not approve. The Americans reassured him that Memorial was just across the street, there was an underground passage, and he would be taken through it for treatment.

By this time Flandrin was exhausted and felt very isolated. After the conference around the bed, he went back to see the Shah alone and asked if he would like him to come to New York.

"You have already done a lot for me," he recalls the Shah saying. "I am sure you have problems of your own. It is not necessary for you to come too." In truth, Flandrin doubted he could be of much use in New York. "I knew the Americans. I knew after the experience of Alam that I'd be able to do nothing in New York. Still I sometimes regret not having gone with him. But the Americans made no effort at all to ask me to go."

He went to say good-bye to the Queen. She gave him a little Mexican silver cup bearing the Pahlavi coat of arms. She said she was sorry she had nothing from Iran, and added with a shy smile, "Perhaps you can put it on your desk for your pencils!"

The Queen was in an impossible position. Like the Shah, she trusted Flandrin, but the Americans were telling her that her husband must go to the States. She did not want to go there any more than he did, but "I didn't want to take the responsibility. Everyone knows the U.S. is the best place for medical treatment, and if we'd had the treatment in Mexico and something had gone wrong, I felt that maybe I would be blamed for not going to the United States. . . ."

That night, October 18, Kean called Dr. Dustin, the State Department's medical officer. He explained his diagnosis and recommendations. He thought his call might have been taped. Kean said he could assemble a team to treat the Shah in Mexico, but it would be much better for him to be flown to New York Hospital. Dustin asked how long they had. Kean replied, "Days yes, weeks probably, months no." Joseph Reed called State with a similar message.

The next morning the issue was discussed at President Carter's weekly foreign-affairs breakfast. Cy Vance had now changed his mind. He had decided that the Shah would have to be admitted for humanitarian reasons. "We were faced squarely with a decision in which common decency and humanity had to be weighed against possible harm to our embassy personnel in Teheran," he wrote later.

Carter still argued that it was against U.S. interests. His chief of staff, Hamilton Jordan, had an eye to the political implications. "Mr. President," said Jordan, "if the Shah dies in Mexico, can you imagine the field day Kissinger will have with that? He'll say that first you caused the Shah's downfall and now you've killed him."

"To hell with Henry Kissinger," Carter replied, "I am President of this country!"

Vance and Brzezinski, together at last, argued on grounds of humanitarian principle. Carter was alone. He asked his advisers to double-check the Shah's condition and to find out from the embassy in Teheran whether its safety could be guaranteed. Vance agreed to do so.

As the meeting ended, Carter asked, "What are you guys going to advise me to do if they overrun our embassy and take our people hostage?"

Over the next forty-eight hours the embassy in Teheran informed Iranian Prime Minister Mehdi Bazargan and the foreign minister, Ibrahim Yazdi, of the Shah's condition and the possibility that he might be admitted to the States. They were clearly surprised. The revolutionaries had been poring through the papers the Pahlavis had left behind and there was every rumor in the world on the streets of Teheran, but there was no talk anywhere now of the Shah having cancer.

Bazargan and Yazdi did not like the idea of the Shah going to the States. Almost all Iranians would interpret it as part of a repeat of the CIA's 1953 plot to restore the Shah. It might weaken their own position vis-à-vis Ayatollah Khomeini, who was pressing for more radical progress toward a theocratic state than the Bazargan administration contemplated. But if he had to go to the States, Texas would be preferable to New York, for then he would not be in the heart of exiled opponents of the regime. Iranians would be convinced that in New York he was plotting a counterrevolution. The Iranian authorities ordered additional police to be placed around the U.S. embassy.

In the meantime, Dr. Dustin at the State Department had talked with the medical adviser to the U.S. embassy in Mexico City. At the time it was said that this man, Dr. Jorge Cervantes, confirmed that he thought the Shah should come to the States. Later, however, the conversation was described in a *New York Times* investigation as "casual" and Cervantes himself claimed that he had told Dustin that all the necessary facilities existed in Mexico City.

Dustin reported to his superiors in State that on the basis of conversations with Kean and Cervantes, he believed that the Shah needed to come urgently to the U.S. But later Kean claimed that he had not told Dustin this. He had said that the Shah needed to be treated "in a few weeks" but not necessarily in the next few days. He also said later that he told Dustin that although he preferred New York, Mexico would be possible. This was not the understanding of the White House.

The medical report which Dr. Dustin submitted to State was more categorical than Kean claims to have been to Dustin. According to the Secret White Paper subsequently prepared and eventually released by the White House, it asserted:

> "Highly technical studies are needed to completely diagnose this lymphoma, to grade it, determine its involvement in the process which has produced the jaundice and decide on further treatment. Adjunctive chemotherapeutic approaches are very likely needed but must be based on a proper diagnostic work-up. These studies cannot be carried out in any of the medical facilities in Mexico." It was also Dr. Dustin's judgment that "the situation is urgent and becoming increasingly so. Each day of worsening jaundice and physiological deterioration lessens the chances of recovery from surgical relief which may well be necessary."

In retrospect, it seems strange that the State Department did not insist on sending a top American oncologist to Cuernavaca (as Flandrin had suggested) or at least ask that Dr. Kean call in the Mexican oncologist whom Flandrin had chosen, to see if adequate care could really not be given the Shah in Mexico. But it was not done.

On October 20, Carter received a "super-sensitive" memorandum from State which said that the Shah had "malignant lymphoma compounded by a possible internal blockage which has resulted in severe jaundice." He needed essential diagnostic tests. "Dr. Kean . . . has advised us that these diagnostic studies cannot be carried out in any of the medical facilities in Mexico, and he recommends that the examination take place in the United States. David Rockefeller has asked that we admit the Shah to Sloan-Kettering Hospital in New York City for diagnosis and treatment. The State Department's Medical Director supports Dr. Kean's recommendation." Kean later denied he had ever said that anything could not be done in Mexico. It was New York Hospital, not Sloan-Kettering, which is part of Memorial Hospital across the street, to which he wanted to admit the Shah.

All the president's men, even to some extent the president himself, had been uncomfortable about denying asylum to America's old ally. For both humanitarian and political reasons, none of them wanted him to die in Mexico because of their refusal to allow him in.

As the State Department later noted, there were adequate facilities in Western Europe if not in Mexico. "However, it was concluded that the same obstacles which appeared in March, during the search for a country to receive the Shah then, would also impede an urgent search for medical treatment six months later. According to the independent medical judgments available within the department, each day of delay could have seriously worsened, perhaps irreparably, the Shah's condition. . . . The great urgency of the request when it came and when its true nature became apparent effectively prevented a United States search for alternative facilities in other countries."

López Portillo, the Mexican president, had been informed of the Shah's illness and had already told him that he could return to the house at Cuernavaca as soon as his treatment was complete. On this understanding Jimmy Carter agreed that he should fly to New York.

The Shah and his party left Mexico in a chartered Gulfstream jet on the night of October 22. He could barely walk from the car to the plane. On the flight, he sat quietly in his seat and, he wrote later, he reflected with sadness on the way in which "a worn, fanatic, old man" was destroying everything he had sought to build. In Iran, he believed, self-confidence was being replaced by defeatism, women were being ground into the dust of the Middle Ages, and many of his projects now "lay fallow."

"But then, what interest could the mullahs have in the nuclear power reactors I was planning and building? . . . I had plans to make Iran the world's largest producer of artificial fertilizer. A litany of shattered dreams!"

Such were the images—of abandoned reactors and unfinished fertilizer plants—that haunted the King as he flew across the Gulf of Mexico to Florida.

They were instructed to land at Fort Lauderdale to clear immigration and customs. "Naturally," said the Queen later, "we had to land at the wrong airport." They were not expected at the airport at which they arrived and there was no one to meet them, save an agricultural inspector who wanted to know if they were carrying any plants and intended to dump garbage. The Shah laughed.

They had to wait an hour until the relevant officials drove across town. "We were not allowed to leave the plane," recalled the Queen. "I just walked up and down the tarmac. It was so hot inside and I wanted to take some air."

Eventually they flew on to New York and landed at La Guardia in the cold hours before dawn on October 23, 1979. The handling company had been told that the plane was carrying valuables from the Bank of Mexico.

The party headed first for the home of the Shah's sister Princess Ashraf, on Beekman Place on the East Side. But as they drew near, there was someone standing at an intersection waving them away; despite the secrecy, there were apparently photographers at the door. Armao ordered the driver to take them directly to New York Hospital instead. "Everyone was so excited and dramatizing everything," said the Queen later. "It didn't make things easy for us."

CHAPTER FIFTEEN

The Operation

New York Hospital–Cornell Medical Center is a great gray complex in the East Sixties, right on the East River. The Shah's car drew around the circle in front of the glass doors. He climbed out, walked through the ornate Art Nouveau lobby, under an inscription which reads, "At the Gate of the Temple which is called Beautiful," and was taken in a private elevator up to the seventeenth floor.

The Shah was admitted by his staff under the name "David Newsome." A plastic tag with this name was clipped to his wrist by a member of the staff. It remained there throughout his stay in New York. Until his death many of the reports written on him by doctors associated with his case were written under the name of "David Newsome." The real David Newsom, the under secretary of state for Political Affairs at the State Department, who had been liaising with the Shah's entourage for months, did not much appreciate this.

The Shah's arrival became public knowledge at once. But during his first few days in the hospital, no one would reveal what was really the matter with him. His aides had decided that a blanket of silence should cover the proceedings. At first, hospital staff were even ordered not to confirm that the Shah had been admitted. This infuriated hospital officials as well as reporters. It was almost certainly a grave mistake, for it gave rise to all manner of speculations and conspiracy theories—both in Iran itself and in the United States.

A State Department spokesman told the press that he was "quite" ill, that his health had deteriorated sharply, and that his doctors had told him that "the attention he needed was available only in the United States." Hodding Carter, Cyrus Vance's spokesman, then said that the United States had a pretty good idea of what was wrong with him—but he would not elaborate. The next day Dr. Lawrence K. Altman, *The New York Times* medical correspondent, wrote that there were reports circulating among doctors at the hospital that the Shah was suffering from lymphoma and that it was worsening. In response to questions, Chris Godek, an assistant in Armao's office, said that she had "no information like that." She had not been told the truth.

In fact, the Shah was at last seeing an American cancer specialist. Ben Kean had asked the physician in chief of the New York Hospital, Dr. Hibbard Williams, for help in assembling a team. They chose a surgeon known for his biliary expertise, and an anesthetist. Two days before "Mr. Newsome" arrived in New York, Dr. Kean had called one of the senior oncologists at the Cornell Medical Center, Dr. Morton Coleman.

According to Coleman, Kean said, "Marty, will you please ask your wife to leave the room. I need to talk to you about something very, very, very important that demands utter secrecy.

"Marty," Kean continued, "there's somebody coming in from Mexico and his admission to the U.S. will have many international implications." As he listened to the rasping voice of his colleague, Coleman looked at the ceiling, rolled his eyes, and said to himself, "More Ben Kean bullshit." Later he laughed when telling the story, "I didn't know how prophetic his words were."

Coleman was a senior physician who specialized in aggressive chemotherapy for lymphomas; not all doctors accepted the treatment he offered. He sometimes described himself as a "country boy from Virginia." Tall, stooping, gregarious, and with a laugh like a horse, he had little patience for the finesse that Dr. Kean had developed in dealing with prominent patients. His style was rather more "Well, how are you feeling today?" than "Good morning, Your Majesty." He thought it was fine for Ben Kean to be in charge of the Shah, even though he was not an oncologist. After all, an important case like this could do with a general physician to serve, as Coleman put it, as a "majordomo" between the doctors. That was how Kean saw his function as well.

When the Shah was brought in, his exact condition was still unclear to the various doctors concerned with him. (Dr. Flandrin, the one man who knew it intimately, was now back in Paris.) Were gallstones blocking his bile duct and therefore causing obstructive jaundice? Or was it lymphoma in the belly? Within hours of his arrival they gave him a CAT scan, which was a diagnostic tool that Armao publicly claimed, wrongly, did not exist in Mexico. They discovered that he did have gallstones and an enlarged spleen.

Dr. Coleman was particularly perplexed. Flandrin had given a complete dossier to Kean, but Coleman thought the Shah's medical history was uncertain. Had the French been right in their original diagnosis of Waldenström's syndrome? He thought the evidence inconclusive. But the alternative was that the Shah had all along been suffering from large-cell lymphoma, and that is a very aggressive disease that probably would not have responded so well to the single drug, chlorambucil, with which the French had been treating him all these years. Coleman performed a bone marrow aspirate and biopsy. He did not see evidence of lymphoma or Waldenström's. Could it be that the enlarged spleen was a result of the malaria he had suffered twenty years before? (It should be said that Dr. Flandrin, who spoke to Coleman by telephone from Paris at this time, thought that the Americans had all the necessary information.)

As for the Shah's present treatment, the key question was whether or not to take out his spleen, which was now three times the normal size. It was a hard call, but Coleman concluded that it should be removed now. Coleman wanted to examine the spleen to determine just what sort of lymphoma and what stage of the disease the Shah was suffering from. Otherwise, there was no way of knowing whether the lymphoma was localized or disseminated.

But then, on October 24, Coleman was astonished to hear that the Shah was already in an operating room having his gallbladder removed. He was the Shah's oncologist, but he had not been told that this operation was about to happen. This was another of the breakdowns of communication between the Shah's medical advisers.

He rushed to the operating room and sent in a message suggesting that the surgeon take out the Shah's spleen as well. According
to Coleman, the reply from the surgeon was "Tell Mort he's a
braver man than I."

This was a crucial decision. Problems with his spleen eventually
killed the Shah. With hindsight, it might be argued that Coleman
was correct, and that if the Shah's spleen had been removed as
soon as he arrived in New York, he would have survived much
longer. Certainly Coleman was, in his own words, "hell-bent" on
taking out the spleen. Later he wondered, "Suppose that wasn't
the Shah, just a person in the clinic, would we have taken out the
spleen? Probably so, because we'd done it on other occasions."
Once more the "famous man" syndrome seemed to be intruding.
The whole world, or much of it, was interested in the Shah's
condition, and so his doctors, perhaps inevitably, tilted toward
caution.

By contrast, Dr. Kean says he was certain that the Shah was
much too weak and jaundiced to have his spleen out at that time,
and that the surgeon was absolutely correct not to try. "The
proper thing was just to get in, relieve the jaundice [by taking out
the gallstones] and get out—as fast as possible." He said he would
never have permitted removal of the spleen then. Nor would Hibbard Williams. "He had been jaundiced for weeks and this was no
time for heroism. We had plenty of time to go back for the
spleen."

Coleman agreed that there was no absolute right or wrong. "It
was a judgment call. The surgeon had to consider that the gallbladder is a dirty organ anyway and that the Shah's gallbladder
was chronically infected. Taking out the spleen as well would have
left a second great hole, on the other side of the abdomen, an open
invitation to invading organisms. An infection could cause a subphrenic abscess, every surgeon's nightmare. The man wielding the
blade has to make the final decision."

During the gallbladder operation, a lymph node was cut out
from the Shah's neck and taken away for biopsy. Kean later said
it showed that he now had large-cell, or histiocytic, lymphoma, a
more serious cancer than that which the French had originally
been treating. But Coleman, his oncologist, was still uncertain
whether this lymphoma was in the spleen as well as the neck. He
assumed it was, but he could not know for certain.

The day after the operation, October 24, the Shah's people

began, grudgingly, to release information. As the Shah lay upstairs on the seventeenth floor and as demonstrators outside shouted "Death to the Shah," Robert Armao gave a news conference. Extraordinarily for a medical briefing at a hospital, no doctors were present. Armao admitted what his staff had the day before denied: that the Shah had lymphoma. He said the Shah had not wanted it known before, "in the best interest of his country." He said the Shah had previously been treated by French doctors. Asked why the Shah had not gone to France, Armao answered that Dr. Kean was on the staff at New York Hospital, and that the Shah had been treated there before. Asked when this had been, Armao did not know. (It was in 1949.) All in all, the press conference was not a success.

The next day the Shah's doctors gave their own press conference. Dr. Coleman was called to it only at the last moment. (He had the impression by now that Ben Kean was not always keeping him au courant.) As the oncologist, he did a lot of the talking. He found it difficult to be exact, because he was still not sure what disease the Shah had originally had, whether the French had treated it appropriately or not, and when the condition had worsened. (Flandrin pointed out later that he and Jean Bernard had given both Kean and Coleman full details of the Shah's medical history.) To the press, Coleman said that the Shah had an enlarged spleen, and that if the spleen proved to be lymphatic, then he would have reached Stage III of the disease and it would be present above and below the diaphragm. Many newspapers missed his qualification and published the news that the Shah had Stage III lymphoma. Coleman also stressed "the potential for cure," saying that the Shah had a 50–50 chance of survival. After all, he had responded "exquisitely" to the earlier treatment by his French doctors. Now, of course, the chemotherapy would have to be much more aggressive. "No picnic," said Coleman.

He thought the Shah should stay in New York. "Good medical practice dictates that you stay with your doctors."

Through all of this, the Queen was under enormous pressure. She was staying with the Shah's twin sister, Princess Ashraf. Their relationship had been difficult at the best of times. Now was the worst of times; Ashraf held the Empress in good part responsible for the Shah's liberalizations in the mid-seventies, and for his refusal to suppress the revolution in a decisive manner. The Princess had not attempted to conceal her views from the Empress.

Like the Shah himself, the Empress had been reluctant to come to New York. She trusted Georges Flandrin and was now keeping in touch with him by telephone. He was concerned about the treatment the Shah was receiving and his concern added to hers. He agreed with Coleman that the Shah's spleen should have been removed.

Adding to the Queen's discomfort was the fact that she had loathed hospitals ever since her father had been taken away from her and had died when she was a child. Now she was especially concerned that her four children not be tortured in the same way. Knowing that "nothing stays a secret in New York, not even in a hospital," she wanted to make sure that she gave them the news before they heard it on television. They were all at different schools. She had them brought to Beekman Place, but everything was such a rush—she was just off to the hospital again and she had only a few minutes to tell them what the disease was and that there was hope for a cure.

She visited the Shah several times a day in his hospital room. It was always melodramatic and often unpleasant. To avoid the aggressive, noisy demonstrators, she had to go in and out by one of the service entrances, "where there is all the machinery, the garbage—all the sad and dirty side of the hospital." There were people around her all the time, never leaving her alone. "I was coming and going from the house, down the corridors, having guards stuck to me, Americans." She was also trying to keep away from the press and from friendly Iranians in exile, who wanted to hear the Shah's views on this, that, and the other. "They couldn't understand that he was sick in hospital and could not have political discussions," she said later.

About a week after the Shah's gallbladder operation, X rays revealed that the surgeons had left one gallstone behind—the bile duct was still blocked. Kean and the Shah's other doctors presented this as a routine complication. Privately, some doctors were aghast. Coleman later recalled another doctor telling him, " 'Everyone's laughing. This big-shot surgeon, he left a gallstone, hah-hah. That's like Babe Ruth not hitting a home run, striking out.' But in fairness," Coleman said, "there were gallstones all over the place. This could have happened to any surgeon." But when Flandrin heard the news in Paris, he was appalled. "There is a standard technique, by applying pressure during surgery, to check whether all gallstones have been removed," he said later. "Why was it not done? It was a major error. It should not have happened. Colleagues of mine who do that operation were shaking their heads with disbelief." Dr. Kean, however, said that such a reaction was out of place; it frequently happens that a gallstone that has been concealed in the liver subsequently descends into the duct.

The doctors considered that a second operation through the diseased tissue of the abdomen would be dangerous. They decided that after the Shah had regained some strength, they would call in a Canadian specialist who had developed a technique for crushing stones by means of a scope inserted through a tube into the bile duct. Such a tube had already been put in the Shah's side during the first operation. The procedure had been used since 1972, but not often in New York Hospital.

While his bile duct was still blocked the Shah could not be given the aggressive chemotherapy that Coleman had outlined. Instead they decided to irradiate the cancer in his neck, where the lymph nodes were still giving him pain. Coleman still did not know whether the lymphoma was localized or disseminated. No matter. If it was localized in the neck, the irradiation might cure him; if disseminated, it could do no harm.

The best facilities were across the street in the Memorial Sloan-Kettering Cancer Center. The Shah's mother had been treated by Memorial physicians for cancer and in gratitude the Shah had given the hospital $1 million. Dr. Kean went over to Memorial to discuss their treatment of the Shah. According to Kean, one or two members of the Memorial hierarchy said they did not want the Shah at all. Kean was outraged. "I exploded," he said subsequently. "I said, 'You were willing to take his one million dollars and now you won't treat him!' " Eventually, and under considerable pressure, Memorial agreed. But they insisted that the tunnel connecting the two hospitals was too busy in the daytime to be secure: the Shah would have to be treated at night. And so, ten times, the Shah was taken down in the elevator and was wheeled through the underground tunnel. It was an unpleasant business; there was a lot of fear. For security reasons the radiologist took a different route from her home in New Jersey on each occasion.

The Queen always accompanied her husband. "They would say it would be at five A.M. I would get up and go to the hospital. They would say, 'No, it's not five A.M., it's ten P.M.' Or, 'The doctor's not here, she's out in the country.' Or, 'Memorial Hospital is afraid to have the King there because they're afraid of terrorist attacks.' "

It was all very exhausting. Still, the lymph nodes shrank, the pain eased, and the Shah grew stronger. But he remained depressed.

He grew more so at the end of the first week of November 1979. On November 4, hundreds of demonstrators poured over the walls of the U.S. embassy compound in Teheran and captured the sixty-six Americans inside. Their leaders announced that they were "followers of the Imam's line," and they demanded the return of "the criminal Shah" to Iran. Thus began one of the most bitter and prolonged battles of recent diplomatic history. The curse of the Flying Dutchman was visited upon the port which he had entered, the United States.

The extent to which Ayatollah Khomeini was aware of the plans to capture the embassy is still obscure. But he immediately embraced the action and seized the takeover as a way of driving his revolution along the path with which he was obsessed. The embassy crisis provided just the opportunity he was seeking to destroy the moderate government of Mehdi Bazargan, which he himself had installed in February to replace that of Bakhtiar, and which he now considered too mild to fulfill the Islamic revolution to which he was so attached.

In 1978, an almost unholy alliance, which had embraced in the end most groups in Iran, had formed to overthrow the Shah. Khomeini had been able brilliantly to dissemble his true ambitions beneath lofty, almost Delphic generalizations. By suggesting that he shared everyone's hopes and beliefs, he had managed to form the broadest possible coalition.

But once the Shah was gone, there was no consensus as to how Iran should be ruled. Khomeini himself had a peculiarly personal vision of an ideal Islamic state led by a *vali-fagih*, or "divine guardian" (himself) according to the laws of traditional Islamic jurisprudence. Many of the so-called "moderates" around Bazargan were religious but sought a return to the Western-inspired constitution of 1906, which emphasized democracy and civil liberties. A third large group, which might be called Islamic "progressives," sought to marry Islamic doctrine to modern political notions, including that of individual freedom. Such ideas had been taken up by the urban guerrillas who fought the Shah and whom the Shah had denounced as "Islamic Marxists."

Both the moderates and the progressives envisaged a subordinate role for the clergy. This was clearly not Khomeini's view. In spring 1979, Khomeini encouraged the proliferation of zealous local "komitehs" tied to the mosques. They took over many of the local functions of government—so much so that Bazargan complained that his regime was like "a knife without a blade."

In August, Bazargan and the progressives suffered further blows when rigged elections resulted in a constituent assembly dominated by followers of Khomeini. It produced a constitution that was almost completely to the ayatollah's liking. Khomeini now set about destroying his opposition. A war against the Kurds, who were still pressing their demands for autonomy, was a distraction for public opinion; opposition newspapers and parties were closed down. Much of this was anathema to Bazargan.

Since taking office, Bazargan had attempted to steer a middle course. He had continued contacts with the U.S. embassy. He had wanted to normalize relations with the U.S.; he hoped that the Army would continue to receive U.S. spare parts and, as an old anti-Communist, he wanted continued U.S. support against the Soviet Union. His manifest reasonableness led some senior officials in the State Department to believe that all would be well with the U.S. relationship to Iran, that business would continue even more successfully than before. On November 1, Bazargan and his foreign minister, Ibrahim Yazdi, met with Zbigniew Brzezinski in Algiers. The harshest U.S. critic of the revolution came away impressed with them, and each side thought that a reasonable relationship could be restored between Iran and the United States. This was not the ayatollah's ambition.

After the Shah's arrival in New York, Khomeini declared that there was a new American plot involving the Shah and Iranian traitors dependent on the West. "These American-loving rotten brains must be purged from the nation," he insisted. When his aides heard of the student plans to assault the embassy on November 4, Khomeini called for action, instructing "students and theological students to expand with all their might their attacks against the United States and Israel, so that they may force the United States to return the deposed and criminal Shah."

As soon as the takeover had succeeded, Khomeini and those around him immediately offered fulsome praise for the students. At the same time Bazargan was charged with having an unauthorized meeting with Brzezinski. He and Yazdi resigned. The last of the opposition to Khomeini was now gone from office. The ayatollah was embarked upon a brilliantly bold attempt to create a major crisis with the United States so as to unite the country and enable him to move fast toward his vision of a theocratic state.

CHAPTER SIXTEEN

The Embassy

The American embassy compound in Teheran, bordered by Roosevelt and Takht-e Jamshid avenues, was all of twenty-five acres. The United States had bought it in 1928 for $60,000 from a family that had used it as a summer country home and had had to sell it to pay off a gambling debt.

By the seventies, the city had spread northward into the hills and was all around the mission. One ambassador's wife described it as an oasis in the center of Teheran.

Outside the walls were the hassle and the bustle and the heat (or the cold), the disappointment and the envy, the riches and the poverty of Iran. Inside were sparkling fountains and freshly mown grass, tall pines and sycamore trees, air-conditioning, parties with prominent people, and a sense of both difference and certainty.

The physical isolation was paralleled by an intellectual severance from the realities of the country. In the embassy the official party line that developed from the mid-sixties onward was one of almost uncritical approval of the Shah. He was a strong leader, a reformer who appreciated the needs of his people and who had a vision of a developed, pro-Western, anti-Communist, prosperous Iran. All of this may well have been true—and may also have been the view of other Western embassies—but its costs were less closely examined.

Nor, it must be said, were they really understood. While the Shah appeared to be unassailable, the downside of his policies had been concealed by a compact between him and Western embassies that allowed little or no contact between foreign diplomats and people beyond a charmed (and often charmless) circle.

The CIA owned in Iran one of its largest operations in the world. It had an unusually close, even intimate relationship with the host government, indeed with the ruler himself. Most of America's allies, and indeed its opponents, tolerate CIA stations within the embassies accredited to them. Agency officials assume covers as cultural, commercial, or consular attachés, but usually the host government knows very well what their real purpose is and, in many cases, watches them accordingly. It is rare for the station chief to have a direct and constant relationship with the head of state. But there are not many rulers who have said to a CIA agent, as the Shah had said to Kim Roosevelt in 1953, "I owe my throne to God, my people, and to you." Ever since, the CIA station chiefs had been a regular part of the Shah's life and of his view of the world. Their meetings with him tended to be more informal and relaxed than the equally regular meetings between the Shah and the U.S. ambassador.

Throughout his reign, the Shah retained a rather touching faith in the importance of his CIA contacts. Many station chiefs served their time in Iran and then followed the example of Kim Roosevelt, returning as businessmen keen to exploit their knowledge and contacts to make rather more money than they made in government service. None of them is known to have been distinguished by his deep understanding of the tensions of Iran. Even so, the Shah expected guidance from the Agency. In his final memoirs, he went so far as to complain that the last station chief, appointed at the end of 1978, came from Tokyo and had absolutely no experience at all of Iran. To the Shah it seemed absurd if not sinister. He could not understand why Langley would send him such an ignorant man. "I was astonished by the insignificance of the reports he gave me."

The problem was deeper than one man's ignorance. The Agency had hundreds, perhaps thousands, of people working for or connected to it in Iran. But they operated under a fundamental restriction. The Shah insisted that his allies, and especially the United States, should have no contact with groups or individuals opposing him. He believed that his opponents would interpret any such contacts as foreign support for them. This may well have reflected a correct understanding of the Iranian psyche. But it had serious implications for intelligence gathering.

No ambassador wished to upset the Shah by disobeying his injunction on contact with those who opposed him. To do so would at the very least have jeopardized his country's export opportunities in Iran. And so American and other diplomats swam in a shallow pool of courtiers, industrialists, lawyers, and others who were somehow benefiting from the material successes of the regime. Not all of them liked the Shah. But all or almost all of them owed him something.

This was not peculiar to Iran. It is hard for diplomats anywhere to make friends en poste. "The natives" tend to get tired of their coming and going; only a certain section of people want to be constantly on the diplomatic circuit, passed on by one political counselor to the next. So it was in Teheran. There, as elsewhere, it was the habit of outgoing diplomats to leave lists of their contacts for their successors. Thus did they tend to perpetuate their dependence on a small circle of people more or less licensed by the Shah. There were no others. As a result, the embassy was like a cocoon for most of its staff.

Throughout much of the period of the Great Civilization, the U.S. ambassador to Teheran was Richard Helms, a career CIA official who had been director of Central Intelligence until his dismissal by Richard Nixon at the end of 1972.

After his spectacular 1972 presidential victory, Nixon had retired to Camp David to restructure his government. Like other senior officials, Helms was summoned there; he was seated between Nixon and H.R. Haldeman, and he was fired. Helms was surprised. He supposed it might be because he had refused to have the CIA help the White House cover up the role of its "Plumbers" in the Watergate break-in. Then Nixon began talking in a desultory way and, on the spur of the moment it seemed to Helms, asked him if he would like to be an ambassador. Helms had never given this any thought—after all, he had not expected to be dismissed—but he said he would think about it, and if he went anywhere maybe Iran would be a good choice. Fine, said Nixon.*

---

* This meant that the incumbent ambassador to Iran, Joseph Farland, had to be ordered to leave the post. He was not pleased. Farland had a long diplomatic history. He had been

Helms and the Shah had been educated at the same school, Le Rosey, in Switzerland, though they had not known each other there. They were first introduced by the CIA station chief in Teheran in 1957. As director of the CIA since the mid-sixties, Helms had both the opportunity and the need to meet and discuss operations with a ruler who, in the broad if not the narrow sense of the word, was an important American "asset." Helms had taken a keen interest in the listening posts along the Iran-Soviet frontier, which enabled the U.S. to eavesdrop over the mountains and spy upon Soviet rocket- and missile-launching facilities in the Soviet Central Asian republics. The U.S. could monitor every electronic activity at these bases, as well as Soviet military moves in the whole arc of territory facing the Persian Gulf. Washington considered such facilities vital to the verification of arms control.

Helm's appointment to Teheran inevitably gave rise to lurid speculations about the nature of CIA control over the Shah. For the Shah's enemies it was clear confirmation that the Shah was merely a CIA puppet. But Helms thought that his long association with Iran meant that he would be able "to hit the ground running" when he arrived in Teheran.

Like previous U.S. ambassadors, Helms was an enthusiastic supporter of the Shah's plans for the rapid development and radical transformation of Iran. But he later came to agree that the Shah had tried to move too fast. He thought one reason was the Shah's frustration at the way in which the oil consortium had held oil prices down till the 1970s. "He had lived so many years hoping that the British and the Americans would allow the price of oil to inch up. But we were ruthless with him. So when he finally got his chance in '73, there was no doubt that he was going to get even. There is no doubt he tried to go too fast. Which led to the ports' congestion and the overheating of the economy."

Helms was also inclined to blame the Queen for pushing too

Eisenhower's ambassador in the Dominican Republic when the CIA was plotting to kill Trujillo. Kennedy then sent Farland to Panama, and later he was ambassador to Pakistan at the time of the Bangladesh war. He endeared himself to Nixon and Kissinger by helping conceal Kissinger's first, secret flight from Pakistan to Peking. He was given the Teheran embassy by way of reward for this service. He succeeded Douglas MacArthur II, who, like Nixon and Kissinger, had seen no value in second-guessing the Shah.

At one stage, MacArthur's view was challenged by a group of younger officers in the embassy, known, inevitably, as the "Young Turks," who argued in a long session with him that Iran was more than the Shah, and the embassy should widen its contacts and perceptions. This was not a view the ambassador shared, and nor did his superiors in Washington.

hard the importance of Western culture. But at the same time he was dismissive of the mullahs, saying that they could only be considered educated by comparison with most villagers, who were completely illiterate. In 1976 Helms noted in a twenty-page study that "contacts with religious leaders by foreigners is [sic] discouraged and SAVAK exerts a great deal of effort monitoring religious activities of even those mullahs friendly to the regime. There is probably less information available to foreigners about the dynamics of this sociological strata [sic] than about any other." Helms concluded, "Religious conservatives are dissatisfied with many apsects of modernization yet remain only potentially troublesome."

Helms thought the Shah's foreign policy was superb. He had established good relations with most countries in the region, he had become close to Mrs. Gandhi, he had sorted out the Helmand River problem with Afghanistan, he was a good friend of Bhutto, and his relations with the Soviet Union were correct. He had restored a relationship with Iraq, and though he and King Faisal of Saudi Arabia "talked past each other," Helms thought their relations were stable. "He would rattle off his arrangements with all the different Gulf States. It was all very impressive. Dean Rusk used to say that he was the best-informed man in the world save the U.S. President. Maybe that's a slight exaggeration."

Helms spent four years in Iran.* He came to realize that he could never understand the Iranians. "They have a very difficult turn of mind. Here would be ladies, dressed in Parisian clothes, made up playing bridge. But before they went on trips abroad, they would ship up to Mashhad in chadors to ask for protection."

Helms and his English wife, Cynthia, visited Mashhad, the site of the tomb of the eighth Imam, and one of the most important

---

* Much of Helms's time in Iran was devoured by trips to Washington to testify to one or another of the various congressional committees investigating the CIA. For several years it seemed that he might be indicted for testimony he had given on Chile. In February 1973, he had been asked by Senator Stuart Symington of the Senate Foreign Relations Committee, "Did you try in the Central Intelligence Agency to otherthrow the government of Chile?"

"No, sir," replied the man who was later called by his biographer "the man who kept the secrets."

In fact he had known that in September 1970 the CIA, on President Nixon's orders, had tried to mount a coup to prevent the confirmation of Salvador Allende's election. There was much talk in the mid-seventies that Helms would be tried for perjury. Eventually and instead, he was fined and given a suspended sentence. President Reagan later awarded Helms the Medal of Freedom.

Shiite shrines in Iran. They were moved and a little disturbed by the fervor displayed by the pilgrims. Helms himself later commented, "It was very impressive and enlightening. People were clamoring, pushing, shoving, to keep their hands on the catafalque. They were worked up into a lather. Trying to move people like that toward the West was no easy job." But he gave the Shah full support in his efforts. "There's no way you can say that a leader shouldn't give his people a vision of a better future," he said later.

Mrs. Helms saw the problem differently in a memoir written after the fall. At one lunch when the Shah was entertaining Henry Kissinger, she realized "how almost European he had become. He had brought his country into the modern world, but in doing this he seemed to have removed himself from its heritage. He came to think of himself as a world leader, and he enjoyed nothing more than discussing international affairs with other leaders of stature." But as he did so, Islam became only a religion, not, as it was intended, a way of life. A religion, moreover, to which the Shah was no longer obviously committed. He was more interested in his own direct relationship with God, and needed no mosque and certainly no mullah as intermediary.

Like his predecessors, Richard Helms rejected advice from some of his staff that the U.S. distance itself from the Shah, give him rigorous counsel, and pursue contacts with serious opponents of the regime. In a 1974 memorandum to Washington he stated, "Foreign contact with dissidents or identification with their point of view is not only discouraged but if pursued vigorously could probably result in one's being PNG'ed [made persona non grata]. Accordingly, political reporting officers must exercise great care and prudence in developing contacts and information of interest and value to us."

In an April 1975 report on the Shah's methods, the embassy described him as

> a larger-than-life figure, a stern, dedicated, modernizing ruler who charts his nation's course and intervenes at all levels of activity to ensure that Iran remains on that course. As his experience and self-assurance have grown . . . the Shah has turned less frequently to others for advice on policy matters. Some observers therefore have assumed that he is isolated from reality; this is not the case. . . .

The memorandum noted, however, that the only people who dared question the Shah were Assadollah Alam, the minister of court, Princess Ashraf, and the Empress.

By 1976 Helms had come to acknowledge some of the drawbacks of the embassy's reporting systems. Discussions with even senior ministers and officials

> are not always as useful as we would like because Iranian government and society are highly structured and authoritarian and all major decisions are made at the top. Often even relatively senior officials are not well informed about policies and plans and have little influence on them. We also have difficulty developing sources about dissidence and even about attitudes among the clergy because of Iranian sensitivities and the GOI's [Government of Iran's] disapproval of foreign contacts with these groups.

That same year John Stempel, of the political section of the embassy, wrote a SECRET cable entitled "Iran's Modernizing Monarchy: A Political Assessment." This acknowledged that Iran's economic expansion "has not produced a concomitant growth in political participation." Too many people were uncertain or cynical about the future. The Shah was now dominant, "but existent and emergent groups will have to be successfully engaged in the political process if Iran is to continue developing in relative stability."

Religious groups were dissatisfied with the Great Civilization "yet remain only potentially troublesome." Nonetheless, Stempel pointed out that

> a sizable minority, perhaps even a slight majority of Iranians, particularly in the rural areas, have neither changed their attitudes nor are inclined to accept "modern" (Western) mores. They reject part of what the Shah has done (such as giving women the vote) as against the will of God and harmful to the true faith of Islam. . . . More important, respectable bazaar merchants, ordinary farmers, and pious Moslems in all areas feel themselves alienated from the regime.

The Shah's change of calendar had angered many people.

> Should a situation of collapsing public order and less decisive leadership than presently exists come about, the mullahs and their followers, including wealthy merchants both in Teheran and in the

provinces, constitute a loosely organized force that could coalesce around an issue or an incident to offer a real challenge. This force is only potential and not well organized. . . .

But even though some senior embassy officials understood the problems, they could not really spend much time with the Shah's critics, for fear, as Helms had put it, of being "PNG'ed." Moreover, it was scarcely worthwhile.

Too much had been invested in the Shah—by European nations as well as by the U.S.—for any real changes in policy. In many senses, he was the keystone of the arch of Western defenses in the Middle East. The United States was his principal armorer, but it was only one of several; and more importantly, there was general agreement in Western Europe that, following the British withdrawal from the Gulf in 1971, only the Shah could be the policeman. One of President Kennedy's entourage, Dave Powers, had once said of him, "He's my kind of Shah." By the mid-seventies, he was everyone's kind of Shah.

He was the only Shah around. He was an ally of more than thirty years, Western oriented, reforming rather than reactionary, a dictator but not even that bloody by contemporary standards, and a marvelous customer to boot. As Captain Gary Sick, the aide to Zbigniew Brzezinski who dealt with Iran, has pointed out, through the sixties and seventies American leaders became convinced that the Shah was master in his own house and that the opposition to him was defeated and irrelevant. Occasional embassy reports that warned about "potential" unrest were small beer. Zbigniew Brzezinski later complained that "Islamic fundamentalism was a phenomenon largely ignored in our intelligence reports." This was, overall, true. But the very relationship that Brzezinski, among so many others, sought for the U.S. with the Shah precluded any such reporting. The Shah would never have tolerated the necessary investigations.

Brian Urquhart, the former under secretary general of the United Nations, has recorded that when Kurt Waldheim and he visited Teheran in January 1978, they asked to meet with members of the opposition. The Shah, clearly irritated, replied, "I will not have any guest of mine waste a single minute on these ridiculous people." Urquhart found the Shah highly opinionated and unable to have an argument—the meeting was a monologue. At lunch with Princess Ashraf, Urquhart found the food excellent, the conversation non-existent. "There was an atmosphere of overwhelming nouveau-riche, meretricious chi-chi and sycophancy. . . . There was an overheated, overstuffed atmosphere in these super-deluxe mini-palaces in the imperial compound which left one gasping for air."

Unable to investigate those excluded from the regime, the CIA and the embassy spent enormous amounts of time on compiling biographies of prominent members of the ruling circles, in particular the Shah's family, courtiers, and leading Iranian businessmen. These were nearly always entertaining, often libelous, and sometimes inaccurate. One of the favorite exercises appears to have been to gather gossip on the rivalry between the Empress and Princess Ashraf and to speculate with which of them various ministers and generals would side in a showdown between the two women.

One 1975 analysis reckoned that

> as long as the Shah lives, Ashraf and her controversial life-style are of little importance except as an ongoing embarrassment to the Pahlavi Dynasty. However, if he should die before the Crown Prince reaches his majority, . . . or is ready to take on the responsibilities of monarchy, Ashraf's urge for power, her delight in intrigue, and her rivalry with Farah are likely to emerge to the detriment of a stable succession.

The embassy found it hard to say exactly which men would align themselves with which woman because "the machinations at court are so complex and convoluted." But, "in the final analysis, we believe that Farah would emerge the victor, if only in name. Ashraf would have an initial advantage but the Empress has certain advantages which we doubt Ashraf could overcome short of violence." These were her legitimacy as regent and her genuine popularity. She was then the only member of the family who could claim to be popular. "Ashraf, on the other hand, is the most controversial and least popular of her line."

Despite its enormous presence in Iran, the Agency apparently did not eavesdrop on the Shah by electronic methods and had no paid asset in the Shah's immediate entourage. A few months before his fall, the Agency asked the embassy to provide information to help it update its psychological profile of the monarch. Among the questions asked were:

1. Concerning the Shah's episodes of depression, were they ever so severe as to significantly interfere with his leadership? Did they seem disproportionate to the circumstances or were rather appropriate discouragement or frustration in the face of severe political problems? What happens to his decision making at these times—does he ever become paralyzed with indecision, tend to delegate to others decisions he might otherwise make himself?

2. How does he pull himself out of these downs? What is his decision making like after a down—is he exaggeratedly decisive?

3. Describe the role of his wife, the degree to which he relies on her.

4. Comments on his time frame would be helpful. In terms of his plan to turn a stable modern Iran over to his son, are there indications from him that he is slipping in his schedule, feeling he will have to remain longer in office in order to accomplish his plan?

When the CIA had sent a team from Washington to review the embassy's work over 1976–77, it found serious shortcomings. A "basic concern" was that

> Washington does not have a clear perception of the Shah's long-range objectives. For example, why is he acquiring such a vast array of sophisticated military hardware? The Shah states adequate defenses against Communist-equipped Iraq are merely precautionary, yet the placement of new bases suggests other interests. In 1985 when oil revenues from Iranian production have peaked and his oil-rich neighbors are just across the Gulf, what does the Shah intend to do with his accumulated weaponry? Will he still claim and demonstrate concern for the stability of the area? Or will he have destabilizing objectives?

The CIA thought that much more serious reporting should be done by the embassy, and better analysis by Washington.

The State Department was more sanguine and argued that the Shah had always told the U.S. a good deal about his aims and tactics and probably would continue to do so. "Given the nature of his state, we will remain largely dependent on his soliloquies and on the ability of our ambassador and others to pose penetrating questions. Realistically, we should not expect to get significantly more information from him than we are receiving now." The CIA thought this was inadequate.

The CIA also felt that Washington needed much more information on what the Shah felt and how he reached decisions. "In this regard it is particularly important to know what subjects are withheld from the Shah and the degree to which reports to him are doctored by subordinates. To what extent do such practices warp his perspective, isolate him, and imperil his regime?" The Agency complained that reporting on the opposition was far too dependent on SAVAK, and there was not even adequate understanding of SAVAK itself.

The process was circular. The CIA and other Western agencies derived much of their information from SAVAK. SAVAK was controlled by the Shah. The CIA reported to the Shah. So did SAVAK. The Shah talked to the ambassador and station chief and there was no independent source that could be used as a check. The embassy had no one close to him, but then there *was* no one close to him—save the Empress. For all these reasons, analysis tended to be both self-confident and self-perpetuating.

The CIA's dependence on SAVAK continued throughout the early seventies, when SAVAK's reputation for torture and repression was at its most disagreeable. There were also allegations that the Nixon administration even turned a blind eye to SAVAK activities—such as the pursuit of Iranian dissidents—in the United States itself although these were probably illegal.*

When Jimmy Carter became president, one of his difficult early decisions was whether or not the SAVAK connection should continue. William Sullivan recalls that before taking up his assignment as ambassador to Iran he specifically asked Carter about future collaboration with SAVAK. The president replied that after examining this question he had concluded that "the intelligence which we received, particularly from our listening stations focused on the Soviet Union, was of such importance that we should continue the collaboration. . . ." But he hoped Sullivan would try

---

* According to cables from Ambassador Helms to Washington, published by Jack Anderson in 1979, the Shah became irritated by critical publicity about the activities of SAVAK operatives in the U.S. in 1976. In one such cable to Henry Kissinger, on November 7, 1976, Helms passed on an Iranian government warning that any American action against SAVAK officials would be reciprocated by moves in Iran against American officials. In a further cable of December 27, 1976, Helms stated, "The Shah is very concerned to maintain the special relationship between Iran and the United States. He contends that no SAVAK representative is operating against the United States or its citizens. Put another way, SAVAK is not authorized to conduct activities counter to U.S. law." On January 3, 1977, Helms quoted the Shah as saying that if anything were done to SAVAK agents in the U.S., he "would not be able to overlook the presence of seventy of your people who are carrying out activities contrary to Iranian law" or of "others whom we do not know about officially."

to persuade the Shah to improve his government's human rights performance. Sullivan did try. As already noted, even before Carter took office, human rights in Iran had improved.

When Sullivan arrived in Teheran, he saw the narrow circle of embassy contacts—courtiers, lawyers, industrialists, and others who were benefiting from the regime—as "the ring around the embassy." Almost all of them were Westernized and were "wealthy, gracious, and entertaining." They had British butlers, Spanish or Filipino maids, and Italian cooks. Some of their salons were amusing. But he did not find them very perceptive.

If he tried to meet people outside the court or its periphery, he discovered "how suspicious they were of foreigners, particularly Americans." He was puzzled; outside the charmed circle around the Shah there seemed to be no adulation or emulation of the United States. He felt that most Shia Muslims found contact with foreigners uncongenial. All in all, Sullivan thought he was more isolated in Iran than in Laos, the Philippines, or any other country in which he had served.

Soon after Sullivan arrived, he and his wife, like the Helmses, visited the shrine at Mashhad. They too were impressed by the emotional fervor of the pilgrims. Sullivan noted also the zeal of the governor of the province, who showed them with pride a film of how he had bulldozed the honeycombed shops and homes of the bazaar around the mosque in the interests of "modernization" but against great popular resistance. (The governor also tried to insist on presenting Mrs. Sullivan with jewelry worth several thousand dollars. The Sullivans protested that they could not, under U.S. law, accept the gift. Officials told them that the shrine was so wealthy as a result of all the jewelry, rugs, and other precious things given it by pilgrims that these jewels were "no greater than a cup of coffee.")

Sullivan saw the tensions between the faithful and the Shah's smooth officials. But when he asked his staff to give him more information on the nature of Shiite beliefs and ambitions, he had found that there was almost no contact between the mullahs and the embassy. No one had thought they mattered. The Shah himself called them corrupt and venal "ragheads." He felt he had crushed them. So did the Soviet ambassador; he told Sullivan that Shiism was insignificant now. That was 1977.

The real relationship between the Shah and the Iranian people remained an area not of darkness, but at least of twilight, for both the intelligence agencies and for the monarch. They all shared in the failure to anticipate, still less to understand, the events of 1978–79. Even as late as spring 1978, after serious rioting in Qom, U.S. diplomats remained complacent. In April, a Soviet embassy official, Victor Kazakhov, described by his U.S. contact, Ralph Boyce, as "a young, hard-charging KGB officer," warned Boyce that there would be an uprising in Iran. Boyce dismissed this: "He gave me a textbook explanation of oppressed masses rising to overthrow their shackles, etc."

Another and revealing image of the Shah's collapse was created by the Polish writer Ryszard Kapuscinski, who saw the Shah as the director and the only character in an epic production called "The Great Civilization." Everyone else—peasants, workers, generals, foreign businessmen and ministers of finance—were mere extras, all obediently responding to the orders of the Shah. Then there is confusion as suddenly the script is thrown away; the black flags of the Shiites appear on stage and the extras begin to storm the upper levels of the stage. "Ministers stuff bags full of banknotes and take flight, ladies grab jewelry boxes and vanish, butlers wander around as though lost." The extras take over and then all the wires and cables are disconnected from the brilliant Peacock Throne and its overpowering occupant. "The brilliance begins to fade and the figure itself grows smaller and more ordinary. Finally, the electricians step aside and an elderly, slim man, indeed the kind of gentleman we might encounter at a movie, in a café or in a line, rises from the throne, brushes his suit, straightens his tie, and walks off stage on his way to the airport."

It is dangerous to be too critical with hindsight. Revolutions are, by definition, unexpected, spontaneous, uncontrolled. Henry Kissinger has said that he once told Western newsmen in the mid-seventies that "a rate of economic advance like Iran's was bound to lead to revolution. But it was idle musing, for I added immediately that apparently the momentum of a very rapid rate of growth could overcome the political perils of industrialization. I was wrong." He has also pointed out that the events of 1978–79 were never inevitable—a different reaction by the Shah and his allies might have produced a very different outcome. He has furthermore suggested that in the West, "we lack a coherent idea of how to channel the elemental forces let loose by the process of development." There was no precedent for a leader like the Shah, commanding a vast army and extensive security forces, to be over-thrown so easily as he was. Almost no other foreign power antic-ipated it. The British did not. Nor did other West Europeans. However, the Israelis, whose secret service, Mossad, is legendary for the length of its tentacles, claim that they did expect it. Mossad and SAVAK had worked together, and conducted joint opera-tions, since the 1950s. Mossad helped to arm the Kurds against Iraq. The Israelis regularly gave Teheran intelligence reports on the internal affairs of Arab countries, and SAVAK reciprocated.

The head of the Israeli mission in Teheran at this time was Uri Lubrani, who had spent much of his career in Africa—Uganda, Rwanda, Burundi, and Ethiopia. He was known to be extremely well informed. He was sending gloomy reports to Tel Aviv since at least the beginning of 1978. On one occasion, after he had been to see the Shah on Kish Island, he met one of the Shah's advisers who said to him, "Have you actually seen His Imperial Majesty?"

"Yes," replied Lubrani.

"Have you *really* seen this epitome of Iranian degradation?"

Lubrani was astonished. "I couldn't believe what I was hearing. It meant there was something rotten at the very core of the base on which the Shah relied."

He later said that he had also foreseen the religious nature of the convulsion in Iran. "Having gone to Iran from Ethiopia, I had seen a monarchy actually in the process of decay. I realized very early in my stay that the only organized infrastructure which had leeway to operate within the country was the religious commu-nity."

In Lubrani's opinion, SAVAK had recruited young mullahs who "at a certain juncture exchanged sides, and they injected into this rather medieval, Byzantine kind of religious infrastructure, modern techniques, modern thought, modern press relations, and so on. When I look at our [Israeli] religious establishment, I see certain similarities."

In November 1979, when the militants seized the U.S. em-bassy, they found there almost seventy people—far more than the "bare bones" staffing that the White House had authorized after the first attack on the compound in February. Over the summer of 1979 each agency had gradually increased its personnel in Iran.

The militants also found thousands of files. At the time of the Shah's fall, Sullivan had prudently ordered all nonessential papers to be shipped out of Teheran. But in the next ten months various agencies had quietly shipped them back, and in November 1979 the embassy shredders had no time to deal with all the documents before the siege was complete.

In fact even shredding was not to prove a protection against the zeal of the militants. Over the next five years Iran published more than fifty volumes of documents seized in the embassy in November 1979. Several of the memoranda quoted in this chapter come from those books. Many of the documents published were fully shredded pages that had been reconstituted. The painstaking, eye-destroying care with which this was done was a testimony to the burning commitment to expose and humiliate the United States.

CHAPTER SEVENTEEN

The Asylum

Soon after the militants captured the embassy, the Pope offered to mediate between Iran and the United States. The ayatollah angrily denounced him. Where was the Vatican, he asked, when the Shah "put our youth in frying pans and sawed off their legs?"

In the United States, public shock over the seizure of the embassy gave way to anger. The Shah's presence in the U.S. was seen by millions of Americans as the cause of the hostage seizure—which itself was taken as a real personal insult.

The Shah himself quickly understood this. On November 8, he sent President Carter a message through David Rockefeller's office to say that he "felt terrible" about what had happened and would "leave the United States today," if it were up to him. But his doctors had said that he was in no position to travel. The State Department learned that he "has been perspiring heavily overnight and could have pneumonia, although a definitive report is not in from the doctors." He would not be able to leave for three or four weeks, until after the last gallstone was removed.

Carter's bitter reflection was that by that time all the Americans in the embassy could be dead. But he said he did not want to endanger the Shah's life and under no circumstances would he allow the Shah to be extradited as the Iranians were demanding.

Across the United States there was outrage over the fact that a
"medieval fanatic," which was how many people saw Khomeini,
could break all laws, sanction the seizure of American diplomats,
and hold the United States to ransom. There was a simultaneous
search for explanations and for scapegoats. Why was the Shah in
the United States anyway?

For those who like conspiracies, the Rockefellers and Henry
Kissinger were easily seen as the arch villains in the "plot" to
admit the Shah. Perhaps not everyone agreed with the statement
from an Iranian spokesman at the United Nations, who described
them as "dehumanized and sinister elements," but they became
easy scapegoats. Robert Armao and Dr. Kean also began to come
in for unfavorable comment; they were portrayed as servants of
the Rockefellers.

In search of the motive, journalists and analysts began to examine the relationship between David Rockefeller's Chase Manhattan Bank and the Shah. Chase had been one of the first banks
to appreciate how much business was to be done in Iran in the

David Rockefeller

fifties and sixties. By the seventies it had become one of the principal foreign banks in Iran, a banker to the National Iranian Oil Company as well as to the Shah himself, and the government's main creditor. In 1974, at a time when Iran was restricting foreign investment in its banks, Chase was allowed to open a joint venture bank called the International Bank of Iran, based in Teheran. After 1975, Chase was regularly chosen by Iran as the managing bank to put together consortiums of lenders when Iran sought to borrow money. Chase had vast Iranian deposits. By 1975 they were said to be about $2.5 billion, or almost 8 percent of the bank's total deposits.

The relationship did not immediately change when the Shah fell. But in the fall of 1979, Iran began transferring its deposits out of Chase into other banks, including the London branch of the Bank of America.*

Chase became increasingly exposed, and this exposure was at the core of the most elaborate conspiracy theory devised to explain David Rockefeller's anxiety to have the Shah come to the U.S. The theory, subsequently expounded in some detail but without clinching evidence by a financial journalist, Mark Hulbert, in his book *Interlock,* was that the Chase needed a serious crisis in U.S.–Iranian relations in order to give it an excuse to "pull the plug" on Iranian loans. This was allegedly why David Rockefeller was so keen to get the Shah into the States—that would guarantee the necessary crisis.

In this context the medical advice on the basis of which the Shah had been secretly spirited into the country was dissected. Some

---

* Between February and August 1979, the National Iranian Oil Company deposited almost $6 billion with Chase's London branch. By the middle of November 1979 Iran's deposits with Chase had dropped to $392 million in London and only $39 million in New York. There was another $30 to $40 million in foreign currencies on deposit in London. At the same time, the offshore branches of Chase carried loans of about $350 million to the government of Iran or Iranian entities.

newspapers and journals made Dr. Benjamin Kean the villain. He was portrayed as a close associate if not a minion of the Rockefellers, and it was alleged that as such he had finessed the Shah's admission, urging it not for strictly medical reasons but to please David Rockefeller and, incidentally, Henry Kissinger.

Parade magazine said that Kean's report to the State Department from Mexico stated flatly that "highly technical studies (for cancer) cannot be carried out in any of the medical facilities in Mexico." *Science* magazine went further and alleged that Dr. Kean's original diagnosis had been flawed and superficial and that he had been acting as an agent of Rockefeller interests. For his part Kean insisted publicly that he knew neither Rockefeller nor Kissinger, and had not been in touch with them at any stage about the Shah. He sued *Science* for its allegations, and the magazine subsequently printed an apology. But *Science*'s further points, that there were adequate facilities in Mexico City, including CAT scans, and in many other countries besides the United States, were beyond dispute.

On the morning of November 14 the financial crisis broke. Just three weeks after the Shah was smuggled into New York and ten days after the hostages were seized, President Carter signed an order freezing all Iranian assets held by U.S. banks within the United States and abroad. This move had been in preparation for several days. The official reason given was that reports had just arrived in Washington that Iran's acting foreign minister, Abolhassan Bani-Sadr, was threatening to withdraw all Iran's assets in American banks. The conspiracy theory, never proven, was that Chase wanted to declare Iran in default of a major loan and that November 14 was a very convenient date for the bank.

The theory went like this. In 1977 a consortium of eleven banks, led by Chase, had made Iranian utilities a loan of $500 million. This was a record loan for Iran, and it was intended to help balance the national budget, which was badly stretched by the Shah's military spending. Chase's share of the loan was $50 million—this was Iran's largest single debt to Chase.

An interest payment of $4 million on this loan was due on November 15, 1979. On November 4, Iran had actually instructed Chase to make the interest payment of $4 million by transferring funds from one account to another. But the Chase did not do so. Then, after President Carter froze all Iranian assets on November 14, Chase refused to make the transfer, giving the presidential order as its reason. (Evidence produced later in court provided no further details on Chase's refusal.)

Thus Chase was now technically in a position to declare the loan in default. Five days later, on November 19, it did so. This infuriated some of its European partners in the syndicate. On November 23, Chase informed the Bank Markazi in Teheran that it had set all of the Central Bank's accounts against the monies that Chase said Iran owed it and its various branches. The Bank Markazi immediately began a lawsuit against Chase in London and Chase brought a countersuit in New York.

David Rockefeller made no direct comment on the allegations. He put out a somewhat Olympian statement on his relationship with the Shah, saying that he had known him for more than twenty years. "I was convinced that he was a real friend to this country for over thirty-seven years." He had been in contact with the Shah since he had left Iran, helping him to find homes. When he heard that the Shah was ill in Mexico, "I then helped to arrange" Dr. Kean's visit. When Kean "confirmed the gravity of the Shah's condition, I assisted in having the results of that examination brought to the attention of the State Department." From then on the decision to admit the Shah or not had had nothing to do with him; it was the U.S. government's alone. Privately, Rockefeller apparently told President Carter that he would like "to escape his responsibilities for the Shah's movements."

Rockefeller's associate in pressing for the Shah's admission, Henry Kissinger, gave an interview in *U.S. News & World Report* criticizing the Carter administration's treatment of the Shah and the handling of the Iranian crisis. But on November 12 he called Cy Vance's office to say that this interview was given several days before the embassy was seized. According to an internal memorandum to the secretary, Kissinger said, he would reiterate the need for support of the president in the current crises in all public statements.

A few days later, in Austin, Texas, Kissinger announced that people were "sick and tired of seeing Americans pushed around" and asked of Carter's foreign policy, "Could it be that there is no penalty for opposing the United States and no reward for friendship to the United States?"

Far from offering support to the president, he stated, "The disintegration of America's ability to shape events cannot be an accident. The challenges to the United States simultaneously in so many parts of the world did not just happen."

There were undoubtedly many Americans who shared Kissinger's dislike of the Carter administration. But his observations were not popular everywhere and his perception that Washington was weak. *The New York Times* called them "repellent." Anthony Lewis wrote in the same paper that the most striking thing about Kissinger's performance was its cowardice. "He urged the Shah's admission to the United States but has taken no responsibility for the result." Privately he had given support to officials, and publicly he had undermined them. His behavior "has produced more revulsion in official Washington than anything to date." This was the view also of George Ball, who called Kissinger's conduct "enormously obnoxious."

As so often happens, crisis spawned examination. By the middle of November 1979, there were dozens of high-powered journalists from the American newspapers and networks scouring Teheran, New York, Washington, Geneva, and elsewhere for evidence of the Shah's misrule. Newspapers and television networks began to run far more detailed coverage of the Shah's reign than ever before. The charges made by his enemies—that he tortured and killed, that he was a dangerous megalomaniac, that the White Revolution had been a catastrophe, that he was an American puppet—were turned over and over in an unprecedented way.

In particular, the investigators were embarked on a long and ultimately frustrating chase after his and his family's wealth. The new authorities in Teheran charged that the Pahlavis had plundered the country. "The Americans must realize that this family, who were only illiterate peasants two generations ago, has stolen much of the national wealth from the country," said one official from the Iranian embassy in Washington. Fabulous figures were bandied around. Lawyers representing the new government charged that the Pahlavis had diverted at least $20 billion in Iranian government funds to their own personal use through the Pahlavi Foundation and other organizations. Other officials said $56 billion.

In Teheran, the new head of the Iranian Central Bank was Ali Reza Nobari, a thirty-two-year-old graduate of the Sorbonne and Stanford. He and his staff produced jumbled stacks of documents and canceled checks to try to enable foreign journalists to document the extent of Pahlavi perfidy.

Oddly, the new regime had done nothing to pursue these trails until after the hostages were captured. Asked why not, Nobari replied, "The culpability of the Shah was so established in the psychology of Iranians" that the new government saw no reason to "dig up documents" or to try the Shah in absentia. In other words, the myth was considered adequate. But now, after the hostage seizure, the government had decided it had to "prove to foreigners" its view of the Shah's rule.

Among the papers that were now produced were photocopies of what appeared to be telexes transferring money abroad in the names of the Shah's sisters. These amounted to nearly $800 million, according to Nobari. He said he was investigating possible payments to the family as "commissions on arms sales" and he said that he thought the Shah had probably sent "suitcases full of cash" out of the country. But there was no documentary evidence of this, and he acknowledged that "we haven't been able to find anything having the Shah's own name on it." The problem, according to Mr. Nobari, was that "the records are scattered all over." He said that most of the relevant documents had been destroyed by bank officials working for the Pahlavis. The task was not made any easier by the disarray among those trying to prove the charges in both Iran and the United States. For example, the lawsuit filed in New York alleging that the Shah had stolen $20 billion was prepared without any real reference to the evidence available in Teheran. The figure represented no more than a guess.

The investigators did find and produce letters from Chase setting up an account for the Shah back in 1946, and photocopies of checks made out to the Shah by Chase, on instructions from the Bank Melli in Teheran, thereafter. These were for amounts ranging from $1,000 to $150,000.

Then the Central Bank found documents showing that Iranian government entities made substantial loans to the Shah and his family—loans that seemed not to have been repaid. They also produced documents relating to the Pahlavi Foundation, which was ostensibly a charity but which in fact used its powers of patronage to considerable effect to underpin the regime.

The foundation had been established in 1958, and the Shah had transferred substantial Pahlavi assets to it in 1961, at a time when the wealth of the royal family was becoming a political issue. The charitable works of the foundation were not insubstantial. By

1977 it had paid for the foreign education of twelve thousand students, who needed to repay only 25 percent of the loans they were given. It also gave food and assistance to the very poor and the disabled, provided pensions for the families of policemen and soldiers killed in the service of the country, ran a book publishing house, and financed orphanages. But its works were political as well as charitable. The publishing house produced works that were Pahlavi propaganda. The orphanages (as in all dictatorships of Right or Left) could be used to provide recruits for the security services.

By the end of the Shah's reign, the foundation's assets included hotels; shares of the cement, sugar, and insurance industries, as well as shipping and automobiles; and most of the casinos in Iran. No one knows the total value, but the foundation was thought to be worth close to $3 billion. It owned 100 percent of Bank Omran, which alone had assets of $1.05 billion. The bank had been set up in 1952 to finance the development and sale of crown lands (as well as to collect debts to the crown), but by the seventies most of its work was in property development, from which various members of the royal family made vast and separate fortunes.

Everything was intertwined. From the documents produced by the Central Bank at the end of 1979, it appeared that the Industrial and Mining Development Bank of Iran had loaned the Shah's relations or enterprises in which the Pahlavi Foundation had an interest more than $570 million—which was more than double the bank's 1978 reported capital and reserves of $215 million. Some of the loan contracts were never registered or secured, contrary to Iranian law. As in so many of the financial deals that the rich arrange for themselves, the trails of money and paper crossed and crisscrossed one another, crossed frontiers, and built up accounts in a bewildering and ultimately stupefying manner. According to the sleuths in Teheran, money from one loan, apparently meant to finance the building of a hotel in Teheran, turned up in the Luxembourg account of an Israeli consulting firm.

Altogether, according to the Iranian investigators, Bank Omran had made unrepaid loans totaling at least $180 million to the foundation—almost three times the bank's reported capital and reserves in 1978.

They found also a construction company called Atisaz to which Bank Omran had made unsecured loans of $138 million. (In 1978 the bank accepted as collateral the Hyatt Teheran Hotel, which was owned by the Pahlavi Foundation. But according to the Iranian investigators, this hotel was worth only about $30 million.) Atisaz was said to have been used by the Shah to launder funds. The job was said to have been done by his personal banker, Mohammed Behbehanian—the man who had come to Aswan to meet the Shah and who had advised him to apologize to the British if he wanted to win back his throne.

Since leaving the Shah in Morocco, Mr. Behbehanian had gone to ground, hounded, he thought, by the new regime and also by the story that he had stolen millions of dollars from his master. When the Shah was in the Bahamas, Behbehanian had spoken to him once by telephone and had wept as he complained to his King that after long years of service his honor had been thus besmirched. The Shah tried to comfort him. Since then Behbehanian had not been in touch.

Years later, Behbehanian said in an interview in his home in Switzerland that Atisaz was a company he had created to build a resort on the Caspian. He said that the money came from the royal estates and that it had therefore profited the Shah. He also said that he had sold the Hyatt Hotel to Bank Omran for $25 million. The Iranian Central Bank investigators claimed that Bank Omran had transferred $15 million in Atisaz funds to a Milwaukee bank and that this had subsequently been sent on to the Swiss Bank Corporation office in New York. Again, cast-iron evidence was not available, and Mr. Behbehanian denied that anything improper had been done. He said that the Shah's principal wealth abroad derived from an investment that Behbehanian had made for him in Spanish property in the sixties. The original money, said Behbehanian, had come from the sale of crown lands. In the early seventies, he said, he had also sold some of the Shah's shares in Iranian companies and had added this money to the Spanish profits kept out of the country. That money represented the bulk of the Shah's wealth abroad.

To counter the allegations that he had stolen billions and billions of dollars from Iran, the Shah saw Barbara Walters of ABC News in his room in New York Hospital. He told her it was absurd to bandy around figures of billions of dollars. People did not realize how much one billion was, let alone twenty-five, which he was accused of having. He was not poor, he agreed, but he was probably no richer than some American millionaires. He had between $50 and $100 million, he said.

He also insisted to her that he had had to come to the States because there was no CAT scan in Mexico. That was untrue.

By this time, the Shah was spending most of the day sitting in his room playing cards, or watching television, which was filled with news and information about Iran. Quite apart from the constant views of demonstrators outside the U.S. embassy in Tehran, acting out rage against the United States, Americans were being told more about Iran, its past relations with the United States, and its present turmoil than they had learned of any country since Vietnam. Day in, day out, expert after politician after journalist after academic came forward to offer analyses. Not all were very accurate, but most were hostile to the Shah, denouncing him as a thief, a torturer, and a megalomaniac.

This fare, added to his natural paranoia, served to convince the Shah that there really had been a Western plot against him. One day he found himself watching Sir Anthony Parsons, the British ambassador who had wept when he said good-bye to the Shah but had then helped persuade Mrs. Thatcher not to allow him into Britain. Parsons was now Britain's man at the United Nations and was apparently suggesting that the new Iranian authorities should come to the U.N. and explain their revolution. "I could hardly believe my ears," the Shah wrote later in his memoirs. "This was the same Parsons who told me in the fall of 1978, when I planned free elections, that if I lost them—and my throne—I would go down in history as a ruler who had lived up to his democratic ideals." He saw Parsons' present "performance" as "a classic example of the West's double standard. As an ally, I was expected to live up to the West's idea of democracy regardless of its unfeasibility in a country like mine. But this so-called Islamic Republic, which makes a mockery of all Western ideals, was cordially invited to the U.N. to educate the delegates in the new 'morality' of the so-called Islamic Revolution."

The Shah wrote later that as he sat in the hospital watching the alternating cries of American fury and incomprehension that followed the seizure of the hostages, "I began to wonder if there had been any coherence to Western policy toward Iran beyond a successful effort to destroy me." He recalled that both British and American hands had laid heavily on Iran—"Western support of my rule had always been tempered by a need to exercise a sufficient amount of control." Ironically, his enemies at home would have agreed precisely with such an analysis.

Even now he had his supporters in the United States. He received scores of cards and letters and bouquets of flowers from ordinary Americans. One man wrote offering a cottage on a lake "where you'll be safe." As he grew stronger, he had visitors who, in some way, represented the different aspects of his relationship with the West. Henry Kissinger came. Kissinger found him "resigned" but concerned that perhaps the administration would send him back to Iran. Kissinger assured him this was inconceivable. The Shah said he thought the whole crisis would end with Khomeini being overthrown by radicals. David Rockefeller came. Gianni Agnelli, the head of Fiat, who himself was part of the international high society that had included the Shah as well, stopped by.

Frank Sinatra came too. He had called Robert Armao to say that he felt very bad about what had happened to the Shah and would love to come to see him. Delighted, said Armao. "Frank came up to see the Shah, had a lovely conversation. He invited the Shah to his home in Palm Springs," said Armao later. "He called me several times thereafter to reiterate the invitation, saying, 'The Shah's my friend, it's a disgrace the way America's treating him, my house at Palm Springs is at his disposal.' He was very gracious to the Shah."

Richard Helms and his wife, Cynthia, came to the bedside. Helms was now running a public-relations firm called Safeer, which is Persian for ambassador, in Washington. He found the Shah obsessed with the way in which both nations and individuals had betrayed him. Why had the West destroyed him? he asked. He talked also of his former minister of court, Assadollah Alam, who had died of the same illness in this same hospital in 1977. "Alam died at the right time," he said.

By the end of November, the Shah seemed strong enough to be moved. Mark Morse went back to Mexico to prepare the house at Cuernavaca. But in the meantime new problems had developed among the Shah's doctors. Dr. Kean had asked Morton Coleman, the only oncologist involved, to leave the case.

Coleman did not understand why this happened. He thought perhaps he had been more forthright with the Shah than was appropriate. "I'm not exactly a shrinking violet, and I go into the guy and say, 'Look, with all respect, I can tell you what you want to hear—which was probably the way Iran was being run—or I can tell you what you need to hear. First off you need that spleen out to know what's going on in there, and secondly you will probably need combination chemotherapy if you want to be cured. Chlorambucil alone will no longer do.' I think the Shah may have gotten a little bit pissed off with me for my having told him what he needed to hear. But perhaps this sort of candor would have been beneficial to him earlier in Iran."

Dr. Kean said in a subsequent interview that this was ridiculous: Coleman was removed because he, Kean, did not want his patient, the Shah, subjected to Coleman's aggressive, radical, and still experimental chemotherapy. He said that originally he thought he could control Coleman's enthusiasm for his own therapy, but then discovered he could not. Coleman said that the Shah, suffering from cancer, was now without a medical oncologist. Kean said this was not so; the Memorial Hospital group, in charge of his irradiation, was more than able to look after him. Coleman's point was that they were radiotherapists, not medical oncologists.

Coleman thought it was self-evident that the Shah, like many rich or powerful patients, was getting fragmented care; Dr. Kean's Peter Smith principle was not being heeded. In order that he should not be accused of having either diagnosed or treated the Shah incorrectly, Coleman wrote Hibbard Williams a letter setting out what he thought was the Shah's present condition and the possible treatments he might be given. It began: "Herein is the final oncology note on Mr. David Newsome." He suggested that the spleen should be removed if possible.

Dr. Kean subsequently asserted that Stage III or Stage IV lymphoma had by now been diagnosed. Coleman was more cautious. He wrote that "the extent of the disease, however, remains uncertain and hinges on the nature of the splenomegaly, since the axillary node biopsy, lymphangiogram, and CAT scan revealed no pathologic nodes as indirect evidence of further spread." If it was confirmed that the Shah did indeed have Stage III or Stage IV histiocytic lymphoma, then a six-month course of aggressive chemotherapy would be needed. But that should not be done unless and until lymphoma in the spleen was confirmed, he wrote.

Subsequently, Coleman heard on the grapevine that despite his instructions chlorambucil was being administered to the Shah, partly because the Shah himself asked for it. Although he was not now involved, he retained the confidence of the Shah's family, in particular of Princess Ashraf, and Dr. Pirnia, the pediatrician.

On November 30 the Shah's odyssey was again disrupted. It was only three days before he was due to fly back to Mexico; Washington had been pushing for him to leave as soon as he was fit. Then Armao received a call from the Mexican consul general. He had to see him at once. Armao agreed to meet him in a restaurant in a few hours' time. The diplomat came straight to the point. "The Shah can't stay in Mexico." He could come for a few days, because he still had a valid visa. But after that, it was out.

Armao could not believe it. President López Portillo had made a solemn promise to the Shah, and everything was arranged. Armao called the Mexican ambassador, who confirmed the news. "That's right, I received a communiqué. The Shah is not welcome in Mexico. You have to understand his presence is becoming a threat to our national interest."

Armao returned to the hospital. It was an hour or so before he could bring himself to tell the Shah. "But why?" the Shah asked.

Armao replied that the Mexican Foreign Ministry had always been against them; now that the U.S. embassy had been seized, he thought it must have finally won the argument.

When Carter heard the news he was outraged. He reckoned that he would never get the hostages out while the Shah remained in the States, and he was extremely anxious for him to leave.

Armao called David Newsom at the State Department and said that the Shah was going to leave the hospital and move into his sister Ashraf's house in Beekman Place. Newsom thought this was a dreadful idea; it would only reinforce Iranian paranoia that the U.S. was bent on restoring the entire Pahlavi family. He told Armao it was impossible. At this Armao lost his temper and shouted that there was only so much that a public-relations firm could do. It was up to the White House now. They had better find the Shah a place to go. Otherwise it was Beekman Place.

Hurriedly, Carter sent his counsel, Lloyd Cutler, up to see the Shah. Cutler managed to persuade him not to go to his sister's home. He asked him instead to fly at once and in secret to Lackland Air Force Base in Texas. There was a good hospital there, said Cutler, and he could wait in secluded comfort until the United States found him another country. The Shah agreed and told the Queen. They had to leave that night, he said.

"I couldn't talk to anyone. Not even my mother. And not to the children, which was so hard," said the Empress later. She had only a few hours to pack and she did not know what to take. She was to leave before dawn. Her youngest daughter, Leila, who was only nine, was in the house. Next morning she came looking for her mother and found her gone.

Sometime before dawn on December 2, Dr. Kean cut from the Shah's wrist the plastic nametag that called him David Newsom; and the Shah was wheeled out of his room and along the subdued corridors of the hospital. He was so surrounded by dark shadows of FBI men with weapons that it all reminded him of a getaway scene in a 1930s gangster movie. They pushed him through the basements, past dirty gray-green walls, piles of broken furniture and machinery, trolleys of trash, into the garage which was filled with agents. The getaway cars roared up the ramp into the dark of 71st Street.

The Queen and the dogs were accorded a similar escort that had been gathering in Beekman Place. The FBI was all over the place, she said, all with their walkie-talkies, their guns, their unsmiling expressions, trying busily to look inconspicuous. For her, younger than her husband, "It was like a James Bond movie. There were FBI and CIA people in my car. And there were laundry vans full of security people in front of us and behind us."

The convoys drove through the dark, cold, and empty pre-dawn streets to La Guardia. There the plane, an Air Force DC-9, was surrounded by more men wearing bulletproof vests and carrying machine guns. They were bundled aboard and the plane took off at once.

The sky lightened as they flew southwest and they landed at Lackland around breakfast time. Here again security was intense. After saluting and shaking hands, the military men pushed them without courtesies into an ambulance which immediately roared off down the airfield, with the Shah and the Queen hanging on grimly inside, swinging back and forth as the vehicle cornered and braked aggressively.

Then came for the Queen the worst moment so far in the long ride across the world. The ambulance screeched to a halt, the doors were opened, and they were asked to step out. Suddenly they found themselves inside the psychiatric wing of the military hospital. There were men in white coats, male nurses who looked like gorillas, bars on the windows, and an overwhelming sense of oppression and finality. This was the safest place on the base, they were told. The Queen exploded.

"My God," she recalled. "After all that pressure, and being up all night, to arrive in a psychiatric ward! Maybe five minutes ago crazy people had been sleeping in those beds. A terrible feeling! My husband was in a room that had no windows."

She looked around her own room. There was a microphone in the ceiling—to give orders to the patients, she supposed. The door had no handle on her side. She felt completely claustrophobic. But at least she had a window. She tried to open the curtains. A male nurse moved to stop her.

"I will go crazy," she said. "I have to see the sky and I have to breathe some air." She pulled open the curtains. The window would open only a fraction and there were iron bars behind it, but it was something. "Suddenly that five centimeters of air was my life."

She was genuinely afraid that the Carter administration had kidnapped them. "Are we in jail?" she shouted at Mark Morse. "Has Carter put us in jail? Are we now under arrest?" Who knew what would happen next? Maybe they would be deported. Sent back to the ayatollah, perhaps. Neither she nor her husband had any faith in Carter.

To her relief she was allowed to use the telephone, so she called friends to tell them where they were. "If you don't hear from us, we are here," she said. Then she sat down at the table in her cell and started to write—something, anything, "to pass the time and to stop going crazy."

It was several hours before they were moved out of their cells. "Later they told me, 'Thank God you didn't see the next room, it was full of chains,' " said the Empress.

CHAPTER EIGHTEEN

The General

Lackland is an open base, no repository of nuclear weapons, for example; it is a training base—many of the Shah's own pilots had been stationed there. Thousands of people come and go every day "as they would through a shopping center," said the Shah himself. This was why the base commander, General Acker, had had the idea of putting the Shah and the Queen behind the bars of the mental hospital.

In view of the Queen's objections, they were given instead a little apartment reserved for visiting officers. There were three small rooms, with garish curtains and carpet and a lurid vinyl couch. Once the dogs had moved in, there was barely room for their owners.

General Acker asked them to please stay inside at all times. The Queen refused, saying, "I have to go outside." So they were allowed to walk around the house, while armed air force security men perched like militant crows in the trees.

Whatever its shortcomings, life at Lackland was much more pleasant than being cooped up on the seventeenth floor of New York Hospital with demonstrators howling in the canyons below and abuse pouring hour by hour from the television. Here the Shah and the Empress seemed, by contrast, almost to be among

friends. General Acker asked them to dinner several times and in
every other way tried to make them comfortable, checking what
food they liked, making sure they were looked after. Several of
the officers had served in Iran and all of them were far more
sympathetic than the people and the pundits of New York. The
Shah had always been knowledgeable about aircraft and he could
talk to these officers. Better, indeed, than to many people. They
in turn actually showed him respect—which was a quality of
which he had seen little since he fled Teheran. "Military people
have different views about the world to politicians," said the
Queen later.

The weather was good; the Shah went for walks and General
Acker found tennis partners for the Queen. The Shah sat and
watched her play. She forced herself onto the court—"just to keep
going." For her the tension was now worse than for the Shah; she
wept a lot and she smoked incessantly. She called Georges Flandrin in Paris and said, "It's not only in Teheran that there are
hostages." She knew that the sanctuary at Lackland, if that was
what it was, would be very temporary. Everyone had made that
clear. She was desperately worried by the same old problem, to
which answers became ever more difficult: Where on earth could
they go next?

The Shah discussed the problem with Steve Oxman, a young
State Department "baby-sitter" whom Washington had sent to
Lackland. The Shah told him that he really wanted to go to a
"mainstream" country, somewhere respectable like Austria or
Switzerland. He did not want to be in some banana republic to
which only pariahs were sent. "I'm not Tamerlane," he said to
Oxman.

On December 7, 1979, Shahriar Mustapha Shafiq was murdered
on a Parisian street as he was carrying groceries home to his sister's
apartment in the Rue de la Villa Dupont, a cul-de-sac in the fashionable Sixteenth Arrondissement. A young man wearing a wrap-
around crash helmet fell in step behind him, pulled out a pistol,
and shot him in the back of the head. As Shafiq fell, the gunman
bent over him, fired another round into his head, and then disappeared among the crowd in the Rue Pergolèse. Two 9-millimeter
cartridges were found on the ground beside Shafiq's body.

In Teheran, Sadeq Khalkhali, the head of the Islamic Revolutionary Tribunal, immediately took the credit for the murder.

Such killings, he said, would continue "until all these dirty pawns of the decadent system have been purged."

Shahriar Shafiq was the Shah's nephew, Princess Ashraf's second son. He was thirty-four and a naval officer; he had been in command of the Persian Gulf fleet of Hovercraft, which the Shah had bought from the British and which those who feared the Shah thought would be used to extend Pahlavi suzerainty over the Gulf. A competent officer, he was well aware of the absurdities of the Shah's massive arms buying program. The Imperial Navy was supposed to protect the Persian Gulf and to safeguard the oil lanes, but he thought it was not being equipped to do either.

Unlike most of his family, he was still in Iran at the time of the revolution. He managed to get hold of a pleasure boat in the port of Bandar Abbas and set off across the Gulf. Revolutionary guards gave chase in two other boats, but a storm forced them back. Shahriar managed to land in Kuwait. He called his mother to say that he was determined to go back to Iran. In fact he remained in exile, attempting to foment opposition to Khomeini.

His sister, Azadeh, was in her apartment when he was shot. Weeping, she immediately telephoned Ashraf in New York. Ashraf said later that if she had not already been numbed by the shocks and tensions of the last year, the news might have totally destroyed her. She issued a statement saying, "I have lost today a son whom I raised and cherished dearly. He was a staunch patriot and a fine and dedicated navy officer who helped raise high the flag of Iran. . . ." That done she was driven to the airport. "I went for comfort where I had always gone since childhood—to my brother."

Robert Armao heard the news early that same morning in Lackland. He hesitated and then went in to tell the Shah when he awoke. The Shah stared ahead of him and then said, "He was a very dedicated officer. He was a patriot." He then issued a statement saying that Shahriar "was loved, respected, and admired by the men who served under him. His policy was to eat, sleep, and work side by side with his men, be it in the heat of the Persian Gulf or at sea. He shunned any privileges of his position. His devotion to the needy Iranian people of the region where he was stationed was well known."

Later that day came a rumor over the telephone that the killing had been arranged by the Shah's old associate Hossein Fardoust. For years Fardoust had been his closest assistant. The son of a palace servant, he had been sent to school in Switzerland with the Shah and had remained with him throughout his rule. Lately, he had been head of the Special Intelligence Bureau, another of the Shah's secret police networks, which functioned independently of SAVAK. He had brought the Shah daily intelligence reports. Like General Nassiri, the head of SAVAK, he was an obvious target for the revolutionaries. But to the Shah's astonishment and horror, he apparently changed sides in early 1979 and took his experience and information to the cause of the ayatollah. What precisely Fardoust was now doing was unclear. But the Shah considered his behavior a deeply tragic personal betrayal, and a national treason. He talked about it constantly in the last months of his life. At times it seemed to obsess him more than almost anything else that had happened. "He was more than a brother to me," he had said to Richard Helms. As for the idea that Fardoust had been involved in the murder of Prince Shahriar, "I can't believe that anyone that close to me would be so low as to do a thing like that. If I believed that, I would have to lose faith in all humanity."

Day by day the White House grew more keen to see the Shah move on. Jimmy Carter's view was that he had been allowed in only for medical treatment, and now that it was complete, he must leave. Carter considered the Mexicans had betrayed him personally. He was convinced that he had to get rid of the Shah to get the hostages home. And home before Christmas was what he still hoped for.

In fact, there was not much reason to suppose that the Shah's departure from the States would secure the hostages' release; Iranian officials constantly warned that only his return to Iran to stand trial for all his "crimes" would secure their freedom. Even so, Carter wanted him out of America, fast.

Another curious thing was happening. The longer the Shah stayed, the more bitter large sections of America seemed to become about him. The longer the hostages were held, the more frustrating and humiliating became America's powerlessness.

Some of the anger sprang from straightforward politics. Thus Edward Kennedy, then just beginning his campaign against Carter for the Democratic nomination, launched into the realms of hyperbole, declaring that the Shah "ran one of the most violent regimes in the history of mankind." Why should "that individual," he asked, be allowed "to come here and stay here with his

umpteen billions of dollars that he's stolen from Iran" while poor
Hispanics, legally settled in the States, had to wait nine years to
bring their children in?

A parallel debate developed in the letters column of *The New
York Times* as to whether and how the Shah should be put on
trial. Some writers suggested an international tribunal. Iranian
revolutionary officials had made reference to Nuremberg. But a
basic principle of Nuremberg had been that the judges were supposed to be independent.

Given the nature of the trials of prominent members of the
ancien régime that had already taken place in Iran, there was every
reason to suppose that a trial of the Shah there would be a prede-
termined farce. Yet the idea began to grow, at least among some
members of the American press and among writers of letters to
editors, that the only decent course left the Shah was to sacrifice
himself and return home for trial. Thus could he redeem himself
as a martyr.

The columnist Jimmy Breslin declaimed from his pulpit in the
New York *Daily News,* "Somewhere there has to be a bugle sum-
moning the man to get up, without coercion or promise, and
perform a solitary act and end the danger for others." Quoting *A
Tale of Two Cities,* Breslin announced that giving himself up
would be a far better thing than the Shah had ever done before.
"He is a man presented with a chance for true nobility, to save
the lives of men who are here now, of children who are yet to be
born."

The Shah gave no sign of having heard any such clarions. "I
have been called many things but I have never been called stupid,"
he had said of the suggestion to Barbara Walters of ABC Television. But, as ever, the question was where else could he go?

The State Department was still scouring the world for a bolt-
hole. The list of possible countries was not very encouraging.
Cyrus Vance told Carter that among those that had not said an
outright no were Costa Rica, Paraguay, Guatemala, Iceland,
Tonga, the Bahamas, South Africa, and Panama. But most of
them were pretty shaky. Guatemala withdrew as a result of the
Kennedy attack. Hodding Carter, Vance's spokesman, told the
press that the administration still hoped he would soon leave, but
until some place was found, he would be free to stay. "We are not
going to put a man in a rowboat and send him out beyond the
continental shelf if he has no place to go."

Of course, there was still Egypt. Immediately after Mexico's rebuff, Sadat had repeated, yet again, his invitation to the Shah to come back. But both Vice President Mubarak and Egypt's ambassador to the United States, Ashraf Ghorbal, advised Washington that his return would only worsen Sadat's already bad relations with the rest of the Arab world. Carter wrote in his diary, "The situation is that I want him to go to Egypt but don't want to hurt Sadat. Sadat wants him to stay in the United States, but doesn't want to hurt me." There seemed to be no solution. But then a rather unusual knight came galloping to Carter's rescue.

General Omar Torrijos, the caudillo of Panama, was watching a Panamanian prizefighter box in Las Vegas when Mexico's refusal to readmit the Shah was announced. In the spirit of Las Vegas, the general asked one of his aides whether he thought that the Shah could be an important card to play. Torrijos was nothing if not a gambler.

Omar Torrijos will live in history if for one reason alone: Graham Greene has written what is almost a love letter to him, his book *Getting to Know the General.*

In the second half of the seventies, Torrijos invited Greene several times to Panama. Quite why was never very clear, but Greene thought it was perhaps so that he could record the great project on which Torrijos was embarked—the creation of a new Panama Canal treaty with the United States.

At their first meeting, Torrijos appeared, perhaps from a tangled bed, in a dressing gown and underpants. A lock of tousled hair fell over his forehead toward his cautious eyes. Greene was struck by his lean good looks. He was effervescent and ebullient, with the charm of an aging boy and the enthusiasms of a cat.

Thereafter, Greene made several trips to Panama, drinking old Bols gin on the direct KLM flight from Amsterdam, and having a whale of a time. Greene fell for Torrijos' charisma, his idiosyncratic style of leadership, his leftish populism, and the gaiety over which lowered a brooding sense of death. Once Torrijos told Greene that he felt the same affection for him as he had felt for Tito.

Torrijos had run Panama since the end of the sixties when, as a colonel in the National Guard, he had put President Arnulfo Arias Madrid on a plane for Miami. The Arias family had dominated Panama politically since the country was conjured into existence at the beginning of the century. Till then it had been a part of

General Omar Torrijos

Colombia. But Theodore Roosevelt's great ambition was for the United States to build and control a canal through the isthmus. In 1903 the United States encouraged a rebellion against Colombia led by a French engineer, recognized Panama as an independent state, and signed a Canal Treaty with the Frenchman which granted the United States all rights and authority in the Canal Zone "which it would possess as if it were sovereign of the territory."

The Canal was then built, with enormous difficulties. It was a stupendous achievement, one of the great wonders of the world. Seven years were needed to dig an eight-mile ditch through the Continental Divide, the mountains that are the backbone of all America. For all those years the path of the Canal was a brilliantly organized chaos of railroad trains, dynamite teams, steam shovels, dirt spreaders, men with picks and spades, dumpers, and, when water was eventually allowed in, dredgers.

Huge lock gates were installed on both the Pacific and Atlantic shores and still today they work exactly as they were built. The great ships are lifted through the locks eighty-five feet above sea level and then pass through the Continental Divide and into a vast man-made lake that was created when the locks retained the waters of several rivers. This lake is dotted with islands that used to be the tops of mountains. Sailing across it evokes the experience of Noah in the Flood; these were the sights he saw as the water receded. The great difference is that the Flood was an act of God, and the Canal a magnificent act of man.

For more than seventy years the original treaty held, and the United States controlled the Canal and the zone through which it ran, absolutely. No Panamanians were allowed into positions of authority and Americans were given extraterritorial rights. It was a straightforwardly colonial situation—as if for five miles either side of the Mississippi River, Panama were sovereign. The resentment of the Panamians grew and grew. There were serious riots against the United States in 1959 and 1964. In 1965 President Johnson agreed to start negotiating a new treaty. But by now U.S. ownership of the Canal was seen by a vast number of Americans as both natural and essential; right-wing opposition to any change of status was intense and the talks proceeded only slowly until Jimmy Carter became president twelve years later.

Carter made a new Canal treaty a priority. It was that too for Torrijos. The U.S. Senate debate on the treaties was passionate. There was widespread, angry opposition. Ronald Reagan, then a leading Republican expected to run in the 1980 election, was among those most fiercely against any concessions to Panamanian sensibilities. (Another leading conservative American, John Wayne, was in favor of the treaty; he had had a Panamanian wife and understood the country rather better than most. He roundly attacked Reagan's crusade.)

The Senate debate was broadcast extensively on Panamanian radio, and Torrijos used to stride up and down the terrace of his house holding a transistor and listening to himself being denounced as a Communist, a drug runner, and a drunk by one opponent of the bill after another. Whenever he was abused in a particularly offensive fashion, he would fling the transistor to the paving stones. He later told the U.S. ambassador that he went through two cases of Sonys that way. He knew that his opponents in Washington were attempting to provoke him into an anti-American outburst. He managed to restrain himself.

In early 1978 Carter managed to push the treaty (actually two treaties) through Congress. The new arrangements allowed for the joint operation of the Canal till the last day of 1999 and entitled the U.S. to defend its neutrality against external threats thereafter. Although less generous than many Panamanians had hoped, the terms were a vast improvement on the previous system. Later Torrijos revealed that he had planned to blow up the Canal if the U.S. Congress had rejected the treaties.

He went to Washington for the signing ceremony, and as a little joke against the States, he included Graham Greene as part of the Panamanian delegation. For years Greene had been denied more than brief tourist visas to the States on the grounds that he had Communist sympathies.

At a private moment during the ceremonies, Torrijos turned to Carter to thank him for helping end generations of frustration and despair among the Panamanian people. He could not finish his statement; he broke down and sobbed in his wife's arms. Carter wrote later that he had great respect and affection for him. Torrijos felt the same for Carter, a President entirely devoid of the *Yanqui* machismo that had so tortured relations between the United States and Central America.

Now, in December 1979, when he realized that Carter was having serious difficulties in disposing of the Shah, Torrijos began to think of helping him. He had already invited the Shah to come to Panama from the Bahamas; but then the Shah had preferred Mexico, and his staff had worried that Panama was only after his money. Now that Mexico was out, Torrijos began to think of playing "the Shah card." Inviting the Shah again might be in Panama's national interest. Torrijos did not want Ronald Reagan (or any other Republican candidate) to win the 1980 election, and he understood how badly the hostage crisis could damage Carter.

Before Torrijos made a formal offer, messages were exchanged. In Miami a Cuban-born businessman, Bernardo Benes, talked with Panama's Vice President Ricardo de la Espriella. He told him "the gringos are looking for a place for the Shah" and asked whether Panama's invitation from last spring still held. The vice president said he thought so. Benes reported this to the State Department and they called the U.S. ambassador in Panama.

This was Ambler Moss, a bright and enthusiastic officer who adored Panama. Moss has a ready laugh and impish good humor. He comes from the Tidewater area of Virginia and is related to Nancy Astor, the formidable American who became the first woman member of the British Parliament. Hispanic affairs are his passion. He had been closely involved in the treaty negotiations and was appointed ambassador in September 1978.

Like Graham Greene, Moss found Omar Torrijos an irresistible character. He appreciated his earthy joie de vivre, his unpredictable, macho personality. The general had many mansions in which he stayed with different ladies when the fancy took him. His main base belonged to a businessman friend named Rory Gonzales; it was on Calle Cinquente (50th Street). There he used to summon Moss, or anyone else he wanted to see. As often as not he would talk to visitors while still in a rumpled bed, a glass of Scotch in one hand, a cigar in the other.

When Moss was called by State to find out if Panama really would take the Shah, he went first to see the vice president, Ricardo de la Espriella. They agreed that Jimmy Carter should make a personal appeal to Omar Torrijos. Carter decided to send his chief of staff, Hamilton Jordan, down to Panama.

Jordan had worked for Carter for thirteen years, all through two long Georgia gubernatorial campaigns; he was a loyal assistant. In Washington he had refused to take local customs and etiquettes very seriously and caused some offense to the resident princelings of the city. He had acquired a not entirely fair reputation as a roughneck "good ol' boy," who drank too much, spilled out of his blue jeans, and peered oafishly down cleavages. This image might have made him seem a strange choice for such a sensitive diplomatic mission. But during the fiendish negotiations over the treaties he had become rather friendly with Torrijos. The Panamanian leader really only trusted people who enjoyed both alcohol and women; Jordan seemed very reliable to him.

Now Carter thought Jordan would be able to discover whether Torrijos' invitation to the Shah was really serious. Jordan called Harold Brown, the secretary of defense, to ask for a military plane, and he called Ambler Moss. He was arriving in a few hours, he said, and he needed to see Torrijos. His visit must be kept absolutely secret.

When Jordan's plane landed at Howard Air Force Base in the Canal Zone that evening, he stepped out in what Moss thought was the perfect disguise for him—a dark suit and dark tie, as well as dark glasses. Moss scooped him into his limousine and took him off to see the general. Drink in hand, Torrijos rose to greet him. "*Buenas noches*, Papa General," said Jordan. They embraced and began to drink the local beer, Balboa.

Jordan was nervous; this was, after all, an important diplomatic mission for him and he was not accustomed to being a diplomat. They talked about sex.

Torrijos said that his idea of security was to keep constantly on the move. "Sometimes I wake up and I don't know where I am."

"Or who you're with," interrupted Jordan. They all laughed.

Then Torrijos asked him, "What brings you here in the middle of the night?" Jordan asked to talk to him alone and they moved out onto the verandah. As Jordan explained Carter's problem with the Shah, Torrijos lit one of the large cigars his friend Fidel had sent him and leaned back in his chair. When Jordan finished, the general was silent and sat drawing on his cigar. Jordan waited nervously, until eventually Torrijos said yes. Jordan wanted to shout for joy.

Although it was the middle of the night, Jordan at once called Carter. "Mr. President, sorry to wake you," he said. "I'm with our friend down south and he's willing to accept that gift."

"Thank God," said Carter, and then thanked Torrijos as well, in Spanish.

Torrijos offered Jordan a bed for the night, but Jordan said he thought he should get straight to Lackland, in Texas, to try to persuade the Shah that Panama would be a suitable new staging post. As Jordan left, the general came running after him and pushed a brown bag through the car window. It was a six-pack of cold Balboa beer. "*Gracias,* Papa General," called Jordan, and Torrijos stood laughing in the drive.

Next morning, after a few hours' rest in Lackland, Jordan called on the Shah. With him went Lloyd Cutler, the White House counsel who had flown down from Washington, and Steve Oxman, the State Department's baby-sitter. They were met by Robert Armao, whom Jordan knew only by reputation—and disliked. Indeed, it is hard to think of two young Americans who would be more antithetical to each other: a rumpled, carousing, southern Democratic pol, and a fastidious eastern Republican courtier. In his memoirs, Jordan described Armao as "a carefully groomed young man in an expensive suit and a sculpted hairdo. He presented the appearance of an elegant man of the world, but he was unable to conceal his nervous anticipation of being center stage in an international drama." Jordan realized that Armao was not in favor of Panama. He did not like what he had heard of Torrijos. He thought the medical facilities would be inadequate, and he was worried that the Shah might be extradited to Iran from Panama.

When they went into the Shah's room, Armao reminded Jordan how to behave. "Be sure to refer to the Shah as 'Your Majesty' when you address him." Jordan felt like a child being told to mind his manners, but it was good advice; the Shah would not listen to anyone who failed to observe the protocol.

Jordan was struck first by the ghastly apartment in which the Shah had been plumped. It reminded him of a $75-a-day "suite" in the Holiday Inn in Peoria. The last time he had seen the Shah was at the White House in 1977. Despite being teargassed on the White House lawn, the Shah had behaved with dignity and aplomb, very much the strong leader of a significant nation.

Now, two years later, the Shah looked shrunken and pale. He seemed to totter as he pulled himself off the vinyl couch to greet Jordan; only his fierce eyes had not changed. He was wearing an air-force-blue dressing gown with "USA" written across the back.

"What brings you to Texas?" he asked. "Usually when I have contact with the U.S. government these days, it is at their request and because they want me to do something."

Jordan replied, "We are not here, Your Majesty, to make a request, but to describe to you the hostage situation as we see it and to review with you possible options for your travel to another country."

The Shah's reply, as recalled by Jordan, was instructive of his priorities. "Well, as I am sure you know, I would like to do everything possible to help your country resolve the hostage crisis. I don't want to be blamed by history for this terrible thing!"

Jordan said the administration thought that the hostage crisis could not be resolved as long as the Shah remained in the States. The Shah said that the people holding the hostages were crazy Communists who could not be dealt with rationally. He said he was prepared to leave, but the question was where to go. "What about Austria and Switzerland?" he asked.

Jordan said they had both refused; the Shah seemed very disappointed. His relations with Bruno Kreisky had always been good, and he had had a house in Switzerland for many years. "It seems that no one wants me," he said to Jordan in a low, grief-filled voice.

"That's not true, Your Majesty," replied Jordan quickly. This might well have encouraged the ex-monarch. But then out of his hat Jordan pulled only Panama.

The Shah was clearly not excited. He complained that Torrijos was "a typical South American dictator." Jordan claimed later that this shocked him; was the Shah not a "dictator" himself? He attempted to sing the praises of Torrijos and said that, apart from

Sadat, he was "the most fascinating person we have met" since Carter took office. Jordan does not record the Shah's reaction to this judgment.

Jordan said also that Torrijos was an honest man who was attempting to democratize his country. He was tempted to blurt out to the Shah that this "dictator" had done the very things that might have saved the Shah's own regime.

The Shah pointed out that while he would be happy to fly straight into somewhere familiar, he knew nothing of Panama. He asked Armao for his advice, and Armao replied that he would want assurances about the security arrangements in Panama, about the medical facilities, and about the Shah's being able to return to the States in the event of an emergency. He made it clear he had a dim view of Panama. He felt that the Panamanians were only after the Shah's money and that the place was unsafe. He made his views very plain.

Jordan was appalled at the idea that Torrijos' generosity and his own diplomacy should be brought to naught by a Manhattan PR man whom he did not trust. He said he thought that reasonable assurances could be given. "But how long will it take to consult your doctors and security people and make a decision?" he asked.

"It will take as long as it takes!" Armao retorted. "Or is there a deadline—and are you telling His Majesty that he has to leave the United States?"

The blunt Georgian glared at the smooth New Yorker, and tried not to show how irritated he was. "Of course not, Bob," he replied.

Armao said he would check first with the doctors and then with the security men to see if they were satisfied with Panama. The Shah said he would talk with the Queen. They agreed that Jordan, Armao, and Colonel Jahanbini should immediately fly back to Panama together to see if there was anywhere suitable for the Shah to live.

Before they left, Jordan asked the Shah for his assessment of what was now happening in Iran. The Shah replied that it was in chaos; everything was being destroyed by Khomeini and his henchmen. "I cannot tell you how bad I felt to pick up the morning papers in the Bahamas and see that men who had worked for me for years and years trying to improve Iran had been executed. I am sure that will be part of your nation's human rights report," he said with a touch of sarcasm.

When Jordan asked him what had gone wrong, the Shah replied that although he had had a lot of time to consider this, he could not really explain it. The advice from the Americans had been contradictory. But, "If I had to do it over again, I would have been firmer. Iran is worth fighting for, and I should have led that fight! If I had, I would still be sitting on the Peacock Throne today and not having to sneak around the world like a criminal!"

There was one lighter moment to the visit. The Empress had been as concerned as the Shah about where they might now go. But she was delighted to show Jordan a present from a friend—it was a roll of toilet paper with Khomeini's face printed on every sheet. She also took great pleasure in playing him a pop record that someone had sent her—it was called "Eenie Meenie Khomeini."

Then Jordan had to leave to give the Shah time to "freshen up," for his sister Princess Ashraf was about to arrive. The Shah commented on her bravery. She had lost her country and her son to Khomeini's assassins, "but her sole concern now is for my health."

Jordan met the Princess in the hall. He held out his hand. She just glared at him with the same black eyes as those of her brother. She swept past into the Shah's room.

Jordan flew back to Panama with Armao and Colonel Jahanbini. They looked at a house in the mountain province of Chiriquí and another on the island of Contadora, which lies some thirty miles off Panama City in the Pacific. This was the holiday home of Gabriel Lewis, a cheerful, engaging Figaro-type businessman who had been Torrijos' own inspired choice as ambassador to the United States during the tortured negotiations over the new Canal treaties in the mid-seventies. His home seemed the most suitable. Security would be easier, yet the mainland hospitals would be only a few minutes' flying time away, and the Queen would like the sea and the resort atmosphere.

Torrijos asked them to come to see him. Jordan embraced the general saying, "Hello, Papa." Armao bowed and said, "It is an honor to meet you, Your Excellency." Jordan almost burst out laughing at this formality, which he considered quite inappropriate for the swashbuckling general. Such courtesy was, however, second nature to Armao. Torrijos asked Armao to tell the Shah, "He will be treated like an honored guest. And if I hear that anyone tries to take advantage of the Shah, I will have that person thrown in jail."

Torrijos then wrote a personal invitation to the Shah. Armao seemed mollifed to Jordan. As they climbed back aboard the plane for Texas, he said, "It's up to the Shah and his doctors now." On the flight back to Lackland he and Jordan discussed what the royal party needed. High on the list was a proper telephone link for the Queen; she had to keep in touch with her friends in order to preserve her sanity, said Armao.

They arrived at Lackland just after midnight on December 14. The Shah had waited up. Armao told him that he did not much like Panama, but it was just possible. Next morning Jordan came by the small apartment and presented the Shah with Torrijos' letter. The Shah seemed, to Jordan at least, delighted and said several times, "I actually have an invitation from this man."

Now, the only outstanding problem was the Shah's health. In the two weeks he had been at Lackland, his spleen had begun to swell again. He was examined by air force doctors who took blood samples that were analyzed under a new medical pseudonym—Raul Palacios. The air force doctor's opinion was that the Shah's spleen should be removed as soon as possible.

Dr. Kean was summoned from New York. He flew down with his colleague Hibbard Williams, and with the Shah's attorney, William Jackson. Kean and Williams agreed with the Lackland diagnosis; the Shah's spleen must come out. Kean talked to the Shah about it.

The Shah asked how long it would take for him to recuperate. Kean said two to three weeks.

The Shah said that was too long. "They want me out of the country. They think it will help the hostages. It won't, but I'm not staying."

Kean said later that this was "the turning point." There was only Panama to go to. "For the Shah to agree to go with a major illness and with the need for a major operation to a strange country of limited medical facilities was a sacrifice."

The Shah asked Kean if chlorambucil might help—it had reduced his spleen when Flandrin first prescribed it. Kean said it might well work again. The Shah said that was what he wanted to try. If it did not work, he could have the surgery in Panama. Kean agreed; chlorambucil was given again, at a higher dosage than before.

Kean went next door to join Cutler, Jordan, and the others. If the Shah did go to Panama, there was one thing on which Kean was absolutely determined. The Shah must be treated at Gorgas Hospital, the U.S. military hospital in the former Canal Zone, not in any ordinary Panamanian hospital. Kean had been stationed at Gorgas himself during World War II. He knew it well, and he trusted it. Like many Americans, he had less confidence in the native facilities down south.

Kean told Cutler and Jordan that he had to have an agreement on Gorgas. And he wanted a promise of U.S. government help if required. "This means I want to know you will give me everything I need, even if it means flying in a B-52 with medical equipment. If this is not possible, then I want assurances that I can bring the Shah back to the U.S. for medical care at Houston or elsewhere."

These were the elements of what later became known as the Lackland Agreement—the U.S. would give the Shah any security or medical support he needed; any operation could take place at Gorgas Hospital, not in Panama City; and in a medical emergency the Shah could return to the United States.

According to Kean, Cutler looked him in the eye and said, "You've got it." But as far as Kean was concerned, "The promises were never to be redeemed." (In his memoirs, Jordan omitted the promise of treatment at Gorgas.)

Greatly relieved, Jordan flew back to Washington to report to the president. The Shah, he said, was now a sad and tragic figure. Carter agreed to call him.

This was the first time that Carter spoke to the Shah since he had telephoned him from Camp David, at Sadat's urging, in September 1978. Now, he repeated the assurance of the Lackland Agreement and wished the Shah well.

Around the same time Carter also asked Henry Kissinger to moderate the criticisms that he was making of the administration's policy toward the Shah. According to Carter, Kissinger promised to refrain from such criticisms during the hostage crisis and said he was satisfied with the Panamanian arrangements. After this commitment, Carter wrote in his memoirs, "Things were better for a few days—and then reverted to their former state."

On the morning of December 15, the Shah, the Queen, his small staff, and his dogs took off for the seventh leg of their drawn-out exile, never to return to the country that for so many decades had succored him, encouraged him, and yet ultimately, he thought, betrayed him. As they flew south, "The American promises were still ringing in my ears," he wrote shortly afterward.

In the White House, Jody Powell, the press secretary, said he hoped the Shah's departure would help bring a peaceful resolution to the crisis. But from Teheran came only further threats to try the hostages as spies, together with denunciations of the "criminal Shah." The Iranian foreign minister immediately embarked upon the process of trying to extradite the Shah from Panama. This gave Omar Torrijos, friend of Jimmy Carter and Fidel Castro, expansive host and reckless high roller, an exhilarating, conspiratorial, and dangerous vision of how he, personally and alone, could solve the crisis now gripping the United States and, therefore, much of the world.

CHAPTER NINETEEN

The Island

Waiting to welcome the Shah on the tarmac at the neat airport of Howard Air Force Base in the former Canal Zone were a clutch of nervous soldiers from Panama's National Guard, Panamanian intelligence officers, Torrijos' closest aide, his doctor, and the U.S. ambassador, Ambler Moss. The last few hours had been somewhat hectic.

The State Department had called Moss only the previous day to inform him that the Shah was flying south the next morning. And he had been told he could not tell anyone in Panama—it was too secret. Jesus, thought Moss, there's so much to do. Eventually, on Friday afternoon, he decided on his own responsibility to tell Torrijos. He started to try to call the general.

Moss had a long, ragged list of telephone numbers of all the houses and apartments that Torrijos used. He tried at least ten. No Torrijos. No one knew where he was. Finally, at about nine o'clock in the evening, an inebriated general called Moss. "Ambler, you've been trying to call me?"

"Yes," replied the ambassador. "You know that special visitor? Well, he's coming tomorrow morning."

Torrijos cursed. "Get yourself over here," he shouted.

By this time the entire U.S. bureaucracy had switched into high gear. Cables were zapping into the political section of the embassy and into the CIA station in Panama. Embassy staff were rushing around trying to fulfill confused and sometimes contradictory instructions.

Moss found Torrijos slumped in the chair in Calle Cinquente, clearly at the end of a six-hour drinking bout. He told the general they had to issue a joint press release and showed him Washington's draft. Torrijos mumbled various changes and then alarmed Moss by telling him he must clear it with the president of Panama, Arístides Royo. The president served at the pleasure of the National Guard and was at almost all times at Torrijos' beck and call. But Torrijos wanted to observe the formalities; the president should know the Shah was coming.

Royo, a good-looking young lawyer, who had a reputation as a playboy, proved elusive also. Eventually Moss found him by telephone and gave him the news. Royo replied, "Well, it sounds pretty crazy to me, but if it's what Torrijos wants, what can I say?"

"Thank you, Arístides, you're a gentleman," said Moss and went back to Torrijos. He was gone. Moss asked the secretary where he was. "Well, sir, he fell asleep and so we put him to bed."

Over an open line from Calle Cinquente, Moss called the State Department's Operations Center and dictated changes to the joint press release. Then he was asked the question he was dreading. "Now, Mr. Ambassador, is everything ready?" For the first time in his life, Moss said later, he deliberately lied to his government. "Those bureaucrats in Washington would never have understood if I'd told them, 'No, nothing's been done. Omar's drunk in his bed.'" So instead he said, "Yes, everything's fine. Send him down." Then he went home to sleep.

His telephone rang at 6 A.M. on Saturday. It was the general. "Ambler," he said, "what were you talking to me about last night? The date and all that?"

"The date, *mio general, hoy*. Today. He's leaving in two and a half hours' time."

"Oh, my God. Get your ass over here."

As Moss was pulling up his pants, Gabriel Lewis called. "Ambler, what the fuck is going on?"

"Gabriel, I haven't got the time to explain it now. Go to Calle Cinquente at once and you'll hear it all from the general."

When Moss himself reached the house, it was bedlam, with

sergeants and captains and majors running around, shouting into different telephones. Gabriel Lewis roared up in his car.

Apart from his short and successful spell as ambassador in Washington, Lewis is a shrewd businessman who has made many fortunes. One of the largest was from providing the United Fruit Company with boxes to pack their bananas in. He was an operator with aplomb, a rascal with a sense of fun, a buccaneer like Torrijos himself.

Now the general told Lewis that the Shah was moving into his house on Contadora in a couple of hours; he had better get over there and clean out his things. And Moss gave him a long shopping list that Washington had sent; it included dog food. Lewis rushed to his private plane at the city airport. Moss drove through the hectic streets of downtown Panama into the manicured peace of the former Canal Zone to await the Shah's plane at Howard Air Force Base. Also there to greet the Shah was Professor José de Jesus Martinez, whom everyone knew as Chuchu.

Chuchu was a professor of Marxist philosophy at Panama University, a poet, a playwright, a sergeant in General Torrijos' security guard, and also the constant companion of Graham Greene on the trips he made to Panama, getting to know the general. Now Torrijos had assigned Chuchu to watch over the Shah's arrival.

Chuchu was schooled in mathematics as well as Marxism. His Marxism he had learned in Panama; his mathematics, at the Sorbonne. He told Graham Greene that he had once published a short book called *The Theory of Insinity*. When Greene had asked him what on earth was "insinity," Chuchu replied, "Oh, well, you see, I had lost a front tooth and when I was lecturing I found I was saying "insinity."

One day Chuchu, an amateur photographer, had gone to take some pictures of the "Wild Pigs," a guerrilla force that Torrijos had created to fight in the jungles and mountains. Chuchu had been so exhilarated by them and by a defiant anti-American song they sang that he had asked to be allowed to join them. They would have rejected him as far too old to withstand the training, but the general happened by and said, "Let the old fool try."

Chuchu survived and Torrijos was so impressed that he made him a sergeant in his own security guard when he was not teaching at the university. He liked the fact that Chuchu was a poet, and a rather melancholy and romantic womanizer as well as a philosopher.

Chuchu was a casual, easygoing man, stocky, with a crop of gray hair and a boxer's nose. He drove around in an old car which had empty beer bottles floating about the floor. He loved flying a small plane—and did it with some abandon. He also loved wine, his various wives, his many children, and Omar Torrijos. He did not love the United States.

In some ways Chuchu was more radical than Torrijos; he had for some time been a courier to the Sandinistas and he would have liked a confrontation with the United States over the Canal, rather than a treaty. This was perhaps what Torrijos too would have preferred; he had told Greene that he signed the new treaties with Carter only "to save the lives of forty thousand young Panamanians."

Now, standing at the airport, Chuchu wondered about the extraordinary invitation that Torrijos had extended. He supposed that one of the main reasons Torrijos had accepted the Shah was shame over Mexico's behavior. "When one Latin American does something bad, other Latin Americans feel ashamed," Chuchu explained later. (*The New York Times* saw it the same way. In a comment on "Panama's Beau Geste," the paper suggested that "the proud Latin-American tradition of asylum used to be championed above all by Mexico." Now, "Mexico's noble history is itself in exile—but not far away.") Then, of course, there was Torrijos' friendship with Carter; Torrijos put a lot of faith in personal relations in politics.

But the main reason, Chuchu thought, was that Torrijos was a gambler and he saw the Shah as a card. He had said as much to Chuchu in Las Vegas. He wanted to be in the game of helping Jimmy Carter get reelected. Having the Shah in Panama at least gave him a seat at the table. It might also be a good hand.

Just before the Shah arrived, the press in Panama discovered that he had left Lackland and was on his way. Telephones at the U.S. embassy in Panama City and in various offices in the former Canal Zone began ringing off the hook, and several journalists drove themselves as fast as they could into the air base. They were held at bay by the National Guard while the Shah's plane landed. "They were mad as wet owls," said Ambler Moss later with a laugh.

Out came the Shah, looking shrunken inside his suit, the Queen, Colonel Jahanbini and his sergeants, Dr. Pirnia, Robert Armao, Mark Morse, the two dogs, the suitcases and a whole load of wooden crates, which became a source of constant speculation among the Panamanians. "He's all yours," said an American officer to Ambler Moss.

It was a casual remark, but it infuriated Chuchu in a way that symbolized the ancient strains in the relationship between Panama and the United States. Such strains were to curse the Shah's stay in the country.

As far as Chuchu was concerned, the Shah was now under Panamanian, not American, protection. So in no way was he Ambler Moss' responsibility. Indeed, the Americans had shed themselves of him; Panama had been gracious where the U.S. had been cowardly. With some asperity, Chuchu insisted that he have one of the few places on the helicopter that was standing by to take the Shah and the Empress over to the island of Contadora.

On the short flight the Shah sat slumped, silent, and expressionless in his seat. The Queen stroked his hair. Even the dogs seemed depressed to Chuchu.

The helicopter passed by the Pacific entrance to the Canal; below were the ships quietly waiting to pass slowly through to the Atlantic. After about fifteen minutes the dim shapes of the Pearl Islands began to emerge below. They are the closest South Sea Islands to the U.S.; there are about one hundred of them. Most are uninhabited, but some have pearl divers and fishermen, often the descendants of runaway slaves, living on them. The Shah said something about Elba to Armao.

Contadora Island had been bought by Gabriel Lewis for a song in the sixties. He built a house there and then sold the rest of the island to a tour operator in the seventies. A rather pretty wooden hotel, modeled on the barracks used by the laborers who dug the Canal, was built. But after the 1973 energy crisis, Contadora never took off as an international holiday place. When the Shah arrived in December 1979, it was more favored by Italian package tourists than by the sort of people with whom the Shah and the Queen used to consort in St. Moritz.

After landing at the airstrip, the helicopter went back for the boxes and suitcases. It took five more flights to cope with them all. The Shah, the Queen, and the rest of their party were driven

along little lanes and up small hillocks, through woods into which Lewis had introduced deer, to his house, Puntalara.

The house was in some disarray, and Lewis was still looking for suitable extra staff and bringing in provisions. But it was an obviously attractive spot. The house was modern, white, with a red-tiled roof and dark wood lining under the overhanging eaves. In the front, a large red-tiled terrace gave onto a lawn running steeply down to the rocks and the sand below.

The terrace was set with comfortable white and yellow garden furniture, a hammock, and a bar. The view over the Pacific past the palms, the hibiscus, and the bougainvillea was superb. Sliding doors opened to a sitting room, a small dining room, and a basic kitchen in the back of the house. Beside the kitchen there was a rather cramped and dark double bedroom decorated in blue. The main bedroom was upstairs, above the terrace and with its own wide balcony overlooking the sea. It had rather dark paneling and a large crucifix above the bed. This was the room the Shah took. The Queen had the room by the kitchen.

There were three more small bedrooms at the back of the first floor and these were taken by Dr. Pirnia, Colonel Jahanbini, and a Panamanian security officer. Other members of the entourage had rooms in a little guesthouse behind Puntalara, or in the hotel, which was about a fifteen-minute walk, on the other side of the airstrip.

Small though it was, Puntalara was infinitely nicer than the officers' vinyl quarters at Lackland and the Shah and the Queen seemed quite pleased. When they had looked around, everyone walked to lunch at the hotel, where the manager, Ralph Tursi, had been warned to expect them. Some of the guests were rather excited; one German kept putting his spaghetti in his ear as he craned to watch the King of Kings.

Over the meal, Ambassador Moss and Gabriel Lewis tried to talk up Panama and the general. They told the Shah that the country was now almost 80 percent literate—far higher than in most parts of Central America. The Shah's response was that he had wanted to educate the Iranians too. Of course, there was a shortage of teachers in Iran. So he had had the idea of putting up an educational satellite that would bring learning even to the most remote rural areas. Every child would go to school and would take lessons from a television screen. Everywhere, in the desert, in the mountains, by the shore, children would thus receive an excellent education, and within one generation the whole of Iran would be literate. But all his dreams had been destroyed by "that crazy man, Khomeini."

Ambler Moss recalled later that he thought to himself, Well, that's all very fine, but I can see how the mullahs would object. At the moment they have the children sitting in the dust reciting the Koran. And the Shah was planning to use super technology to remove that power from them. As the Shah talked, Moss thought that he had had good intentions but an inadequate grasp of reality. Perhaps that helped explain why he had become so hated.

After lunch, the party walked back to Puntalara. The Shah said how pleased he was to be on his feet. "You know, when I was flat on my back in New York, not only could I not walk, but I could not speak," he said to Ambler Moss.

The next day General Torrijos flew over to see the Shah. The general had been looking forward to meeting the King; he thought they would have a lot in common and would enjoy talking about the business of government. Torrijos was longing to know what had gone wrong in Iran.

But the meeting went badly; there was no chemistry between the shy, arrogant monarch and the exuberant, populist dictator. Torrijos was too effusive; the Shah, too reserved. Torrijos told his friend Rory Gonzales, "He's the saddest man I ever met. But I can't really blame him, falling off the Peacock Throne onto Contadora." Torrijos also saw him as a *chupón*—an orange with all the juice and the flesh squeezed out. No use even to animals now. "This is what happens to a man squeezed by the great nations. After all the juice is gone, they throw him away," said Torrijos.

In fact the only thing that Torrijos really liked about the Shah was his wife, Farah. He found her very desirable. He told Chuchu to tell her that he would provide her with anything she wanted. "So I went to the Queen and told her, and the next day, the general said, 'Tell her again.' I said, 'But my general, I did it yesterday.' 'Go again, go again!' "

As in many of the countries that the Shah visited in his exile, his arrival in Panama brought violent protests. Unfair though it might be, he had come to symbolize, through so much of the world, both the excesses of American power and its ultimate weakness. Many left-wing Panamanian students felt that their country was once again being exploited by the States—this time as a dustbin for an unwanted dictator. At the same time the Shah's presence gave an excuse for opponents of the regime, both Right and Left, to express their dissatisfaction with Torrijos. The bourgeoisie were unhappy because they had hoped that the Canal treaties would bring them an infusion of U.S. investment and dollar prosperity; they had not. On the Left they denounced Torrijos as a "peon of imperialism" and "a man of the Pentagon." For a few days there were nasty riots in the streets.

The general was not much moved. He had expected such demonstrations when he agreed to Hamilton Jordan's original request. "It was preferable this cost be paid by Panama and not the world," he said later. "We knew there would be problems in Panama, but nothing we couldn't handle." The disturbances were abruptly suppressed by the National Guard, and scores of people were arrested and beaten up.

On Contadora the Shah was insulated from such realities. He was heavily protected not only by his own staff but also by the Guard. There were probably more agents on the island than tourists. They were all under the control of Colonel Manuel Antonio Noriega, a short, almost feline man who had been allied to Torrijos ever since Torrijos seized power. He had run G2, army intelligence, since the early 1970s.

As such, Noriega was naturally involved with the CIA, but he was also believed to have his connections with Cuban intelligence and with the services of various other countries, including Israel. He was also thought by U.S. officials to be involved in both the laundering of money and the smuggling of drugs.

Panama is in some ways a louche and tropical Switzerland. All business can be transacted there. Panama provides a flag of convenience for a large part of the world's shipping, a secretive banking system, and corporation laws that allow companies to hide the names of their principals. Panama is, in other words, a gangster's wonderland. All of this, on top of its location halfway along one of the world's great trade routes (Latin America to the U.S.) make it the obvious and ideal place for the laundering of profits of one of the world's fast-growing industries—narcotics. Colonel Manuel Noriega was said to be at the heart of the "Panamanian Connection," a "facilitator," the man who eased shipments and made payoffs.

According to intelligence officials in Washington, who made the information public only in 1986, Noriega was involved in selling weapons to the left-wing M-19 revolutionaries who were trying to overthrow the Colombian government. His name came up time and again in intercepts.

Such behavior was considered regrettable, but offsetting it for the CIA was the fact that since the early seventies Noriega had been willing to spy on Cuba for the United States. (Later he also allowed the Panamanian embassy in Managua to collect information on the Sandinistas for Langley.) CIA station chiefs in Panama knew that he was in turn supplying the Cubans with intelligence on American activities, but if challenged by headquarters, they could claim that on the whole he gave better information to Washington than to Havana. By the end of the decade, it seemed that both the Americans and the Cubans considered him valuable. Whatever else, Noriega was clearly a skillful intelligence official, an operator without ideology, a conscientious manipulator unburdened by conscience.

In December 1979, the nature of Colonel Noriega was not public, but it was well known to the senior American officials who entrusted the Shah to his care. Of course, they had little alternative.

Noriega had the National Guard watch all Panama's ports. People arriving from countries known to be opposed to the Shah were carefully surveilled. Tourists arriving on Contadora were screened before they reached the hotel and regularly while they stayed there. The hotel's business suffered accordingly and its manager later complained that he lost about $1 million during the Shah's sojourn.

At first there were about two hundred National Guardsmen assigned in four shifts to protect the Shah. Many of them were young men in jeans and T-shirts who loitered around the house. The Shah was very concerned about an attack from the sea, so gunmen were stationed on the beach and frogmen in the water. An antiaircraft gun was set up behind the house. Even more dramatically, sonar devices were planted on the seabed to detect either boats or divers approaching the bay. When the Queen went water-skiing guardsmen were there in other speedboats.

The whole National Guard operation was coordinated from a trailer beside Gabriel Lewis's house. In the basement the guardsmen had a tape recorder with which they recorded all telephone conversations in the rooms above.

Proper communications had been part of the Lackland Agreement. The Contadora telephone system was so bad that Ambler Moss had the U.S. Army and the Panamanians install a radio link as well. The telephone was the Queen's line to reality—to her friends.

Manuel Antonio Noriega

When they arrived in Contadora, the Queen looked wretchedly haggard. She worked the phone much of the day and night. Day-time calls would be to the States. At about ten in the evening she would switch to the Middle East, where dawn would be breaking, and talk especially to Mrs. Sadat, who proved the truest of all her powerful friends, and sometimes to King Hussein. As the sun moved west she called friends in Europe around their breakfast times.

All these conversations, and many others by the Shah's staff as well, were intercepted, recorded, and transcribed by Colonel No-riega's men. When Princess Ashraf came, all her activities were an open book. The National Guard knew everything: there was no privacy for the Shah or his entourage on Contadora.

In spite of this, for the first few weeks life on the island settled into a fairly easy and quite pleasant routine, at least compared with what had gone before. The Shah's health seemed to improve; or at least his illness went into remission and his spleen began to subside. He sunbathed, walked along the beach, and allowed him-self to be photographed with tourists dripping wet from the sea.

The children came from the States for the Christmas holidays. The younger son, Ali, used to enjoy impersonating Khomeini waving his arms and shouting. The Shah himself rarely let his emotions show. But when the children left, the staff noticed that both he and the Queen became very much more depressed. When she was not on the telephone, she read a lot—including all the magazine articles about them.

She seemed to some of the Panamanian staff to be pleasantly surprised by the hospitality and friendliness shown to them on Contadora, but sometimes appeared unsure whether it was genu-ine. She went often to the hotel to play tennis. Sometimes the Shah came to play as well—until his illness caught up with him again.

Once Torrijos invited the Pahlavis to lunch along with Mike Harari, a general in Israeli intelligence who spent a good deal of time in Panama, advising the National Guard. Torrijos was close to the Israelis; indeed, Panama had been the only Latin-American state to cast its U.N. vote in Israel's favor over the Entebbe affair. As a result the Israelis had offered all manner of cooperation, as they do almost anywhere that friends of Israel can be gathered and cherished. Torrijos had asked Moshe Dayan a personal favor. Torrijos was not a faithful husband, but he was fond of his wife, to whom he had been married for more than twenty years. She was the daughter of a New York Jewish businessman, who had been horrified by her marriage to the young and raffish Panamanian soldier. He had refused to speak to her ever since their wedding. So Torrijos asked Dayan to intercede. Even this did not have an immediate effect on the old man, but on their twenty-fifth wedding anniversary, he called his daughter for the first time and she went to New York to see him. Torrijos was much moved by this and so was Graham Greene, who recounts the story in his memoir of Torrijos.

During the lunch party, the Shah and General Harari had an argument about the Shah's oil price policy. Torrijos tried to put the Shah at his ease by saying, "I want you to feel at home in Panama. I know you have a reputation of being a wealthy man. If anyone here tries to get into business with you or asks you for money, just let me know, and he'll be punished."

Chuchu found the Shah sad. On one occasion he tried to cheer him up by telling him that the general liked Persian art. This was a complete fantasy; a year or so later, when they were together in the British Museum, Chuchu pointed out a piece to Torrijos, saying, "Look, this is what I told the Shah you liked so much."

Everything about the Shah seemed to Chuchu to be European, not Persian—his wife, his pride, his melancholy. He found his political conversations with the Shah a trifle disappointing. But in other ways, like his courtesy to wet and curious bathers on the beach, Chuchu thought the Shah was poignantly dignified. After all, not so long ago, people had kissed his shoes. "I knew he was a murderer, but he was so beaten up, he was so purified, the cancer he had inside, the sadness of loss of power, and also the sadness of having to leave a still beautiful and loyal wife behind. . . ."

The Shah talked kindly to Chuchu, but only of unimportant things. "He was like a leftover," said Chuchu. "We were all conscious of the horrible tortures and oppression of his people. But none of that remained. You could see that he himself was being tortured—by life. He was having a very slow death, facing his own life—it was like seeing a political prisoner being tortured."

Many of the Panamanians who met with him found it incomprehensible that the Shah still had dreams of returning to his throne. He seemed to think that Khomeini was older and even more ill than he himself, and that when he died he, the Shah, or his son, would be invited back by popular acclaim. He would often talk of his White Revolution and how much he had achieved for Iran. He spoke of himself as being imbued with a kind of mysticism whereas Khomeini was possessed by some sort of devil. He would say of the hostage crisis, "That madman's plans and government are so weak that he had to create a diversion like the hostages to keep people's minds occupied. All he ever talks about is the Shah, what the Shah did, what the Shah took, etcetera, and he does not bother about the practical matter of governing the country."

Colonel Noriega visited the Shah frequently, arriving on the terrace in his dark glasses, carrying his black briefcase, and giving his simpering smile. The Shah, said Noriega later, understood that he was being well protected and was therefore friendly. Noriega, who affected a certain mysticism himself, said later, "I had the feeling that he was programmed to see himself as an extraterrestrial person, like the son of the Sun, not as a human being. A sort of divinity."

President Royo found the Shah's sense of dignity and dynasty extraordinary. Even on Contadora he referred to himself as a direct descendant of Darius. On one occasion he complained that Gabriel Lewis's house was very small and so Royo began to lecture him about Napoleon. After all his palaces, Napoleon ended up in St. Helena, where the authorities were not very kind to him —unlike in Panama.

The Shah replied that the difference was that Napoleon knew his empire was finished. "Mine is intact. All the powers of Europe, led by Metternich, bit off pieces of Napoleon's empire. But my dynasty will prevail."

Royo, in some amazement, asked who would call him back. "The people," replied the Shah. "I won't go back. But my son will."

Torrijos found the Shah well nigh impossible. At one of their meetings the Shah said to him, "My father left me a country, my inheritance." This was not a concept Torrijos would accept. Everything about the Shah's manners and sense of importance irritated the general. The Shah talked about protocol all the time. "But there was not enough space for protocol in the place he was staying!" said Torrijos later, with exasperation.

"I said, 'Look, Señor Shah'—that's what I called him; a lot of

The Shah with a Panamanian security guard and Robert Armao in Contadora

people talked about Your Majesty, someone said, 'Your Excellency,' and he didn't like that because it was wrong, so I always said Señor Shah—'weren't you aware that your people wanted a change?'

"And the Shah said to me, 'Yes, I was going to change. I was going to give them an alternative. I was going to leave my son.'"

Torrijos could hardly believe his ears and asked the Shah whether he wanted to save the monarchy or the people. The Shah replied, "Saving the monarchy is saving the people."

Torrijos looked the Shah in the face and saw that he was completely sincere. "I couldn't talk more because he was talking in A major and I was talking in A minor—we weren't on the same key."

Whereas the Panamanians found the Shah perplexing, they found his American advisers infuriating. By this time, Robert Armao and Mark Morse had come to see themselves as the Shah's principal defense against a cruel and treacherous world. They were there to protect him and his family and whatever was left of his fortune.

As with so much money passing through Panama, some of the Shah's cash arrived in suitcases carried by Robert Armao or someone on his staff. The rest came by electronic transfer. Daily expenditures on Contadora were handled by Mark Morse. He thought the Shah was constantly gouged. The Panamanians by contrast tended to think that Morse's vigilance impugned their national honor. Within days of the Shah's arrival, Colonel Noriega suggested to him that he get rid of Armao and Morse. They interfered with his security efforts, he said. The Shah declined to dismiss them, but he did agree to Armao's going back to New York for a time.

When he was on the island, Chuchu was diligent in demanding that the Panamanian sovereignty and rights be respected. He also thought there was too much involvement with the CIA. (He thought both Morse and Armao were CIA.) "I got mad. I said something like if the Shah wants snow, we cannot give him snow because for snow you have to go to the United States." On one occasion he asked the Shah to tell Ambler Moss to come to the island in a Panamanian helicopter, not an American one. Another time, when Armao asked Moss for a typewriter, Chuchu said, "You should be asking us." He called up Torrijos' base and had one of the general's typewriters sent over.

Apart from Gabriel Lewis's house, the Shah rented a smaller house next door, which was known as the Bunker House, because it was where U.S. Ambassador Ellsworth Bunker had stayed during the Panama Canal talks. He also rented a house belonging to Lewis farther inland. Nonetheless, he needed to keep rooms at the hotel on a constant basis, both for his staff and for visitors.

Early on, the butler, Cristobal Valencia, had gone overboard in buying a set of silverware that he thought was fit for a king and a queen. (Armao had been storing some of the Shah's own silver from Teheran in a warehouse on New York's West Side; it was stolen.) After that, Mark Morse insisted that Valencia account for every small item of expenditure; so the butler used to prepare little slips for stallholders to sign in the vegetable market. He resented it. The Panamanians thought that the Shah's American advisers kept him in a constant state of anxiety about money. Torrijos told Hamilton Jordan later, "That sissy [Armao] and his friend [Morse] get paid a commission by the Shah every time they accuse someone of overcharging him." It struck the Panamanians as ironic that the Shah and the Queen never seemed to have any money of their own. It all seemed to be controlled by the Rockefeller people. But then, kings and queens rarely carry loose change.

Of the two young Americans, the Panamanians had more time for Morse; none of them found Armao an easy interlocutor. Dalys Varga, the secretary whom Torrijos sent over to help out, liked Morse. (He thought she was probably a Torrijos spy.) She found him young and ambitious and far too right-wing in his views for her, but she thought he was decent and she enjoyed having dinner with him. On one occasion she sat Morse down and tried to explain Panamanian history and psychology, and just why it was that the Panamanians did not much like having *Yanquis* come in and order them around. She suggested that he take it easy.

But as the weeks went on, Morse became increasingly frustrated on the island; he felt he was merely helping out Robert Armao and it was doing his own career little or no good. He still felt loyal to the Shah, but he became increasingly edgy with the Panamanians.

The National Guard provided its men free. But the Shah had to pay for the food; they all ate at the hotel where the Shah's monthly bill amounted to over $21,000. The first bill for the entire security system and the equipping of the house came to $68,000. Mark Morse was constantly complaining that it was far too much. Chuchu called such complaints "very vile." But he acknowledged that the security men were always hungry and that they were not used to eating in such luxury as the hotel provided. So, perhaps, they sometimes treated themselves to some of the delicacies on the menu. Who would not, in such a position? After all, Chuchu said, the Shah really did need protection. Sadeq Khalkhali had said when the Shah arrived in Panama that the Shah's children had now been added to the death list. "Our commandos exist, are numerous, and have been trained in different countries, especially Palestine, but also everywhere, including the United States." Wasn't even the Shah's wife being encouraged to murder him?

On at least one occasion the National Guard believed that a hit squad was waiting in Costa Rica. On another, an unidentified plane flew right over the island, giving rise to fears of a kamikaze attack. As far as Chuchu was concerned, Panamanian soldiers were being asked to lay their lives on the line for the Shah. None of them shared his belief in himself. Why shouldn't they eat decently?

Since Armao spent a lot of time in New York, Mark Morse bore the brunt of the tension. Noriega claimed later that he was always provoking them—turning up without his ID card, bringing strangers to the house, taking photographs of the guards, that sort of thing. "They would build traps for him, which he'd inevitably fall into," said Dalys Varga later. For his part, Morse considered Noriega and his men totally untrustworthy. On one occasion they went after him.

According to the Guard, Morse had parked his car in front of the house. The guards told him to move it. He refused, saying, "I'll only be a minute inside." When he came out they told him he was under arrest. The reason, they said, was that he had put everyone in danger by blocking the route in case anyone had to make a quick escape. (Noriega later said that Morse had provoked a confrontation by calling one of the Panamanian security officers "a motherfucker." Morse denied this.)

They gave him no time to make any calls, but bundled him onto a plane and flew him to Panama City. On the short flight a Frenchman, whom Morse had met at the hotel and believed to be a drug runner, said he could see Morse was in trouble and would follow to see what happened to him in Panama City. At the airport Morse was bundled into an old Pontiac with four or five large guardsmen and was driven to their headquarters. The Frenchman called the U.S. embassy.

At the headquarters, Noriega upbraided Morse. Meanwhile, Robert Armao had been called in New York from Contadora and told that Morse had been taken away. He telephoned the White House and Ambler Moss and threatened to hold a press conference.

Ambler Moss then called Noriega and agreed that if Morse was released he would not return to the island till the following day. When he did return, Morse said to the Shah, "I think we are in trouble here."

"Yes. If they arrest you, an American, what's in store for me?" asked the Shah, sitting in a borrowed cottage on an island in an ocean far from home.

CHAPTER TWENTY

The Game

There was another, more serious, underlying cause of tension. Extradition.

In December 1979, while the Ayatollah Khalkhali was still threatening to kill the Shah, other arms of the Iranian government were beginning to try to use the law to get him back. The new foreign minister, Sadegh Ghotbzadeh, was particularly interested. Along with the noisome mobs outside the U.S. embassy in Tehran, Ghotbzadeh had now become a nightly feature on the American network news. His assiduous charm, smart suits, and silk ties made him seem an incongruous spokesman for either the angry demonstrators or the stark ayatollah. He had long been an exiled opponent of the Shah, and in 1978 he had been one of the "modern" young men who surrounded Khomeini in Paris and contrived to give him a benign and humanist aura. He was a fierce rival of another of Khomeini's disciples, Abolhassan Bani-Sadr. He was anxious to have the hostages released, and believed that if he were seen to be securing the Shah's extradition, his own power—and his prospects in Iran's forthcoming presidential election—would be immensely enhanced.

Iran had no embassy in Panama, so just before Christmas 1979, Ghotbzadeh sent there two unlikely intermediaries, a left-wing

French lawyer, Christian Bourguet, and an Argentinian adventurer, Hector Villalon. They had been friends of his during his time of exile in Paris. Bourguet in particular had taken up the cause of Iranians fighting the Shah.

They had arrived in Panama (unbeknownst to the Shah's party) just as Robert Armao was leaving for his "holiday" in New York. On Christmas Day 1979, they met with President Royo and with Marcel Salamin, one of Torrijos' political counselors, a friend of the Cubans and the Sandinistas. (Torrijos liked to surround himself with people of opposite political views—thus, for example, Salamin's socialist views were offset by Gabriel Lewis's capitalist ones.) To establish their bona fides, Bourguet and Villalon had brought with them copies of letters that the Iranian government had sent through more formal channels to President Royo and to Torrijos. After three and a half hours of talks in the presidential suite of the Holiday Inn, they managed to convince the Panamanians both that they really did represent Ghotbzadeh and that they had brought at least the possibility of some sort of action over the Shah that might hasten the hostages' release.

The response of President Royo, a lawyer, was to say, in effect, "We don't have a treaty of extradition between Panama and Iran, but Panama does have its own extradition law, and if the Iranians want to file a case under our law, we can't prejudge the issue. Make your complaint, enumerate the actual crimes for which the Shah should be extradited, find the witnesses and the evidence, write up the indictments. File it all with the Foreign Ministry."

On December 28 Royo made a public announcement to this effect.

> We are sure that Iran will not be able to fulfill these requirements [he said]. Inasmuch as we are a country which complies with international law we are going to insist that Iran complies with the laws which recognize and consecrate the right of asylum and diplomatic immunity, laws which have been violated in the case of the taking of the hostages and the occupation of the American Embassy in Teheran.

The Panamanians had different interests to the Iranians, but some of them coincided. First, there was a need to protect Panama's image in the world, particularly in the Third World. Panama, they would point out, had taken risks rejected by Mexico and by every country in Western Europe, formally or not. The Shah was widely seen in the Third World as a symbol of Western decadence and U.S. imperialism and giving him refuge did not immediately win Panama many new friends. Moreover, no one knew whether the ayatollah might not retaliate against any of the thousands of ships flying the Panamanian flag of convenience. The least the Panamanians could do was to appear to consider seriously, within the context of their own legal system, any request from Iran for the Shah's extradition.

Undoubtedly, the unfolding of the drama can also be explained in terms of Torrijos' own personality. He wanted to become an international hero, the man who ended the hostage crisis and thus saved the United States and his friend Jimmy Carter from humiliation. He dreamed of standing on the podium of the United Nations, or before a joint session of Congress, to be applauded as the man who had resolved the world's most dangerous deadlock. For Torrijos, dealing with extradition was a wonderful game.

But it was one with a serious purpose; to help Jimmy Carter be reelected. Ronald Reagan, the most likely Republican contender, had not only campaigned against the Canal treaties, he had also called Torrijos "a tinhorn dictator." It was above all for this reason that Torrijos had accepted the Shah in the first place. Now, by getting involved with extradition, he was merely trying to play his hand.

Marcel Salamin said later that he and Torrijos had assumed there must be Iranian leaders who wanted to end the crisis and they thought that Bourguet and Villalon had come representing them. "They proposed a fiction. That they should ask for extradition and Panama should ask for the release of the hostages." The problem was that the fiction could develop into reality.

As 1979 turned to 1980, the hostages remained interred, and the Soviet Union invaded Afghanistan, an event that Jimmy Carter saw as a personal betrayal by Leonid Brezhnev, and that the Shah, with a sigh, described on Contadora as a Soviet attempt, in face of a weak American president, to realize the old Russian dream of a warm-water port. At the beginning of the year the U.N. secretary general, Kurt Waldheim, flew to Teheran in a catastrophic attempt to negotiate an end to the hostage crisis. Teheran papers published old photographs of him with the Shah and Princess Ashraf. He was assailed by people with mutilated limbs who claimed they were victims of SAVAK, and his visit to a cemetery of the martyrs of the revolution was so violent that he ran away in fear of his life.

Waldheim returned to New York convinced that no sanctions would ever convince the radicals to surrender the hostages. One reason for this was given to Cyrus Vance by a senior Islamic statesman who said, "You will not get your hostages back until Khomeini has put all the institutions of the Islamic revolution in place."

A few days after the Waldheim fiasco, Marcel Salamin flew to Teheran along with Romulo Escobar Bethancourt, who had been Panama's chief negotiator on the Canal treaties. They were nervous and Salamin said later that the only reason they decided to go was because they believed that Rockefeller and Kissinger were trying to destroy any contacts between the Carter administration and Iran for electoral reasons.

They were put up in the almost empty Intercontinental Hotel in Teheran and Salamin tried to conceal the fact that they were Panamanians; they were scared that they would be taken hostage for the Shah. Eventually they got to see Ghotbzadeh, and explained to him Panama's position and its unique, delicate relationship with the United States. In talking about the Shah's extradition, Ghotbzadeh was ambiguous. "He never said whether he considered it to be real or false, a game or reality," said Salamin later. The Panamanians realized that the power struggles in Iran were still fierce and that Ghotbzadeh himself was in a precarious position. He told them that Iran was going to begin a formal extradition request; they reminded him that under Panamanian law the whole process could simply be halted by the president.

The next day, when the Panamanians returned to the Foreign Ministry, they realized that the Iranian officials had no idea how to start the extradition proceedings. So they spent several hours explaining the details of Panamanian law and helped to prepare the initial papers. In a second meeting with Ghotbzadeh, Salamin says they told him that Panama would seek to draw out the process in order to give Iran and the United States as much time as possible to solve their problems. Salamin said later, "We made it clear we would never extradite the Shah." It is not evident that the Iranians understood this. The Panamanians left Iran convinced both that Ghotbzadeh himself sincerely wanted to resolve the hostage crisis and that the Shah-Panama card might just win the game. The next thing was to get Washington into play.

• • •

Chuchu called Hamilton Jordan as he was having dinner at Camp David on January 11, 1980. "Papa General" wanted Hamilton to come to Panama the very next day, said Chuchu. It was really important. No, he could not talk about it on the phone. And it could not wait. He repeated, "The general thinks it's important."

Jordan talked to Carter. The president said that he had better go. Jordan called Chuchu back. But instead of his flying to Panama, they agreed it would be more discreet for Jordan to meet Chuchu at Homestead Air Force Base in Florida. Next day Jordan flew south.

It was not Chuchu but Gabriel Lewis who came to see him, together with Marcel Salamin. "I bring you greetings from your 'Papa,' " said Lewis with a smile as he and Jordan embraced. Then Salamin said, "I have just returned from Teheran where I met with Foreign Minister Ghotbzadeh." Jordan was astonished. For weeks Washington had been trying to open a direct channel to the Iranian government. State, the NSC, the CIA—all had failed, but here was he, the White House chief of staff, with just such a route being spread before him.

Salamin explained how Bourguet and Villalon had arrived in Panama with a request to extradite the Shah. He said that as far as Panama was concerned, they had no hope of succeeding, but he thought the process could be used to help defuse the hostage crisis. He said also that the Iranians wanted to make contact with Jordan himself and not with the State Department.

"Why?" asked Jordan.

"Because they believe that the State Department is controlled by Kissinger and Rockefeller," said Salamin. Jordan made no reply. But as he listened he became convinced that the Panamanian connection might really be worth pursuing.

He went next door to call Carter with the news. The president said to carry on talking. Back with the Panamanians, Jordan reminded them that there must be no misunderstanding. Torrijos had assured him that under no circumstances would the Shah be extradited, whatever the appearances might be. Appearances might make problems enough. "If the Shah gets scared and asks to come back to the States, we'd have to accept him."

Salamin responded that this was not a problem. He did not think the Iranians really wanted the Shah back; it would cause them too many problems just deciding what to do with him. (This was a favorite Panamanian theory—and an unlikely one.) Salamin had been struck by the fact that although the Iranians talked of extradition, they had done absolutely nothing about it. Before he had gone to Teheran, not a single document had been prepared. That surely showed they were not serious. Christian Bourguet had been equally astonished at how little the Iranian authorities had done to prepare any case against the Shah. In Teheran he had asked a judge, "What precisely will you accuse the Shah of?" The reply had been, "Abuse of trust. Abuse of confidence."

Jordan agreed that the Panamanians should make another trip to Iran and explore further the possibilities of a deal. He returned to Washington very excited and wrote a long Top Secret memorandum to the president, with copies to Vance and Brzezinski.

By now there were, in effect, all the elements of a conspiracy. Ghotbzadeh, Bourguet, Villalon, Jordan, and the Panamanians had set into motion a complicated game of bluff and double bluff in which no one was really ever to know who was fooling whom. Two days later Carter himself outlined the dimensions of the problem to Jordan, saying he hoped the Panamanians would not get "carried away with this extradition thing."

"Torrijos wouldn't do that to us," said Jordan.

"I don't think he would either," the president replied. "But if the Shah got the notion that he was going to be extradited and wanted to leave Panama, we would be in one hell of a fix." Moreover, said Carter, Cy Vance was worried that the Panamanians really did want to extradite the Shah. Vance knew that Noriega was dangerous. Jordan should tell the Panamanians that the U.S. just wanted to use Panama as an open door through which the Americans could talk directly to the Iranians. No more.

A few days later Gabriel Lewis called Jordan, who was immersed in Carter's campaign to fend off a primary challenge by Senator Edward Kennedy, and persuaded him that it was essential that he fly to Europe to meet with Bourguet and Villalon. Jordan was not keen, but Carter agreed, and so the White House chief of staff, together with Hal Saunders, the experienced assistant secretary of state for Near Eastern and South Asian Affairs, flew by Concorde to London. They traveled under false names.

Jordan was surprised by his interlocutors; Villalon looked the part of a screen Latin-American adventurer, immaculately and expensively dressed in a light-brown suit and handmade shoes. He wore a thin black mustache and, above his large aquiline nose and his thick eyebrows, his hair was slicked straight back. He gave them a long and quite well-informed exposition of the political forces in Teheran at the moment.

Then Bourguet arrived, fresh off the plane from Teheran. He was a complete contrast to Villalon, a shaggy dog of a man with long, unkempt hair and beard and thick-rimmed glasses. He too looked his part—a left-wing Parisian intellectual.

Bourguet immediately startled the Americans by announcing that the Shah was a very evil man. When Jordan asked how the hostages were to be freed, Bourguet said without hesitation, "You must return the Shah to Iran!"

Jordan replied that this was absolutely impossible, to which Bourguet responded, "Is America not a country of law? This evil man must return and face his crimes."

Jordan said there was little point in their discussing the nature of the Shah's character. But, according to Jordan, Bourguet insisted that, "The Shah returned—or the Shah dead—is the key to the problem. Nothing can be done unless this problem is solved. Regardless of whether it had figured in the original taking of the hostages, now, in the public mind, the Shah's extradition or his death has become the central issue. It's not a question of saying it's good or bad. It's a fact."

Bourguet went on to explain that so long as the Shah was alive, the Iranians would always think that he was plotting to return, as he had in 1953. No one in Iran believed that he had really gone to New York for medical reasons; obviously it was all part of the CIA's new plan to restore him. There was nothing for it but for "the problem to disappear."

The details of such contacts and conversations were not made public until long after the event. Even so, on Contadora Island the Shah knew very well that the Iranians hoped to extradite him from Panama. And if Cy Vance was worried about how far the Panamanians could be trusted, then the Shah had every right to feel concerned. At Lackland, Carter's counsel, Lloyd Cutler, had assured him that he could not and would not be extradited. But neither he nor his American aides were assured. Robert Armao was contemptuous of Carter anyway and would not have been in the least surprised to have his charge betrayed by the president.

General Torrijos, President Royo, and Gabriel Lewis all did

their best to assure the Shah that he was in no danger. Yes, there were contacts with the Iranian regime, but it was all a great game, they said. They pointed out that under Panamanian law political crimes were not extraditable. They told him that no one could be extradited from Panama if he could not expect a fair trial. Did Hoveyda have a fair trial? He did not. And no one expected that the Shah would have anything approaching a fair trial. More likely he would be torn apart on the tarmac. So of course he was safe in Panama; there was no way the extradition request could be granted.

Moreover, there was no capital punishment in Panama itself, and Panamanian law did not allow extradition of anyone who might face the death sentence elsewhere. This was another guarantee against extradition.

Such were the ways in which the Panamanians attempted to smother the doubts of the Shah when news of Panamanian intrigue with Iran surfaced. They were not entirely successful. Ambler Moss, the U.S. ambassador, thought that the Shah's concerns were being fueled by Armao. "That sneaky little guy would go charging off and if anything would go wrong he would tell his friends in New York and would bring out press releases and embarrass the administration and all this kind of thing." Armao said he never issued releases though he often threatened to reveal how the Shah was being treated. Moreover he considered his concerns for the Shah in the hands of Torrijos and Noriega were well-founded. He saw himself as the Shah's defense attorney.

There was one way in which the Shah could have overcome all risks of extradition; he could have asked for political asylum in Panama. He was advised by one Panamanian lawyer to do this, but he never agreed, both because he thought it humiliating and, even more important, because he thought it would have involved his renouncing the throne—not only for himself but also for his son.

On January 23, 1980, the Foreign Ministry in Teheran announced jubilantly that the Shah had been arrested in Panama pending extradition. This happened after a telephone conversation between Ghotbzadeh and President Royo in which Ghotbzadeh persuaded Royo to say that the Shah was "under the surveillance" of the Panamanian authorities. This was clearly already the case, and so Royo agreed to it. In order to enhance his own prospects in the imminent election for the Iranian presidency, Ghotbzadeh then proclaimed the Shah's arrest.

In the White House, Hamilton Jordan was appalled. He immediately called Gabriel Lewis, who tried to placate him, saying that nothing had changed, the Shah was still in his house on Contadora. But, said Lewis, an Iranian warrant for the Shah's arrest had just arrived in Panama, and under Panamanian law, he therefore had to be detained. Since Noriega's men were protecting him anyway, it was easy to claim that he was indeed now "detained."

Jordan was terrified that the Shah would be so scared by it all that he would insist on returning at once to the U.S. "Gabriel, you must tell the General and President Royo that they are playing with fire," he said.

Torrijos was himself furious with the announcement from Teheran, and the Panamanians issued a statement saying it was completely untrue and they never had any plans to arrest the Shah. Later, almost all the Panamanians involved in the extradition procedure—Arístides Royo, Rory Gonzalez, Marcel Salamin, Gabriel Lewis—insisted that this was always true: Torrijos would never have allowed the Shah to be extradited from Panama to Iran. One person who was not so sure was Chuchu Martinez. He said later that if Torrijos had been certain that by putting the Shah on a plane to Teheran, he could have freed the hostages and guaranteed Carter his reelection, he would have done it. According to Armao, Torrijos himself on one occasion reassured the Shah he would never be extradited but said, "I might have to arrest you and photograph you behind bars. But it will only be propaganda, just to deceive the Iranian government." The Shah said to Armao, "When one is not well, such things are a strain."

Late one February afternoon, Ambler Moss hit the panic button. A call had come through from Robert Armao. He sounded unhappy.

"I want to alert you to something very serious," said the Rockefeller man. "They've taken away the Shah. I think he has been kidnapped."

Oh, God, here we go, thought Moss.

The danse macabre of extradition was still proceeding. The Shah was nervous, some of his people were very nervous, and Armao seemed to Moss to be just about hysterical. (And that was without Armao's knowing anything about Jordan's secret meeting with Bourguet and Villalon.) It was not just Armao. There were others, in the Republican Party, in State, and even in the White House,

who were intensely suspicious of Torrijos. No way could he be
relied upon. He was a drunk, a coke addict, probably also a Communist (after all, he was a friend of Castro). Even Zbigniew Brzezinski was worried that Torrijos might be fooled into handing
over the Shah against the promise of the hostages' release.

Ambler Moss had had no such concerns—or at least not many.
After all the tortuous negotiations over the Canal treaties, he
thought he knew Torrijos pretty well. He was absolutely certain
he could be trusted; or at least he would have been certain if others
had not been so paranoid and had not seized on every opportunity
to instill doubts. Nervousness is infectious. When Armao told him
the Shah had been taken off alone, he felt his legs go weak. "What
do you mean?" he asked Armao, trying to sound calm.

"You know he was scheduled to go over tomorrow morning to
look at some real estate?" said Armao.

"Yes," said Moss.

"Well, Colonel Noriega's people just came along and said that
he'd have to spend the night in Panama [City] and start from there
first thing in the morning."

"Really?" said Moss.

"Yeah, that's what they told him. And so they took him away,"
said Armao. Moss began to mop his brow.

The Panamanians had been keen to persuade the Shah to invest
in the country—indeed, Armao and Morse both felt that one of
the principal reasons that Torrijos had invited him was to get his
hands on the Pahlavi fortune. Several of Torrijos' girlfriends had
come over to the island offering real estate on the mainland. The
Shah and the Queen went to look at some properties. Members of
the Panamanian bourgeoisie would show them around their mar-
bled halls in the suburbs or on the mountain slopes, while the
Queen made polite comments and the Shah peered over his spectacles, saying nothing. But there was an obvious problem. The
Shah and the Queen would need a fully furnished house. Not
many Panamanian millionaires actually wanted to move out and
dispose of their furniture, their linen, their silver, their china, their
glass, their pictures—everything—unless it was really made worth
their while. If the Shah had come along and offered $5 million for
an $800,000 house, that might have been worth some inconve-
nience—it would finance a trip to Tiffany's. But the Shah never
made an offer that a right-thinking rich Panamanian could not
refuse.

Moss knew that since the Shah was living only a few minutes from the Contadora airstrip and the flight to the mainland took only a few minutes more, the idea that he had to leave the previous night to make an early appointment made no sense at all. Armao knew it too. That was why he was alarmed.

Armao said he had tried as hard as he could to get on the aircraft with the Shah. But the National Guard had refused absolutely to let him. He had never trusted the Panamanians and now he was convinced they were harming the Shah. "I'm going to call Jo Reed [David Rockefeller's assistant]," he told Moss. "And he'll call Kissinger, and they'll alert the press and call the White House. We're going to raise hell."

"Wait," said Moss. "Don't do anything yet. I'll try to find out what's happening." He put down the receiver in a state of some distress. Could they really have kidnapped the Shah? Was he already in a box being loaded by a forklift truck into a transport plane, or being wheeled heavily bandaged and drugged across the tarmac, like a Soviet embassy official whose plan to defect has gone hideously wrong and who finds himself in the care of KGB nurses? Could Torrijos really have made some sort of deal with Khomeini? It was impossible. What about Noriega? He was far more unscrupulous than Torrijos. Might he have cut his own deal with Teheran? The possibility was too horrendous. Moss started to call around the city to try to discover what was happening.

He spent an hour and a half on the telephone. Complete blank. Torrijos was unavailable. With a woman, probably. Noriega could not be found. No one else knew anything.

Should I call Washington? Moss wondered. It was tempting, but it would be insane. He knew that if he was in a panic, State would have a coronary. My God, would they send the marines? There'd be B-52s over Panama City within hours.

Finally at about eight-thirty in the evening, Moss reached the last person he expected to know anything—President Royo. He was at home. "Where is the Shah?" asked the ambassador.

Usually they spoke together in Spanish. But this time the president replied in English. Odd, thought Moss.

"Ambler, don't worry about it," said Royo. "We've got everything under control."

"What do you mean? I must know what's happening," said Moss.

The president replied, "I'm speaking English because I'm sitting here watching television with my wife."

Moss waited.

"Isn't a man entitled to a good time?" asked the president of Panama.

"What do you mean?" asked the ambassador of the United States.

"You know what I mean. Everyone likes to have a little fun now and then."

Moss was not really in the mood. "By God, I don't get it," he said.

President Royo was a little impatient. "Oh, don't be naive," he said. "I'm talking about a woman."

Moss almost fell off his chair. "What? The Shah?" he cried.

"Yes."

"Oh, Jesus, Arístides, thank God," said Moss, as relieved as he was astonished. He called back to Armao on Contadora and said, "Look, Bob, I can't talk because this is an open line. But I know that the Shah is all right. I can assure you as ambassador. Please don't call anybody. There's no problem whatsoever and I'm sure that His Majesty will explain it all to you when he gets back to the island."

Noriega later explained that he had indeed been responsible for this night on the town. He claimed that in one of their conversations on the terrace at Contadora the Shah had made it clear how bored he was becoming on the island. Noriega began to explain the macho ethic of Latin America; every man in Panama had a mistress as well as a wife. The Shah responded favorably to this concept and said he would like to see a little more of Panamanian life.

So the National Guard had booked a suite at the Panama Hotel, the city's largest establishment, and arranged for a young woman to come to dinner. She was not a whore, Noriega insisted, but someone of good family. When they had pried the Shah away from Armao, they took him straight to the hotel by plane. He had dinner with his guards and the woman and then retired for the night.

The incident appears in the final version of the Shah's last memoirs, which were rewritten as he lay dying in Egypt, somewhat differently. Speaking of Panamanian attempts to isolate him, he wrote, "On one occasion I flew to Panama City for a secret meeting with the American Ambassador who said he had a message from President Carter. My adviser, Robert Armao, planned to come with me to the capital, but Panamanian officials refused to let him attend."

Had Ambler Moss served in the U.S. embassy in Teheran he would not have been surprised by the Shah's escapade. The court reeked of sex. Everyone talked incessantly about who was the latest favorite of the Shah. The love life of his sister Princess Ashraf was subject to even more lurid gossip and speculation, as she herself complained. Only the Queen was thought to be chaste.

Pimping was a highly developed art form in Teheran. One assiduous young courtier now living well in the Belgravia area of London, recalls that "you had to pimp to progress." Business and sex were inextricably intertwined. Several of the Shah's closest advisers found girls for the Shah. Almost everyone around him encouraged him.

The stories were legion. The Shah insisted on making love to a minister's daughter in a helicopter while it hovered over Isfahan; he had a love child in France; one of his mistresses sent a bill for couture clothes to the embassy in Paris; he shamelessly embarrassed the Queen by flaunting his infidelities. When they arrived together at St. Moritz she would go to their Villa Suvretta while he repaired to the Hotel Suvretta to make love to the latest procurement. Whenever the reception area was stuffed with SAVAK agents, it meant that the Shah was in bed in an upstairs suite. Everyone knew. Giulio Andreotti, the former Italian prime minister, has recalled that once, when the Shah arrived at the Venice Film Festival, he shocked the local prefect by asking for a woman for the night. The Italian prefect replied, "That's a job for the chief of police." Andreotti felt the Shah's request lacked "noblesse oblige."

Of European girls, it was said that he preferred blondes with large mouths. Lufthansa hostesses were favored at one time. But for many years a lot of his girls came from the redoubtable Madame Claude, who ran one of the most successful and prestigious call-girl networks in Paris. Many of her girls were amateurs and some subsequently married extremely well.

One of Claude's girls, a tall, well-built blonde, Ange (not her real name), spent several months in Teheran in 1969. She flew there first class and was met at Teheran airport by a young man from the Ministry of the Court. They drove to the Hilton in a

Mercedes with smoked windows. She was given a suite next door to his. He was good-looking and he tried to seduce her, but she had been warned that if she agreed, she would be on the next plane out. The Shah wanted his girls untouched by Iranian hands. She knew that all the hotel staff knew just why she was there. For the Shah.

For three days nothing happened except that in between trying to bed her the man from the ministry taught her to curtsey. This was essential when she met His Majesty, he said. It would be lèse-majesté if she failed to curtsey.

She was driven to a villa in North Teheran, where there was a conceited-looking flunky whom she took to be a grand chamberlain, several guards, but no Shah. She was shown into a room that had a table laden with food—and a bottle of Chivas Regal. She was very nervous, and the Shah was very late. "Over the next two or three hours I drank Chivas. When he finally arrived I was completely drunk."

She stood up and tried to curtsey as she been taught—and fell over. "*Oh, merde,*" she said, and tried to pick herself up.

The Shah laughed and simply shook her hand.

"But I have to curtsey," said Ange. And so she did. The Shah laughed again.

Claude had told her that the Shah liked to dance and to drink. She poured him a large glass of Chivas, and another for herself. He put on the hi-fi and they did a tango.

Then, drunkenly, she said, "*Alors, baisons,*" and dragged him upstairs past the guards. The Shah was laughing; the guards were not. By the time the Shah left he was very late for a meeting with the Queen at the airport. Ange heard later that there was a terrible scene.

They got on so well together that the Shah insisted that the weekend be prolonged. For the next few months, Ange saw him twice a week. "He was always very nice to me; kind, gentle, and generous. Not like the Arabs."

She made him laugh a lot. "I think that was why he liked me. I used to call him 'Shahmajesté.' " They used to play tag in the bedroom; the French name of the game is *Chat* (Cat), so she used to chase him around the bed shouting, "*Chat*—Shah—*Chat*—Shah." He enjoyed that too, but he seemed to her to be an extraordinarily sad man.

When Ange was not with the Shah, life in Teheran was very boring. She was caged in her suite at the Hilton and was not even able to go to the pool without a guard. Other than the Shah, the only person she was allowed to see alone was the man from the ministry, who continued in his attempts to sleep with her. He would have her to dinner in his suite and then appear from the shower with his dressing gown open. "No one will know, I promise," he insisted. But she always said, "No, I am here for His Majesty." There were other propositions from American businessmen in the hotel, offering her thousands of dollars a time; she says she turned those down as well, but kicked herself for not at least taking their numbers for a later date, out of Iran. "If only I had been a better businesswoman!"

After six months she could not stand it any longer. The man from the ministry was furious when she said she was leaving. "But you please His Majesty. You cannot leave." She insisted and there was a row. "I suppose I was stupid. But if I am bored I can't do it. For some girls sex is OK just below the waist. But I like to engage the head and heart as well. Claude warned me that I was a fool."

She did not see the Shah again. When he came to Paris for de Gaulle's memorial service in 1970, his staff asked Madame Claude to send Ange to him. But Ange was fishing in the country with her boyfriend and refused to go. Claude was very cross.

Other girls were sent to the Shah throughout the seventies. He seemed to need them principally for the relaxation and companionship they could provide—a release from the strains of government and the servility that he himself demanded from his court. It was said that he was not so much interested in sex. Rather, he would spend hours in their company while he simply talked about himself. Like Ange, most of them found him sad.

Apart from Princess Ashraf, there were numerous other visitors to Contadora. The high-spirited, rich daughters of Assadollah Alam, the late minister of court, came. So did Abolfath Mahvi, one of those Iranian businessmen who had made millions out of his dealings in the boom years of the Great Civilization. He was reported to be one of the richest men in Iran—Standard Oil, Boeing, Honeywell, McDonnell Douglas, the catering for Iran Air, nuclear power—Mr. Mahvi was in all of them until, for a time, one of his rivals had him blacklisted and excluded from deals.

At the time of the revolution, says Mahvi, the Shah owed him

$3 million for unspecified services. When he arrived on Conta-
dora, the Shah said, "If you have come for your money, I don't
have it."

"Oh, no, Your Majesty," Mahvi says he protested. "I just came
to see you. Three million dollars is nothing compared to the loss
of the country."

The Shah told Mahvi that he had very little money left and that
he even had to worry about the cost of his wife's long-distance
calls. Mahvi did not know how much the Shah really had. "Probably not more than fifty million dollars—er, five hundred million," he said later.

But perhaps the most interesting visitor was the British television personality David Frost, who, during the Shah's rule, had
been one of the Western journalists close to the throne. He had
produced an epic series on Iran called *The Crossroads of Civilization*, which had not been as well received as many of his productions.

Now, in January 1980, the Shah felt strong enough to try to
explain himself "for posterity." Within the small world of television celebrities, the competition for the right to cross-examine him
was, understandably, intense. Among those who felt they de-
served such an exclusive was Barbara Walters of ABC Television.
She had seen him in New York Hospital and was taking part in a
large documentary on the hostage crisis masterminded by Pierre
Salinger, who worked for ABC in Paris and who was already in
touch with Christian Bourguet, Ghotbzadeh's French lawyer.

Mike Wallace of CBS thought that he should have the interview. He, unlike Walters and Frost, had subjected the Shah to
some fairly aggressive interviews during his reign. But Armao
decided that of all the suitors for the Shah's confidences, David
Frost was the most attractive—first because of his long connections with the Shah, and secondly because of the success of his
interviews with Richard Nixon. There was, however, one problem: Henry Kissinger.

In fall 1979 Kissinger had published the first volume of his
memoirs, *White House Years*. He was then a paid consultant to
NBC News and NBC contracted Frost to interview him. The
memoirs were tightly guarded; Frost was allowed to read parts of
them and take notes in a New York bank vault. He then asked
this author to help him prepare questions on Kissinger's policies

toward Cambodia. When the interview was recorded, Frost began
with a long series of questions on Cambodia. He refused to accept
Kissinger's answers at face value, and the former secretary of state,
who was used to gentle handling by the media, was outraged.
After the session he realized that he had performed badly and
demanded that the interview be rerecorded. NBC News managers
acceded to this demand, but Frost refused to do so. Alleging an
attempt at censorship, he resigned from the project and told *The
New York Times* the story; in order not to appear to be Kissinger's poodle, the following week NBC News announced that it
would broadcast the original interview to which Kissinger had
taken such violent exception. He reacted with what one NBC
official, Nigel Ryan, called "hysteria," making scores of phone
calls to try to have at least some of the more damaging exchanges
deleted. NBC, in the face of intense scrutiny from other news
media, refused.

When, only a few weeks later, Kissinger heard that Frost had
been chosen to interview his friend the Shah, he made his displeasure known. The Shah did not change his mind.

A member of Armao's staff, Chris Godek, went down to Contadora to prepare the Shah for the interview. Playing the part of
Frost, she asked him tough questions on all aspects of his rule—
SAVAK, corruption, oil prices, and the CIA. The Shah remarked
that he had never been briefed so well while he was on the throne.

An extraordinary encounter took place at the beginning of the
interview. Frost had employed as his principal adviser Andrew
Whitley, a British journalist who had been the BBC's man in
Teheran through the Shah's final days of power. The Shah and
many of his advisers considered that the BBC World Service,
acting as mouthpiece of the British government, had conspired
with Khomeini to destroy him. He detested Whitley's reporting
and had asked the British embassy to have him withdrawn. When
this failed, he had considered expelling him from Iran, but did not
do so.

In January 1980 the Shah still felt bitter about the role of the
BBC. When he heard that Whitley was helping Frost prepare the
questions, he was upset. Armao was furious and came close to
canceling the interview. But the Shah decided to go ahead nonetheless. Unlike many Western statesmen, he had never cut short
an interview in the past, nor refused to answer a question, nor,
like Kissinger, demanded that a whole interview be remade. He

had asked for no ground rules and no questions in advance from Frost.

Whitley and the Shah met on the stairs of the hotel on Contadora. The Shah behaved with courtesy, and shook Whitley's hand gravely. They treated each other like old battlefield adversaries meeting for the first time after the war was over.

The interview was taped over four days. The Shah wrote in his last memoirs that he enjoyed the challenge that it presented, but according to his aides he was disappointed to find Frost rather more reverential than he had been in his interrogations of Nixon and Kissinger. They said that he had looked forward to an opportunity to defend himself in a robust exchange. Nonetheless, he seemed to one of Frost's other advisers, John Birt, who had taken part in both the Nixon and Kissinger interviews, to be honest. "Unlike Nixon or Kissinger, the Shah was trying to tell the truth as he saw it," said Birt later.

The Frost team had come armed with great briefing books and filled with theories as to why the Shah had fallen. The Shah had none. "I tell you, Mr. Frost," he said over and over again, both on camera and off, "that I still cannot understand—I will repeat that—I still cannot understand what has happened."

When Frost asked him if he had not made the mistake of thinking that anyone who opposed him was an enemy of the state, the Shah paused: "That might be true," he said, but then continued, "But these same people today . . . where are they? Either outside the country or in hiding."

When Frost asked if SAVAK had become a state within a state, the Shah replied, "No, I don't think so . . . they had secrets, maybe. And they could eventually impose what they thought was good for the country, and they could have been quite wrong."

And at the end, they were really not much help? asked Frost.

"They were doing nothing."

"They didn't predict anymore than anyone else did that the threat would come from the mullahs?"

"No. They could claim that they had their wings clipped. But I think they were in the dark."

"Did your advisers tell you how unpopular and feared SAVAK was?"

"Oh, yes, surely. The Empress was every day telling me."

The Shah rejected absolutely Frost's suggestion that he might have suffered from any *"folie de grandeur."* Iran was a country

with almost forty million people. Britain, with a similar population, was once "ruling the waves, and you had such a vast empire
that was unprecedented in the history of the world. . . . I don't
see where there is *folie de grandeur* if an advanced nation with
fifty million people could contribute to the stability of the Indian
Ocean region."

When David Frost left Contadora, he left a man brooding on
history but finding in distant mirrors no reflection to help him
really understand his own fate. Frost himself thought that the
Shah was not so much evil as a vain and unconfident King who
dared only to surround himself with sycophants. As such he had
remained tragically oblivious to the changing nature of the society
over which he presided and of the people whose loyalty he took
for granted.

Frost's team left Panama on the same plane as Robert Armao
and Crown Prince Reza. At the Panama City airport they were
told that their flight to New York would be several hours late.
For the sake of security, they were driven in a fast motorcade to a
suite in the Panama Hotel. In a dark room, which was filled by
the usual scruffy armed guards and which grew hot despite an old
ceiling fan, the Crown Prince insisted that everyone play black-
jack.

The British television men sat around the table. So did the local
head of Pan American's security, a funny, flashy man with gold
teeth and a gun in his belt, who was obviously enjoying himself
immensely.

The Crown Prince wanted to be the croupier. The stakes were
matchsticks that cost a dollar each. Reza played as if the bank
were worth a million. After two hours he had won five dollars
and he walked away from the table in triumph.

CHAPTER TWENTY-ONE

The Quarrel

The highest point in Panama City is Ancon Hill. It stands above the Pacific entrance to the Canal and is a far more prominent landmark than, say, Capitol Hill in Washington. Its slopes are sharp and covered with trees—and until 1978 it belonged to the United States. After the U.S. obtained the rights to the Canal and the Canal Zone "in perpetuity" in 1903, the Stars and Stripes flew on top of the hill—a visible and infuriatingly haughty symbol to Panamanians of the extent to which sovereignty over part of their nation had been taken away from them. Melancholy songs and angry verses celebrated the loss of Ancon Hill. To be able to "walk up Ancon Hill" became a litmus of independence. During the new treaty negotiations, the Panamanians fought desperately for the return of Ancon Hill.

Dotted across the hill were several of the buildings that the United States considered essential to the safe running of the Canal —the Canal Company's administration building, the governor's house, the headquarters of Southern Command, and Gorgas Hospital. They are fine cream-painted structures with red-tiled roofs.

The hospital was named after William Gorgas, a brilliant American physician who managed to bring the malaria and yellow fever under control, making the building of the Canal possible.

Throughout the first half of the twentieth century Gorgas was the best-equipped hospital in Panama. It was by and for Americans. Ordinary Panamanians did not have access to its facilities. Like the hill on which it was built, Gorgas Hospital became a symbol of occupation.

Under the Canal Treaties signed by Jimmy Carter and Omar Torrijos, Ancon Hill was returned to Panama. But the U.S. flag was not removed; instead, a huge Panamanian flag was placed beside it. The United States retained many of its rights in what was now "the former Canal Zone." It continued to run Gorgas Hospital, with many Panamanians on the staff.

By this time there were many other hospitals in Panama City. Probably the best of them was the Paitilla Medical Center, a low, white modernistic building in the new business sector of the city by the sea. This was a private hospital, staffed and owned by a group of Panamanian doctors, some of whom were close to Omar Torrijos.

Before the Shah came to Panama, his New York doctor, Ben Kean, had insisted that if he needed hospital treatment he must be taken to Gorgas and nowhere else. This had been agreed to by Lloyd Cutler, Jimmy Carter's counsel, and was part of the Lackland Agreement negotiated between the U.S. government and the Shah's entourage.

Kean said later that having served in Panama during World War II, he understood Panamanian nationalism. He knew that the racism practiced by many American Canal Zone employees was deeply offensive to Panamanians. "They had to have resentments against us," he said. Therefore, he said, he was especially careful in the way he behaved with them in regard to the Shah.

But to hear the Panamanians tell it, when the Shah needed hospital treatment, Ben Kean acted as the archetypal ugly American, a latter-day Teddy Roosevelt, charging up Ancon Hill and scattering all Panamanian sensibilities and pride before him.

Once again, medical politics and personalities interfered with the Shah's treatment, and in ways that were even more astonishing than those that had already occurred. What happened next was not a comedy of errors; it was a fiasco. The doctors' perceptions of what happened are irreconcilable.

When the Shah had first arrived in Panama, Omar Torrijos had told his surgeon general and his personal doctor, Carlos García

Aguilera, that he wanted him in charge of the case.

"Charlie García," as he is known, has a somewhat unhappy reputation in Panama City. A square, tough, dark-haired man, he had been looking after senior officers of the National Guard for years. Like most Panamanian physicians, he was trained in the United States; his wife was the daughter of a U.S. naval surgeon, and his son joined the U.S. Air Force. He is not, therefore, known as a radical; he loves the macho life of the military and charges around town in a curtained roadster with medicine and rifles and uniforms littering the back. Some of his colleagues speculate that he might have links to the CIA. He is widely reputed to have a stubborn, almost truculent temperament. After Torrijos' death he remained as doctor to General Noriega.

Dr. García had gone to watch the Shah land with his wife and dogs and staff at Howard Air Force Base. He thought the Shah looked desperately ill. A few days later he flew to Contadora to examine him. He found the Shah's spleen enlarged and he took a blood sample. As far as Charlie García was concerned, he was now in charge of the Shah. This was Panama, and the general had assigned him. It was a Panamanian, not an American, show. García said he appointed a young oncologist, Adán Ríos, to take care of the Shah's cancer treatment.

On December 26, Ben Kean and Hibbard Williams flew down from New York to arrange for the Shah's care—based around Gorgas. The next day they drove up Ancon Hill and met at Gorgas Hospital its American superintendent, its chief of medicine, and Charlie García and Adán Ríos. As well as working at Paitilla and other Panamanian hospitals, Ríos was a consultant at Gorgas so he was acceptable to Kean. Ríos was told that he would draw the Shah's blood at regular intervals and bring it to Gorgas for analysis.

Kean said later that it was he, not Charlie García, who appointed Ríos. He said that García was at the meeting as a representative of the Panamanian government, and that to his relief, García behaved very quietly, saying that Torrijos wanted to cooperate fully. García later recalled, by contrast, that he did not like the way Kean tried to take charge and tried to appoint Ríos himself. He said that he protested, "Dr. Kean, how can you appoint anyone? You're in Panama. You appoint in New York, not in Panama."

This disagreement over who had actually "appointed" Adán Ríos as the Shah's oncologist was symptomatic of the difficult relations that grew between the American and Panamanian doctors in general and between Drs. Kean and García in particular. Each thought he was in charge. Neither was used to being subordinate.

The young man in the middle, Adán Ríos, had trained at M. D. Anderson Hospital, which is part of the Texas Medical Center in Houston and is one of America's leading cancer hospitals. Ríos said that Kean told him he would be in charge of the day-to-day oncological aspects of the case. Ríos later recalled asking Kean, "I want to be sure I understand correctly; you are telling me I am in charge of him?" To which Kean replied, "You are going to be his physician."

Throughout the next six weeks, Ríos made several visits to the house on Contadora. The Shah continued to take chlorambucil, the drug that his French doctors, Jean Bernard and Georges Flandrin, had originally prescribed six years before. His health improved in the dry warmth of Contadora. He gained about twenty-four pounds. Ríos was young—too young, Dr. Pirnia thought—but he was discreet; he never spoke to the press about his patient. Indeed, no one knew that he was involved with the Shah.

At first he spoke frequently to Dr. Kean on the telephone about the patient; as the weeks went on, he did so less. The Panamanians were assuming more control.

At the beginning of February Ríos checked the Shah into Paitilla Medical Center, not Gorgas, for a discreet checkup. No one, not even Dr. Kean, knew about it. The Shah was satisfied. (The tests at Paitilla were done under yet another pseudonym for the Shah. The name used was that of Manuel Antonio Noriega, the Panamanian chief of security.)

By the middle of February it was clear that the Shah's spleen was beginning to grow again; Ríos decided it would not be possible to postpone a splenectomy much longer.

Very soon after that, the Shah developed a respiratory infection, probably as the result of a virus. His white cell count and platelet count both fell dramatically. White cells are needed both to provide immunities from disease and to kill bacteria; now the Shah simply did not have enough to do either. The platelets are essential for clotting the blood; the Shah could now bleed to death even without an operation. It was clear to Ríos and García that there was a new crisis. They were alarmed. So was Dr. Kean when he was informed in New York.

The Queen was also worried about her husband. She called Georges Flandrin in Paris and asked him to come at once. He told his wife he would be back in a couple of days; it was weeks before he returned.

On March 2, Flandrin took the Concorde to New York, intending to transit direct to Panama. But he was greeted at JFK with a message to call Robert Armao, who asked him to stay in New York to meet with the doctors from New York Hospital. Flandrin was not very pleased by the delay, despite the courtesy of the "dapper" Armao and his charming wife. The next day Armao took him to Dr. Kean's offices. There too was Hibbard Williams, the physician in chief at New York Hospital. (Flandrin remembered that the Queen called Kean and Williams "Dupont and Dupond," after the two comic, bowler-hatted detectives in the Tintin books.) Also there was a man Flandrin did not know— he thought he might be CIA. He was in fact Dr. Bayard Clarkson, the chief of hematology-lymphoma service at Memorial.

To Flandrin it felt like a "council of war." He thought the Americans were hoping to stop him from proceeding to Panama. "They were irritated that anyone else should be involved in the Shah's medical problems. Everyone else had been removed, but the problem was that the Shah insisted on my coming. I said it was very difficult, that the Queen had invited me and I could not but go."

However, he suggested that after he had examined the Shah he would fly straight back to New York and report his findings. The Americans agreed to this and Flandrin left, still perplexed. "I didn't really understand what they wanted—except that I should not go to Panama."

Dr. Kean's recollection of the meeting is different. He said that he and his colleagues had no wish to stop Flandrin traveling to Panama and that they had merely wished to consult him before his trip. Dr. Clarkson's notes of the meeting confirm this. They show that the doctors thought the Shah should have a splenectomy, but that the risk of death was about 10 percent.

On Contadora, Flandrin met the Shah's Panamanian doctors. He did not like Charlie García, but Adán Ríos seemed both competent and apolitical. Ríos liked Flandrin too. "He was the Shah's true physician," he said later. "He didn't look for glory. The rest of us were just geographical accidents, no matter how big we wanted to play our roles. It was unfortunate that Georges did not have more power."

As soon as Flandrin examined the Shah, he realized that his condition was once again very serious. The spleen had become enormous, and Flandrin confirmed that both the Shah's white blood count and his platelet count were dangerously low. People in such condition can die within hours if they get an infection. Antibiotics are essential. Flandrin gave him a transfusion of two units of packed red cells. He aspirated a bone marrow sample, which, to his relief, appeared completely normal. That meant that the Shah still had a chance. But it was essential to take out the spleen at once, give him a blood transfusion, and then radiotherapy immediately afterwards.

All this Flandrin realized the day he arrived in Panama. He says he called New York to tell Armao and Kean that "I could not leave the Shah; if they wanted to check his condition, they would have to come themselves." Meantime, he had begun to get a whiff of the arcane and frightening extradition negotiations being conducted over and around the Shah.

What he did not hear, and no one at the time knew, was that Charlie García was convinced that the Iranians had been encouraging him to murder the Shah.

Torrijos had sent García on one of the Panamanian delegations to Paris to negotiate with Christian Bourguet and Hector Villalon, the emissaries of Sadegh Ghotbzadeh, the Iranian foreign minister, the question of the Shah's extradition. According to García, Villalon asked him a series of questions as to how best to kill a person. Would you use curare, strychnine, things of that nature? García said later that though the questions were indirect, "I knew exactly what he was trying to tell me. I knew he was only dealing with one person. The end of the story was that 'If you kill the dog, you get rid of the rabies. If the Shah disappears, the problem of the hostages disappears.' "

It seems that the murder of the Shah was being proposed quite seriously at this time. In his book, *Crisis,* Hamilton Jordan recounts a secret meeting he had in Paris on February 17 with an Iranian whose name he had promised not to divulge.

Jordan asked him why Iran could not put aside its grievances against the Shah. The Iranian replied, "But, Mr. Jordan—we *cannot* put aside the case of the Shah! That man is so evil, he has tortured and murdered so many of our people, he has stolen so much of our money! The Shah and Kissinger and Rockefeller made our country an instrument of U.S. foreign policy. The Shah is the reason for the hostages! You must understand that!

[H]olding fifty-three Americans is a slight injustice compared to the killing and torturing of thousands and thousands of Iranians by the criminal Shah!"

Jordan decided it was futile to argue about the past and asked how the present crisis could be resolved.

It was easy, came the reply. "All you have to do is kill the Shah."

"You're kidding," said Jordan, shocked.

"I am very serious, Mr. Jordan," came the reply. "The Shah is in Panama now. I am not talking about anything dramatic. Perhaps the CIA can give him an injection or do something to make it look like a natural death. I'm only asking you to do to the Shah what the CIA did to thousands of innocent Iranians over the past thirty years!"

Jordan said he responded, "That's impossible! It's totally out of the question!"

Subsequently, Jordan's interlocutor was revealed as Sadegh Ghotbzadeh, the Iranian foreign minister.

Under the supervision of Charlie García, Flandrin and Ríos began to prepare, in secrecy, for the operation. The Shah himself had no objections to their choosing Paitilla instead of Gorgas. Ambler Moss, the U.S. ambassador, was all in favor of the Shah's being taken there rather than back onto what was virtually U.S. territory; he knew that it could not be kept secret and that it would not play well in Teheran.

The next thing was to find a surgical team. Splenectomy is not usually a difficult operation. But in the case of hypersplenism, complications can arise. With such a serious platelet deficiency, the Shah was in danger of simply bleeding to death during surgery or in the immediate postoperative period. This risk could be diminished by platelet transfusions before surgery or at the moment of splenic artery interruption. There was also a risk of even more serious infection than he now suffered; that risk could be lessened by white cell transfusions. A third possible complication was thromboembolism due to an increase in platelets after splenectomy.

Anticipating these problems, Adán Ríos put in a call to his alma mater, the M. D. Anderson Hospital and Tumor Institute at the Medical Center in Houston, Texas. He spoke to Dr. Jeane Hester, an associate professor of internal medicine. He asked her to become part of the medical team he was assembling to operate on the Shah. She agreed.

Jeane Hester, a tall, willowy woman, is an experienced oncologist whose particular expertise is in treating leukemia patients with transfusions of supportive blood components. She was an obvious and well-qualified person to have on any medical team treating the Shah.

In every milliliter of blood there are supposed to be about 5 million red cells, 250,000 platelets, and 5,000 white cells. Just as the differences in concentration are enormous, so are the differences in life span. Red cells live 120 days, platelets live 10 days, and white cells live 6 hours. The red cells carry oxygen, white cells fight infection, and platelets initiate clotting. All of them come from the bone marrow in pelvic bones, ribs, breastbone, and vertebrae. The bone marrow of leukemia patients is unable to manufacture the right number of cells, and so the patients risk dying of hemorrhage and infection while being treated. Hester's job was to stop that by giving patients a transfusion of white cells and platelets from normal donors. Since the early seventies she had assisted at hundreds of operations. She had also been working on a research project with IBM to develop machinery to separate blood cells. She was as knowledgeable as anyone about the technical advances.

From what Ríos told her, Hester realized that the Shah's counts were so low that he would never, unaided, be able to support major surgery or the intensive chemotherapy that, she suspected, would be needed after the splenectomy.

She knew that in theory the Shah's illness might be localized in an enlarged spleen—and that its removal could cure him. But given his history of chronic leukemia and the involvement of his lymph glands, it was more likely that the disease was systemic, and would be found wherever there were lymph nodes—all over the body. That would require intensive chemotherapy, perhaps for two years. And that itself would suppress the bone marrow and so lead to a further reduction in the blood count. She was sure she would need equipment to provide massive transfusions of platelets and probably white cells as well.

She called IBM and asked for their help. They agreed to provide her with an IBM 2991 blood cell washer, which would purify the concentrations of red cells, and an IBM 2997 blood cell separator, which is used to prepare the leukocytes and platelets.

Blood separators have become still more sophisticated since the Shah needed them. But even in 1980 they were extraordinary machines. If you transfuse complete red cells to a patient, he often develops antibodies against the white cells and platelets, which will make the transfusion ineffective. The IBM separator used centrifugal forces to wash the white cells and platelets out of the red cells—rather like decaffeinating coffee.

The machines were delicate, and since there was an obvious danger that they might be damaged in transit or might not conform to the Panamanian electricity supply, IBM sent an engineer with them to Panama.

Rather than go as a member of the university, which might have led to embarrassing political complications, Hester decided to take vacation time to travel to Panama. Before she left Houston, she got a call from Ben Kean in New York. This confused her somewhat; she knew very little about the Shah's medical history. She had no idea that Dr. Kean considered he was in charge of the case and, she said later, he did not then directly inform her of this.

The Panamanian doctors later alleged that when he heard of the plans that were being made for an operation, Kean intervened with the State Department, with the army medical command in Panama, and with IBM, to stop the machines being sent to Panama. Kean himself denied he had done any such thing—and the machines certainly arrived. But he said that he had asked that the machines be sent to Gorgas rather than to any hospital in Panama City. He too flew down to Panama.

When Hester arrived there on March 6, she met Dr. Flandrin, whom she immediately liked. She thought he was a dedicated physician; she had no disagreement with him on how the case should be managed. She examined the bone marrow that he had aspirated from the Shah. If a patient is anemic, the first question to ask is: Is he bleeding? There was no suggestion that that was the Shah's problem. There were two other possibilities: that his red cells were being destroyed in the spleen or by circulating antibodies, or that the bone marrow was not producing any. The cells grow in the bone marrow, so it is relatively easy to count them there to see whether they are correctly balanced. At this stage about 75 percent of the Shah's bone marrow cells were red; the normal figure would have been only 25 percent. Why would the bone marrow be producing red cells so fast? If he was not bleeding, it must be because they were being destroyed in the spleen.

That day Flandrin, Rios, and Garcia recommended a splenectomy as soon as possible. According to Flandrin and the Panamanian doctors, Dr. Kean was "the sole dissenter" and recommended embolization of the splenic artery or radiotherapy. Kean says that while he did mention these as theoretical alternatives to splenectomy in a general medical discussion, he always considered splenectomy inevitable—and quite dangerous. According to the Panamanians, the Shah was entirely happy with the recommendations that they and Flandrin made and was also happy for a surgeon to be brought from M. D. Anderson Hospital. He said he did not want a surgeon from New York Hospital. The Panamanians, Hester and Flandrin considered asking Dr. Charles McBride, a well-known surgeon at M. D. Anderson, to take part in the operation.

Kean's view of what was going on in Panama is very different from that of the Panamanian doctors. Although he had not been back to Panama since just after the Shah's arrival, he considered that the Shah was still "his" patient. Rios, Flandrin, and any other doctors possessed only such authority as he was prepared to delegate. He was already angry (he said later) that in recent weeks he had been getting only secondhand reports that the Shah was feeling unwell. He complained that Rios had not returned his calls. He was infuriated that the Shah had been taken to Paitilla for a checkup without his knowledge, rather than to Gorgas. Now that he was in Panama he decided that nothing was as it should be. He decided that the problem was that "Dr. Torrijos had taken charge."

In a later interview and in his subsequent authorized account, published in *American Medical News,* the journal of the American Medical Association, Kean acknowledged that the Shah himself had made no objections to an operation at what Kean called "General Torrijos' Hospital," Paitilla. But as far as Kean was concerned, the Carter administration had promised the Shah he would be treated at Gorgas, and that was that. Later he acknowledged that he wanted the Shah in American, not Panamanian, facilities.

He confronted the Panamanian physicians with this. National as well as professional pride was involved on both sides. The Panamanian doctors considered that if the Shah were taken to Gorgas, it would be seen throughout the world as evidence of their own incompetence. They therefore insisted on Paitilla. The Americans and the Panamanians were both chauvinists.

The pretty wooden hotel by the sea on Contadora provided the first scene for the new crisis. Dr. Kean met there with Charlie García and with Adán Ríos. According to Kean's account, they were on the lawn in front of the hotel when Gárcia told him it was Paitilla or nowhere. They went up to Robert Armao's room to argue. García was obdurate.

Kean was outraged. His ruddy face whitened and he seemed to have difficulty controlling himself. "I dare you to tell this to the Shah," he said.

García apparently responded, "Take me to him. This is an order from the general."

The doctors strode together, not speaking, past the airstrip and along the lane to Puntalara. It was a tiring hike. At the house, breathing heavily, they were shown into the Shah's presence.

According to Kean, "Dr. García proceeded to spit out the ultimatum to the Shah. It was Paitilla or nowhere. The Shah just listened. I was disgusted."

Adán Ríos then said, "Let's get the best man possible," and he reached for the telephone. Kean stopped him, saying, "I consider this a betrayal."

At that point the Shah stood up, said, "Good day, gentlemen," and left the room.

Charlie García remembers this encounter rather differently. He said later that the Shah actually took him aside and said, "If you think that Dr. Kean is making trouble, I will get rid of him."

García insists that he never gave an ultimatum of Paitilla or nowhere. But he says that when Kean asked for Gorgas, "I reminded him, 'Dr. Kean, the Shah of Iran is in Panama as a guest —because fifty to sixty Americans are hostage in Teheran. If you put the Shah in Gorgas, you might as well take him to New York. But if that is done, you won't know what will happen to the hostages.' " García also said that once the Shah went to Gorgas, he would not be allowed back into Panama itself. He tried to convince Kean and Armao that taking the Shah to Gorgas would be terribly damaging for the hostages. "There was no way we could convince Kean and Armao of that. They didn't give a shit about the hostages."

This was not how Kean and Armao saw their positions.

Robert Armao felt less strongly than Kean about Gorgas; he considered that Paitilla was a pretty good hospital. But Kean insisted that Panamanian nationalism should not be allowed to interfere with the Shah's treatment. He began to think about how he could regain control.

"I needed a new solution," Kean said later. He talked it over with Armao at dinner in the hotel that night and came up with the idea of finding a medical superstar. "I needed a surgeon so big that no one would dare buck him. I needed a man of international acclaim," he said later.

He fixed upon Dr. Michael DeBakey, who was the most distinguished heart surgeon in the world. (Dr. Christiaan Barnard had perhaps been more famous.) There was nothing wrong with the Shah's heart; it was DeBakey's name and fame that Kean coveted.

After dinner, according to Kean, he went upstairs to Robert Armao's room and called DeBakey. The surgeon was unavailable, but he called back late that night. He agreed to come to Panama to operate on the Shah. But he said he would want to bring his own medical team. (There is another element of confusion here; DeBakey later said that Kean first called him on March 4—in other words, two days before the row on Contadora. Kean said later that this was one of the few occasions on which DeBakey was mistaken.)

Kean was delighted. Dr. Hester and Dr. Flandrin were dubious when they heard of the plan. Hester, who was trying to get the IBM blood separator working properly, said at the time, "Dr. DeBakey's a fantastic surgeon. But I haven't worked with him; I don't know how he'll approach this situation, and we tend with cancer patients to use oncologic surgeons." Dr. Hester was beginning to think the Shah's situation was all very odd. Why weren't cancer specialists in charge of his care? Why get a heart surgeon to operate in the abdomen? Dr. Flandrin felt similarly, that a cancer patient with a greatly enlarged spleen should be operated on by a surgeon with precise oncological experience. He had wanted to bring in a surgeon from Dr. Hester's hospital, M. D. Anderson. Once again he felt powerless.

Dr. Coleman also said later that he thought Dr. DeBakey, whatever his skills, was not the right choice of surgeon for the Shah. But Dr. Kean argued that a surgeon as brilliant as DeBakey could easily take out a spleen, and, after all, his forte was abdominal aneurysm. "I considered him a universal surgeon, not just a

heart man," said Kean later. "Not only that, but one of the problems with taking out the spleen is bleeding, and he is a vascular
surgeon."

When the Shah was being examined by Hester on Contadora,
he asked her what she thought of DeBakey. She now realized that
there were many different political and medical interests involved
in the case and replied cautiously, "He is a marvelous cardiovascular surgeon." *

The Shah said, "Well, I'm certain if Dr. DeBakey couldn't take
out my spleen he would have said so—or they would have told
me."

Next day, March 7, Kean met again with Charlie García in
Panama City. Also there was Dr. Gaspar García de Paredes, the
dean of the University of Panama Medical School and one of the
country's senior surgeons. García de Paredes, a member of one of
Panama's oldest families, had trained in the United States; indeed,
in the late 1950s, he had studied under Ben Kean at Cornell. As
chief of surgery at Paitilla, he had been involved in the discussions
about assembling a team to operate on the Shah.

Until now, everything had been calm from García de Paredes'
point of view. That was how he liked it. He was quite unlike his
far more political and aggressive colleague Charlie García. García
de Paredes was a soft, owl-faced man with gold-rimmed spectacles
and graying sideburns. He had an altogether soothing bedside
manner.

Now, said García de Paredes later, Kean asked them merely if
DeBakey could be "on the team."

---

* Hester thought that the actual surgery would be the least of the problems—much more
serious would be the postoperative care. In particular, she feared that the anesthetic would
lead to a recurrence of his pneumonia. Postoperative infection of the lungs was more dangerous and more likely than hemorrhage, she thought. She also began to wonder whether anyone
had told the Shah that he was suffering from systemic malignancy and that his troubles would
not necessarily end with the removal of his spleen.

She explained that she wanted to do blood tests on his family and security staff to see
whose blood type would be most suitable for providing platelets for him. Hester hoped that
Ashraf, his twin, would be the ideal donor. But after examining the Princess, she decided
against that idea; Ashraf's veins were too small. Hester took blood samples from the Queen
and Colonel Jahanbini and other members of the entourage, as well as from the Shah himself.
When they were analyzed, she discovered that she shared some typing antigens with the Shah
and so decided that it would be appropriate for her to act as a donor. It was better that he
should develop antibodies against her rather than his family, because they would be almost
certainly be needed at a later stage.

"Ridiculous!" said Kean later. "Would I call DeBakey at midnight to be 'on a team'?"

DeBakey himself said that Kean and Hibbard Williams "both made it very clear that I was to have complete responsibility and asked me to bring whatever personnel and equipment I needed. Without that assurance, I would not have agreed to go and certainly would not have taken my surgical team and equipment with me."

There is a clear and obvious conflict between what the American and the Panamanian doctors recalled. The Panamanians later stated that they had agreed to DeBakey's coming, in what they called "a spirit of cooperation and aware of the grave responsibility when dealing with the health of such a personage." Garcia de Paredes said later that he understood DeBakey might, at most, bring a scrub nurse. He said Kean never suggested that he was going to take over the entire operation. The Panamanians insisted that they would never have agreed to that; they had to bend the law even to allow a foreign doctor to "participate" in an operation.

Kean and Armao flew back to New York, Hester to Houston. Suddenly, the delicate discussions between medical men were upset by articles in the American press revealing that the Shah was gravely ill and that he needed "sophisticated" medical attention that was unavailable in Panama. "Friends of the ex-monarch" were quoted in the New York *Daily News* as saying that "he should be admitted to the Gorgas Army Hospital or another in the United States."

The Panamanian doctors had said nothing to the press, so they presumed that these stories came from Dr. Kean or Robert Armao, and they were outraged. They believed that they were being denigrated in order to get the Shah either into Gorgas or back to the United States. (Like other Panamanian officials, Charlie García professed to believe that Kean and Armao were both Rockefeller minions and that the Rockefellers wanted the Shah back in the U.S. so as to damage Jimmy Carter further.)

Then the American press got wind of the fact that DeBakey was to do the operation. Rightly or wrongly, the Panamanian doctors came to the conclusion that their competence was being called into question. It looked as if there was no one in Panama capable of taking out a spleen. There was uproar throughout the medical community in Panama City, according to García de Paredes. "We can take out spleens with the left hand, the right hand tied behind our backs," said Charlie García to Dr. Flandrin.

Charlie García and García de Paredes asked Mark Morse to call Armao and tell him how appalled they were. Morse warned Armao that as far as the Panamanians were concerned they had only invited DeBakey and his scrub nurse to work with them, not to replace them.

Quite apart from questions of honor, the news leak caused serious security problems for Panama. Scores of journalists flocked to the country to witness, from nearby, the Shah being subjected once more to the knife. More serious was the possibility of terrorist attack. Iranian officials were still publicly vowing to murder the Shah—as well as privately soliciting it. Now that his operation had been announced, Paitilla Hospital had to be put under heavy guard. Armed soldiers were placed on the roof, in the basement, and at all doors and corridors. The life of the hospital was completely disrupted.

The Panamanians were still prepared to compromise, and on Thursday, March 13, the Panamanian Council of Health authorized DeBakey "to act as an observer and surgical consultant, exclusively in the case of Mr. Mohammed Reza Pahlavi." The next day, the Shah and his wife flew from Contadora to Panama City and checked into a third-floor room at Paitilla, a room that Colonel Jahanbini and the Panamanian National Guard had made as secure as possible. Iron plates had been fixed over the windows, so the room was practically in darkness. The whole wing was cordoned off; there were soldiers quartered directly above and below the room. It was relatively comfortable.

That afternoon, the New Yorkers—Armao, Kean, Hibbard Williams—flew south in a private plane. They stopped at Hobby Airport, Houston, to pick up Jeane Hester and Dr. DeBakey and his substantial medical team. The plane took off with all these important people aboard. The real storms were only now about to break—chiefly, though perhaps not entirely fairly, about the person of Michael DeBakey.

CHAPTER TWENTY-TWO

The Cutter's Dilemma

According to popular stereotype, surgeons are supposed to think of themselves as God. This is a cliché that the story of Michael DeBakey does nothing to diminish. He is a god with especially divine hands.

Dr. DeBakey is to heart surgery as Muhammad Ali was to boxing, Frank Sinatra to crooning, or Lyndon Johnson to Democratic politics—a genius with a vast and sometimes uncomfortable ego.

In his private conference room in the hospital he runs in Houston, the walls are covered with green suede and festooned with just a few of the trophies, citations, awards, and photographs of DeBakey with the Good, the Not So Good, and the Great whom he has, on various occasions, treated or saved. He has operated on the ex-king of the Belgians, Guy Lombardo, the Duke of Windsor, Joe Louis, and many, many more. Howard Hughes died en route to the hope of salvation in DeBakey's hospital.

On DeBakey's wall there is also a copy of a mural tracing the history of medicine. It begins with Esculapio and ends with DeBakey. By the front door of the building stands a bronze statue of him erected by ex-King Leopold and Princess Lilian of Belgium in 1978 "in recognition of one who served so many." It shows the great cutter in surgical gown and cap, arms clasped across his chest, gazing impassively down, almost, it seems, at a body on a table before him. His hands are large, long-fingered, and supple. The legend describes him as "Surgeon, Educator and Medical Statesman." In Panama his statesmanship was to be tested.

DeBakey has been at Texas Medical Center in Houston since 1948; he and the center have grown together in stature. When he took over the department of surgery at Baylor College of Medicine, a part of the center, he had certain ambitions. He wanted to be a great surgeon and he wanted to construct a fabulous medical school and a hospital. He wished, in the words of one writer, "to be a national leader, perhaps the national leader, in the formulation of health policy, and the most prominent authority on all matters medical." All that, and more, he achieved in the next thirty years.

By the end of the seventies, the Medical Center had become, appropriately enough for Texas, one of the biggest and most advanced group of medical facilities in all America. It had more than four thousand beds, a plant worth more than $600 million, and an annual operating budget of $552 million. It had dozens of different institutions on its campus and it took patients from all over the world. Houston was oil and Houston was the Medical Center.

Part of the center's worldwide reputation derived from the fact that it concentrated on the most sensational and expensive kinds of individual medical rescue operations. Such an emphasis obviously created huge baronies and reputations for the top doctors at the center. Indeed, as the center grew, it became, in many ways, the sum of the reputations of its most brilliant and successful practitioners. They were the stars, the prima donnas on the stage that the center provided. And of them all, none was so great a star as Michael DeBakey.

He became a celebrity because he did more operations, and particularly, more spectacular operations than any of the other doctors. He also did many of them in a bright halo of publicity. Thus when he performed the first implant of an artificial left ventricle, there was a *Life* magazine photographer in the operating room; DeBakey gave a network interview as he left the operating theater.

Every famous surgeon has to be known for the particular, and DeBakey developed as his speciality vascular surgery, repairs to the blood vessels. He would cut open arteries that had become occluded by fats built up by too much cholesterol, too much smoking, high blood pressure, or by genetic factors. Then he

Dr. Michael DeBakey

would scrape out the blockage and either sew the artery back together or bypass it by attaching another channel to the vessel. At the same time, he developed an effective technique for dealing with aneurysms. (This is when the wall of a vein weakens and balloons and is in danger of bursting.) In both operations De-Bakey began to use Dacron as a patch. Indeed his skilled use of Dacron became almost a signature.

DeBakey was a brilliant pioneer. By the mid-sixties he had already become one of the country's leading "medical statesmen," which meant not only performing spectacular operations but also raising large amounts of money, and becoming involved in medical and national politics. He was on the cover of *Time* magazine, he frequently testified before congressional committees, and his friend Lyndon Johnson made him chairman of the President's Commission on Heart Disease, Cancer and Stroke. He became a frequent and superb public speaker, able to explain in simple language and a delightful, slow Louisiana accent the most intricate and arcane details of a surgeon's work. Audiences were always enraptured.

To the public, to politicians, to his patients, and to celebrities, even to most of the press, DeBakey seemed almost perfect—a man of infinite charm, who was totally, sincerely dedicated to his life-giving work. A gentleman, a genius, and a saint to boot.

Inevitably, some of those who worked for him or with him had a slightly different view, but it was not one they often chose to make public. "He is a very powerful man. I don't want to criticize him publicly," said one doctor at the Medical Center. This other picture of DeBakey that some of his colleagues gave was of a restless, arrogant creature endlessly driven to ever greater achievements and public recognition. A domineering man who was not always quite sensitive to the needs of his associates.

He worked extraordinarily hard and slept little. It was said that he needed only two hours a night, or that he catnapped during the day and did not sleep at night at all. He expected others to live the same punishing sort of life, even though all the glory of it went to him. The medical students at Baylor used to say that one of De-Bakey's residents had asked permission to be with his wife when she had a baby. "Fine," said DeBakey "two hours off will be enough, won't it?" He was a living legend.

By March 1980, he was seventy-one and he had a young wife and new baby of his own. He was a good-looking man who wore heavy horn-rimmed spectacles and walked with a slight stoop. He looked a little like an avuncular but sprightly turtle, with a pleasant smile and a quiet bedside manner. He had fantastic energy, and his hair, which had once been graying, was deep black. An article in *Texas Monthly* by Nick Lemann described how De-Bakey used to stride into the operating theater in white cowboy boots with high platform heels. Every other surgeon at the Medical Center wore regulation hospital green scrub suits. DeBakey had his own special royal-blue scrubs with his initials embroidered on the breast pocket.

On the flight south to Panama, the doctors sat around talking about the Shah's case. In retrospect it seemed to Hester that the one thing not adequately discussed was whether DeBakey was to be formally in charge of the surgery or whether he was technically a consultant to the Panamanians. DeBakey himself apparently had no doubt that he would be in charge and he believed that the Panamanian doctors understood that.

"I had said beforehand that if I was going to operate there, I was going to bring my team and therefore I needed to be sure that the doctors at the hospital are in agreement with that. Not only were they in agreement, I got a message from one of the doctors that they also wanted to host a little party for me," he said. Such an invitation had indeed been extended, but the Panamanian doctors subsequently denied that there had been any agreement that DeBakey was to be in charge, let alone that he was to bring his own large team.

Ben Kean later acknowledged that even he was surprised by the size of DeBakey's team, and thought he himself might have been the source of the misunderstanding. "Discussing it with the Panamanians, I didn't say, 'DeBakey and team,' I said, 'DeBakey.' It could be that they were surprised." Kean said also that he assumed DeBakey would, as a courtesy, invite Dr. Gaspar García de Paredes, the senior surgeon at Paitilla, to join his team and "scrub"—that is to say, wash his hands carefully and get gloved. That is the ritual that transforms an observer into a participant. But the Panamanians had a very different view. It was their hospital and they thought it was their right to invite DeBakey to scrub, not the other way around.

By the time the plane arrived in Panama on Friday evening, the Panamanian doctors were in a high old state. The leaks of information from the U.S. had infuriated them. They had publicly authorized DeBakey to come to Panama "to act as an observer and surgical consultant" in the case of the Shah. Yet here he was arriving in a private plane with an assistant, an anesthetist, and a nurse, quite apart from all the other doctors.

Usually DeBakey is welcomed in foreign countries, if not as a head of state then certainly as one of the world's most senior "medical statesmen." But that evening in Panama, no one came to meet the plane. General Torrijos himself had called Charlie García to suggest that he had better do so, but García had refused. "I was feeling pissed off and disgusted and said to Torrijos, 'As far as I am concerned, they can jump in the lake,' " said García later.

Dr. Kean subsequently described their anonymous arrival at the Panama City airport as "disgraceful," "embarrassing," and "devastating." "I had persuaded DeBakey that he would be welcome, as everywhere else in the world." Instead, the great surgeon was insulted as he landed. The troupe of American doctors had to find their own way to the Holiday Inn. That too irritated at least the male doctors. Worse was to come.

Paitilla Hospital is close to the Holiday Inn, in the most modern part of Panama City. Dr. Flandrin had moved to the Holiday Inn from Contadora. After the American doctors had checked into the hotel, the men—without Dr. Hester—walked across the road to see the Shah. To their fury, they were refused admission.

No one had told them that security at the hospital was now made draconian. The place was crawling with young men in T-shirts carrying submachine guns. Everyone had to wear identity cards. (At Dr. Pirnia's request, Dr. Flandrin had been given one that called him *Médico del Rey*, Doctor of the Shah.) The Americans were supposed to pick up their badges at the Holiday Inn, but they had not done so. When the Panamanian guards were obdurate, the Americans became outraged. "Only by resorting to counterthreats was I able to straighten things out," said Kean later. Torrijos himself had to be called before they were allowed in. Kean said he heard that the general was drunk. Perhaps inevitably some of the Americans saw the incident as further proof of a Panamanian conspiracy against the Shah. The Panamanians saw it as another example of American arrogance. "They went to see our patient at our hospital, to decide what to do without consulting us," said García de Paredes later.

While they were waiting for permission to get into the wing where the Shah was being guarded, Kean, Williams, and DeBakey wandered around the rest of the hospital. Kean later claimed that they were able to walk into the surgical units, the transfusion area, and the intravenous supply rooms. He said that this made a mockery of the security arrangements, for it would have been simple for someone to slip something into the materials that were to be injected into the Shah.

Meanwhile Adán Ríos, the Shah's Panamanian oncologist, was looking for Jeane Hester, whom he had invited to take part in the operation. She was still at the hotel. She was annoyed at the discourtesy of her colleagues in not telling her they were going to see the Shah. She thought it reflected their lack of enthusiasm for her involvement, because she had been chosen by the Panamanians. She was right.

Eventually the DeBakey team and Dr. Kean were allowed upstairs to the Shah's room. They gathered around his bedside. Georges Flandrin was also there. So was the Queen. So was Dr. Ríos. The Queen remembered later being struck by his appearance. "Poor Ríos! He was the only Panamanian doctor there at that moment. He looked dreadful. I had the feeling that something was going on. I think there was a conflict between his ethics and the politics of the place. He didn't know what to say. He just sat there, completely white, not saying a word. He was so nervous—that was my feeling."

DeBakey examined the Shah. Afterwards, as the others were leaving, the Shah asked Flandrin to stay behind. "Dr. Flandrin," he said, "you are like the Swiss, a neutral between the belligerents. Can one have confidence in these arrangements? Do you think I should let myself be operated on here?"

Flandrin had thought that DeBakey was the wrong choice of surgeon, but he now found him very impressive—"a man of finesse and subtlety, with great intellectual and medical qualities." But the tension between the Panamanians and the Americans was appalling.

"Certainly not. I have no confidence given what has happened," he said.

"I agree with you," said the Shah, with resignation.

Later that same Friday evening Kean and DeBakey decided to bring forward the surgery, from Sunday morning to Saturday afternoon. This alarmed Dr. Hester. "I don't know if I can get the blood ready by then," she said. Volunteers at Gorgas Hospital had given blood, but it had not yet been washed or processed. Nor had a missing pump for the IBM machine yet arrived; the IBM engineer, Pete Greco, was due to fly in with it that evening.

"I won't know till tomorrow morning whether I can get the blood ready for the afternoon," she said. They agreed that everyone should meet again at 9 A.M. on Saturday. Hester had a long night ahead of her. It was one in which, she said later, "My professional career just about went down the drain."

She and Adán Ríos drove out to the airport to meet Pete Greco, the IBM engineer. They missed him. When they finally found him at the hotel at about 11 P.M., he had bad news. He had been to Gorgas Hospital to fit the new pump he had brought—there was a pin missing and it could not be mounted.

"You won't believe my frenzy," said Hester. She called IBM in the States and dragged someone out of bed. He said they would mail a replacement. No way, she said. He must get several replacements and "you put them on someone's lap and send them down on a plane."

At midnight, she and Greco returned to Gorgas. Hester had originally helped IBM design the machine, so she now tried to redesign it, to make it work even though it was incomplete. They spent most of the night working. The problem was that the inadequate pump made it impossible to mix the blood with the anticoagulant smoothly.

By Saturday morning, she was quite exhausted. At breakfast she told Dr. Kean that the machine was not yet repaired. "He looked at me and he was just furious. And he said, 'I knew you couldn't do it.' "

Hester was not pleased. After all, she had originally been told that the blood would be needed on Sunday, not Saturday. "I told you I could do it by Sunday morning, and I will do it by Sunday morning," she replied. She said she was going to give it one more try this morning. "I will let you know by noon whether there are platelets available for the surgery this afternoon."

Pete Greco went off to the airport to catch a flight to Miami to pick up another pump. Hester returned to the machines and the blood at Gorgas.

After breakfast, Kean, DeBakey, and Hibbard Williams crossed the road to Paitilla for a meeting in the hospital library with their Panamanian counterparts. It was an unhappy occasion.

Kean still wanted the Shah operated on at Gorgas, as the Lackland Agreement had promised. But Colonel Mims Aultman, the U.S. commander at Gorgas, was reluctant. He knew Panama and understood the nationalist feelings involved. He feared there would be immense security problems, if not riots by those same students who had already protested the Shah's admission to Panama and who would now be enraged by the additional insult of a takeover by *Yanqui* imperialist medicine. This time the government would be for them, not against them.

The Panamanian doctors believed on that Saturday morning that Kean had again been in touch with the U.S. authorities at Gorgas, trying to get the Shah transferred there. On every score, the Panamanian doctors were terribly upset. Here was DeBakey arriving in their country with a full team, with its own equipment and instruments. "So we felt," said García de Paredes later, "they're coming to our hospital and making us look like a bunch of idiots before the whole community."

The meeting was chaired by Gaspar García de Paredes. Usually his manners are impeccable. But, he said later, he was angrier now than he had been for many years. When he studied under Ben Kean at Cornell in the fifties, he had admired him greatly. Now he felt that Dr. Kean was behaving abominably toward him and toward Panama. He said he had lost pounds that week trying to avoid the hordes of press, to ensure tight security at the hospital, and to calm other doctors at Paitilla who were furious that Americans should have been allowed to come at all.

There were also different and competing paranoias. Torrijos had emphasized to his doctors that on no account was the Shah to die in Panama. Yet there were so many people who wanted him dead. The Iranians, through intermediaries, had seemed to offer massive bribes to any doctor who terminated him. Hit squads were said to be after him. There were even rumors in Panama that the CIA itself was out to kill him—in order to end the hostage crisis. And yet David Rockefeller and Henry Kissinger wanted him back in the States. Charlie García was convinced that all this talk of the Lackland Agreement was a smoke screen for trying to ensure a Republican victory in 1980. "These people didn't give a shit about the hostages," said Charlie García later.

There was paranoia on the Shah's side as well. Some of his entourage had real fears of an "accident" on the operating table. Alternatively, while the Shah was under anesthetic, he might be carted off to the airport in a box and flown to Teheran, to awake under the vengeful smile of the ayatollah.

Gaspar García de Paredes tried to appear calmer than he felt as he opened the library meeting, sitting across the room from the Americans. "I was so mad. I was so mad," he later recalled.

He began by telling Kean that he was not authorized to practice in Panama and that he could not participate in any way in the operation. He said that they were all furious about the press leaks that cast doubt on their competence and had caused them security nightmares. That was why DeBakey had been invited only as "observer and surgical consultant."

Turning to DeBakey, whom he considered more innocent than Dr. Kean, García de Paredes said, "We invited you here to work with us and we will stick by that. You are welcome." But he went on to add a phrase that infuriated the Americans. He said to one of the most famous surgeons in the world, "You know the American College [of Surgeons] frowns on itinerant surgeons."

Itinerant surgeons are carpetbaggers. They are jobbing "cutters"—men who descend from big cities onto small rural towns, "cut" whomsoever the local doctor has lined up for them, and move on to the next town, their fees in their pockets. They do not provide either preoperative or postoperative care. Any mistakes they make are left in the hands of the local doctor. This was not how Dr. DeBakey was usually seen.

It was a grave insult, but DeBakey responded calmly and politely, saying, "Well, you know, I've just come here to help."

The tone of the meeting degenerated when Charlie García, the surgeon general, stormed in. He was convinced that Kean, whom he now loathed, was still trying to get the Shah moved to Gorgas. Tempers flared. Kean and Armao said that the U.S. government had made commitments and nothing should or could be changed. This infuriated the Panamanians even more. García de Paredes told the Americans to remember that "you are not in Afghanistan." This was an odd metaphor, but he meant that Panama was not an occupied country where invaders could do as they pleased. The meeting broke up.

Later that morning the Panamanians asked to meet alone with DeBakey. They tried to be conciliatory and told him that they had no quarrel with him personally; indeed they had the highest regard for his reputation. They would be glad for him to be part of the team. Their quarrel was only with Dr. Kean.

According to the Panamanians, DeBakey replied that he had not originally understood what his role was to be. He had not known that the Panamanians were themselves assembling a team. He said he was used to being in complete charge of his cases; if this was not possible, he would rather withdraw at once. They thought he had been misled by Dr. Kean. However, DeBakey said later he would never have agreed to go to Panama at all unless Kean had made it clear that he would have full responsibility for the care of the Shah. "Dr. Kean told me that he had been told by the Panamanian physicians who were taking care of the Shah that I and my team would be welcome to the country." It is evident that DeBakey had had no inkling that his arrival with a large team could upset the Panamanians.

Meanwhile, Jeane Hester was still up Ancon Hill at Gorgas, struggling with the defective IBM machine to produce platelets for the Shah. By midday Saturday she had succeeded. They were not the best platelets she had ever separated, but they were good enough. From Gorgas she called Kean to tell him that the operation could go ahead that afternoon. To her consternation he replied that problems had arisen and that surgery would probably have to be canceled for today. She assumed then that it would take place as originally scheduled, on Sunday. She continued working. She did not know that her colleagues were on the point of deciding not to have the operation in Panama.

Ambler Moss was presiding over a provincial U.S.A. Day Country Fair when he heard of the crisis. In the middle of a toast proposing indelible Panamanian-American friendship, he was interrupted by an aide and told to call the embassy at once. "Let me finish my toast and drink my champagne," he replied. When he did call, he was told, "Get back here fast; there's real trouble with the Shah."

When Moss heard what had happened, he came to the quick conclusion that the big doctors had been behaving as big doctors so often do—as prima donnas. "Good God, ballet dancers are nothing compared to the top of the medical profession as far as egos are concerned. Unbelievable, towering egos!"

That Saturday afternoon Moss started shuttling back and forth between DeBakey's suite at the Holiday Inn and Gaspar García de Paredes' home nearby. He found the latter exhausted. His wife had insisted that he take a Valium—something he never did—and so he had gone to bed.

Nonetheless he and Moss, and Torrijos' adviser Marcel Salamin, sat on the porch and tried to talk out a solution. García de Paredes told Moss that DeBakey could still be involved, but it could not be a purely American team; it had to be a combined Panamanian-American effort.

Then the ambassador rushed around to see DeBakey who, he thought, was probably the blameless party in the whole dispute. Moss thought that Kean had misled DeBakey into thinking that he would be totally in charge. "The truth was that that was only what Kean wanted to happen." Moss gave the medical statesman a potted history of U.S.–Panamanian relations—the tensions, the fight over the Canal treaties, the latent fears and hostilities. DeBakey seemed to take it all on board.

That evening, Moss brought García de Paredes and DeBakey together. The Panamanian surgeon apologized to the American for calling him an itinerant surgeon and said he had been very upset that morning. According to Ambassador Moss, DeBakey for his part said words to the effect that "you are very distinguished people and I wouldn't think of coming in here and taking things over. I would just offer advice." He autographed a copy of his book *The Living Heart* for García de Paredes.

De Paredes declared that he found himself in the presence of a great master. "And so if you were in on this operation, then of course there would be no one among us who would dare to question your word." DeBakey said later that the Panamanians "emphasized to me that their hostility was not to me personally and they apologized for the political situation that had arisen."

"It was all love and kisses," said Ambler Moss. "They were sort of throwing bouquets at each other."

According to García de Paredes, DeBakey agreed to join the Panamanian team as an equal. But then he proposed that given all the problems and since the Shah was now suffering from a respiratory infection, it would be best to postpone the operation for a couple of weeks. García de Paredes assented; they agreed that all the doctors involved should meet on Sunday morning.

Jeane Hester knew nothing of all this; she was still working to produce blood components at Gorgas. That night the IBM engineer, Pete Greco, arrived back from Miami, exhausted, but with the right pump. For the first time, the machine worked properly. Hester took some blood from Greco and was going to give some herself. But around midnight she was finally told that Sunday was off as well. Exhausted, she returned to the Holiday Inn.

At breakfast the next morning, Sunday, Dr. Kean asked her if the machines could be moved to another country. Yes, she said, but they would have to be recrated and the supplies repacked—it would take a few days. She did not ask where or what Kean had in mind. Greco pointed out they would have to be certain about the local voltage and cycles.

After breakfast the Panamanian and American doctors gathered in a friendly meeting and agreed unanimously that the operation should take place on March 30, Palm Sunday. This was the Panamanian choice, because the schools would be closed and many of the students would be out of town. DeBakey and García de Paredes agreed to a press statement saying that the Shah's doctors had unanimously decided to postpone the operation. Everyone was asked to say nothing else to the press. Before DeBakey left the country he and García de Paredes met again amidst great cordiality. "See you in a fortnight," said García de Paredes.

But the delay was an American ruse. DeBakey felt, as indeed did Flandrin, that given what had happened, the Shah could no longer receive optimal care in Panama. None of the American doctors wanted to abandon the Shah—they wanted to get him out of Panama. Quite apart from the medical crisis of the last few days, there was uncertainty over Torrijos' intentions, and the specter of extradition. Because of their fear that the Shah might be arrested pending extradition, they and Armao felt that they had to keep any plans for removing him secret.

The Shah had been in the hospital all weekend while this medical tempest raged around him. It cannot have been pleasant to have been told by his doctors that his cancer was getting worse and that a major operation was essential at once; to have agreed to it, despite fears of those around him that he might be murdered or kidnapped under the anesthetic; to spend a couple of days in the hospital while his doctors screamed at one another; and then to be told it was off after all.

On Sunday, Michael DeBakey came to his room and told the Shah that he thought he should either personally withdraw or do the operation outside of Panama. "I told [him] that I'd decided that if I was going to do it in Panama, I wanted to be in complete charge of everything, but that I would prefer not to do it in Panama itself, at this particular hospital."

Kean and Armao told the King that they wanted him to leave Panama. They suggested he return to Gabriel Lewis' house on Contadora for the time being.

Jeane Hester came to see the Shah that morning also. She brought a bag of yellow platelets that she had intended to use, just to show him what they looked like. He seemed very worried. "But don't you think it's dangerous, Dr. Hester, for me to wait with my white count so low?"

She wondered what on earth she could say. As a physician, she did indeed think it might be risky; he could have another attack of pneumonia. But she had also been worried about operating the previous day, Saturday, when he was suffering from an infection and she was unsure of the blood components. Could she now say, "Sir, I have no control over what's happening to you. I'm just being drawn along to provide for you when they tell me they are going to operate. I mean I'm not part of the decision-making team." Could she say that? she wondered. She felt she could not.

So instead, all she said was "We'll be back. Things will work out all right." The Shah smiled at her.

In the final version of his memoirs, the Shah called all this "a medical soap opera." He could not understand how the Panamanians could let their "false nationalist pride override the well-being of a patient." He wrote, "I considered their attitude insane. My life was in jeopardy and I was not about to lose it to the personal insecurities of the Panamanians."

Jeane Hester still knew nothing about the plan to move the Shah out of Panama for the operation. "Of course we did not tell her," said Kean later. "Hester meant Ríos, who meant García, who meant Torrijos." She flew back to Houston with DeBakey, expecting to return with him to Panama in a fortnight. When she subsequently learned that DeBakey and Kean had no such intention, she was horrified and expressed a point of view very different from that of the other American physicians. She thought highly of the Panamanian doctors and considered the facilities at Paitilla more than adequate. But she thought the Shah was being looked after by committee. Not even by one constant committee, but by a whole range of floating committees with doctors coming and going, burnishing their own egos and those of their nations as much as caring for the Shah's body.

She felt so strongly about this that she subsequently wrote to Torrijos apologizing for the whole melodrama. She said, "It is unfortunate that the political disruption created by Dr. Kean and the professionally inappropriate behavior on his part interrupted what should have been routine medical and surgical management of a patient with a malignancy."

She said she had also spoken to Hamilton Jordan about it all,

so at least someone in our government is aware that other physicians have been involved in the case whose opinion differed from that of Dr. Kean and Dr. DeBakey. The fact that a cardiovascular surgeon and a professor emeritus of tropical medicine were directing the care of a patient with cancer is known in the medical community in this country. Questions about the medical expertise of such physicians to provide appropriate oncologic management are being asked.

Subsequently, in an interview for this book, Dr. Hester explained that she had not meant to question DeBakey's undoubted skill as a surgeon. She pointed out that she had instead referred to "oncologic management." She thought that if Dr. Kean or Dr.

DeBakey had had cancer they would have insisted on oncologists being in charge of them.

When Dr. Kean was asked about the criticisms expressed by Dr. Hester in her letter, he replied that he would not dignify such an attack with a response. Dr. DeBakey, however, described her comments as "completely erroneous, nonfactual, misleading, prejudicial, and gratuitous. If she had bothered to review my medical background, she would have learned that I have published many articles on the surgical treatment of malignancies. Her glib statements reflect an abysmal ignorance of qualifications and my publications in my areas of expertise."

CHAPTER TWENTY-THREE

The Second Flight into Egypt

Throughout the melodrama, the Empress had been spending a good deal of time on the telephone to Jehan Sadat in Egypt. In one such call during the middle acts, as the doctors were squabbling center stage, she said, "Jehan, our situation is desperate." The Shah needed an operation at once, or else he would die. But it just could not be done in Panama. "I cannot trust anyone here."

Mrs. Sadat asked, "Why, Farah, why?"

The Queen replied that it was hard for her to discuss it over the telephone. Mrs. Sadat realized she was afraid of being overheard. "But we must leave Panama immediately. There are ominous reports." Mrs. Sadat said later that she knew the Queen was referring to the rumors that Torrijos was cooperating in Iranian attempts to extradite the Shah.

The Queen said that she had to get her husband out of the Panamanian hospital; she simply could not have confidence in what might happen. Panama would not allow American doctors to operate. Could the U.S. government not help? asked Mrs. Sadat. "The U.S. government?" replied the Queen with bitterness. "We have had enough of their help to last a lifetime."

Mrs. Sadat wrote later that her immediate reaction was to insist that the Shah come to Egypt for his operation. "If we give this man shelter, God will never leave us, I thought to myself. This was not a matter of politics. It was a matter of principles."

She called her husband and he assured her she had said the right thing, even if it made trouble in Egypt. "It will please God," she recalled him saying.

According to Mrs. Sadat, the Queen could not believe it when she called back to confirm that they could indeed come to Egypt for the operation. "You will allow the American doctors to operate? You are sure?" she asked. "Are you sure?"

"Yes, Farah, yes," replied Jehan Sadat, several times. The Queen was persuaded.

Meanwhile, Ben Kean, back in New York, had spoken to Lloyd Cutler, the White House counsel with whom he had framed the Lackland Agreement on the Shah's treatment in Panama and his right to return to the U.S. if necessary. Kean wanted him back in the States. Cutler, in the midst of the White House's agony over the hostages, made it clear that the Shah's return would not be helpful. In Kean's view this meant that the Lackland Agreement no longer held. As far as he was concerned, that made Egypt all but inevitable.

But that idea also alarmed the White House, on account of both Sadat and the hostages. If the Shah left Panama, then any slim hope of securing the hostages' release through the complicated extradition discussions, which were about to reach a climax in Panama, would be lost.

Hamilton Jordan still believed that the negotiations could be gotten back on track; Hector Villalon was about to go to Iran with a letter from Jordan to Abolhassan Bani-Sadr, who had just roundly defeated Sadegh Ghotbzadeh in the presidential election. Jimmy Carter was less sanguine and told Jordan he thought the Iranian leaders were unreliable "bastards."

Jordan and the White House were at that moment engaged in the Illinois primary, which was the first test for Teddy Kennedy's presidential challenge against Jimmy Carter in a major industrial state. At the same time Jordan was meeting with his lawyers to prepare for his appearance before a special prosecutor on charges that he had snorted cocaine at a New York nightclub, Studio 54. In the event, Carter defeated Kennedy in Illinois—and eventually the charges against Jordan were dismissed.

Brzezinski called Jordan to tell him of an intelligence report that the Shah was about to leave Panama for Egypt. When Jordan asked what could be done, Brzezinski replied, "Hamilton, Panama and the Shah are your specialty. I'm in charge of current leaders and big countries—you're in charge of former leaders and small countries."

On March 20, Jordan flew down to Panama, via Houston, in an attempt to persuade DeBakey of the overriding national importance of the Shah's staying in Panama. Remembering that the U.S. government had had very little independent medical advice at the time the Shah was admitted from Mexico, he took with him Dr. Norman Rich, a senior surgeon from Walter Reed Army Hospital in Washington. With them on the flight to Houston was a State Department official, Arnie Raphel, who had served in Iran. Rich warned Jordan to be subtle with DeBakey, because the surgeon would obviously feel that his first responsibility was to his patient. However, he, Rich, felt that the Shah's spleen could be safely removed in Panama.

They saw DeBakey in his conference room. He was adamant that his duty lay with the Shah. "I'll operate where I have to, but I cannot be pleased about the prospect of doing it in Panama. And even if you could satisfy me, Mr. Jordan, I'm not sure if anyone can persuade the Shah to have it done there."

DeBakey said that he had told Jordan that doing the surgery in Panama would increase the risk several fold. "Therefore, I said that I could not recommend that it be done there. However, if the situation reached the point that there was no other way out—like operating in an emergency situation on a battleship—and there was nothing else to do, I would do my best to be of service." He said also that it was still not certain how much control he would have and for safe surgery, "you can't have more than one captain of the ship." When Jordan asked him to think of the hostages, he replied, "Mr. Jordan, that is your problem and the president's problem. The Shah's health is my problem." Jordan decided he just had to go on down to Panama and try to change the Shah's mind. But getting there was not so easy.

They took off from Houston in their U.S. Air Force plane; it developed radar trouble and so they landed in New Orleans. There they had to wait for another plane to be sent down from Washington. This one developed a different malfunction. They had to return to New Orleans and wait. A third plane eventually arrived and they took off, climbed, and headed south over the

Gulf of Mexico toward Panama. An hour into the flight there was a loud explosion, the plane dived toward the ocean, the cabin filled with smoke, and the floor began to heat the soles of the passengers' shoes. Finally, the pilot managed to level out the craft just above the waves, turn it around, and limp back to New Orleans.

By the time they took off in their fourth plane, it was 2:30 A.M.; they had been out of Washington for fourteen hours. Jordan's temper was frayed. "Dammit," he thought to himself (so he wrote later), "we almost got killed on this flight—the least the Shah can do is to consider the effect of his operation on our hostages. But maybe he doesn't care . . . maybe the tragic figure I talked with at Lackland is as cold and uncaring and even as cruel as his critics say."

They finally arrived in Panama at breakfast time on Friday, March 21. After a couple of hours' sleep in the U.S. ambassador's fine old residence—a place that always made Jordan think he was in a Graham Greene novel—Jordan embarked on what he said at the time was "the worst weekend in my life," the weekend that he failed to stop the Shah escaping from Panama. "It was like the final act of an opéra bouffe," said the U.S. ambassador, Ambler Moss. "You had all the maids fluttering around and a prima donna at center stage. Several, perhaps."

After Jordan awoke, Omar Torrijos, Chuchu, and Charlie García all came to see him.

Torrijos and Jordan, with Chuchu as translator, sat in wicker chairs on the veranda, while Charlie García told Dr. Rich about the Shah's medical crises. "We've got problems, Papa General," said Jordan. "We have information that the Shah has decided to leave Panama and go to Egypt."

Torrijos was displeased. "That would be bad for everyone—for the hostages, for the Shah, and even for Panama," he said as he lit a large Cuban cigar, which had been customized with his own name on the band. "What can we do to change his mind?"

Jordan suggested that perhaps the Shah would stay if the Panamanian doctors could allow DeBakey to perform the actual operation. Torrijos pondered and said, "Doctors are strange animals with big skills and big egos."

Jordan replied that he had once considered becoming a doctor, to which Torrijos riposted, "Your ego alone qualifies you."

But Torrijos was not certain that the doctors could solve the problem. The three of them sat on the veranda while the general thought. He then spoke harshly about the Shah. "I'll do whatever you want me to—just tell me. We can let the Shah go or keep him here—and I'll make him stay here even if he doesn't want to. I have observed this king—he cares about no one but himself. He does not have the right to jeopardize the lives of fifty-three others. All I care about is helping the president solve the problems of the hostages." Jordan was worried that if the Shah were forced to stay in Panama against his will, it might not play well at home.

Torrijos said that he would have the Panamanian doctors call DeBakey and ask him officially to return. Then he himself would call the Shah and pretend that he was aggrieved that after all the hospitality Panama had offered, the Shah was now wanting to leave. "If he is really scared about being extradited, then I still have some leverage on him." As Chuchu translated, Torrijos stood up, paced around, and then left, surrounded by his entourage.

Ambler Moss then told Jordan that Robert Armao had called to find out when Jordan was coming to see the Shah on Contadora. This made Jordan nervous. He told Moss he had made a real mistake in agreeing at Lackland that the Shah could return to the U.S. for medical treatment if necessary. He was afraid that the Shah now wanted to collect on that promise.

Jordan went up to Moss' office. Carter's White House counsel, Lloyd Cutler—who had actually negotiated the Lackland Agreement with Robert Armao and Dr. Kean—was arriving in Panama City. He too had had trouble with his U.S. military plane; it lost an engine on landing. "I'll never again oppose increases in the defense budget," said Jordan.

Cutler was not amused by the notion that Torrijos might actually prevent the Shah from leaving. "That's just talk, isn't it? He wouldn't really do that—would he?"

"Don't underestimate the general," replied Moss. "If we gave him the nod, or even winked, he'd do it all right."

They called Washington and spoke to the president. He insisted, as he had already done before, that if the Shah could not be persuaded to stay in Panama, then he must return to the States. At all costs he must not go to Egypt. "Anwar's got enough problems without having us dump the Shah in his lap."

Jordan was appalled and told Carter that this could endanger the lives of the hostages. But Carter was adamant—the Shah must not go to Egypt. "It's not fair to Sadat," he said.

This attitude horrified Cy Vance and other State Department officials dealing with the hostage crisis as much as it did Jordan. Hal Saunders, the assistant secretary of state, called Jordan to warn that if the Shah did return to the U.S., the Iranians might kill the hostages. The U.S. would have to react and that could lead to a war in the Gulf. "That will be bad for our country *and* for Sadat." Saunders, unlike Carter, thought that Sadat was the best judge of what he could and could not endure. He could not be more isolated in the Arab world than he was now. Saunders told Jordan that the best thing would be to persuade the Shah to stay in Panama.

Jordan then decided that he should not go to see the Shah himself; Arnie Raphel and Lloyd Cutler had better go without him. First, his personal contact with the Shah might jeopardize his ability to negotiate with the Iranians. Secondly, Arnie Raphel suggested that Jordan's refusing to see him would persuade the Shah that he would never be allowed to return to the States. On Contadora the Shah did indeed interpret Jordan's failure to appear as a signal that Carter was cutting whatever slim commitment he still had to him.

For Jordan a serious shock was in store.

The extradition game had been proceeding apace, with its various players more and more enthusiastically involved. Torrijos had appointed a senior Panamanian jurist, Juan Materno Vasquez, to represent Iranian government interests in the case. Materno Vasquez had traveled to Teheran and become a dedicated partisan of the revolution, determined to do all he could to secure the Shah's extradition. The Shah, he believed, was a truly evil man and Panama's best interests would be served by his being sent straight from Panama to Teheran for trial. Most of the Panamanian participants insist that such zealotry was not quite what Torrijos had had in mind.

But Materno Vasquez' views were well suited to the enthusiasm with which Christian Bourguet and Hector Villalon, Jordan's two Parisian interlocutors, had been pursuing the Shah throughout.

Bourguet had arrived back in Panama on Thursday, March 20, armed at last with all the documents needed to file Iran's extradition request with the Panamanian Foreign Ministry. It had taken the Iranians a long time to prepare these papers; they all had to be translated into Spanish and there were few Spanish translators in Teheran. Under Panamanian law the papers had to be filed within sixty days of the original extradition request; this meant that Monday, March 24, was the deadline. Today was Friday.

When Bourguet arrived, Materno Vasquez assured him that once the papers were filed, the Shah would have to be arrested and that there was now every chance that the extradition request would ultimately be successful. Of course, Iran would have to agree to "recompense" Panama for all that it might lose by incurring the displeasure of the U.S.

There was, however, one problem. The papers could not be presented by Bourguet; they had to be formally delivered by an Iranian official. There was no Iranian diplomat in Panama; one had to fly down from New York. The man in question, Farough Parsi, had not yet left New York. He intended to arrive in Panama on Monday, the final day allowed. Bourguet was concerned, but there was nothing he could do.

That Friday, Bourguet was summoned to Torrijos' office. In came Hamilton Jordan. Jordan was very surprised to see the Frenchman and, he wrote later, asked, "My friend, what the hell are you doing here?"

"I am here to file the extradition papers," replied the Frenchman. "The deadline is next Monday. What the hell are *you* doing here?"

"Christian, the Shah wants to leave Panama," Jordan replied.

Bourguet was upset. "That is very bad news, Hamilton," he said. "Where will he go?"

Either to Egypt or the States, replied Jordan. Bourguet started. "To the States? Not to the States! You cannot allow it. They will kill the hostages."

Jordan explained to Bourguet the nature of the Shah's medical problems and the promise of the Lackland Agreement. Then Torrijos jumped up from the sofa, flourishing his cigar, and began to talk excitedly to Chuchu in Spanish. "I can keep the Shah here if I want . . . whether Hamilton likes it or not, I can keep him here for the operation." On another occasion he said he thought the Shah "should take a helicopter or a beautiful white horse and ride into Persia and die like a king on a sword."

But, he told Bourguet, "I will not do it unless the hostages are transferred from the militants to the government. Tell that to your friends in Iran . . . tell them that they have twenty-four hours to move the hostages or the Shah will leave!''

Jordan said nothing as Torrijos made this threat to detain the Shah against his will. Bourguet announced that he had to go back to his hotel to call Ghotbzadeh. Torrijos said he would give Bourguet twelve hours.

Torrijos then took Jordan into another room to introduce him to the Panamanian doctors involved in the case, declaring, "There are three doctors here, but twenty-five different opinions." He made the point that they had all been trained in the States and, acting like a surgeon sawing off a limb, he said, "They learned side-by-side with the American doctors how to carve up the body." Everyone laughed. Then he complained that the Panamanian doctors had been insulted by the way in which the American doctors had tried to take the Shah away from them, but ended by saying that DeBakey was welcome to return and to be "the general of the doctors".

Back at the embassy, Jordan made another call to Carter and to Vance. Carter again told him that he wanted the Shah to stay in Panama for the operation, but if that could not be arranged, then he must come back to the States. He must not go to Egypt.

Cy Vance then came on the telephone and suggested that if the Shah really did have to come to the States, then at least Washington should insist that he abdicate. Vance thus did not contradict Carter's insistence that the Shah be allowed back if he left Panama —but he imposed a condition which the Shah would be unlikely to accept. "Good old lawyer Cy," thought Jordan. "Never dishonorable but often sly."

With this new proposal, Lloyd Cutler and Raphel then left for the airport and Contadora to see the Shah. It was now nine o'clock in the evening.

The Shah, the Queen, Robert Armao, and Mark Morse had been awaiting them all day. They had each become more nervous and unhappy with Panama since the incidents at Paitilla Hospital. They felt the Shah was being fleeced; by now their bills on the island amounted to several hundred thousand dollars. Rumors of the extradition proceedings abounded, though no one on Contadora had any idea how far they had progressed. They still knew nothing of Jordan's contacts with Bourguet and Villalon. Everyone had continually tried to reassure them. But often Armao replied, "Can you really be certain about a man like Torrijos, who is always high on coke or booze?" Or about Noriega, indeed?

The Queen felt that in the last few days increasingly strange pressures were being put upon them. The telephone was, for a time, cut off—and they were told it was because they had not paid the bill. Then Torrijos sent a message saying that as she was a student of architecture she should come with him to visit buildings on one of the other islands. She said she would wait until her husband was better and they could both come, to which the reply was that she should come alone. "You know, that was weird," she said later. "This low voice in the corner, and only me. I said, 'What do they have in mind?' I go somewhere, and they do whatever they want with my husband. Is that the idea?"

When Cutler and Raphel arrived at the house, Cutler asked to see the Shah. The Queen made it clear that she was going to remain with him. She was afraid that by pleading the cause of the hostages, the Americans might persuade the Shah to change his mind and stay in Panama. "I wanted to be there, because I didn't want my husband to change his mind; we had to leave for Egypt."

Armao also wanted to be in on the meeting. He felt that Cutler would try to bully the Shah and that the Shah would be far too mild and humble. But Cutler said, "Bob, I hope you don't mind my seeing the Shah alone, because I have some personal messages from the president." Despite Armao's protests, the Shah agreed to Cutler's request. "So I stayed outside," Armao said later, "and I was wild. I was ranting and raving." (Jordan subsequently wrote that he was delighted that someone had "taken the opportunity to put the cocky Armao down.")

On the terrace under the stars, Cutler outlined the choices that they had—remaining in Panama, returning to the States, or proceeding to Egypt. The Shah made it clear that his preference was Egypt. "I realize I am a dying man, so my concern is for my family and my country. But I want to die with honor, not on the operating table . . . because of a mistake or a bribe."

Even so, Cutler brought up the possibility of abdication in the event the Shah returned to the States. The Shah said it did not matter to him, he was dying and his son could have the throne. This was not quite what Cutler had in mind; there was a long pause and then Cutler said that the U.S. would think about it. According to Raphel, the Queen then interrupted in Persian (which Raphel spoke) and said, "Don't you dare abdicate! Think of our son and our people! The people would never understand!"

The Queen's recollection of this conversation is a little different. She recalls Raphel turning to them and saying, "In your speeches you have many times said that you are ready to sacrifice your life for the good of your country and your people." She was not sure what he meant but wondered if he was proposing that the Shah should sacrifice himself for the hostages. "Then, when Cutler spoke of abdication, I said, 'If you're talking about the reaction of the Iranian government if my husband abdicates, my son will be there to claim his rights. And if it was not my elder son, there is my second son. And if my second son is not there, there will be another person from the family. So nothing will change.' It was ridiculous."

Cutler put the case for Panama as strongly as he could, saying that the Panamanians had made a lot of concessions and that it would now even be possible to have DeBakey operate at Gorgas Hospital in the Canal Zone, fulfilling the letter of the Lackland Agreement. He also warned of the harm that might be done to Sadat if the Shah insisted on going to Egypt. When Cutler had finished, the Shah said he would let them know his decision in the morning. He was still inclined to go to Egypt. Later, in the final version of his memoirs, he wrote, "I did not seriously consider the American offers. For the last year and a half, American promises had not been worth very much. They had already cost me my throne and any further trust in them could well mean my life."

Just as Cutler and Raphel were about to leave, the telephone rang. After the Shah hung up, he told the Americans that it was one of the Panamanian doctors, calling to complain that he had not been paid for his last visit. Cutler asked how much the bill was. "Eighteen hundred dollars," said the Shah. He smiled and said, "You wonder why I want to leave this place?"

After Cutler and Raphel had left for the mainland, the Shah told Armao and Morse of the proposal that he abdicate. They were furious and suggested that the Shah should tell Cutler he would consider abdication, go to the States, and once he was there say, "To hell with you."

The Shah replied, "I would feel more comfortable among friends. We'll go to Egypt."

The next morning, Saturday, March 22, Jimmy Carter called Anwar Sadat to tell him of his concern over the Shah's possible arrival. Sadat apparently replied, "Jimmy, don't you worry about Egypt. You worry about your hostages." Cutler and Raphel flew back to Contadora. The Shah said he would leave the next morning for Cairo.

Sadat had offered to send his own plane, but it had not yet left Cairo. Cutler judged that if the Shah was leaving, the sooner he did so the better. So he suggested that the U.S. find a plane that could make a through flight. The White House contacted at least two charter companies. Eventually the contract went to Evergreen International Airlines, which had had CIA affiliations. Some American officials thought this connection was unwise. The final charge to the Shah was enormous—$250,000, said Armao.

On Contadora the entourage spent the last day packing—and paying bills. In Panama City, Jordan lay much of the day in Ambler Moss' pool, avoiding the press. Christian Bourguet was on the telephone to Teheran from his hotel. Several times he called Jordan to report that Torrijos' offer to keep the Shah in Panama had galvanized the Revolutionary Council in Teheran and that they were on the verge of removing the hostages from the hands of the militants. Jordan says he listened politely but noncommittally.

Bourguet thought he had a more responsive audience in Torrijos, but on Saturday Torrijos told him that he could not keep the Shah more than another few hours. And he would have to have good reason to detain him. Teheran must do something to show progress on the hostages. What was going on there?

Bourguet called Iran again to speak to his colleague Hector Villalon and to Ghotbzadeh. The leadership was still locked in argument over how or how not to remove the hostages from the militants. Ghotbzadeh, who had invested more than any of the others in the Panamanian connection, was all for using force. The new president, Bani-Sadr, refused. Nothing was done. The hours before Torrijos' deadline raced away.

On Sunday morning the Shah's luggage was carted to the little airstrip by the hotel to be loaded onto a light plane for the flight to the mainland. There was more baggage than when he arrived; it included the big packing cases that had so intrigued Torrijos. The plane had to make several trips. Then it was apparently called off the job. Finally, it returned. The Shah, the Queen, Dr. Pirnia, Colonel Jahanbini, Colonel Nevissi, Robert Armao, Mark Morse, and the valet, Amir Pourshoja, flew to the mainland. So did the

dogs. Beno, the Great Dane, was sick. The Shah said to Armao, "Perhaps we should leave him behind."

Armao replied, "Your Majesty, over my dead body will Beno be buried in Panama."

The Shah left Gabriel Lewis a handwritten note saying, "The Empress and I have difficulty to find words to thank you and Mrs. Lewis for your unparalleled hospitality and graciousness and helpfulness. My regret is that I don't have a country where I could invite you and your family to repay part of what you have done for us. . . ."

All morning, Bourguet's partner, Hector Villalon, was calling from Teheran on behalf of Sadegh Ghotbzadeh to beg the Panamanians to delay the Shah a little longer. Even Ambler Moss, who trusted the Panamanians more than almost anyone, became a little concerned. Were the delays deliberate? Was the luggage being held on purpose? American journalists were swarming all over town, furious at not being able to see the Shah or to find out what was happening. Jordan was waiting for word that the Shah had left, so that he too could leave, and all the time the siren song from Teheran was being repeated over the ether. "The hostages are being moved right now. Don't worry. Just hang on to him."

The Evergreen Airlines plane had arrived at Panama's Tocumen Airport that morning. It was quite unsuitable—a huge DC-8 with more than three hundred narrow seats crammed in to carry as many tourists (or soldiers) as possible. Armao complained and was told that it was the only plane available.

Colonel Noriega was at the airport to see them off, all smiles, and wishing even Armao well. They boarded the uncomfortable old plane and finally, just before 2 P.M., on Sunday, March 23, the Shah flew out of Panama. It was just three months after he had arrived. Fifteen minutes later, the pilot informed his passengers that they had left Panamanian airspace. Armao walked back and congratulated the Shah. The course was set for the Azores where the plane was to be refueled.

Even now Sadegh Ghotbzadeh had not given up hope. Yet again he called Christian Bourguet to assure him that the hostages would be released if only the Shah could be prevented from reaching Egypt. Once more Bourguet called Torrijos and Torrijos summoned Moss. Torrijos was excited; perhaps he was drunk.

"Right now, at this very moment," he told Moss, "the hostages are being moved. If you can keep the Shah from getting to Egypt, they'll deliver them."

"Oh, my God," said Moss, and raced back to the embassy. He called Hamilton Jordan, who had just taken off in a USAF plane and was headed back to Washington. Now, at the very end of this saga, Jordan was presented with yet another apparent opportunity to rescue the hostages. Arnie Raphel said it was just like the Iranians to wait until the last moment before doing a deal.

Moss said, "Is it possible that the fuel stop in the Azores be prolonged into a forty-eight-hour stay for a physical checkup or a blood test or a medical or whatever, because it looks like the hostages are being moved."

Jordan called the secretary of defense, Harold Brown, in Washington. Speaking carefully for fear of interception, he said, "Harold, as you know, our friend is en route to Egypt. I would like you to hold his plane in the Azores when they land there for refueling. It is very important and could resolve our problem." Brown did not ask on whose authority Jordan was making this request; he agreed to it.

• • •

While Jordan headed north, the Shah's plane flew east toward the night. Although every passenger could have had a dozen rows each, it was not a restful flight. The heating was inadequate, the seats were painful, the food was wretched. There were, however, blankets.

The Shah was not feeling at all well. He had reason to be worried. "Medically, time was of the essence; I was running a fever; my blood count was dangerously low; the blood platelet count dropped to less than 10% of normal. . . . If I cut myself at so high an altitude, I might well bleed to death."

When they landed in the Azores, a cold wind filled the plane; Colonel Jahanbini lent the Shah his pullover. A small group of Portuguese and American officials came on board to greet the Shah. "Though sick and feverish," wrote the Shah later, "I rose, straightened my clothes and prepared to see them, as protocol required."

The plane was refueled. But it did not take off. They waited at least two hours on the tarmac. The Queen became concerned. "The plane was getting cold and my husband had a very, very high fever. They told us the delay was because they were getting permission for the route." She did not believe this; obviously the flight plan must have been filed and cleared long before. She began to get worried, and paced up and down the tarmac, waiting. Inside the cabin, the Shah asked Armao what was wrong. Armao went out and asked an American officer why the plane was being held. He then asked to call New York. Finally, the plane was cleared to leave.

What had happened was that Torrijos and Jordan had both finally lost patience with the promises emanating from Ghotbzadeh and Christian Bourguet. In one call to Ghotbzadeh, Torrijos had said, "The Americans may be able to stop the Shah, now you tell me where the hostages are." Ghotbzadeh replied, "Well, I can promise you, my friend, that in twenty-four hours I'll have them moved." At which point Torrijos had apparently uttered an expletive and slammed down the phone.

He called Ambler Moss and said, "Ambler, forget the whole thing. I told Ghotbzadeh to go to hell. It's all over."

When Jordan received this message, he ordered the Shah's plane to be released from the Azores. Later he claimed that the delay had been so short that the Shah and his party had not noticed it. (When Jimmy Carter learned of Jordan's free-lance activity, he was, in Jordan's phrase, "livid," and told his chief of staff that he had greatly exceeded his authority.)

Freed by Jordan, the Shah's old plane took off once more, from the Azores to Cairo. On this final leg, Armao had Colonel Nevissi sit in the cockpit to make sure that they were being flown in the right direction and not toward Teheran. "What do I do if we are going the wrong way?" asked Nevissi. "Shoot the pilot?"

In his memoirs, Carter recorded that the American and Panamanian press blamed the Shah's second flight into Egypt on Kissinger and Rockefeller. "Regardless of who might have been responsible," he wrote that he had opposed the move because of the adverse effects it might have on Sadat. "But this consideration did not seem to concern the Shah, who claimed falsely that he was in danger in Panama."

On Monday morning in Panama, Christian Bourguet and the Iranian diplomat from New York hastened to the Foreign Ministry to present the extradition documents charging the Shah with crimes against the Iranian people. The foreign minister himself scuttled out a back door of the building. The Frenchman and the Iranian found it difficult to locate anyone at all willing to deal with the matter. Eventually they managed to present the papers formally to a junior official. The documents were filed away.

Also this morning, Torrijos had one last order, one which the Queen found very offensive when she later heard of it. He sent word to Contadora that the Queen's room was not to be touched. "I didn't sleep with her, but at least I'll sleep in her sheets," he told one of his friends.

CHAPTER TWENTY-FOUR

The End

Anwar Sadat and his wife, Jehan, were at Cairo airport to greet their guests.

When Mark Morse informed the Shah that the Egyptian president was there, the Shah left his seat and, without waiting for his wife, walked as fast as he could to the door of the plane. At the bottom of the steps, Sadat embraced him and said, "Thank God you're safe."

Mrs. Sadat was shocked by the Shah's appearance. He was so thin that his suit seemed two sizes too big for him. His face was white. She thought that if any man ever needed friends, it was he. "Looking at him, I was struck by the callousness of the Americans. Thank God my husband had the courage to treat the Shah with humanity, welcoming him to Egypt personally."

The two couples flew together by helicopter to the Kubbeh Palace. Sadat wanted to show the Shah that a residence and not just a hospital room was being prepared for him. Then the helicopter took them on to the Ma'adi Hospital.

During the flight, the Shah wept. "I have done nothing for you," he said to Sadat. "Yet you are the only one to accept me with dignity. The others whom I have helped have offered me no help in return. I cannot understand."

Mrs. Sadat told him to think nothing of it. Would he not have done the same for her husband had he needed it? Mrs. Sadat believed that the United States had decided to send the Shah back to Teheran from Panama, and that had he not flown out on Sunday, he would never have reached the safety of Egypt.

The doctors began to assemble. At the Queen's request, Georges Flandrin flew in from Paris. Looking out the Shah's window with its distant view of the Nile and the Pyramids, he recalled his ancestor, Joseph Flandrin, whom Napoleon had appointed governor of Cairo.

On March 26 Dr. DeBakey arrived with a team of six people to perform the operation for which the Shah had been waiting since December. Sadat had ordered the Egyptian doctors, who included his own son-in-law and personal physician, to allow DeBakey to do as he wished. The Egyptians—Dr. Zachariya el Baz, Dr. Taha Mohamed Abd el Aziz, and Dr. Amin Mohamed 'Afifi—assisted. DeBakey had not invited Jeane Hester along; instead he had taken his own blood-bank pathologist, together with blood separators. Nonetheless, Dr. Kean had asked Hester to supply DeBakey with the results of her own tests on the Shah's blood.

By this time the Shah's blood counts had deteriorated to what DeBakey called "a very serious condition." Before the operation, his team transfused two units of whole blood and several units of packed red cells and platelets. The surgery took place on the evening of Friday, March 28.

The operation lasted an hour and twenty minutes. There were problems with one of the blood machines but DeBakey said later that these were insignificant and that "it all went about as smoothly as you could make it."

The Queen, her children, Colonel Jahanbini, Ardeshir Zahedi and others watched the surgery on a video monitor just outside the operating room. Dr. Kean gave them a running commentary. When the spleen was brought out it was seen to be grossly oversize—ten times as big as the normal fist size, according to DeBakey; twenty times, according to Dr. Kean, who later described it as "one foot long, literally the size of a football."

Splenectomy in a patient in the Shah's condition can be complicated. For example, the tail of the pancreas fits right into the spleen, and there is always a risk that it will be damaged when the spleen is removed. In the case of a swollen spleen which surrounds the pancreas, this can very easily happen. The pancreas then releases powerful enzymes that destroy the tissue around it. Fluid collects. When a patient is immunosuppressed, as the Shah was, this can lead to an abscess developing in the abdomen. Often a drain is placed in the abdomen to prevent this occurring. That was not done when the Shah's spleen was removed. Dr. DeBakey said later that it was not necessary because there was no damage to the pancreas.

After the operation Sadat awarded the doctors decorations. DeBakey was given the First Order of the Republic, the highest civilian award in Egypt, and the other doctors were given the Second Order. (DeBakey gave out copies of his book.) As they moved through the reception line, Dr. Kean, ebullient as ever, said to Sadat, "When the history of the twentieth century is written, there will be two towering figures—Churchill and Sadat." At this Sadat merely nodded. But when Kean recounted the incident to the Shah after he had recovered from his anesthetic, the Shah replied, "Ah, but such an odd pair. Remember, Churchill once imprisoned Sadat!"

The spleen and a sliver of liver removed during the operation were taken to the pathology lab for examination. The Egyptians invited Dr. Kean to examine the tissues. As soon as they cut the liver, Dr. Kean looked at the Egyptian pathologist. A healthy liver would have been dark red. The Shah's was mottled white—invaded with cancer. At that moment, Kean said later, he knew that the Shah would die soon.

He and DeBakey were not in full agreement at this moment on the Shah's prognosis. As far as DeBakey was concerned the important thing was that the Shah's bone marrow was normal. He said in an interview that the future was "difficult at this time to assess," but because the bone marrow was healthy, and there was no retroperitoneal lymph node involvement, he was "hopeful" that the Shah could resume chemotherapy, to which he had responded well in the past. In another interview soon after the operation, he said the Shah was making a "beautiful" recovery and that he was "very hopeful . . . reasonably hopeful" that the Shah could be treated successfully. His blood counts had already returned to normal without transfusions. "We are hopeful because his bone marrow is normal, he can resume chemotherapy, and he had a good response to chemotherapy in the past," DeBakey told *American Medical News*, the journal of the American Medical Association, soon after the operation.

Dr. Kean did not share such optimism. The liver was so far gone that he thought chemotherapy had no chance. He said that the morning after the operation he told the Queen and Princess Ashraf that they should cut back on the chemotherapy and let the Shah spend his remaining months in as much comfort as possible. He told them that the Shah might live to see another Christmas, not the most obvious landmark for Muslims. But he felt that the Shah should be allowed to die in peace and that there should not be too much officious striving to keep him alive. "Then," Kean said in a later interview, "I paid final respects to my patient, sparing him the bad news, and left." He turned the Shah's care over to the Egyptians, with Dr. Flandrin, in whom the Queen still had confidence, acting as consultant. Kean said later that he felt he could not be in charge of the case from New York. Furthermore, he now felt that there was very little that could be done.

In an interview given much later for this book, DeBakey took a position closer to that of Kean and far from his own original qualified optimism. He said the biopsy showed the liver to be "full of lymphatic cells that were malignant. We had no idea before there was that much malignancy. That was really quite shocking . . . So we were again between the two problems of depressing his immune process [by chemotherapy] and thereby subjecting him to infection, or allowing the malignancy to rapidly gallop forward."

⋅ ⋅ ⋅

The hostile reaction throughout the Middle East to the Shah's arrival in Egypt, which Jimmy Carter had feared, began at once. Ayatollah Khomeini declared, "Satan is now attempting a new political project to perpetuate his domination. . . . Satan must know that to support the Shah is to support his great betrayal, and his pillage, and to have sent the Shah, enemy of Islam and Iran, to another enemy is to deceive the Muslims of the whole world." Sadat privately scoffed at such abuse—the ayatollah was a lunatic, he said. He went on television to explain himself publicly and said that it was against Islamic law to pursue a sick and homeless man. The Egyptian People's Assembly overwhelmingly approved his decision to admit the Shah. But Muslim fundamentalists throughout Egypt protested and demonstrated. In Assiut, the center of Egyptian fundamentalism, an antigovernment demonstration became also anti-Christian and several Coptic Christians were killed. The Coptic Patriarch canceled all Easter celebrations. At the beginning of April, more anti-Copt demonstrations took place, and on April 8 two more Copts were killed and thirty-five were wounded when they were attacked by Muslims in Minia. The tensions and the violence grew worse throughout the spring, partly as a result of the failed American military attempt to rescue the hostages from Iran on April 24. But Sadat managed, for the time being, to control it.

Ten days after the surgery, the chemotherapy was begun again. Then the Shah left the hospital and was driven to the Kubbeh Palace, which is usually home to heads of state visiting Egypt. He and the Empress lived there in somewhat faded but very pleasant surroundings. For a few days he seemed to be recovering. But then he began to complain of pains in his stomach, nausea, and vomiting. He developed a fever. X rays showed fluid building up above the diaphragm. The Egyptian doctors aspirated some and found that it was infected. His white cell count had dropped alarmingly.

Now more serious arguments set in among his relations. In particular, the long-standing tensions between his sister Princess Ashraf and his wife, Queen Farah, developed into disagreements as to how he should be treated and by whom. Ashraf in particular was unwilling to accept Dr. Kean's recommendation that her brother be allowed to die.

Consulted by telephone in Paris, Georges Flandrin said he

thought it sounded as if the Shah had developed a subphrenic abscess. He recommended that DeBakey be recalled from Texas.

Princess Ashraf was not content. She summoned from New York Dr. Morton Coleman, the oncologist who had originally seen the Shah when he had arrived at New York Hospital. Coleman informed Kean that he was going to Cairo; Kean was not pleased, but he told Coleman to go ahead. When he subsequently learned that Coleman had also brought in Kean's former assistant, Dr. Thomas C. Jones, Kean was annoyed. He wrote to Georges Flandrin in Paris to apologize. He told Flandrin that when Coleman called him to tell him of the invitation from Ashraf, "I expressed displeasure at his involvement and asked him to stop in Paris to see you before proceeding to Cairo. . . . I am distressed by the manner in which the Princess has acted. . . . The man has suffered a great deal, and it is difficult for a loving sister to understand that he would get the best medical attention by following proper protocol. . . . *

By this time, the Shah had had at least eight separate teams of doctors: his original Iranian physicians, the French, the Mexicans, Kean's team, the American doctors at Lackland, the Panamanians, the Kean-DeBakey team in Cairo, and now finally revolving sets of different doctors all with different ideas of how he should be treated and might or might not be saved.

When Coleman arrived in Cairo he found the Shah had a fever and pain in his abdomen. He too thought the problem might be a subphrenic abscess. "The Egyptians told me that the pancreas had been involved in the splenectomy and that they felt a drain should probably have been put in." Coleman called DeBakey and said that he also thought the surgeon should return.

At the end of April, DeBakey flew back to Cairo and saw the Shah once more. According to Dr. Pirnia, the Iranian pediatrician, the Shah was fully dressed and "very brave, very dignified, very erect." He was feeling a little better than he had a week before and he told DeBakey he had no pain. DeBakey examined him and said later that he found no distension, abdominal tenderness, or rigidity. "I found no evidence of a subphrenic infection or abscess

---

* Coleman said later that he had specifically gone to Kean to ask his permission to travel to Egypt. "I said, 'Ben, you asked me on the case, and you have the right to ask me off the case. I won't go without your permission.' " He said that Kean gave his permission and asked him to call Flandrin, not to stop in Paris. He said he was unable to reach Flandrin by telephone.

or pancreatic cyst, and all the other physicians in attendance agreed with me that there was none. My publications on subphrenic infections and abscess are considered classics in this field." He thought that the Shah had reacted badly to the chemotherapy. He and the Egyptian doctors decided that the treatment should continue but with a reduced dosage for the time being. This was the last time DeBakey saw the Shah.

Once again there was no consensus among the doctors. Georges Flandrin, in Paris, and Morton Coleman still thought the Shah was suffering from a subphrenic abscess that should be drained. DeBakey had found no evidence of this. Kean in New York felt that chemotherapy should be shelved. The oncologists—Flandrin and Coleman—believed that, after a pause, it should continue. Indeed, Coleman thought that aggressive chemotherapy, which he practiced, could save the Shah. "I really wanted to have a crack at curing this guy," he said later, "and aggressive chemotherapy was the only way!" He said later that Kean's pessimism "reflected the old misguided conception of what cancer is all about." He recommended the addition of two further drugs when the treatment was resumed in May. Flandrin's prescription was milder. In the event, there was confusion between the dosages at the hospital; neither was administered correctly.

Once again, disagreements among doctors had become critical. The Egyptian doctors were trying to care for the patient while all sorts of different opinions were being invited by different members of the family. Calls from the United States and from France all offered distinct and sometimes incompatible advice. At this time, said Coleman later, "It seemed that Ashraf was calling the shots. She was U.S.–oriented. The Queen was French-oriented."

The Queen found this all very upsetting. DeBakey had assured her in April that there was no abscess. But subsequently the Shah became much iller. "He couldn't eat anymore, and they wouldn't find any more veins; they had used all of them, on his hand, his arm, his leg. . . . Then he was so sick we had to take him back to the hospital. I couldn't find DeBakey. At the end of June, I asked Flandrin to come."

Flandrin was on holiday in the Loire. "I felt bad about it all," he said later. "I had looked after him for so long." When the Queen's summons reached him, he hurriedly tried to assemble a French medical team; it was not easy because the summer holidays were approaching. He had to rely on people he did not know.

In Cairo, Flandrin found the Shah's condition *"épouvantable"* but the Shah still tried to joke about Flandrin's youthful appearance. He had been running a fever for weeks, and it seemed likely to Flandrin that he was still suffering from the subphrenic abscess that he had suspected as long ago as April.

Flandrin was now convinced that an operation to drain the abdomen was urgently required. He called Paris in search of a surgeon and eventually he selected Dr. Pierre-Louis Fagniez, a *"spécialiste de seconde-main."* This is a surgeon who, in effect, attempts to deal with postoperative complications. He brought a team to Cairo. They told the Shah that he needed another operation. He said, "Well, let's take the bull by the horns."

Meanwhile, Dr. Coleman had returned once more. He and the French doctors had terrible rows. "The French could not have been more arrogant, more awful," he said later. "They treated me like a nun in a whorehouse." Flandrin says that at one stage he took Coleman by the lapels and said, "One of us is *de trop*." The Queen was astonished to see the normally calm Frenchman so upset. He explained to her that, as in football, it was sometimes necessary to tackle one's opponent. He said, "Your Majesty, have we finished mucking about with the Shah's health?"

"There were so many doctors," said the Queen later. "Egyptians, French, Americans, and they didn't want to take the responsibility of a decision. So they left the decisions to us. Some were saying the French doctors were not good enough; others were saying the Americans were no good."

In one sense, the positions were now reversed. In Mexico, a few months before, Flandrin had been excluded by American doctors. Now in Egypt there were several French doctors and only one American, Coleman. He was uneasy about operating on the Shah, given his weakened condition. Coleman was also doubtful about the French operating team. In retrospect, he agreed that the French were correct, though he considered that the Shah's postoperative problems justified his misgivings. He said later that the French and the Egyptians were "at each other's throats and I was in between. As people, I really liked the Egyptians; I couldn't stand the French. They were utterly impossible." Flandrin said later that there was some friction subsequently between the Egyptians and the French, but at this moment the only disagreement was with Coleman who alone opposed surgery.

The Queen was in an agony as to what to do, but decided that the French must operate. On June 30, Pierre-Louis Fagniez opened the Shah's abdomen and drained it. A liter and a half of pus was removed, together with pancreatic debris. Flandrin felt vindicated but outraged. He considered the debilitating infection and weakness the Shah had suffered for the last three months could have been avoided altogether. He thought that after the spleen had been removed, a drain should have been left in the wound so that it could have been washed daily. He left the theater and told the Queen the news. She was pleased that the operation had not been a mistake. "Go and sing the 'Marseillaise' in Fagniez' ear," she said. But Flandrin knew there was little to celebrate.

After this operation, relations among the doctors deteriorated further. Ashraf wanted new opinions. Dr. Pirnia asked Coleman to put together a team. Robert Armao also began to assemble a medical team in New York. Dr. Kean started to plan his return. But then he had a call from Armao saying that there had been "a palace revolution" and he was not now wanted. The Egyptians— like the Panamanians before them—became angered that all responsibility for the patient was being removed from them. They were senior physicians but were being treated like medical students.

They began to complain about the behavior of a member of Flandrin's team who had brought his girlfriend and drunk champagne to celebrate a birthday just two doors from the Shah's hospital room. Some of the French behaved, said Mark Morse later, as if they were on holiday in Cairo. The French doctors became offended and threatened to leave. The Queen asked Flandrin to intervene with them. "We should put aside these problems," she said. "Then I realized the French did want to leave and we had no other doctors. It was a horrible situation."

All the doctors held a meeting. "Nobody wanted to take a decision," said the Queen. "Always at a critical moment it had to be a member of the family who decides." President Sadat was asked to intervene; he apparently told the Egyptians that since it was now clear that the Shah was going to die, they should stand back. Flandrin said that Sadat had confirmed that he, Flandrin, was in charge.

In early July, the disagreements began to surface in the Egyptian press. The leading Egyptian paper, *Al-Ahram*, reported that during the operation to remove the Shah's spleen, the pancreas was injured. "In the search for something to attach the surgical

knot to when the operation was over, a surgical instrument accidentally hit the tail of the pancreas and created a cyst. . . . The
area became infected because the anticancer drug treatment the
Shah had been receiving reduced his body's white blood cell
count, hampering its ability to combat infection."

Such reports, which were picked up by the American media,
were labeled inaccurate by Dr. DeBakey in Houston. The Shah's
condition was now improving, he said in an interview on July 8,
1980. He had been frequently in telephone contact with Cairo and
"I never got the impression in discussions that he is dying." He
denied that the pancreas had been damaged by accident during the
splenectomy. "There was no way a surgical instrument could have
accidentally pressed the end of the pancreas. We dissected the
exposed tip of the tail of the pancreas and sewed over the area.
Everything was clean and sterile." He said that when he visited
the Shah at the end of April "there was absolutely no sign of any
infection from the operation." He blamed the Shah's current
problems on too much chemotherapy, which had lowered his
resistance to infection. No chemotherapy had been given since
May.

Later, in responding to queries for this book, Dr. DeBakey
said, "The Egyptian doctors were astounded to see [the *Al-Ahram*
report] as we were, and they assured us that no one at the hospital
gave that information, since it was not true. . . ." DeBakey also
asked for comments from Dr. Gerald Lawrie who was the surgeon
assisting him in the operation on the Shah. Dr. Lawrie confirmed
Dr. DeBakey's view.*

Dr. Flandrin said that he was also convinced that the Shah had
been suffering from a subphrenic abscess. "When Dr. Pierre-
Louis Fagniez operated at the end of June, he found a necrosis of

---

* Dr. Lawrie wrote: "The pancreas had clearly experienced a recurrent pancreatitis at some
stage because the pancreas was extremely fibrotic secondary to recurrent inflammation. The
tail of the pancreas was deeply embedded in the hilum of this massive spleen which was itself
a tumor made up of extensive infiltration with hystiocytic lymphosarcoma. The splenic
vessels were controlled by clamping the tail of the pancreas with vascular clamps and dividing
the tissue in this area. It was well-recognized that pancreatic tissue was divided during this
maneuver and the tail of the pancreas was carefully identified and meticulously oversewn.
Because of the fibrotic nature of the tail of the pancreas and the excellent hemostasis and
good apposition of the pancreatic tissue obtained by this maneuver, it was not felt that
drainage was indicated. As we frequently do at Baylor College of Medicine, the splenic bed
was not drained but instead the peritoneum over the splenic bed was meticulously reapprox-
imated. . . ."

the tail of the pancreas. This could only be due to traumatic lesion of the tail of the pancreas during the splenectomy. I don't want to call it a mistake, but rather a problem which can happen to any surgeon. Furthermore, it is impossible to have a localized precise lesion of the pancreas, and a pancreatic abscess because of excess chemotherapy." While there is no evidence that a surgical instrument accidentally hit the pancreas, an infection could have developed from the clamps which came into contact with the pancreas in the normal course of the operation.

In early July 1980 DeBakey said he was "guardedly optimistic." But the Shah's condition deteriorated throughout July. He had to have several operations to try to stanch internal bleeding. He was fully conscious and some of the time was able to sit in a chair. But for most of the time he was laid out on a hard stretcher bed. He could scarcely eat. Georges Flandrin was ashamed at the pain he had to endure.

Radio Teheran responded to the news of the Shah's relapse by accusing President Carter of plotting the "elimination" of the Shah to help him win the U.S. election. But, according to Teheran, "the murder of the deposed Shah in Cairo will never solve his problem."

The Shah's children were now in Egypt but spent a good deal of time in Alexandria rather than at his bedside. In daily attendance were the Queen and Mark Morse, who was hastily helping the Shah rewrite his memoirs. Every day Morse would ask him whether he agreed to this or that characterization or recollection. As the Shah grew weaker, Morse had to lean close to him to hear his replies. This final, American version of the memoirs was in several respects different from the editions published in France and Britain. It was published posthumously and it stated at the front, "It is my intention that the American version of *Answer to History* be the definitive text." In this version the Shah gave himself more credit for stopping SAVAK's torture than he had in his original edition of the book. He added the claim that Richard Nixon and Henry Kissinger had written asking him to rescind oil price rises, he was generally more critical of American "weakness" in the face of Soviet threats.

Ardeshir Zahedi was the only senior official in the Shah's government to come to Egypt in the last weeks of the Shah's life. He brought the Shah a private message from Soraya. Zahedi operated

rather as the master of ceremonies, handing out cigars and trying
to keep abreast of—and to contain—the fights and intrigues between courtiers and doctors in the corridor outside the bedroom.
He saw the competition between the French and American doctors as a symptom of the fight between his old enemy Ashraf and
the Queen to prove their respective loves for the Shah. Ashraf was
behaving very emotionally, said Flandrin. Among all his siblings
only Ashraf had throughout demonstrated utter, passionate loyalty to him.

By the end of July, Coleman had walked out after failing to
convince the French of his point of view. "It had degenerated into
a circus with the French the principal clowns," alleged Coleman.
"I knew that the Shah was going to die." DeBakey and Kean had
not returned. Now, at the end, Georges Flandrin was quietly
ministering to the Shah, as he had for most of the last six years.
The Shah was losing blood, and he was in agony. Those around
him then say that he was very patient. Flandrin said, "He just
talked about his country. I admired him a lot then."

"During all this period," said the Queen later, "everyone was
complaining and my husband never, never complained, never said
anything against anybody. Sometimes he would say, 'I don't understand why.' But being angry, insulting people—never. In a
way he had elevated himself so much above everything. I think he
was a man of integrity, dignity. He was a civilized human being.
And when you have suffered so much, seen so much, what is
there to say? Words cannot express your feelings."

When Mrs. Sadat visited the Shah just before his death, she too
was struck by his stoicism. "God must have loved this man to
give him the strength to bear hardships so gracefully, I thought as
I stood by him in the intensive-care unit." She said to him that he
would soon be better and they would all have a lovely time together in Alexandria. Looking at the tears in Farah's eyes, she said
to her, "Be brave. Don't show him your feelings. He is very
intelligent and will understand."

The Shah's end was brutal. On July 26, his temperature soared
as his body was invaded by a new infection. He began to hemorrhage badly and went into shock. It was clear that he was near
death. Flandrin told the Queen and Princess Ashraf. The Queen,
in great distress, begged him to call the children back from Alexandria. Ardeshir Zahedi called them also. They drove through the

hot, oppressive night to Cairo. When Farahnaz, then seventeen, saw her father, she flung herself on her knees by his bed, seized his hand and cried, "Baba, Baba!" On the other side of the bed, throughout the night Flandrin monitored the Shah's blood pressure and other vital functions. But after transfusing eleven packed units of blood, he decided further fight was useless and stopped what he called "obstinate therapy."

Princess Ashraf later gave her own account of her brother's death to *Paris Match*. She said she watched her brother's electrocardiogram as if her own life depended on it. "Following the movement of the needles, I felt my own heart beat, my own pulse run." By midnight it was clear that his heart was beating more and more slowly. Ashraf said, "My spirit was completely confused, but one thought dominated all others; I must leave with him. I must not stay." She asked Dr. Pirnia how long she gave him. Five or six hours was the reply.

I told myself that I ought to take something at once if I wanted to leave at the same time as him. . . . All that I wanted was to end our life as we had begun it—together. Like a robot I went to my room and swallowed a mixture of sleeping pills and Valium. I lay down as if to go to sleep. But sleep did not come. I stayed wide-awake and I asked myself the question which had been haunting me for months, "What kind of justice is it that forces my brother to live his last moments in exile, in a little hospital bed, far from everything he loves?" I know today that it is a question to which I will never find an answer.

After lying there, thinking of all her brother's qualities, she decided she must go back to his side. It was 5 A.M.

He was still alive and breathing very fast. I looked at the electrocardiogram and then at his face. Suddenly the machine stopped. I took my brother's hand in mine and that was all. . . . Like a sleepwalker, drunk with remorse, I took him in my arms and did what I had never dared to do while he was alive—I kissed him as much as I wanted, all over—his feet, his hands. . . . I did not want to leave him. I stayed with him so long that I suddenly felt his hand go cold. Then I lost consciousness. I was carried to the palace and when I woke up, I took ten more pills, thinking, This time it will work. But nothing happened and I finally had to accept that when God does not want you, he does not take you.

Others who were there that night have other memories. Colonel
Jahanbini said that Ashraf sat on a chair by the bed staring at her
twin's face. She was clearly traumatized by the loss of the love of
her life.

The Queen and the children came to the bedside at various times
during the night. Dr. Pirnia was also there, and so was the Shah's
valet, Amir Pourshoja, who had served him for twenty-five years,
had a weak heart, and was in a state of total grief about his master.
Ardeshir Zahedi remained in the room all night. Before the Shah
lost consciousness, Zahedi said to him, "You are in shock. You
will get better."

The Shah replied, "No, you don't understand. I'm dying." He
held Zahedi's hand and watched the drip going into his arm. Before dawn he went into a coma. He died just before 10 o'clock in
the morning of July 27, 1980.

At the moment of death, Zahedi and Mark Morse were standing
at the end of the bed. Amir Pourshoja leaned his head against the
wall and began to weep so fiercely that the others were afraid for
him.

The doctors removed the drips from the Shah's body. The
Queen asked Dr. Pirnia to take off the Shah's ring and give it to
her. She also took a small copy of the Koran from under the
pillow. An Egyptian nurse closed his eyes. Farah and his son Reza
kissed him on the cheek. His body was taken to the morgue;
someone snatched a photograph and sold it to *Paris Match*.

The United States acknowledged the Shah's death in a desultory
manner, making no mention of the long alliance between him and
the United States. The statement noted merely that the Shah had
been "a leader of Iran for an exceptionally long period of time—
38 years." History would record that he led his country at a time
when "profound changes were taking place. His death marks the
end of an era in Iran."

Henry Kissinger was kinder, saying, "He was a good friend of
the United States who stood by us in every crisis," adding that he
died abandoned by all his friends except Sadat. Richard Nixon
said, "I think the handling of the situation by our own administration will be regarded as one of the black pages of American history."

David Rockefeller gave it as his opinion that history would
recognize the Shah "as a modernizing leader who worked assidu-

ously over several decades to bring economic and social progress for his beloved Iran."

John J. McCloy, who, like Kissinger and Rockefeller, had campaigned to have the Shah admitted to the States, said, "I think he was entitled to better treatment by the United States. Our treatment was undignified."

In Iran, the Shah's death was greeted with indifference. Demands for his return had now ceased—except among those politicians like Sadegh Ghotbzadeh who reckoned that they might gain specific personal kudos from it. But even for Ghotbzadeh the thrill of that chase had worn off. A few days before, he had said, "Nobody cares about the Shah because he is nearly finished. I myself do not care. The man is dying. When he is in his grave, he must explain all his crimes to God."

On his death, Radio Teheran declared, "Mohammed Reza Pahlavi, the bloodsucker of the century, has died at last." The official Iranian news agency announced, "Mohammed Reza Pahlavi, 'King of Kings' and the pharaoh of his time, died. The treacherous Shah lies next to the tomb of ancient Egyptian pharaohs and in the asylum of Sadat in disgrace, misery, and vagrancy, in the same state of despair in which the pharaoh and his army were drowned in the sea."

"No state funeral was grander," wrote Mrs. Sadat of the obsequies her husband arranged for the Shah. Sadat said that the Shah "had often spoken of a simple funeral but in appreciation of all he did, we will bid him farewell with the same amount of honor and respect as we greeted him with when he arrived here." The tomb had been prepared in el-Rifa'i Mosque, where Reza Shah had been temporarily buried during World War II, before his son had his remains taken back to Iran.

It was a blistering hot day. The coffin, covered with an Iranian flag, was borne on a horse-drawn gun carriage. Before it walked three Egyptian officers carrying three decorations on three cushions. Two were Iranian and one was Egyptian. The many other foreign decorations, awarded the Shah during his reign, were kept in the box in which Amir Pourshoja had carried them around the world—because those nations had not accepted him during his exile.

Behind the coffin, the funeral cortege walked three miles through the streets to the mosque. Mrs. Sadat kept close to Farah

(Top) Farah Diba, Richard
Nixon and Crown Prince Reza

(Bottom) Princess Ashraf
with Anwar Sadat

Diba. "Do whatever Farah does," Sadat had told her. "We must
help her get through this most sad and difficult day." On the other
side of Mrs. Sadat was Princess Ashraf, wearing dark glasses and
a veil and leaning on Colonel Nevissi.

The most prominent of the mourners was Richard Nixon. Ex-
King Constantine of Greece also came. The United States, West
Germany, and France were represented by their ambassadors;

Britain sent its chargé d'affaires. The only Arab nation represented was Morocco. Israel sent its first ambassador to Egypt.

As the procession walked through the crowded slums, military helicopters clattered overhead and thousands of troops and police kept watch on the populace. At one point, people had to be beaten back and kept away from the mourners by commandos with electric crowd-control sticks.

A few days later, the Empress issued a statement in which she said that before he died the Shah had asked that his remains be entombed with his slain generals "after the liberation of Iran." She reported that in one of his last statements he had said, "I commend the great Iranian people into the hands of the Crown Prince. God protect him. And this is my last wish."

Epilogue

The death of the Shah had no effect upon the fate of the American hostages in Iran. Eventually they were released, after complicated financial agreements were made in Algiers between the American and Iranian governments, minutes after Ronald Reagan took over the U.S. presidency from Jimmy Carter on January 20, 1981.

Since then much of the world has continued to be dominated by the legacies of the Shah and the visions of the ayatollah.

After the death of the Shah, Farah Diba and her children stayed in the Koubbeh Palace in Cairo until early 1982. Reza, the new Shah, then moved to Morocco, partly in order to stress that he was independent of his mother. In 1984 when he was twenty-three years old, he moved to the United States and took up residence outside Washington. Ostensibly, he devoted his time to attempting to restore the monarchy. But he did not have much visible success. In 1986 it was reported that, like his father before him, he was receiving the support of the CIA. He and his mother did not always agree on the direction that his campaign should take.

The Queen and her three younger children, Farahnaz, Ali Reza and Leila, moved to the United States in 1982, and the children completed their education. By 1988 the Queen divided her time between Connecticut and Europe.

Princess Ashraf continued to divide her time between New York and Paris. Throughout, she dressed in mourning for her brother, eschewing society, saying, "Why pretend to gaiety when your heart is bleeding?" She lived a lonely life, spending much of the day in bed, often rising only in the afternoon for a massage. In the evenings she sometimes went to the cinema with members of her entourage; as in the old days of the palace, films remained a passion. After the movies came dinner and the indulgence of another Pahlavi enthusiasm—card playing until the small hours, when she finally tried to sleep. Ashraf established the Foundation for Iranian Studies in Washington. This was intended to help keep Iranian culture and history alive among a few of the million or so Iranians now in exile. She continued to support some Iranians who, unlike her, had been financially ruined by the revolution. Other relatives and some other officials of the Shah continued to prosper. Thus, Hushang Ansary, the Shah's minister of finance, made more millions in New York. He had his friend Henry Kissinger join the board of Sun Resorts, a company Ansary promoted in the Virgin Islands.

Robert Armao continued to work for Princess Ashraf, though not for the Queen. His name was linked with Roberto Calvi, the Italian banker and member of the P2 Masonic Lodge who was found hanged under Blackfriars Bridge in London. Before Calvi's death, Armao was asked to put together a consortium to buy Calvi's Banco Ambrosiano. He did business in the Seychelles and was slightly involved with Mrs. Aquino during the Philippine revolution. By 1988 his company was also working in Indonesia and Korea.

Mark Morse left Armao's employ. He went to work for a management consultancy group in Washington. He stayed in touch with the Queen.

Dr. Pirnia, Colonel Jahanbini, Amir Pourshoja and other Iranian members of the small party which traveled with the Shah were all found homes in the United States.

Ardeshir Zahedi returned to the home on the banks of Lake Geneva which his father had bought in the 1950s after the Shah had dismissed him as prime minister.

The doctors returned to their practices. Many of them have revealed details of what happened; some of these histories were hard to reconcile one with the other. Of the principals, only Dr. Flandrin remained silent for years.* He had wanted to reply to other accounts of the Shah's treatment but, he said, the Queen had cautioned him, "Do you not think that we already have enough enemies." Until he agreed to be interviewed for this book, he said nothing publicly but comforted himself with the knowledge that the Queen continued to show confidence in him. He recalled also that Napoleon's Irish surgeon on St. Helena, Barry O'Meara, had been criticized after the death of the emperor. He had finally set down his own account of Napoleon's death, saying, "This is my opinion, which is not produced by the indignation of the moment, but was developed a long time ago. Now I make it known in precise and clear terms." In 1987 Flandrin did the same, describing the Shah's illness and death in long letters to his professor, Jean Bernard.

Flandrin wrote that he was anxious not to abuse his Hippocratic oath of confidentiality, but he felt that so much that was wrong had already been published that it was important that the record be corrected. He also felt that his observations on the Shah's behavior in his last days might help the reputation of a man who had been much attacked. "It is possible that these brief remarks may be important later, for her Majesty the Queen, who lived this drama as sovereign, as wife, as woman and as mother. . . . Decency would seem to demand absolute discretion from me, but in fact that would mean that the only accounts on the record would be those contemporary versions in various papers, which did not reflect the reality—at least not that which I had experienced."

---

* Immediately after the Shah's death, Georges Flandrin wrote to Dr. DeBakey recounting the Shah's last weeks. "Despite the long-delayed diagnosis [of the subphrenic abscess], the favorable evolution of the abscess allows one to state that the patient did not die directly from the postsplenectomic infection but from the evolutive return of the malign syndrome. . . . The interruptions of the chemotherapy during these two months, made inevitable by the uncontrolled infectious state and by the long-delayed diagnosis of the subphrenic abscess, unfortunately allowed the evolutive resumption of the malign lymphoma. . . ."

In response, Dr. DeBakey wrote to Flandrin that when he had visited the Shah at the end of April, he and the Egyptian doctors had agreed "that there was no clinical or laboratory evidence of a subphrenic infection (I have some experience with this process, as you may observe from the enclosed reprint) and that all his symptoms were probably caused by a reaction to the cancer chemotherapy, including the signs of foot drop, ileus, and gastrointestinal upset. Accordingly, it was suggested that the chemotherapy be started again in about five days, but at a reduced dosage, and then the dose be gradually increased over a period of time, depending on his reaction. . . . It would thus appear that the patient was caught between the weakened immune system caused by cancer chemotherapy, resulting in development of a generalized infection producing several localized infections, and the necessity of discontinuing the cancer chemotherapy, resulting in progression of the cancer."

* * *

In Egypt, popular dissatisfaction with Anwar Sadat's rule increased month by month through 1980 and 1981. His peace with Israel seemed stalled; it had isolated Egypt in the Arab world, but had not brought tangible benefits to most of the Egyptian people. On the international stage, Sadat still had what the Egyptian journalist Mohammed Heikal called "superstar status," but he was becoming more and more remote from Egypt itself. Even the American media began to compare his problems with those of the Shah. In September 1981, Sadat arrested hundreds of his critics and opponents. On October 6, 1981, during a military parade, he was assassinated by members of the Muslim Brotherhood. His funeral was attended by a galaxy of foreign leaders, including three former American presidents and the prime minister of Israel. Very few of his own countrymen were among the mourners. Subsequently, his wife Jehan went to live in the United States.

King Hassan remained securely on his throne. Lynden Pindling was re-elected prime minister of the Bahamas in 1986. Lopez Portillo was replaced as president of Mexico in 1982.

General Omar Torrijos was killed in August 1981 when his plane crashed into a mountain in bad weather. Graham Greene wrote that when he heard of Torrijos' death, "it was as though a whole section of my life had been cut out. . . . I have never lost as good a friend as Omar Torrijos . . ."

Torrijos was succeeded as de facto ruler of Panama by Manuel Antonio Noriega, who had been head of intelligence when the Shah was on Contadora Island. Noriega ruled with none of the populist enthusiasm of Torrijos. He was, in short, a thug.

In 1986, he was accused in *The New York Times* of running drugs, working for Cuban intelligence as well as the CIA, and of complicity in the murder of a civilian Panamanian politician, Dr. Hugo Spadafora. He published a booklet in response to such attacks. Among many pictures of himself, it contained a speech of his which began, "Today I want to begin this conversation with the spiritual guide of the Psalmist who says: 'Those who trust in Jehovah are like Mount Sion, which does not move, yet it is forever unswerving . . .' "

In 1987 a senior officer of the National Guard repeated the charges against Noriega and asserted that Noriega had sabotaged Torrijos' plane. Panamanians rioted against Noriega's rule; the disturbances were suppressed by force. Gabriel Lewis flew to Washington where he campaigned against Noriega's rule.

In early 1988 a grand jury in Miami indicted Noriega on charges of drug running. More accounts of his murderous rule surfaced, and the United States began to apply financial and diplomatic pressures upon Panama to ensure his removal from power. U.S. agencies had known for years about Noriega's abuses of power; but up to now his conduct had been relatively silent as well as convenient. The publicity which now attended his activities, particularly his drug running, rendered him an embarrassment.

In Iran itself, Ayatollah Khomeini consolidated a theocratic state which was less pretentious but infinitely more authoritarian and arbitrary than that of the Shah. All opposition was destroyed. According to Amnesty International, which had been critical of SAVAK under the Shah, thousands of political prisoners were detained in Khomeini's Iran, torture was "commonly inflicted" (and in some periods and places was "routine"), there was no right to a fair trial, and death was a penalty all too often imposed.

In 1987 Amnesty reported, "Thousands of people have been executed in Iran since 1979. Many of the victims died simply because the authorities believed they belonged to opposition organizations. . . . Most executions in Iran are by hanging or firing squad. Stoning to death is also prescribed for certain offenses. Stoning is designed to cause pain to the victim before death. The Islamic Penal Code of Iran states: 'In the punishment of stoning to death, the stones should not be too large, so that the person dies on being hit by one or two of them; they should not be so small either that they could be defined as stones.' " Amnesty also reported that the Iranian authorities had announced the introduction of a new machine—an electric guillotine to amputate the fingers or hands of convicted thieves; the official press claimed that it could sever a hand in less than one-tenth of a second. Furthermore, "Criminal trial proceedings leading to flogging or mutilation are often brief and lacking in vital legal safeguards. . . . Amnesty International has received reports of pregnant women who had miscarriages after being flogged." In many ways the atrocities inflicted by the ayatollah's secret police seemed more appalling than those attributed to SAVAK. And whereas the Shah showed himself susceptible to foreign concern, the leaders of the Islamic revolution demonstrated no such inclination.

Throughout the period, Iran was engaged in a bloody war with its neighbor Iraq. This war was begun in September 1980 by the

Iraqis—traditional enemies of Iran with whom the Shah had come to terms. Iraq's leader, Sadam Hussein, hoped to take advantage of the post-revolutionary confusion in Iran to destroy Khomeini's Islamic regime. The Iraqis underestimated the strength and tenacity of the Iranian armed forces, and the war continued eight years, with Khomeini vowing that it would not end until the death or overthrow of Sadam Hussein. On the Iranian side, the war was characterized by the dispatch of thousands upon thousands of young boys to instant "martyrdom" on the battleground. Much of the war was fought unseen, far from Western television cameras; there were few reliable statistics about its destructive effects. But it was a total war for both sides. One estimate was that at least 300,000 Iranians and 100,000 Iraqis were killed. Under the Shah, no Iranians were at war, save those who fought in the short campaign to destroy the Marxist rebellion in Oman.

The war with Iraq was closely related to the export of the Shiite revolution. Indeed, fear of this revolution was one of the reasons which led the Iraqis to attack Iran in the first place. Most other Arab states, particularly those of the Persian Gulf, have been as frightened as Iraq by the specter of Shiite fundamentalism.

The only Arab country to support Iran in its war was Syria, whose leader, Hafez Assad, had long been an opponent of Sadam Hussein. At the same time, the only mass uprising to claim inspiration from the Iranian revolution took place in Syria. In 1981–82 the Muslim Brotherhood organized a rebellion in the town of Hama. The Syrian Army surrounded the town and shelled it. Soldiers then went in and gassed individual houses. About 25,000 people were thought to have been killed in one weekend. The event received very little attention in the West. Like the war between Iran and Iraq, it was hidden from our eyes and, unlike SAVAK, was not therefore an assault upon our consciences.

The war, and Iranian needs, led to the restoration of what seemed a most unlikely alliance—between fundamentalist Iran and Israel. The Shah's unobtrusive but strong links with Israel had been roundly denounced by the ayatollah before he came to power. Soon after his return, the PLO took over the Israeli mission in Teheran. It was clear throughout the eighties that Iran had the closest links to some of the most radical groups in South Lebanon which saw Israel and the United States as equal Satans. Indeed, Iran evidently controlled the taking of many of the hostages in Beirut.

But in 1981, Iran quietly re-established contact with Israel. The Iranian clerics had found, as the Iranian Shah had found before them, that they had certain interests in common with Israel—and against the Arabs. Israeli leaders had similar perceptions. Ideologies may change like weather vanes. But the size of nations, their geographical position, their fears, their ambitions, their views of their regional destiny—such factors do not quickly alter.

Iran needed spare parts for the American weapons which had been purchased by the Shah. Israel was eager to supply both these and its own arms products to a country fighting one of its most intransigent Arab enemies, and at the same time to restore some of the links which the two countries had found so beneficial in the time of the Shah. One problem was that a U.S. embargo on arms transfers to Iran, imposed at the time of the seizure of the embassy, had never been removed. In January 1984, George Shultz, the U.S. secretary of state, designated Iran a sponsor of international terrorism. From then on, the United States actively pressured its allies not to ship arms to Iran.

But by that time many U.S. officials had become concerned about U.S. policy toward Iran after the death of Khomeini. For five years now there had been virtually no link between the United States and Iran. Yet for almost forty years before that, the links had been intimate. There was clearly a vacuum.

The central fact for the United States, and all other Western countries, remained that Iran was a vast country containing enormous oil resources and bordered by the Soviet Union, in the most volatile area of the world. The ayatollah might denounce the United States as The Great Satan, and President Reagan could respond by saying that the Iranian leaders were "loony tunes," but at the same time officials of each country could still perceive that its present needs from the others were similar to those it had in the past.

In 1985, under the rubric of making contact with Iran's "moderates," U.S. officials allowed Israeli middlemen to draw them into a relationship under which U.S. arms were to be transferred, through Israel, to Iran. Ostensibly this was to enhance the authority of those "moderate" Iranian leaders who sought an opening to the West, and to the United States in particular. In reality the initiative became a deal whereby American arms were to be traded for the release of American hostages held by pro-Iranian groups in Beirut. It was also in clear violation of U.S. law. When these dealings were revealed at the end of 1986, they became known as "Irangate." And so it happened that, like Eisenhower, Kennedy, Nixon and Carter, Ronald Reagan became the latest in a long line of American presidents to be confronted with his own particular "Iran crisis."

Vietnam was an artificial crisis; the country faded into relative obscurity once America had been expelled. Despite all the exhortations and the suffering of that terrible war, Vietnam was really peripheral to underlying Western interests. That could never have been said of Iran.

During the course of 1987, U.S. hearings on "Irangate" were completed, Iranian fundamentalists attacked other Muslim pilgrims in Mecca, more hostages were seized in Lebanon, and the war in the Gulf disrupted the shipping lanes on which the world depends for a large proportion of its oil. In an abrupt turnaround from being Iran's secret arms supplier, President Reagan declared that the United States must become guardian of the Gulf in order to protect international shipping from Iran. Several Kuwaiti tankers were reflagged with the Stars and Stripes.

In early 1988, Iran remained one of the most intractable of the world's crises. The ayatollah's fundamentalist regime was seen as a threat not only in the West, but also in the Soviet Union where there are 55 million Muslims. The two superpowers continued to have enormous interests in the future of the country. Iranians remained, as they always have been, deeply suspicious of outside interference and manipulation. The ayatollah declared, "The U.S. is worse than the Soviet Union and the Soviet Union is worse than the U.S."

When the Shah had declared that Iran was the geopolitical center of the world, he was correct. Iran has been deemed a vital crossroads ever since the Silk Route passed just north of where the city of Teheran was later built. For centuries this vast, heterogeneous country has been a bridge between East and West, a buffer between Russia and the Persian Gulf, a source and a cause of constant competition and friction. The interests that other nations have in it inevitably transcend the fate of one man, however loyal an ally he may have striven to be. It was a part of the Shah's tragedy, and Iran's, that he did not understand this. The Shah may well be remembered more kindly in the future than he is today. He could claim considerable achievements—not the least of which was that for over thirty years, apart from his foray into Oman, he

kept his country out of war. (He exploited the Kurds as merce-
naries instead.) His regime was much less violent than that which
succeeded it. He genuinely hoped to improve the condition of his
countrymen, but until 1976 he viciously punished all those who
dissented from his methods.

His understanding of both his own people and his allies was
often poor. He was correct to view the Ayatollah Khomeini and
his lieutenants as fanatical and cruel; yet he failed to comprehend
the widespread popular grievances which brought them to power
and himself to destruction. One must remember that most of Iran,
not just a narrow section, was suffused with joy at his fall in
1979. He continually placed personal relationships—above all, to
his corrupt and ineffective family—before the requirements of the
nation. From that single delusion followed much that was most
cruel and most fanciful about the Pahlavi regime. His downfall
was that his allies, particularly the Americans and the British,
seeing Iran as the keystone of the region, encouraged him in his
conviction that he alone mattered in Iran. Inevitably, he came to
believe that they would never abandon him. When, as a result of
his errors, he was turned adrift in the world, he was genuinely
baffled that the personal loyalties by which he had set so much
store were not the standards applied by most statesmen. Yet he
himself saw loyalty as a class affair. Thus he did not understand
that he had betrayed Amir Abbas Hoveyda, because Hoveyda was
his servant. But since he was the peer of Jimmy Carter and other
leaders, their rejection of him was indeed betrayal.

The Shah's friend Henry Kissinger was right to call him a Flying
Dutchman. His last ride around the tarnished rim of the Western
world was a punishment for hubris. He behaved during that forlorn and tawdry journey with both courage and dignity. But his
appearance was seen by many of his former friends and allies as a
curse.

Acknowledgments

This book grew from conversations with Alice Mayhew about loyalties between states. I researched and wrote it over the period 1984–87, principally in Britain, France and the United States. Many Iranians gave generously of their time and their recollections to me. I am especially thankful to the Shah's widow, Empress Farah Diba, and to other members of the Shah's small entourage on his final flight around the world. These include Dr. Lucy Pirnia, Colonel Kiumars Jahanbini, Kambiz Atabai, Robert Armao, and Mark Morse.

Many of the Shah's medical advisers discussed with me the problems of treating his cancer. They included Drs. Georges Flandrin, Ben Kean, Morton Coleman, Gaspar García de Paredes, Carlos García, Jeane Hester, Michael DeBakey, Adán Ríos, Dr. el Baz Rihan. Many of them talked with me or corresponded with me over a considerable period. When I first asked Dr. Flandrin to speak with me, he sought permission from Empress Farah Diba. She agreed and Dr. Flandrin asked her what he should say. "Why, the truth," she replied. Dr. Flandrin also shared with me letters he had written to his professor, Jean Bernard, about the care of the Shah. He said he felt that the Queen and her children had a right to know what had happened in this extraordinarily byzantine case. But as he himself acknowledged, and as I discovered, it was often hard to discover precisely what had taken place.

My interest in Iran began in the 1960s. Ardeshir Zahedi, the Shah's ambassador to London, became a firm friend of my family then, and has remained so since. He and many other Iranians were very helpful in the research for this book, but they may well not agree with its conclusions.

Among those Iranians to whom I am grateful are Shusha Guppy, Parviz Radji, Naz Alam, Hossein Amir-Sadeghi, Medi

Samii, Firooz Zahedi, Parvin Farmanfarmayan, Farhad Sepabhodi, Shaul Bakhash, Leila Emami, Amir Aslan Afshar, Amir Khosro Afhsar, Fereydoun Hoveyda, Fereshteh Razavi, Mahnaz Zahedi, Darius Homayoun, Hale Bakhash, Sharam Chubim, Barry Chubim. No one was more generous than Cyrus Ghani whose knowledge of Iran and its relations with the West is truly encyclopedic and whose book *Iran and the West* is a resource to treasure.

Among the other books which I have found most useful and on which I have drawn for this work are *All Fall Down,* by Gary Sick; *America Held Hostage,* by Pierre Salinger; *Crisis,* by Hamilton Jordan; *Paved with Good Intentions,* by Barry Rubin; *The Shah,* by Margaret Laing; *Roots of Revolution,* by Nicki Keddie. I have also made use of the *Documents from the Den of Spies.* This is a collection of volumes, more than fifty now, compiled by the militants who occupied the U.S. embassy in Teheran in November 1979. They consist of memoranda from the State Department, the Central Intelligence Agency, the Department of Defense and other U.S. agencies stretching back over thirty years. They are a unique resource. Other U.S. government documents that I have used were declassified in a more orthodox fashion under the Freedom of Information Act.

As usual, I am very grateful for the help of other writers and journalists who assisted me to understand this subject and gave me of their time, memories or files. They include Edward Behr, David Housego, Seymour Hersh, Terry Smith, Lawrence Altman, Chris Dickey, Karen de Young, Barry Chubin, Jeff Gerth, Robert Graham, Jonathan Randall, Jon Swain, Strobe Talbott, Brooke Shearer, Dan Morgan, Walter Pincus, David Leitch, Rosie Boycott, Avi Schlaim, Pierre Salinger, Gaia Servadio, Anthony Terry, Martin Woollacott, Mauri Woollacott, Anthony Sampson, Magnus Linklater, Lesley Blanch, Clare Hollingworth, Gary Sick, Frank Manitsas, Bernard Diederich, John Birt, Clive Irving, Alan Hart, Gavin Young, Fred Halliday, Scott Armstrong, Bob Woodward, Eric Hooglund, Mark Bloch, Caroline Gathorne Hardy, Geoffrey Phillips, Steven Erlanger, Chris Godek. The reporting of Dennis L. Breo and Brenda Stone in *American Medical News* was also very valuable. Charles Moore was very patient. Lucretia Stewart arranged my trip to Panama. Gerald Rafshoon kindly gave me access to interviews he and his associates had conducted of the Shah's exile. Josephine Wallace did research in New York; John Meakins organized many journeys with aplomb; Heather Laughton transcribed endless taped interviews with skill.

My father, who was once president of the Iran Society in Britain, was unfailingly kind in many ways and I thank him. Among the many others who gave me generously of their time, their knowledge or their hospitality during the research are Olga Polizzi, Tony and Christiane Besse, David Cornwell and Jane Cornwell, Mary Brabin, Ben Bradlee and Sally Quinn, David and J. B. Greenway, Kevin and Gail Buckley, Richard Sennett, David Puttnam, Roland Joffe, Charles Peck, John Dewe Matthews and Marina Warner, Denis Wright, Charles and Marjorie Whibley, Pamela Egremont. I also thank especially Lynn Nesbitt who knows, I hope, how much I value her friendship.

My time in Panama was much enhanced by the fact that Graham Greene gave me an introduction to his friend Chuchu Martinez who had not only been Greene's guide in *Getting to Know the General,* Omar Torrijos—but had also helped look after the Shah during his sojourn in Panama. Gabriel Lewis, the former Panamanian ambassador to the United States, was very hospitable and flew me to see his house on the island of Contadora, where the Shah had lived. He also arranged for me to meet with General Manuel Noriega. In 1987, Ambassador Lewis fled Panama for Washington, DC, where he helped coordinate the opposition to General Noriega.

This is the third book which I have been lucky enough to write with the help of Alice Mayhew, my editor at Simon and Schuster. As usual, it has been a delightful and rewarding experience, and one that I hope will be repeated. At Simon and Schuster I am also grateful to Richard E. Snyder for his consistent encouragement and support. I had frequent and essential assistance from Henry Ferris and David Shipley. The copyediting by Patricia Miller and Marcia Peterson was a tour de force. My thanks also to Eric Rayman, and the incomparable Sophie Sorkin, Frank Metz, and George Hodgman.

In London, Elaine Greene has been as supportive, in many ways, as she has always been. I thank her. At Chatto and Windus, Carmen Callil was every bit as stimulating a publisher and editor as reputed and Jeremy Lewis gave unstinting help throughout.

I am indebted to all of these, and to many more.

William Shawcross,
London, 1988.

Notes

PROLOGUE

PAGE

13. Kissinger on Flying Dutchman: *The New York Times,* April 23, 1979.

CHAPTER ONE

PAGE

17. Ashraf's son on her paintings: Parviz Radji, *In the Service of the Peacock Throne* (London: Hamish Hamilton, 1983), p. 241.
18. Central Bank employees: Ibid., p. 268.
18. Radji's diary extract: Ibid., p. 228.
18. Fox joke: Ibid., pp. 309–10.
19. Ansary and Henry Kissinger: U.S. Embassy cable, Teheran 10695, November 2, 1978.
20. Dr.Shakhar story: Author's interview with Kambiz Atabai, November 20, 1985.
20. Saddiqi story: British diplomat's diary, provided confidentially to the author.
21. President Carter's telephone call to Shah: Gary Sick, *All Fall Down* (New York: Random House, 1985), p. 51.
22. Michael Blumenthal meeting: Interview with CBS News, 1980.
23. Habib Olahi story: Interview with the author, October 9, 1985.
23. Amir Aslan Afshar story: Interview with the author, July 13, 1985.
24. Kambiz Atabai story: Interview with the author, November 20, 1985.
26. Marenches and the Shah: Christine Ockrent, Comte de Marenches, *Dans le secret des princes* (Paris: Stock, 1986), pp. 241–58.

28. Parsons memoirs: Anthony Parsons, *The Pride and the Fall* (London: Jonathan Cape, 1984), pp. 40, 71, 125.

29. Sullivan memoirs: William H. Sullivan, *Mission to Iran* (New York: Norton, 1981), pp. 156–57.

30. Sullivan suggests the Shah leave: Ibid., pp. 230–31.

31. Amir Aslan Afshar's reaction: Interview with the author, July 13, 1985.

32. Shah on Sullivan looking at his watch: Mohammed Reza Pahlavi, *Answer to History* (New York: Stein and Day, 1982), p. 172.

32. ". . . like a dead mouse": Ibid., p. 173.

33. Description of Shah's office: Lesley Blanch, *Farah Diba* (London: Collins, 1978), pp. 90–91.

33. Shah and bust of his father: Amir Aslan Afshar, interview with the author, July 13, 1985.

34. Queen on breathing space: Interview with the author, March 26–27, 1986.

34. Farewells at palace: Amir Aslan Afshar, interview with the author, July 13, 1985.

37. Shah's speech at airport: *Daily Telegraph*, London, January 17, 1980.

37. Shah's emotions at airport: M. R. Pahlavi, *Answer to History*, pp. 173–74.

CHAPTER TWO

39. Christopher Marlowe's line: See, for example, *Life*, October 15, 1971.

41. Construction of tents: See, for example, Blanch, *Farah Diba*, pp. 133–35. Also *The Washington Post*, August 29, 1971.

42. Shah and artichoke: *The Washington Post*, August 29, 1971.

43. Alexander and Persepolis: See Mortimer Wheeler, *Flames over Persepolis* (1979). Cited in Cyrus Ghani, *Iran and the West* (London and New York: Kegan Paul International, 1987), pp. 393–94.

44. Blanch on Army: Blanch, *Farah Diba*, p. 134.

44. ". . . Cecil B. De Mille's": Fereydoun Hoveyda, *The Fall of the Shah* (London: Weidenfeld and Nicolson, 1980), pp. 83–84.

44. "a mighty empire . . .": Edward Mortimer, *Faith and Power* (London: Faber and Faber, 1982), p. 34.

45. Footnote on travelers to Persia: Ghani, *Iran and the West*, pp. 322–33; in discussion of E. Denison Ross, et al, *Sir Anthony Sherley and his Persian Adventure*, London, 1933.

46. Omar Khayyám and Edward FitzGerald: Discussed by Ghani, *Iran and the West;* in reviews of "Edward FitzGerald, 1809–1909, Centenary Celebration Souvenir," *East Anglian Daily Times*, Ipswich, March 19, 1909; Robert Bernard Martin, *With Friends Possessed: A Life of Edward FitzGerald* (London: 1985), pp. 477–78, 511–12, 533–34.

46. Shah's speech at tomb of Cyrus: Hoveyda, *The Fall of the Shah*, p. 84.

47. Shah's interview on Persepolis: R. K. Karanija, *The Mind of a Monarch* (London: Allen and Unwin, 1977), pp. 21–22.

CHAPTER THREE

49. Description of flight: Author's interviews with Amir Aslan Afshar, July 13, 1985; Kambiz Atabai, November 20, 1985; Kiumars Jahanbini, November 8, 1985.

50. Dr. Pirnia's position: Interview with the author, October 2, 1985.

50 . Queen on palace: Interview with the author, March 26–27, 1986.

51. Reza Shah's background: See Ghani, *Iran and the West*, pp. 375–78 and 395–398; Richard H. Ullman, *The Anglo-Soviet Accord* (Princeton: Princeton University Press, 1972); Donald N. Wilber, *Riza Shah Pahlavi: The Resurrection and Reconstruction of Iran, 1878–1944* (Hicksville, N.Y.: Exposition Press, 1975); Blanch, *Farah Diba*, pp. 27–30; Margaret Laing, *The Shah* (London: Sidgwick and Jackson, 1976), pp. 34–42.

51. Reuter concession: Nikki Keddie, *Roots of Revolution* (New Haven: Yale University Press, 1981), p. 59.

52. Knox D'Arcy concession: Ibid., pp. 38, 78.

52. Iran and World War I: Ghani, *Iran and the West*, pp. 375–78, 395–98.

53. Ironside and Reza Khan: Ibid., p. 376; Denis Wright, *The English Amongst the Persians* (London: Heinemann, 1977), p. 182.

53. ". . . a turning point in Iranian history": Keddie, *Roots of Revolution*, p. 87.

54. "Persia" versus "Iran": Ghani, *Iran and the West*, p. 166, discussing A. H. K. Hamzavi, *Henceforth Iran* (London, 1936).

56. Mohammed Reza and miracles: M. R. Pahlavi, *Answer to History*, pp. 56–61.

56. Mohammed Reza on democracy and discipline: Quoted by Ghani, *Iran and the West*, p. 123, discussing Karl Eskelund, *Behind the Peacock Throne* (London, 1965).

57. Mohammed Reza on his father and marriage: Laing, *The Shah*, p. 68.

58. Cecil Beaton on Princess Fawzia: Ibid.

58. Colville on Persia: John Colville, *The Fringes of Power* (London: Hodder and Stoughton, 1986), pp. 14–15.

59. Reza Shah to Mohammed Reza on abdication: M. R. Pahlavi, *Answer to History*, pp. 67–68.

59. British hesitation on succession: Wright, *The English Amongst the Persians*, pp. 212–14.

60. Ashraf quoting her father: Ashraf Pahlavi, *Faces in a Mirror* (New York: Prentice Hall, 1980), p. 43.

60. Fawzia finds life intolerable: Laing, *The Shah*, p. 96.

60. Mohammed Reza appeal to Roosevelt: Barry Rubin, *Paved with Good Intentions* (Oxford and New York: Oxford University Press, 1980), p. 19.

60. Roosevelt to Cordell Hull: Ibid., p. 22.

60. Hurley and Churchill: Ghani, *Iran and the West*, pp. 79–80, discussing Churchill and Roosevelt, *The Complete Correspondence* (Princeton: Princeton University Press, 1984).

61. Azerbaijan crisis: See, for example, Rubin, *Paved with Good Intentions*, pp. 27–28.

61. Shah's escape from assassination: Laing, *The Shah*, pp. 97–98; M. R. Pahlavi, *Answer to History*, p. 59.

62. AIOC exploitation: See, for example, Keddie, *Roots of Revolution*, p. 133.

62. Mossadeq on British deciding everything: Vernon Walters, *Silent Missions* (New York: Doubleday, 1978), pp. 247–52.

63. Dean Acheson on Mossadeq: Rubin, *Paved with Good Intentions*, p. 59.

63. Mossadeq on no need for settlement: Laing, *The Shah*, p. 122.

64. Mossadeq banishes the Queen Mother and Ashraf: *The New York Times*, March 3, 1953.

64. British diplomat's lunch with Shah: From John Walker, Teheran, January 19, 1951, Public Records Office, London, EP 1015/9.

64. Anglo-American paper: November 8, 1951, Public Records Office, London, EP 1024/10.

64. Harriman and Mossadeq: Walters, *Silent Missions*, pp. 241–63.

64. Soraya on the Shah: Laing, *The Shah*, pp. 125–26.

65. American interest in Soviet threat: C. M. Wodehouse, *Something Ventured* (London: Granada, 1981), p. 117.

65. British plan put on hold: Rubin, *Paved with Good Intentions*, p. 77.

65. Meeting with Allen Dulles: Ibid., p. 81.

65. Roosevelt recruits brothers: Ibid., pp. 78–79.

65. Footnote: Wodehouse, *Something Ventured*, p. 112.

66. State Department information on the Shah: Cable from British ambassador, Washington to Foreign Office, May 21, 1953, Public Records Office, London, FO 371/104659.

66. Churchill's advice to Shah: P.M.'s personal minutes, May 22, 1953, Public Records Office, London, M.151/53.

66. Henderson meeting with Shah: Cable from British ambassador, Washington to Foreign Office, June 2, 1953, Public Records Office, London, FO 371/104659.

66. Churchill takes over Operation Boot: Wodehouse, *Something Ventured*, p. 125.

66. Churchill message to Shah: Public Records Office, London, FO 371/104659.80648.

67. Soraya on Ashraf's mission: Laing, *The Shah*, p. 131.

67. Roosevelt and Shah: Kermit Roosevelt, *Countercoup: The Struggle for the Control of Iran* (New York: McGraw, 1979), pp. 69–77, 91–95, 111–13, 199.

67. Zahedi: Fitzroy Maclean, *Eastern Approaches* (London, Jonathan Cape, 1949), pp. 266–75.

67. Coup and countercoup story: See, for example, Rubin, *Paved with Good Intentions,* pp. 81–86.

68. British ambassador to Baghdad cable: Public Records Office, London, FO 371/104659.80648. EP 1943/4.

69. British diplomat in Rome letter: Public Records Office, London, FO 371/104658.80648. EP 1941.

69. State Department's instruction to Shah in Rome: Telegram, August 17, 1953, No. 488; Public Records Office, London, FO 371/104659.80648.

69. Notes in Winston Churchill's files: Public Records Office, London, FO 371/104659. 80648. EP 1943/EG.

70. Shah's behavior in Rome hotel: Public Records Office, London, FO 371/104658. 8064. EP 1941.

70. Eyewitness to street scene in Teheran: *Saturday Evening Post*, November 2, 1954; quoted in Wodehouse, *Something Ventured*, p. 129.
70. Shah's reaction to the news: Laing, *The Shah*, p. 137.
70. Shah's gratitude to Roosevelt: Roosevelt, *Countercoup.*
72. Shah on "true election": M. R. Pahlavi, *Answer to History*, pp. 90–91.

CHAPTER FOUR

73. Sadat to Shah: Jehan Sadat, *A Woman of Egypt* (New York: Simon and Schuster, 1987), p. 398.
74. Sadat's relationship with Shah: Ibid., pp. 339–42.
74. Shah's remark to minister: Samuel Seger, *The Iranian Triangle, The Secret Relations between Israel-Iran-U.S.A.*, (Tel Aviv, 1981), p. 125.
74. Mrs. Sadat's misgivings about Iran: Sadat, *A Woman of Egypt*, pp. 341–42.
75. Mrs. Sadat's invitation to Shah and Empress: Ibid., pp. 389, 396–97.
76. Shah's comment to Sadat: Ibid., p. 398; author's interview with Mrs. Sadat, January 27, 1985.
76. King Constantine on Shah: Radji, *In the Service of the Peacock Throne*, p. 314.
77. Flandrin trip: Author's interviews with Georges Flandrin, February 26, 1985 and April 4, 1985.
77. Behbehanian visit: Author's interview with Mohammed Behbehanian, December 2, 1985.
79. Persian tolerance of Jews: Robert Reppa, *Israel and Iran* (New York: Praeger, 1974), p. 86.
80. Iran's recognition of Israel: Uri Bialer, *Middle East Journal* 39 (Spring 1985).
81. "Crashing thrones": Rubin, *Paved with Good Intentions*, p. 98.
82. Shah and Dulles: Memorandum of conversation by the secretary of state, March 9, 1956, 110.11.DU/3-956, State Department document.
83. Dulles suggestion that Eisenhower "flatter" the Shah: Cable, January 25, 1958, State Department, No. 15269.
83. U.S. ambassador's telegram to State: November 7, 1957, State Department, 611.88/11-757.
83. Dulles on Shah's "blackmail": Cable to U.S. ambassador, Teheran, January 16, 1958.
83. Nikita Khrushchev warning: Rubin, *Paved with Good Intentions*, pp. 101–2.
84. Soraya's lament: Leonard Mosley, *Dulles* (New York: Dial Press, 1978), pp. 326–27.
84. Shah's divorce from Soraya: *The Washington Post*, March 22, 1958; May 21, 1963.
85. Shah and Arabs: Rubin, *Paved with Good Intentions*, p. 103.
85. Kennedy and Khrushchev: Ibid., p. 107.
86. Shah on "increased U.S. intrigue": M. R. Pahlavi, *Answer to History*, p. 146.
86. National Intelligence Estimate (NIE): June 5, 1961. Secret: The Prospect of a Neutral Iran, quoting NIE 3-4-61, February 28, 1961.
86. Shah and Amini: Ibid., pp. 22–23.
86. State Department cable: October 22, 1961, No. 13827.
86. Presidential Task Force view: June 5, 1961.

86. Kennedy's remarks to Shah: Memorandum of conversation, April 13, 1962.

87. Justice Department and Shah: Arthur M. Schlesinger, Jr., *Robert Kennedy and His Times* (Boston: Houghton Mifflin, 1978), pp. 435–36.

87. Shah's dismissal of Amini: Rubin, *Paved with Good Intentions*, p. 106; M. R. Pahlavi, *Answer to History*, p. 23.

89. Shah to Abba Eban: Seger, *Triangle*.

89. Sadat on Nasser's death: Sadat, *A Woman of Egypt*, p. 249.

89. Mrs. Sadat on King Hassan's motives: Interview with the author, January 27, 1985.

89. Carter's reaction: Jimmy Carter, *Keeping Faith* (London: Collins, 1982), pp. 447–48.

90. Departure scene: *Daily Telegraph*, London, January 30, 1979.

CHAPTER FIVE

91. CIA report on Shah's family: Ernest R. Oney, *Elites and the Distribution of Power in Iran*, CIA Secret, PR 76.10017, February 1976, p. 27. Reprinted in "Documents from the Den of Spies," Teheran.

91. U.S. Embassy study: *The Iranian Imperial Family*, Amembassy, Teheran, January 19, 1975, Tab A2. Documents from the Den of Spies.

92. Queen's views on leaving Iran: Interview with the author, March 26–27, 1986.

92. Farah at her father's death: Blanch, *Farah Diba*, p. 40.

93. Farah's engagement and marriage: Ibid., pp. 30–40.

95. Director of clinic: Ibid., p. 17.

96. Gilda story: author's interviews with court and government officials; also *Daily Express*, London, March 19, 1979.

97. Court rumors on Queen and Shah: Oney, *Elites and the Distribution of Power in Iran*, pp. 72–73; author's interviews with courtiers.

97. Oriana Fallaci interview: *New Republic*, December 1, 1973.

98. Queen and culture: Parsons, *The Pride and the Fall*, p. 26.

98. Queen's later comments on Persepolis: Interview with the author, March 26–27, 1986.

99. King Hassan's palace sources: *The New York Times*, January 22, 1979.

100. Shah on Hassan: M. R. Pahlavi, *Answer to History*, p. 137.

101. Guests at the Mamounia: *The New York Times*, February 3, 1979.

103. U.S. ambassador on General Walters: Author's interview with Ambassador Parker, November 12, 1985.

103. Shah to Salinger: Pierre Salinger, *America Held Hostage* (London: Deutsch, 1982), p. 16.

104. State Department biography of Zahedi: *Decisionmaking in Iran*, Amembassy, Teheran, July 22, 1976, Enclosure I, pp. 10–11.

106. Carter's commitment to Zahedi: Salinger: *America Held Hostage*, p. 39.

107. Plot to seize Khomeini's plane: Author's interviews with Ardeshir Zahedi, December 3, 1985; Kambiz Atabai, November 19, 1985; and Kiumars Jahanbini, November 8, 1985.

108. Attempted coup in Teheran: Author's interview with Admiral Habib Olahi, October 9, 1985.

CHAPTER SIX

110. For a succinct analysis of Iranian Shiism, see Mortimer, *Faith and Power*, pp. 296–376.

112. Rubin quote: Rubin, *Paved with Good Intentions*, p. 6.

113. Khomeini's early sermons and views: See Shaul Bakhash, *The Reign of the Ayatollahs* (London: I. B. Taurus, 1985), pp. 19–40.

114. 1963 riots: Ibid., pp. 29–30; Rubin, *Paved with Good Intentions*, p. 109.

115. Extraterritoriality: *Ghani, Iran and the West*, p. 434.

117. Shah in palace in Marrakesh: Author's interview with the Empress, March 26–27, 1986; and with Amir Aslan Afshar, November 20, 1985.

118. Queen's memory of February 11, 1979: Author's interview, March 26–27, 1986.

118. Shah and Robert Trent Jones: *International Herald Tribune*, June 13, 1985.

118. Sullivan's riposte to Brzezinski: Sullivan, *Mission to Iran*, p. 253.

119. Account of embassy siege: Ibid., pp. 246–68.

120. Vance's reason: Cyrus Vance, *Hard Choices* (New York: Simon and Schuster, 1983), pp. 342–44.

120. Sullivan visit to Bazargan: Sullivan, *Mission to Iran*, pp. 271–73.

120. Pine-box warning: Author's interview with Charles Naas, January 28, 1985.

CHAPTER SEVEN

121. Moroccan opposition to Shah: *Daily Telegraph*, London, February 16, 1979.

122. Diplomatic corps gossip: Author's interviews with Ambassador Parker, November 12, 1985; Mohammed Behbehanian, December 2, 1985; and Ambassador Sepabhodi, September 6, 1985.

122. Moustachio story: Author's interview with Ambassador Sepabhodi. See also Sick, *All Fall Down*, p. 177.

123. Clare Hollingworth story: Author's interview with Hollingworth, June 18, 1985; *Daily Telegraph*, London, February 16, 1979.

123. *Private Eye* rows: Radji, *In the Service of the Peacock Throne*, pp. 17–20.

124. Chalfont article: *Times*, London, March 1, 1976.

124. Barbara Walters interview: *The New York Times*, March 7, 1979.

124. Shah's bewilderment: Author's interview with Ambassador Sepabhodi, September 6, 1985.

124. Sepabhodi's summons: Author's interview with Ambassador Sepabhodi, September 6, 1985.

124. Shah's aircraft story: Author's interview with Amir Aslan Afshar, July 13, 1985.

125. Return of staff to Teheran: Author's interviews with Amir Aslan Afshar, July 13, 1985, and Colonel Jahanbini, November 8, 1985.

125. Captain Moezzi's hands: Michael Ledeen and William Lewis, *Debacle* (New York: Alfred A. Knopf, 1987), pp. 216–17.

125. Departure of staff: Author's interviews with those concerned.

126. Shah's February 22 message: Sick, *All Fall Down*, p. 177.

126. February 23 meeting of NSC committee: Ibid., p.177.

126. Brzezinski's view: Ibid., p. 178.

126. Zahedi's call: Ibid., p. 178; also, author's interview with Zahedi, December 3–4, 1985.

126. Carter's reaction: Sick, *All Fall Down*, p. 178.

127. Shah's 1977 visit to Washington: Ibid., p. 28; Hamilton Jordan, *Crisis* (New York: Berkley, 1982), p. 78.

129. Carter's New Year's Eve visit to Teheran: Sullivan, *Mission to Iran*, pp. 130–136; Sick, *All Fall Down*, pp. 29–31.

130. Ashraf's reaction: Ashraf Pahlavi, *Faces in a Mirror*, pp. 198–99.

131. Sullivan and Shah at airport: Sullivan, *Mission to Iran*, pp. 135–36.

131. Shah's ordering publication of attack on Khomeini: author's interview with Darius Homagoon, former minister of information, January 27, 1985.

132. Aaron's warning: Sick, *All Fall Down*, p. 178.

132. Zahedi and Swiss: Author's interview with Zahedi, December 3–4, 1985.

133. Zahedi on Giscard d'Estaing: Author's interview with Zahedi, December 3–4, 1985.

133. Shah and Giscard's telephone call: Author's interview with Amir Aslan Afshar, July 13, 1985.

133. Carter on Guadeloupe: Carter, *Keeping Faith*, p. 445.

133. Rosalynn Carter on Gaudeloupe: Rosalynn Carter, *First Lady from Plains*, pp. 307–8.

133. Giscard's intervention at Guadeloupe: Rubin, *Paved with Good Intentions*, pp. 245–46.

134. Marenches in Morocco: Marenches and Ockrent, *Dans le Secret des Princes*, pp. 257–58.

135. "Other accounts" of Hassan's views: Sick, *All Fall Down*, p. 178; Carter, *Keeping Faith*, p. 452; author's interviews with Ambassador Parker.

135. Vance request to Kissinger: *The New Yorker*, June 9, 1980.

135. Vance's current view: Vance, *Hard Choices*, p. 344.

135. Carter's view: Carter, *Keeping Faith*.

135. Vance request to Kissinger and Rockefeller: *The New York Times Magazine*, May 17, 1981.

136. Moustachio's second visit: Author's interview with Ambassador Sepabhodi, September 6, 1985.

136. Parker's interview: Author's interview with Ambassador Parker, November 13, 1985.

137. Don Agger's role: Author's interview with Agger, October 10, 1985.

138. Finding the Bahamas: *The New York Times Magazine*, May 17, 1981; author's interviews with Robert Armao, February 13, 1986; and Mark Morse, November 11, 1985.

138. Queen's comment: Author's interview, March 26–27, 1986.

CHAPTER EIGHT

139. Shah's friendlessness: Laing, *The Shah*, pp. 139–40.

140. Description of Rockefeller: See Joseph Persico, *The Imperial Rockefeller* (New York: Simon and Schuster, 1982), passim.

140. World Trade Center arrangement: Ibid., p. 44.

140. Rockefeller in Isfahan bazaar: Ibid., p. 190.

140. Caspian games: Author's interview with Mahnaz Zahedi, October 5, 1985.

141. Profiles of Robert Armao: *The New York Times*, August 14, 1979; *Interview*, February 1982; *Avenue*, September 1984.

141. Armao as "mystery man": Persico, *The Imperial Rockefeller*, p. 312.

142. Armao on unlisted number: *The New York Times*, August 14, 1979.

142. Armao on "low profile" and "Anonymity is bliss": *Interview*, February 1982.

142. Armao on inspiration of Rockefeller: Ibid.

142. Armao leaves "greeter's" job: *The New York Times*, August 9, 1979.

143. Armao on his dispatch to Shah: *Interview*, February 1982; *Avenue*, September 1984.

143. Zahedi's view of Armao: Author's interview with Zahedi, December 3–4, 1985.

144. Armao's view of Carter administration: *The New York Times Magazine*, May 17, 1981; Salinger, *America Held Hostage*, passim; author's interview with Armao, November 14, 1986.

144. Carter's view of Armao. *The New York Times Magazine*, May 17, 1981.

144. Sick's view of Armao: Sick, *All Fall Down*, p. 179.

144. Morse's role: Author's interview with Morse, November 11, 1985.

145. Armao at "21" Club: *Avenue*, September 1984.

145. Landing at Nassau: Author's interview with Morse, November 11, 1985.

145. James Crosby and Resorts: *The Wall Street Journal*, November 14, 1985.

146. Pindling and Resorts: Ibid.

146. Colonel Jahanbini on Crosby's house and Pindling: Author's interview, November 8, 1985.

147. *The New York Times* report: *The New York Times Magazine*, May 17, 1981.

147. "Free steak dinner": *The New York Times*, March 31, 1979.

148. Trapped Israelis: Sullivan, *Mission to Iran*, pp. 270–71.

148. Arafat's threats and Bahamian chief of police comment: *Daily Telegraph*, London, April 28, 1979.

148. Jahanbini's views: Author's interview, November 8, 1971.

150. Queen on being treated like a criminal, on Crosby's house, and on Bahamian foreign policy: Author's interview, March 7–8, 1985.

CHAPTER NINE

151. Kissinger's call to Brzezinski: Zbigniew Brzezinski, *Power and Principle* (London: Weidenfeld and Nicolson, 1983), p. 473.

151. McCloy background: Anthony Sampson, *The Seven Sisters* (London: Coronet, 1975), p. 179.

152. Vance's lament on McCloy: *The New York Times Magazine*, May 17, 1981.

152. Kissinger's campaign, Sick, *All Fall Down*, p. 179. Kissinger's views were expressed in detail in *The Economist*, London, February 10, 1979.

153. Administration linkage of Shah and SALT: *The New York Times Magazine*, May 17, 1981.

153. Brzezinski's suggestion Kissinger call Carter: Ibid.

153. Kissinger on his conversation with Carter: Ibid.

153. Carter on his conversation with Kissinger: Ibid.

153. Jordan's account: Jordan, *Crisis*, p. 22.

154. Kissinger on "shame": Kissinger, *Years of Upheaval* (London: Weidenfeld and Nicolson, 1982), p. 667.

154. Carter's irritation: Brzezinski, *Power and Principle*, p. 473.

154. Rockefeller's meeting with Carter: *The New York Times Magazine*, May 17, 1981.

155. Carter's reaction: Carter, *Keeping Faith*, pp. 452–53.

155. Kissinger on Flying Dutchman: *The New York Times*, April 23, 1979.

156. Nixon's euphoria: Sick, *All Fall Down*, p. 13.

156. Nixon on Shah in 1950s: Richard Nixon, *Memoirs*, p. 133.

157. State Department briefing paper: Secret/Exdis s/s 7208277, May 12, 1972.

157. U.S. officials' impressions: Author's interview with Harold Saunders, November 14, 1985; State Department cable, NEA/IRN: T. L. Eliot, Jr: CSI 4/3/69. NSSM 66, July 12, 1969.

158. Takeover of islands: Rubin, *Paved with Good Intentions*, p. 133.

158. Arms sales figures: Ibid., pp. 158–89; State Department White Paper on U.S.-Iranian relations.

158. INR June 1970 Research Study: The External Threat to Iran, June 9, 1970 Secret, No Foreign Dissem, Controlled Dissem.

159. Shah's methods of government and Amouzegar example: Letter to Ambassador Helms from John Washburn, second secretary of the U.S. Embassy, Teheran, August 11, 1973.

160. SAVAK background, including Bakhtiar story: Rubin, *Paved with Good Intentions*, p. 108–9.

161. SAVAK's reach: Ibid., pp. 177–82.

162. Dissidence increasing: Shahrough Akhavi, *Religion and Politics in Contemporary Iran* (New York: State University of New York Press, 1980), pp.161–62.

162. Shah's preparations for Nixon visit: Author's interview with Douglas Heck, former deputy chief of mission, U.S. Embassy, Teheran, July 4, 1985.

162. Kissinger on Shah's "melancholy": Henry Kissinger, *The White House Years* (Boston: Little, Brown & Co., 1979), p. 1263.

162. Kissinger and belly dancer: *The Washington Post*, May 31 and June 1, 1972.

163. Nixon's talks with Shah: See George Ball, *The Past Has Another Pattern* (New York: Norton, 1982), pp. 453–55; also, author's interview with George Ball, June 12, 1980. See also Sick, *All Fall Down*, pp. 13–15; also, author's interview with Gary Sick, September 17, 1985.

163. F-14 and F-15 fighters: Rubin, *Paved with Good Intentions*, p. 134. See also Robert Graham, *Iran: The Illusion of Power* (London: Croom Helm, 1978), p. 171.

163. Pentagon's studies: Sick, *All Fall Down*, p. 14.

163. Nixon and Kissinger's decision: This has been widely described. See, for example, Sick, *All Fall Down*, pp. 13–15; Rubin, *Paved with Good Intentions*, pp. 134–35.

164. Sick on Shah's crackdown: Sick, *All Fall Down*, p. 23; also, author's interviews with Gary Sick, September 17, 1985 and George Ball, June 12, 1980.

164. Anti-American violence: *The Washington Post*, June 1, 1972.

164. Ronald Ziegler statement: Ibid.

164. Shah to Afshar: Author's interview with Amir Aslam Afshar, July 13, 1985.

164. INR Intelligence note: "Secret: Iran: Internal Dissidence—a Note of Warning," INR, June 12, 1972.

165. Kissinger's "remarkable" memoranda: SECRET, for the secretary of state and the secretary of defense, June 15 and July 25, 1972.

165. Footnote on Kurds: Pike Committee Report, published in *The Village Voice*, February 23, 1976; William Safire, *The New York Times*, February 12, 1976 and December 19, 1977.

166. Dismay in Pentagon: Sick, *All Fall Down*, p. 14.

166. Shah on ambition to be Air Force general: Radji, *In the Service of the Peacock Throne*, p. 200.

166. The Empress on speed: Laing, *The Shah*, p. 191.

167. George Ball comment: Interview with the author; Ball, *The Past Has Another Pattern*, pp. 453–58.

167. Kissinger's comments: Kissinger, *The White House Years*, p. 1072; *Years of Upheaval*, pp. 669–70.

168. U.S. arms sales: Figures from State Department White Paper on U.S.-Iranian relations, prepared for President Carter.

168. Sick on arms sales: Sick, *All Fall Down*, pp. 13–19; Kissinger memorandum for President Ford, "Strategy for your discussions with the Shah of Iran," Secret-noDis. May 13, 1975.

CHAPTER TEN

169. French doctor's visit: Author's interviews with Dr. Georges Flandrin, February 26, 1985 and thereafter.

169. Letter to laugh about: Author's interview with Colonel Kiumars Jahanbini, November 8, 1985.

169. PLO and Khalkhali threats: *Daily Telegraph*, London, May 14, May 23, June 18 and June 22, 1984.

170. Rockefeller remark: *The New York Times Magazine*, May 17, 1981.

170. Carter's reaction: Carter, *Keeping Faith*, p. 452.

170. Bahamian criticism of Shah's stay: *Daily Telegraph* (London), April 28, 1979.

171. Oil history: See, for example, Keddie, *Roots of Revolution*, pp. 89–90, 132–140.

171. Shah's pressure in 1966 and 1968: Rubin, *Paved with Good Intentions*, p. 110.

172. Wave finger remark: Ibid., p. 140.

172. "Why should we cut it?": *U.S. News & World Report*, May 6, 1974.

173. Shah's "blast-off": Author's interview with Hussein Amir Sadeghi, June 5, 1985.

173. Shah's criticism of Western waste and sloth: *U.S. News & World Report*, May 6, 1974.

173. Shah's decision to double spend: Graham, *Iran: The Illusion of Power*, p. 78.

174. "Hyperboom" comment: Ibid., p. 83.

174. Hoveyda's view: Interview with Eric Rouleau, *Le Monde*, October 3–4, 1976.

174. Shah sipping tea: *Fortune*, October 1974.

174. Shah on blasé societies: Ibid.

175. British ministers: *Guardian*, London, January 24, 1974; *Daily Express*, London, January 25, 1974.

175. Kissinger and Joint Economic Commission: Kissinger cable to Helms, State 073527, EXDIS, 11022242 April 1974.

176. Missile coproduction: In a September 16, 1974 interdepartmental memorandum, Kissinger's aide Laurence Eagleburger wrote, "HAK has indicated a strong personal interest in the matter of Iranian requests to coproduce certain weapons systems." He wanted a decision "rapidly."

176. Shah's comment that he took the decisions: Helms cable to Kissinger, EXDIS, Teheran 2958, 1709372.

177. Arms bonanza: See Rubin, *Paved with Good Intentions*, p. 159; Sick, *All Fall Down*, pp. 15–18; State Department White Paper, p. 15.

177. Major weapons systems: State Department White Paper, p. 12.

178. Bell employee behavior: *The Washington Post*, December 12, 1978.

179. Yamani's complaints: James Akins, Memorandum for the File; U.S.-Persian-Israeli-cooperation, August 28, 1975, Ref: Jidda 6009.

179. Akins remark: Letter from Akins to Senator Charles Percy, September 4, 1975: "I have been told that Kissinger dislikes me and that certain aspects of my reporting have 'annoyed' him. . . . [apparently] my reporting doesn't fit in with what the secretary wants to hear."

179. Simon on Shah as "a nut": *The Washington Post*, March 2, 1974.

179. Simon's advice to Ford: Memorandum for the president, U.S. policy toward OPEC.

179. Schlesinger's proposal for a review and its delay: Sick, *All Fall Down*, pp.15–18.

179. Kissinger's memo to Ford: "Strategy for Your Discussion with the Shah of Iran." May 13, 1975; Secret/NODIS.

180. Ford's intervention: Jack Anderson, *Parade*, August 26, 1979.

180. Kissinger and oil prices: On May 4, 1980, CBS "60 Minutes" broadcast charges by James Akins, former U.S. ambassador to Saudi Arabia, and others, that there was collusion between sections of the U.S. government and the Shah to drive up oil prices in order to facilitate Iranian arms purchases. Kissinger called such charges "untrue and malicious."

180. Shah on American corruption: Walter Pincus and Dan Morgan, *The Washington Post*, January 20, 1980.

180. Shah on "chicanery": *The Washington Post*, January 2, 1977.

180. Senate White Paper: Staff Report of Senate Foreign Assistance Subcommittee of Foreign Relations Committee, August 2, 1976.

180. Kissinger's flight to Teheran: *Times* (London), August 5, 1976.

181. Shah's comments and Kissinger's announcement: *The Washington Post*, August 7, 1976, and Rubin, *Paved with Good Intentions*, p. 175.

181. Shah and Kissinger's exchange of messages: State 252342, October 1976.

181. Carter's conclusions: PD-NSC 13, May 12, 1977.

182. Shah to Gavin Young, *Observer*, London, November 16, 1975.

182. Fiftieth anniversary celebration: Parsons, *The Pride and the Fall*, pp. 23–24.

183. Iranian economic figures: Graham, *Iran: The Illusion of Power*, pp. 93–103.

CHAPTER ELEVEN

185. Ashraf successfully sues *Le Monde* and gets retraction from *The Washington Post*: Ashraf Pahlavi, *Faces in a Mirror*.

185. Stories about Ashraf: Related by many members of the court to the author. See also Ashraf Pahlavi, *Faces in a Mirror,* pp. 189–90; Oney, *Elites and the Distribution of Power in Iran,* pp. 64–66.

186. Ashraf on looking after her brother: Harpers and Queen, Interview with Shusha Guppy, 1988.

186. Ashraf on being unwanted: Ashraf Pahlavi, *Faces in a Mirror,* pp. 1 and 6.

186. Photograph of the children: Ibid.

187. Comparison of Shah and Christ: Ashraf interview with Barbara Walters, ABC television, 1980.

187. On Mohammed's school in Switzerland: Ashraf Pahlavi, *Faces in a Mirror,* p. 19.

187. "like faces in a mirror": Ibid., p. 20.

187. Photograph of Ashraf and Mohammed: Ibid.

187. Ashraf's cable and Reza Shah's response: Ibid., p. 23.

187. Ashraf on first husband: Ibid., p. 36.

187. Ashraf on her second marriage: Ibid., pp. 76–77.

188. Ashraf and Stalin: Ibid., pp. 86–87.

188. Ashraf instructs Prime Minister to resign: Ibid., p. 90.

188. Ashraf in U.S.: *New York Post,* September 24, 1974.

189. U.S. Embassy 1951 report: Teheran Desp. 736, December 20, 1951. SECRET p. 7. Quoted in Oney, *Elites and the Distribution of Power in Iran,* CIA study, SECRET, PR 76 10017, February 1976, p. 65.

189. Ashraf as diplomat: Oney, Ibid., p. 65.

189. CIA 1976 report: Ibid., pp. 27–29, 64–66.

190. Radji's lament: Radji, *In the Service of the Peacock Throne.*

190. Iranian bank governor to U.S. Embassy: Oney, *Elites and the Distribution of Power in Iran,* p. 66.

190. Ashraf on her attempted murder in Juan-les-Pins: *The Washington Post,* April 25, 1980.

190. Ashraf's denial of CIA accusations: *The Boston Globe,* February 12, 1980.

190. Ashraf's statement she would combat calumnies: *The New York Times,* January 11, 1980.

191. Ashraf on "second Japan": Repeated often, including interview with author, February 16, 1986.

191. CIA on Prince Shahram: Oney, *Elites and the Distribution of Power in Iran,* p. 66.

191. Ashraf on final days: Radji, *In the Service of the Peacock Throne,* p.226, and Ashraf Pahlavi, *Faces in the Mirror,* p. 205.

191. Saunders on Ashraf: Memorandum to David Newsom, April 18, 1979.

192. Businessmen's bonanza: Graham, *Iran: The Illusion of Power,* pp. 77–92.

193. Madame Afshar on nouveaux riches: Author's interview, July 13, 1985.

194. Description of Kish and Shah's home life there: Blanch, *Farah Diba,* pp. 138–142.

194. Development of Kish: Graham, *Iran: The Illusion of Power,* pp. 159–60.

195. Assurance to British ambassador on British call girls: Author's interview with Sir Anthony Parsons, April 2, 1985.

196. Radji with warm vodka: Radji, *In the Service of the Peacock Throne,* p. 102.

197. Radji on mullahs: Ibid., p. 228.

197. "out . . . like mice": Kayhan, Teheran, October 26, 1976.

198. Development of SAVAK: Rubin, *Paved with Good Intentions*, pp. 177–81, and Graham, *Iran: The Illusion of Power*, pp. 142–47.

199. SAVAK's methods: International Commission of Jurists report, *Human Rights and the Legal System in Iran*, 1976; Amnesty International report, 1975–76; Reza Bahareni, *The Crowned Cannibals*, (New York: Vintage, 1977), pp. 131–218.

199. Parviz Raein story: Memorandum of conversation between Raein and Roger Brewin, counselor for economic and commercial affairs, U.S. Embassy, February 12, 1978.

200. Shah's *Le Monde* interview.

200. Shah's CBS interview: Mike Wallace and Gary P. Gates, *Close Encounters* (New York: William Morrow & Co., 1984).

200. Figures of those killed by SAVAK: Rubin, *Paved with Good Intentions*, pp. 176–81.

201. Shah and the International Committee of the Red Cross: Author's interviews with senior ICRC officials, Geneva, March 12, 1985.

201. Golestan story: Radji, *In the Service of the Peacock Throne*, p. 87.

202. Queen's views: Author's interview, March 26–27, 1986.

202. Shah on women to Oriana Fallaci: *New Republic,* December 1, 1973.

202. Queen to Quinn: *The Washington Post,* May 19, 1975.

203. Dislike of Shah's men for Queen's circle: Author's interview with Amir Aslan Afshar, July 13, 1985; Radji, *In the Service of the Peacock Throne,* p. 194.

204. Queen's views on 1978: Author's interview, March 26–27, 1986.

CHAPTER TWELVE

205. Shah shuts himself up for a day: M. R. Pahlavi, *Answer to History,* p. 185.

205. Murder of the Baha'is: Mortimer, *Faith and Power,* p. 110; and Keddie, *Roots of Revolution,* p. 52.

206. Description of Hoveyda: See, for example, Parsons, *The Pride and the Fall,* pp. 29–30, and Radji, *In the Service of the Peacock Throne,* pp. 5–6.

206. Helms and the Soviet ambassador: Widely told; see, for example, Rubin, *Paved with Good Intentions,* p. 187.

206. Hoveyda and General Arfa: Ghani, *Iran and the West,* pp. 19–20.

207. The Cabinet and the Shah: Parsons, *The Pride and the Fall,* pp. 29–30.

207. Hoveyda and PEN and the ICJ: *The Washington Post,* June 9, 1976.

208. Hoveyda on future successes of Iran: *Fortune,* October 1974.

208. Hoveyda on rich businessman: Author's interview with Fereshteh Razavi, Hoveyda's niece, March 20, 1985.

208. Hoveyda on regime dying inside: Hoveyda, *The Fall of the Shah,* pp.79–80.

209. Hoveyda and Parsons: Parsons, *The Pride and the Fall,* p. 62.

210. Alam's advice: Author's interview with Amir Khosro Afshar, April 12, 1988.

210. Deaths of Nassiri and Khademi: Ibid., p. 100.

211. Parsons and the Shah on Hoveyda: Ibid., pp. 100–101.

211. Leila and the generals: Author's interview with Leila Emani, March 20, 1985.

211. Parsons' interview with the Queen: Parsons, *The Pride and the Fall,* p. 118.

212. "It's out of our hands": Author's interview with Fereshteh Razavi, March 20, 1985.
212. Hoveyda and Shahgoli: Author's interview with Shahgoli, November 14, 1984.
212. Hoveyda's removal by ambulance: Author's interview with Fereshteh Razavi, March 20, 1985.
213. Development of komitehs: See Bakhash, *The Reign of the Ayatollahs*, pp. 56–63.
213. Interrogation of Hoveyda by Yazdi: *The New York Times*, March 15, 1979.
213. Nassiri's state: *The New York Times*, February 12, 1979.
214. Bazargan's denunciation of trials: Bakhash, *The Reign of the Ayatollahs*, p. 61.
215. Fereshteh Razavi's account of Hoveyda in prison: Author's interview, March 20, 1975.
215. Ockrent's account of her visit to Hoveyda: *Paris Match*, April 20, 1979.
215. Fouquier-Tinville: Christopher Hibbert, *The French Revolution* (London: Penguin, 1980), pp. 240–41.
217. Criticisms of Ockrent: *Le Figaro*, April 9, 1979; *L'Aurore*, April 9, 1979.
217. Ockrent's self-defense: *Paris Match*, April 20, 1979.
218. Hoveyda's trial: *Le Monde*, April 10, 1979.
218. Shah in *Le Monde:* April 26, 1979.
218. Shah on "clarifications": M. R. Pahlavi, *Answer to History*, p. 185.
219. Khalkhali's account of Hoveyda's execution: V. S. Naipaul, *Among the Believers* (London: Deutsch, 1981), pp. 54–57.

CHAPTER THIRTEEN

220. Stilemans: Author's interview with Mohammed Behbehanian, December 2, 1985; press reports; *Daily Telegraph*, London, March 29, 1979.
220. Shah on no compliments: Radji, *In the Service of the Peacock Throne*, p. 102.
221. Queen Elizabeth's suggestion: Author's interviews with British officials and with Richard Parker, U.S. ambassador to Morocco, October 8, 1985.
221. David Owen's statement: *Daily Telegraph*, London, February 21, 1979.
221. George V and Czar Nicholas II: Kenneth Rose, *George V* (London: Weidenfeld and Nicolson, 1983), pp. 211–18.
222. Difficulties of security: *Daily Telegraph*, February 21, 1979.
222. Alan Hart's role: Author's interview with Hart, July 16, 1986.
223. Queen Farah on Mrs. Thatcher: Author's interview, March 26–27, 1986.
223. Robert Armao on Mrs. Thatcher: Author's interview, February 13, 1986.
223. Sir Denis Wright's mission: Author's interview, June 27, 1985, and subsequent correspondence.
224. Foreign Office objections: Author's interview with Sir Denis Wright, June 27, 1985, and correspondence and interviews with Sir Anthony Parsons.
225. Cyrus Ghani on Wright: Ghani, *Iran and the West*, pp. 404–5.
225. Wright's obituary of the Shah: *Spectator*, London, August 2, 1980.
226. Atabai on Wright: Author's interview, November 16, 1985 and subsequently.
227. Armao on Shah's reaction: Author's interview, February 13, 1986.
227. Iranian conspiracy theories on British behavior: Author's interviews with many Iranians.

227. Shah on British intent: M. R. Pahlavi, *Answer to History*, p. 15.

228. Sadat's renewed invitation: *Daily Telegraph*, London, May 25, 1979.

228. Austrian possibilities: *The New York Times Magazine*, May 17, 1981.

· 228. Mexican overtures: Ibid.

229. Armao's arrangements: Author's interview with Armao, February 3, 1986.

CHAPTER FOURTEEN

This account of the Shah's illness is in large part derived from substantial interviews and correspondence with Dr. Georges Flandrin for the period 1974–79, and with many of the Shah's other doctors for the years thereafter, including Dr. Lucy Pirnia, Dr. Benjamin H. Kean, Dr. Morton Coleman, and others.

231. Queen on Shah's body: Author's interview, March 26–27, 1986.

231. Flandrin's care for Shah: Author's interviews and correspondence, 1985–87.

239. Safire on Nixon: *The New York Times*, July 26, 1979.

240. Shah's statement on his "anguish": *Daily Telegraph*, London, July 30, 1979.

240. Khalkhali threat: *The New York Times*, June 17, 1979.

240. Revoking of Shah's passport: *The New York Times*, June 24, 1979.

241. Kissinger, Mondale, and Brzezinski: Sick, *All Fall Down*.

241. Carter on "blank the Shah": *New York Times Magazine*, May 17, 1981.

241. Brzezinski on Kissinger: Brzezinski, *Power and Principle*, p. 274.

241. Brzezinski on "third-rate regime": Ibid.

242. Brzezinski on Ashraf's letter: Ibid., p. 474.

242. The involvement of Dr. Benjamin Kean in the care of the Shah has been written about extensively. See, inter alia, *The New York Times Magazine*, May 17, 1981; Salinger, *America Held Hostage;* Jordan, *Crisis;* Kean's interview with Dennis Breo, *American Medical News*, August 7, 1981, reproduced in Dennis L. Breo, *Extraordinary Care* (Chicago: Chicago Review Press, 1986), pp. 72–92.

242. Kean as "boulevardier": *American Medical News*, August 7, 1981.

243. Kean's account of his summons to Cuernavaca: *American Medical News*, August 7, 1981; also author's interview, April 23 and 25, 1987, and subsequent correspondence.

245. Flandrin's view: Author's interview, February 26, 1985.

245. Armao's reaction: Salinger, *America Held Hostage*, p. 14.

246. Kean meets Flandrin: Kean's account, *American Medical News*, August 7, 1981; Flandrin's account, author's interview, February 26, 1985.

248. Queen's view: Author's interview, March 26–27, 1986.

249. Vance's view: Vance, *Hard Choices*, p. 371.

249. Jordan's question: Jordan, *Crisis*, p. 24.

249. Carter's question: Ibid.

250. Reactions in Teheran to the Shah's proposed trip: Sick, *All Fall Down*, pp. 184–85.

250. Dr. Dustin and Dr. Cervantes: *The New York Times Magazine*, May 17, 1981.

251. Carter agrees to Shah's admission to the U.S.: Carter, *Keeping Faith*, p. 456.

252. Shah's thoughts as he flew to Florida: M. R. Pahlavi, *Answer to History*, p. 18.

252. Queen on wrong airport: Author's interview, March 26–27, 1986.

252. Arrival in New York: *The New York Times*, October 24, 1979; Salinger, *America Held Hostage*, p. 26.
252. Queen's comment: Author's interview, March 26–27, 1986.

CHAPTER FIFTEEN

253. David Newsome alias: author's interview with Dr. Kean, April 23 and 25, 1986.
254. Silence over Shah's illness: State Department statement, *The New York Times*, October 23, 1979.
254. Godek remark: *The New York Times*, October 24, 1979; author's interview, November 14, 1984.
254. Coleman and Kean: Author's interview with Dr. Coleman, October 31, 1985.
254. Coleman on "country boy": Author's interview, October 31, 1985.
254. Coleman's questions: Author's interview, November 12, 1985.
256. Kean's view on spleen: Author's interview, April 23 and 25, 1986.
257. Armao's press conference: *The New York Times*, October 25, 1979.
257. Doctors' press conference: Ibid.
257. "Good medical practice . . .": *The New York Times Magazine*, May 17, 1981.
258. Queen's predicament: Interview with the author, March 26–27, 1981.
259. Coleman on gallstones: Author's interview, October 31, 1985.
259. Kean on gallstones: Author's interview with Dr. Kean, April 23 and 25, 1986.
260. Memorial Hospital and irradiation: Author's interview with Dr. Kean, Ibid.
261. Khomeini's priorities: Sick, *All Fall Down*, pp. 198–205.
261. "Knife without a blade": Bakhash, *The Reign of the Ayatollahs*, pp. 52–70.

CHAPTER SIXTEEN

263. Origins of U.S. Embassy: Cynthia Helms, *An Ambassador's Wife in Iran*, (New York: Dodd Mead, 1981), p. 11.
264. Shah's complaint about station chief: M. R. Pahlavi, *Answer to History*, p. 170.
265. Helms offered an embassy: Thomas Powers, *The Man Who Kept the Secrets* (New York: Alfred A. Knopf, 1979).
266. Helms "hit the ground running": Author's interview, October 10, 1985.
266. Young Turks: Author's interview with Douglas Heck, July 4, 1985.
267. Helms on Shah's oil motive, on Queen's influence, on Shah's foreign policy, and on Mashhad: Author's interview, October 10, 1985.
267. Helms on Chile: Powers, *The Man Who Kept the Secrets*, p. 297.
268. Mrs. Helms on Shah at lunch with Kissinger: Helms, *An Ambassador's Wife in Iran*, p. 192.
268. Embassy letter from John Washburn to Ambassador Helms, August 11, 1973.
268. April 1975 embassy report.
269. Stempel memorandum.
269. Helms 1976 memo: "Postmemorandum for Inspectors." To Chief Inspector Herbert F. Propps, May 27, 1976.
270. Gary Sick's comment: Sick, *All Fall Down*, p. 32.

270. Urquhart's view: Brian Urquhart, *A Life in Peace and War* (New York: Harper and Row, 1987), pp. 283–84.

271. 1975 analysis of Ashraf: "The Iranian Imperial Family," January 29, 1975, signed by Jack Miklos.

272. CIA questions: Jerrold M. Post, M. D., October 6, 1978.

272. CIA review: Memorandum by David Blee, National Intelligence officer for the Middle East, for Ambassador Edward S. Little, chairman, Human Resources Committee, November 4, 1976, FOCUS *Iran.*

272. State Department and CIA attitudes: CIA's Human Resources Committee, Assessments Subcommittee, FOCUS *Iran,* December 27, 1976.

274. Sullivan and Carter: Sullivan, *Mission to Iran,* pp. 21–22.

274. Sullivan's impressions of embassy and Iran: Ibid., pp. 35–620.

275. Soviet Embassy warning: From U.S. Embassy documents, published in *The Observer,* London, July 14, 1985.

275. Kissinger's comments: Kissinger, *Years of Upheaval,* pp. 671–74.

275. Kapuscinski's images: Kapuscinski, *Shah of Shahs* (New York: Harcourt Brace Jovanovich, 1985).

276. Lubrani's views: *Times,* London, April 16, 1985.

CHAPTER SEVENTEEN

278. State Department information: *The New York Times,* October 24, 1979.

279. "dehumanized . . . elements": *Times,* London.

280. Chase and Iran: *The New York Times,* November 16, 1979; Mark Hulbert, *Interlock* (New York: Richardson and Snyder, 1982), passim.

280. Chase's exposure: *The New York Times,* November 11, 1979.

281. *Parade* magazine: December 9, 1979.

281. *Science* magazine: January 18 and August 29, 1980.

281. *Science* apology to Kean: May 29, 1981.

282. Rockefeller's statement: *The New York Times,* November 17, 1979.

282. Rockefeller remark to Carter: Carter, *Keeping Faith,* p. 468.

282. Kissinger's attitudes: *The New York Times,* November 29, 1979; SECRET memorandum from Ben Read to Cyrus Vance, following call from Kissinger, November 12, 1979; *Times,* London, November 27, 1979; Carter, *Keeping Faith,* p. 470.

282. Kissinger in Texas; Anthony Lewis on Kissinger: *The New York Times,* November 26, 1979.

283. Iranian official on Shah's plunder: *The New York Times,* November 25, 1979.

284. Ali Reza Nobari's views: *Euromoney,* January 1980.

284. Documents discovered: *The New York Times,* December 5, 1979.

284. Pahlavi Foundation: Graham, *Iran: The Illusion of Power,* p. 156–58; *New York Times,* November 15, 1979.

286. Behbehanian's denials: Author's interview, December 2, 1985.

286. Shah to Barbara Walters: Salinger, *America Held Hostage,* p. 61.

287. Shah on Parsons: M. R. Pahlavi, *Answer to History,* pp. 21–22.

288. Kissinger's visit: SECRET memorandum from Ben Read to Cyrus Vance, November 12, 1979.

288. Frank Sinatra's visit: Author's interview with Robert Armao, February 13, 1986.

288. Helmses' visit: Author's interview with R. Helms, October 10, 1985.

289. Coleman leaves the case: Author's interviews with Coleman and Kean, October 31, 1985, April 23 and 25, 1987.

289. Coleman's letter to Williams: November 26, 1979.

290. Armao and Mexican consul general: Salinger, *America Held Hostage,* and author's interview with Robert Armao, February 13, 1986.

290. Armao to Newsom: Salinger, *America Held Hostage,* p. 65.

290. Cutler's visit: Ibid., p. 66.

290. Queen's account: Author's interview, March 26–27, 1986.

291. Shah on "getaway scene": M. R. Pahlavi, *Answer to History,* p. 25.

292. Queen on asylum: Author's interview, March 26–27, 1986.

CHAPTER EIGHTEEN

294. Queen on life at Lackland: Author's interview, March 26–27, 1986.

294. Shah to Oxman: Author's interview with Oxman, November 12, 1985.

295. Ashraf on her son's death: Ashraf Pahlavi, *Faces in a Mirror,* p. 220.

296. Shah on Fardoust's betrayal: M. R. Pahlavi, *Answer to History,* p. 64.

296. Carter on Mexican betrayal: Carter, *Keeping Faith,* p. 468.

296. Edward Kennedy's remarks: *Times,* London, December 4, 1979.

297. Jimmy Breslin's views: *Times,* December 12, 1979.

297. Shah to Walters: Salinger, *America Held Hostage,* p. 67.

298. Carter's diary: Carter, *Keeping Faith,* p. 469.

298. Torrijos in Las Vegas: Author's interview with Chuchu Martinez and Dalys Varga, November 20, 1986.

300. John Wayne versus Ronald Reagan: William J. Jorden, *Panama Odyssey* (Austin: University of Texas Press, 1984), pp. 487–90.

301. Graham Greene in Washington: Graham Greene, *Getting to Know the General: The Story of an Involvement* (New York: Simon and Schuster, 1984), p. 131.

301. Torrijos breaks down: Ibid., p. 132.

301. Carter on Torrijos: Carter, *Keeping Faith,* p. 161.

301. Torrijos seeks to help Carter: Author's interview with Chuchu Martinez, November 12, 1986.

301. "The gringos are looking for a place . . .": Tad Szulc, *New York Magazine,* May 5, 1980.

301. Ambler Moss background and views: Author's interview, November 19, 1986.

303. Hamilton Jordan's mission: Jordan, *Crisis,* pp. 63–76, and author's interview with Moss, November 19, 1986.

304. Jordan on Armao and Shah at Lackland: Jordan, *Crisis,* pp. 76–83.

304. Shah on Switzerland and Austria: M. R. Pahlavi, *Answer to History,* pp. 25–26.

305. Jordan and Armao exchange: Jordan, *Crisis,* p. 81.

308. Kean on Lackland Agreement: *American Medical News,* August 7, 1981.

308. Carter's call to Shah: M. R. Pahlavi, *Answer to History,* p. 27.

308. Carter and Kissinger: Carter, *Keeping Faith,* p. 470.

CHAPTER NINETEEN

310. Moss searches for Torrijos: Author's interview with Ambler Moss, November 19, 1986.
312. Chuchu Martinez's background and views: Greene, *Getting to Know the General,* passim.
314. Preparations on Contadora: Author's interview with Gabriel Lewis, November 22, 1986.
316. Lunch at the hotel: Author's interviews with Ambler Moss, November 19, 1986; and Gabriel Lewis, November 22, 1986.
317. Torrijos on the Shah: Author's interview with Chuchu Martinez, November 20, 1986.
318. Noriega's background: *The New York Times,* June 12, 1986.
319. Guarding the Shah: Author's interviews with General Noriega, December 3, 1986; Chuchu Martinez, November 20, 1986.
320. Tape-recording: Author's interviews with Mark Morse, November 11, 1985; and Robert Armao, February 13, 1986.
320. Life on Contadora: Interviews conducted on behalf of Hamilton Jordan with Cristobal Valencia, the butler of Puntalara; author's interviews with Ambler Moss, Gabriel Lewis, Chuchu Martinez, and Dalys Varga.
320. Torrijos' lunch party: Author's interview with Gabriel Lewis, November 22, 1986.
321. Torrijos and Moshe Dayan: Greene, *Getting to Know the General,* p. 73.
321. Chuchu on the Shah: Author's interview, November 20, 1986.
322. Noriega on the Shah: Author's interview, December 3, 1986.
322. Shah to President Royo: Author's interview with Aristides Royo, November 23, 1986.
323. Torrijos on the Shah: CBS News, December 20, 1980.
325. Mark Morse's problems: Salinger, *America Held Hostage,* p. 188; author's interviews with Mark Morse, Robert Armao, Dalys Varga, and Ambler Moss.
326. Shah on "What's in store for me?": Author's interview with Mark Morse, September 17, 1987.

CHAPTER TWENTY

328. Mission of Bourguet and Villalon: Author's interview with Christian Bourguet, September 26, 1985; also Salinger, *America Held Hostage,* pp. 103–4; Sick, *All Fall Down,* pp. 252–53.
328. Royo's response: Author's interview with Ambler Moss, November 19, 1986.
328. Royo's announcement: *Times,* London, December 29, 1979.
329. Waldheim in Teheran: Sick, *All Fall Down,* p. 247–48.
330. Senior Islamic statesman to Vance: Ibid., p. 249.
330. Salamin's visit to Teheran: Author's interview with Marcel Salamin, December 3, 1986.
331. Chuchu's call to Jordan: Jordan, *Crisis,* p. 90.
331. Jordan's meeting at Homestead AFB: Ibid., pp. 92–96.
331. Jordan and Carter: Jordan, *Crisis.*

332. Bourguet's views on Iranian extradition plans: Author's interview, September 26, 1985.

332. Jordan's trip to London: Ibid., pp. 102–7.

334. Moss on Armao: Interview with Ambler Moss by Hamilton Jordan's researchers.

334. Teheran's announcement of the Shah's arrest: Author's interview with Arístides Royo, November 23, 1986; Jordan, *Crisis*, p. 111.

335. Denials that extradition was possible by Royo, Gonzalez, Salamin, Lewis: Author's interviews, November–December, 1986.

335. Chuchu Martinez's doubts: Author's interview, November 20, 1986.

335. Ambler Moss hit panic button: Author's interview, November 19, 1986.

336. Shah's real-estate inspections: Author's interview with Mark Morse, October 9, 1985.

337. Moss' conversation with Royo: Author's interviews with Ambler Moss, November 19, 1986; and Arístides Royo, November 23, 1986.

338. Shah's version: M. R. Pahlavi, *Answer to History*, p. 29.

339. Andreotti story: Giulio Andreotti, *Lives* (London: Sidgwick and Jackson, 1988), pp. 107–8.

339. Shah's love life: Author's interviews with many courtiers. See also CIA reports, including Oney, *Elites and the Distribution of Power in Iran.*

341. Story of "Ange": Author's interview, Paris, September 28, 1985.

342. Mahvi's visit: Author's interview with Abolfath Mahvi, Geneva, March 12, 1985.

342. Quests for interview with Shah: Author's interviews with Mark Morse, September 17, 1987; and Robert Armao, February 13, 1988.

342. Frost and Kissinger: Author participated in the preparation for the NBC interview.

343. Godek and the Shah: Author's interview with Chris Godek, November 14, 1984.

343. Shah meets Whitley: Author's interview with John Birt, April 22, 1985.

344. Frost and the Shah: Transcripts and author's interview with John Birt and Clive Irving, April 24, 1985.

345. Crown Prince plays cards: Author's interview with John Birt, April 22, 1985.

CHAPTER TWENTY-ONE

347. Kean on Panamanian resentment: Author's interview with Ben Kean, April 23 and 25, 1987.

348. Charlie García's mission: Author's interview with Dr. García, November 25, 1986.

349. Kean's meeting with García and Ríos: Author's interviews with Ben Kean, April 23 and 25, 1987; Charlie García, November 25, 1986; and Adán Ríos, November 4, 1985.

349. Ríos' recollection: Author's interview with Adán Ríos, November 4, 1985.

349. Ríos decides for splenectomy: Article by the Panamanian doctors, "The Strange Case of Mohammed Reza Pahlavi: An Incident in the Medical History of Panama." *Revista Medica* 13 (January 1981): 231.

350. Queen and Flandrin: Author's interview with Georges Flandrin, February 26, 1985.

350. Flandrin's encounter in New York: Author's interviews with Georges Flandrin, February 26, 1985; and Ben Kean, April 23 and 25, 1987.

350. Ríos and Flandrin: Author's interview with Adán Ríos, November 4, 1985.

351. Flandrin on Contadora: Author's interview with Georges Flandrin, February 26, 1985.

351. García and Villalon: Author's interview with Charlie García, November 25, 1986.

351. Jordan on suggestions the Shah be murdered: Jordan, *Crisis*, pp. 148–54.

352. Revelation of Ghotbzadeh: *The Washington Post*.

352. Flandrin and Rios prepare: Author's interviews with Georges Flandrin, February 26, 1985; and Adán Ríos, November 4, 1985.

353. Hester's role: Author's interview with Jeane Hester, November 3, 1985.

355. Kean's views: Author's interviews; Salinger, *America Held Hostage*, p. 191; *American Medical News*, August 7, 1981.

356. Confrontation at the hotel: Author's interviews with Ben Kean, Charlie García, Robert Armao, Mark Morse; *American Medical News*, August 7, 1981; Salinger, *America Held Hostage*, p. 192.

357. Kean on "new solution": *American Medical News*, August 7, 1981.

357. Kean on DeBakey: Ibid.

357. Coleman on DeBakey: Author's interview with Morton Coleman, November 12, 1985.

358. Garcia de Paredes' position: Author's interview with Gaspar Garcia de Paredes, November 24, 1986.

358. Hester's problems: Author's interview with Jeane Hester, November 3, 1985.

359. Panamanians' agreement to DeBakey: *Revista Medica* 13 (January 1981): 231.

359. Panamanian outrage at publicity: Ibid.

359. Charlie García's views: Author's interview with Dr. García, November 25, 1986.

CHAPTER TWENTY-TWO

362. DeBakey background: *Texas Monthly*, April 1979.

365. DeBakey's view that he was in charge: Author's interview with Michael DeBakey, November 4, 1985, and subsequent correspondence; Brenda Stone's interview with Michael DeBakey in *American Medical News*, April 25, 1980.

365. García's refusal to go to the airport: Author's interview with Charlie García, November 25, 1986.

369. Doctors' confrontations: Author's interviews with Ben Kean, Michael DeBakey, Georges Flandrin, Jeane Hester, Adán Ríos, Charlie García, Gaspar García de Paredes, Lucy Pirnia, Ambler Moss, Robert Armao, Mark Morse, and the Queen; *American Medical News*, April 25, 1980 and August 7, 1981; DeBakey letter to author, March 21, 1988; Flandrin letters to Professor Jean Bernard.

372. DeBakey and de Paredes reconcile: Author's interviews with Ambler Moss, November 19, 1986; and de Paredes, November 24, 1986.

372. The American ruse: Author's interviews with Ben Kean, Michael DeBakey, Robert Armao, and Mark Morse; *American Medical News*, August 7, 1981; Salinger, *America Held Hostage*.

374. Shah on "medical soap opera": M. R. Pahlavi, *Answer to History*, p. 30.
374. Hester's letter: April 4, 1980.

CHAPTER TWENTY-THREE

376. Queen and Jehan Sadat: Author's interviews with the Queen, March 26–27, 1986, and Mrs. Sadat; Sadat, *A Woman of Egypt*, pp. 423–24.
377. Kean and Cutler: *American Medical News*, August 7, 1981; author's interview with Ben Kean.
377. Jordan's hopes: Jordan, *Crisis*, pp. 185–89.
378. Jordan's flight: Ibid., pp. 189, 196–97.
378. DeBakey on "battleship" conditions: *The Washington Post*, April 4, 1980.
379. Moss on "opéra bouffe": Author's interview with Ambler Moss, November 19, 1986.
380. Jordan and Torrijos: Jordan, *Crisis*, pp. 197–99.
381. Jordan and Carter and Saunders: Ibid., p. 202.
381. Raphel's suggestion: Interview with Hamilton Jordan's researchers; Jordan, *Crisis*, pp. 202–3.
381. Materno Vasquez's zeal: Author's interview with Juan Materno Vasquez, November 26, 1986.
382. Materno Vasquez and Bourguet: Author's interviews with Christian Bourguet and Juan Materno Vasquez; Salinger, *America Held Hostage*, p. 211.
383. Jordan and Bourguet: Author's interview with Christian Bourguet; Jordan, *Crisis*, p. 203; Salinger, *America Held Hostage*, p. 212.
384. Queen's fears: Author's interview with Queen, March 26–27, 1986.
384. Cutler meets the Shah: Jordan, *Crisis*, pp. 205–6; author's interview with Queen, March 26–27, 1986.
384. Shah on Cutler's offers: M. R. Pahlavi, *Answer to History*, pp. 32–33.
385. Carter calls Sadat: Jordan, *Crisis*, p. 207.
386. Cutler suggests charter plane: M. R. Pahlavi, *Answer to History*, p. 33.
386. Evergreen Airlines and CIA: *The Washington Post*, March 25, 1980.
386. Bourguet calls Teheran: Author's interview with Christian Bourguet; Salinger, *America Held Hostage*, p. 213; Jordan, *Crisis*, p. 210.
387. Armao and Beno: Author's interview with Robert Armao, November 14, 1987.
388. Armao and Noriega: Author's interview with Robert Armao, November 14, 1987.
388. Moss, Torrijos, and Jordan's final demarche: Author's interview with Ambler Moss, November 19, 1986; Jordan, *Crisis*, pp. 210–11.
389. Shah on flight: M. R. Pahlavi, *Answer to History*, p. 33.
389. Delay at Azores: Author's interview with Queen, March 26–27, 1986.
389. Torrijos and Ghotbzadeh: Author's interview with Ambler Moss, November 19, 1986; Jordan, *Crisis*, pp. 210–11.
389. Carter livid: Jordan, *Crisis*, p. 211.
390. Carter memoirs: Carter, *Keeping Faith*.
390. Monday at the Foreign Ministry: Author's interviews with Ambler Moss, Christian Bourguet, Aristides Royo, and Juan Materno Vasquez.
390. Queen's sheets, Torrijos to Bernard Diederich: Author's interview with Bernard Diederich, November 18, 1986.

CHAPTER TWENTY-FOUR

391. Landing at Cairo: Author's interviews with Mark Morse, the Queen, and Jehan Sadat; Sadat, *A Woman of Egypt*, p. 425; M. R. Pahlavi, *Answer to History*, p. 33.

393. The operation: *American Medical News* interviews with Ben Kean and Michael DeBakey, August 7, 1981, and April 25, 1980. Author's interviews with Ben Kean, Michael DeBakey, Georges Flandrin, Lucy Pirnia. Georges Flandrin's letters to Professor Jean Bernard are also quoted in this chapter.

393. Problems with blood machines: *American Medical News* interview with Michael DeBakey, April 25, 1980; DeBakey letter to author, March 21, 1988.

393. DeBakey on spleen: *The New York Times*, March 31, 1980.

393. Kean on spleen: *American Medical News*, August 7, 1981.

393. Involvement of pancreas: Dennis L. Breo's interview with Michael DeBakey in *American Medical News*, July 18, 1980.

393. Kean to Sadat on Churchill, Shah's response: *American Medical News*, August 7, 1980.

394. DeBakey's "hopeful" prognosis: *American Medical News*, April 25, 1980.

394. DeBakey on Shah's "beautiful" recovery: *The Washington Post*, April 4, 1980.

394. Kean's pessimism: *American Medical News*, August 7, 1981; author's interview with Ben Kean, April 23 and 25, 1980.

394. Kean pays final respects: *American Medical News*, August 7, 1981.

394. DeBakey's interview for book: Author's interview with Michael DeBakey, November 4, 1985.

395. Hostile reaction to Shah's arrival in Egypt: Sadat, *A Woman of Egypt*, pp. 426–28.

395. Ashraf versus Queen: Author's interviews with Ben Kean, Georges Flandrin, and Morton Coleman.

396. Ashraf summons Coleman: Author's interviews with Ben Kean and Morton Coleman.

396. Kean to Flandrin: Kean letter to Flandrin, July 8, 1980.

396. Coleman on pancreas: Author's interview with Morton Coleman, October 31, 1985.

396. Pirnia on DeBakey's visit: Author's interview with Lucy Pirnia, November 2, 1985.

397. DeBakey on his visit: Author's interview with Michael DeBakey, November 4, 1985; letter to author, March 21, 1988.

397. Coleman on chemotherapy: Author's interview with Morton Coleman, October 31, 1985.

397. Coleman on Ashraf and Queen: Author's interview with Morton Coleman, October 31, 1985.

397. Queen on Shah's plight: Author's interview with Queen, March 26–27, 1986.

397. Flandrin summoned by Queen: Author's interview with Georges Flandrin, February 26, 1985.

398. Flandrin on pancreatic cyst: Author's interview with Georges Flandrin, February 26, 1985; Flandrin's letters to Bernard.

398. Coleman rows with French: Author's interviews with Georges Flandrin and Morton Coleman.

398. Queen's predicament: Author's interview with Queen, March 26–27, 1986.

398. Coleman on French and Egyptian doctors: Author's interviews with Morton Coleman, October 31, 1985, and Georges Flandrin, February 26, 1985; Flandrin's letters to Bernard.

399. Kean plans and then cancels his return: Author's interviews with Ben Kean and Robert Armao.

399. Behavior of some French doctors: Author's interviews with Morton Coleman, Mark Morse, and Georges Flandrin.

399. Queen's request to Flandrin: Author's interview with Queen, March 26–27, 1986.

399. *Al-Ahram* reports on Shah: July 6–11 and 20, 1980.

400. DeBakey disputes reports of pancreatic involvement: *American Medical News,* July 18, 1980; letter to author, March 21, 1988; Dr. Lawrie's letter to Dr. DeBakey, undated, written February/March 1988.

400. DeBakey's view of *Al-Ahram* article: Interview with the author, April 23 and 25, 1987.

401. Flandrin's view: Interview with the author, February 26, 1985, and confirmed in subsequent correspondence and interviews, April 1988.

401. Shah deteriorates: Author's interviews with Georges Flandrin, Lucy Pirnia, and Mark Morse.

401. Final version of memoirs: Author's interviews with Mark Morse, Ardeshir Zahedi, and Chris Godek.

402. Queen on Shah's stoicism: Author's interview with Queen, March 26–27, 1986.

402. Mrs. Sadat's view: Sadat, *A Woman of Egypt,* p. 432.

402. Death of the Shah: Author's interviews with the Queen, Lucy Pirnia, Ardeshir Zahedi, Mark Morse, and Georges Flandrin; Salinger, *America Held Hostage,* pp. 261–62; Flandrin's letter to Bernard.

403. Ashraf's account: *Paris Match,* April 3, 1986.

404. Pourshoja's lament: Salinger, *America Held Hostage,* pp. 261–62.

404. State Department on Shah: *The New York Times,* July 28, 1980.

404. Kissinger, Rockefeller, and McCloy on Shah: *The New York Times,* July 28, 1980.

405. Ghotbzadeh and Radio Teheran on Shah: *Times,* London, July 28, 1980.

405. Mrs. Sadat on funeral: Sadat, *A Woman of Egypt,* p. 433.

EPILOGUE:

409. Hushang Ansary and Henry Kissinger: *Forbes,* June 2, 1986.

412. Amnesty views: Iran Briefing, Amnesty International, London, 1987.

Index

Index

PHOTO CREDITS

Pp. 40 (top and bottom), 57, 69, 71, 76, 82, 93, 105, 114, 147, 167, 185,
    189, 237, 241, 277, 278, 297, 321, 361, 385: AP/Wide World Photos
Pp. 61, 127, 128 (bottom), 256, 390, 405 (top and bottom): UPI/Bettmann
    Newsphotos
Pp. 128, 317: Sygma
P. 36: Patrick Chauvel/Sygma
P. 37: Abbas/Magnum
P. 55: Henri Cartier-Bresson/Magnum
P. 94: Sergio Larrain/Magnum
P. 102: Andrew Coulman/Camera Press
P. 148 (top): P. Slade/Gamma Liaison
P. 149 (top and bottom): Hires/Gamma Liaison
P. 152: Andanson/Sygma
P. 209: Setboun/SIPA
P. 232: Ginies/SIPA
P. 313: Desaunois/Gamma Liaison
P. 405: J. P. Laffont/Sygma

About the Author

William Shawcross is the author of *The Quality of Mercy*, for which he was awarded the 1984 World Hunger Media Award. He won the 1980 George Polk Book Award and the 1979 Sidney Hillman Foundation Prize Award for *Sideshow: Kissinger, Nixon and the Destruction of Cambodia*. His previous books include *Dubcek*, and *Crime and Compromise: Janos Kadar and the Politics of Hungary Since Revolution*. He has written for *The Sunday Times, The New Statesman, The Spectator, The New York Review of Books, Rolling Stone, The Washington Post*, and other papers.